New Religions

New Religions

Emerging Faiths and Religious Cultures in the Modern World

VOLUME 2: M–Z

Eugene V. Gallagher and Lydia Willsky-Ciollo

ABC-CLIO®

An Imprint of ABC-CLIO, LLC
Santa Barbara, California • Denver, Colorado

Copyright © 2021 by ABC-CLIO, LLC

All rights reserved. No part of this publication may be reproduced, stored in a retrieval system, or transmitted, in any form or by any means, electronic, mechanical, photocopying, recording, or otherwise, except for the inclusion of brief quotations in a review, without prior permission in writing from the publisher.

Every reasonable effort has been made to trace the owners of copyright materials in this book, but in some instances this has proven impossible. The editors and publishers will be glad to receive information leading to more complete acknowledgments in subsequent printings of the book and in the meantime extend their apologies for any omissions.

Library of Congress Cataloging-in-Publication Data

Names: Gallagher, Eugene V., author. | Willsky-Ciollo, Lydia, author.
Title: New religions : emerging faiths and religious cultures in the modern
  world / Eugene V. Gallagher and Lydia Willsky-Ciollo.
Description: Santa Barbara, California : ABC-CLIO, 2021. | Includes
  bibliographical references and index. | Contents: v. 1. A-L — v. 2. M-Z.
Identifiers: LCCN 2020015897 (print) | LCCN 2020015898 (ebook) | ISBN
  9781440862373 (v. 1 ; hardcover) | ISBN 9781440862380 (v. 2 ; hardcover)
  | ISBN 9781440862359 (hardcover) | ISBN 9781440862366 (ebook)
Subjects: LCSH: Cults.
Classification: LCC BP603 .G356 2020 (print) | LCC BP603 (ebook) | DDC
  209—dc23
LC record available at https://lccn.loc.gov/2020015897
LC ebook record available at https://lccn.loc.gov/2020015898

ISBN: 978-1-4408-6235-9 (set)
     978-1-4408-6237-3 (vol. 1)
     978-1-4408-6238-0 (vol. 2)
     978-1-4408-6236-6 (ebook)

25 24 23 22 21   1 2 3 4 5

This book is also available as an eBook.

ABC-CLIO
An Imprint of ABC-CLIO, LLC

ABC-CLIO, LLC
147 Castilian Drive
Santa Barbara, California 93117
www.abc-clio.com

This book is printed on acid-free paper ∞

Manufactured in the United States of America

Contents

Alphabetical List of Entries   vii

Guide to Related Topics   xiii

Preface   xix

Introduction   xxiii

Chronology   xxix

A–Z Entries   1

Index   691

Alphabetical List of Entries

VOLUME ONE

Adi Da Samraj

Aetherius Society, The

African New Religious Movements

Ahmadiyya Movement, The

Alamo, Tony

Ali, Noble Drew

Al-Qaeda

Amana Society

Amish, The

Anamadim

Anthroposophy

Anticult Movement, The

Apostates

Applewhite, Marshall, and Bonnie Lu Nettles

Art and New Religious Movements

Asahara, Shoko

Ásatrú

Aum Shinrikyō

Aurobindo, Sri

Ayahuasca

Baba, Meher

Babism

Bahá'í

Ballard, Guy W.

Bey, Hakim

Black Judaism

Blavatsky, Helena Petrovna

Book of Mormon, The

Brahma Kumaris

Brainwashing

Branch Davidians

Breatharianism

Caddy, Eileen

Candomblé

Cao Dai

Cayce, Edgar

CESNUR (The Center for the Study of New Religions)

Channeling

Chaos Magick

Charisma and Leadership in New Religious Movements

Chen Tao

Children and New Religious Movements

Children of God (The Family International)

Chinese New Religious Movements

Christadelphians

Christian Identity

Christian Science

Church of All Worlds, The

Alphabetical List of Entries

Church of Jesus Christ of Latter-day Saints, The

Church of Satan, The

Church of the Lord (Aladura)

Church Universal and Triumphant, The

Conspiracy Theories

Conversion

Cosmotheism

Course in Miracles, A

Courts and New Religious Movements

Crowley, Aleister

Crystals

Cult

Cult Awareness Network

Cultic Milieu

Damanhur

Deprogramming

Diamond Mountain Center

Diamond Way, The

Dianetics

Disaffiliation and Ex-membership in New Religious Movements

Divine Principle

Druidry

Dudeism

Eckankar

Eco-Paganism

Eddy, Mary Baker

Elan Vital (Divine Light Mission)

Environmentalism and New Religious Movements

Essene Groups

Exclusive (Plymouth) Brethren

Exit Counseling

Falun Gong

Farm, The

Farrakhan, Louis

Father Divine

Findhorn Foundation, The

Food and New Religious Movements

Fortune, Dion

Fourth Way, The

Fox, Kate, and Margaret

Fraud and Deception in New Religions

FREECOG (Free the Children of God)

Freemasonry

Freezone Scientology

Fundamentalist Mormons

Gardner, Gerald

Gender and New Religious Movements

Ghost Dance Movement (Wovoka)

Ghosts, the Paranormal, and New Religious Movements

Globalization and New Religious Movements

Gnostic Groups

Goddess Worship

Grant, Kenneth

Guénon, René

Gurdjieff, G. I.

Hassan, Steven

Healing, Health, and New Religious Movements

Heaven's Gate

Hermetic Order of the Golden Dawn, The

Hermeticism

Hindu New Religious Movements

Holy Order of MANS, The

Holy Piby, The

Hoodoo

Hubbard, L. Ron

Alphabetical List of Entries

I AM Activity, The

Indigo Children

Info-Cult/Info-Secte

INFORM (The Information Network on Religious Movements)

Insider/Outsider Problem, The

Integral Yoga

International Cultic Studies Association, The (The American Family Foundation)

International Peace Mission Movement

International Society for Krishna Consciousness (ISKCON)

ISIS

Japanese New Religious Movements

Jediism

Jews for Jesus

Jones, Rev. Jim

Judge, William Quan

Kabbalah

Kardecism (Spiritism)

Kimbangu, Simon

Knight, JZ (Ramtha)

Kopimism

Korean New Religious Movements

Koresh, David

Landmark Forum, The (est)

LaVey, Anton Szandor

Law Enforcement and New Religious Movements

Lee, (Mother) Ann

Lévi, Éliphas

Love Israel Family, The

VOLUME TWO

Magic and New Religious Movements

Malcolm X

Marian Apparitions

Marriage and Relationships in New Religious Movements

Mathers, Samuel Liddell

Media and New Religious Movements

Mediums

Membership and New Religious Movements

Mesmerism

Messianic Judaism

Messianism and New Religious Movements

Millennialism

Miller, William

Millerites, The

Moon, Rev. Sun Myung

Moorish Science Temple of America, The

Movement for the Restoration of the Ten Commandments of God, The

Movement of Spiritual Inner Awareness

Muhammad, Elijah

Mungiki

Music and New Religious Movements

Mysticism

Nation of Gods and Earths, The (The Five Percent Nation)

Nation of Islam, The

Nation of Yahweh, The

Native American Church, The

Neopaganism

New Age, The

New Cathar Church, The

New Church, The

New Religions on/and the Internet

New Scriptures and New Religious Movements

Alphabetical List of Entries

New Thought

Noyes, John Humphrey

NXIVM

Oahspe

Occultism and Esotericism

Odinism

Olcott, Henry Steel

Oneida Community, The

Order of the Solar Temple, The

Ordo Templi Orientis

Otherkin

Ouspensky, P. D.

Parsons, John Whiteside

Pastafarianism (The Church of the Flying Spaghetti Monster)

Patrick, Ted

Pentecostalism

Peoples Temple

Prabhupada, A. C. Bhaktivedanta

Prophecy in New Religious Movements

Prophet, Elizabeth Clare

Pursel, Jach (Lazaris)

Quimby, Phineas

Race and New Religious Movements

Raëlians, The

Rajneesh, Shree Bhagwan/Osho

Rajneesh/Osho Movement, The

Ramakrishna Mission

Rastafari

Rosicrucianism

Ross, Rick Alan

Russell, Charles Taze

Salafism

Santería

Satanic Panic

Satanism

Sathya Sai Baba Movement, The

Science and Health with Key to the Scriptures

Science Fiction and New Religious Movements

Science, Technology, and New Religious Movements

Scientology

Sect

Seekers

Self-Realization Fellowship (Yogananda)

Seventh-day Adventism

Sex, Sexuality, and New Religious Movements

Seymour, William

Shakers, The

Shamanism

Shembe, Isaiah

Singer, Margaret Thaler

Smith, Joseph

Soka Gakkai

Spiritual but Not Religious

Spiritualism

Starhawk

Steiner, Rudolf

Subud

Sufi New Religious Movements

Swedenborg, Emanuel

Tantrik Order, The

Temple of Set, The

Thelema

Theosophical Society, The

Theosophy

Thoreau, Henry David

3HO

Transcendental Meditation

Alphabetical List of Entries

Transcendentalism
Twelve Tribes, The
UFO Religions
Umbanda
Unarius Academy of Science, The
Unification Church, The
Unitarian Universalism
United Nuwaubian Nation of Moors, The
Unity School of Christianity
Urantia Book, The
Utopianism in New Religious Movements
Valley of the Dawn, The
Vampirism
Vedanta Society, The
Violence and New Religious Movements
Vivekananda, Swami
Vodou
Vorilhon, Claude (Raël)
Waite, Arthur Edward
Watch Tower Bible and Tract Society, The (Jehovah's Witnesses)
White, Ellen G.
Wicca
Women in New Religious Movements
World Church of the Creator, The
World's Parliament of Religion, The
Yoga
Yogi, Maharishi Mahesh
Zionist Churches (Africa)

Guide to Related Topics

GROUPS AND MOVEMENTS

Aetherius Society, The

African New Religious Movements

Ahmadiyya Movement, The

Al-Qaeda

Amana Society

Amish, The

Anamadim

Anthroposophy

Anticult Movement, The

Ásatrú

Aum Shinrikyō

Ayahuasca

Babism

Bahá'í

Black Judaism

Brahma Kumaris

Branch Davidians

Breatharianism

Candomblé

Cao Dai

CESNUR (The Center for the Study of New Religions)

Channeling

Chaos Magick

Chen Tao

Children of God (The Family International)

Chinese New Religious Movements

Christadelphians

Christian Identity

Christian Science

Church of All Worlds, The

Church of Jesus Christ of Latter-day Saints, The

Church of Satan, The

Church of the Lord (Aladura)

Church Universal and Triumphant, The

Cosmotheism

Crystals

Cult Awareness Network

Damanhur

Diamond Mountain Center

Diamond Way, The

Druidry

Dudeism

Eckankar

Eco-Paganism

Elan Vital (Divine Light Mission)

Essene Groups

Exclusive (Plymouth) Brethren

Falun Gong

Guide to Related Topics

Farm, The

Findhorn Foundation, The

Fourth Way, The

FREECOG (Free the Children of God)

Freemasonry

Freezone Scientology

Fundamentalist Mormons

Ghost Dance Movement (Wovoka)

Gnostic Groups

Goddess Worship

Heaven's Gate

Hermetic Order of the Golden Dawn, The

Hermeticism

Hindu New Religious Movements

Holy Order of MANS, The

Hoodoo

I AM Activity, The

Indigo Children

Info-Cult/Info-Secte

INFORM (The Information Network on Religious Movements)

Integral Yoga

International Cultic Studies Association, The (The American Family Foundation)

International Peace Mission Movement

International Society for Krishna Consciousness (ISKCON)

ISIS

Japanese New Religious Movements

Jediism

Jews for Jesus

Kabbalah

Kardecism (Spiritism)

Kopimism

Korean New Religious Movements

Landmark Forum, The (est)

Love Israel Family, The

Marian Apparitions

Mesmerism

Messianic Judaism

Millerites, The

Moorish Science Temple of America, The

Movement for the Restoration of the Ten Commandments, The

Movement of Spiritual Inner Awareness

Mungiki

Mysticism

Nation of Gods and Earths, The (The Five Percent Nation)

Nation of Islam, The

Nation of Yahweh, The

Native American Church, The

Neopaganism

New Cathar Church, The

New Church, The

New Thought

NXIVM

Odinism

Oneida Community, The

Order of the Solar Temple, The

Ordo Templi Orientis

Otherkin

Pastafarianism (The Church of the Flying Spaghetti Monster)

Pentecostalism

Peoples Temple

Raëlians, The

Rajneesh/Osho Movement, The

Ramakrishna Mission

Guide to Related Topics

Rastafari

Rosicrucianism

Salafism

Santería

Satanic Panic

Satanism

Sathya Sai Baba Movement, The

Scientology

Self-Realization Fellowship (Yogananda)

Seventh-day Adventism

Shakers, The

Soka Gakkai

Spiritual but Not Religious

Spiritualism

Subud

Sufi New Religious Movements

Tantrik Order, The

Temple of Set, The

Thelema

Theosophical Society, The

Theosophy

3HO

Transcendental Meditation

Transcendentalism

Twelve Tribes, The

UFO Religions

Umbanda

Unarius Academy of Science, The

Unification Church, The

Unitarian Universalism

United Nuwaubian Nation of Moors, The

Unity School of Christianity

Valley of the Dawn, The

Vampirism

Vedanta Society, The

Vodou

Watch Tower Bible and Tract Society, The (Jehovah's Witnesses)

Wicca

World Church of the Creator, The

Zionist Churches (Africa)

PEOPLE

Adi Da Samraj

Alamo, Tony

Ali, Noble Drew

Applewhite, Marshall, and Bonnie Lu Nettles

Asahara, Shoko

Aurobindo, Sri

Baba, Meher

Ballard, Guy W.

Bey, Hakim

Blavatsky, Helena Petrovna

Caddy, Eileen

Cayce, Edgar

Crowley, Aleister

Eddy, Mary Baker

Farrakhan, Louis

Father Divine

Fortune, Dion

Fox, Kate, and Margaret

Gardner, Gerald

Grant, Kenneth

Guénon, René

Gurdjieff, G. I.

Hassan, Steven

Hubbard, L. Ron

Jones, Rev. Jim

Judge, William Quan

Kimbangu, Simon

xvi Guide to Related Topics

Knight, JZ (Ramtha)
Koresh, David
LaVey, Anton Szandor
Lee, (Mother) Ann
Lévi, Éliphas
Malcolm X
Mathers, Samuel Liddell
Miller, William
Moon, Rev. Sun Myung
Muhammad, Elijah
Noyes, John Humphrey
Olcott, Henry Steel
Ouspensky, P. D.
Parsons, John Whiteside
Patrick, Ted
Prabhupada, A. C. Bhaktivedanta
Prophet, Elizabeth Clare
Pursel, Jach (Lazaris)
Quimby, Phineas
Rajneesh, Shree Bhagwan/Osho
Ross, Rick Alan
Russell, Charles Taze
Seymour, William
Shembe, Isaiah
Singer, Margaret
Smith, Joseph
Starhawk
Steiner, Rudolf
Swedenborg, Emanuel
Thoreau, Henry David
Vivekananda, Swami
Vorilhon, Claude (Raël)
Waite, Arthur Edward
White, Ellen G.
Yogi, Maharishi Mahesh

TERMS

Apostates
Brainwashing
Conspiracy Theories
Conversion
Cult
Cultic Milieu
Deprogramming
Dianetics
Exit Counseling
Insider/Outsider Problem, The
Mediums
Millennialism
New Age, The
Occultism and Esotericism
Sect
Seekers
Shamanism
World's Parliament of Religion, The
Yoga

TEXTS

Book of Mormon, The
Course in Miracles, A
Divine Principle
Holy Piby, The
Oahspe
Science and Health with Key to the Scriptures
Urantia Book, The

THEMES

Art and New Religious Movements

Charisma and Leadership in New Religious Movements

Children and New Religious Movements

Courts and New Religious Movements

Disaffiliation and Ex-membership in New Religious Movements

Environmentalism and New Religious Movements

Food and New Religious Movements

Fraud and Deception in New Religions

Gender and New Religious Movements

Ghosts, the Paranormal, and New Religious Movements

Globalization and New Religious Movements

Healing, Health, and New Religious Movements

Law Enforcement and New Religious Movements

Magic and New Religious Movements

Marriage and Relationships in New Religious Movements

Media and New Religious Movements

Membership and New Religious Movements

Messianism and New Religious Movements

Music and New Religious Movements

New Religions on/and the Internet

New Scriptures and New Religious Movements

Prophecy in New Religious Movements

Race and New Religious Movements

Science Fiction and New Religious Movements

Science, Technology, and New Religious Movements

Sex, Sexuality, and New Religious Movements

Utopianism in New Religious Movements

Violence and New Religious Movements

Women in New Religious Movements

Magic and New Religious Movements

Often, the word "magic" conjures top hats and white rabbits or sinister figures working spells on screen—not religion. In fact, many major religions, particularly Western traditions such as Christianity, have distanced themselves from magic, which implies human manipulation of the supposedly supernatural. Belief in magic has been cast as superstition, at best, or demonic influence, at worst. This has also served to inoculate certain Western traditions against accusations that biblical or historical events that seem magical—such as Jesus turning water into wine—are in fact miraculous. The difference between "magic" and "miracle," in this view, is that one results from human tricks and the other from divine intervention. As the field of anthropology and comparative religion expanded during the late nineteenth century, this view of magic was reaffirmed by theorists who viewed other religions through a Western, Judeo-Christian lens. People who practiced magic were cast as "primitive," and thus lower on the global hierarchy of religious practice.

In his book *Witchcraft, Oracles, and Magic Among the Azande* (1937), British anthropologist E. E. Evans-Pritchard (1902–1973) came to the conclusion that magic, witchcraft, and religion were intertwined and not distinct categories as many theologians and anthropologists had claimed. The Azande, a North Central African tribe, believed that they could participate mystically in the world around them, engaging with the supernatural realm through established rituals, which, theoretically, could allow them a means of controlling things like the success of crops, the health of their families, and the protection of their tribe from attack. In fact, even the notion that separate words must exist to characterize certain practices as "magical" was nonsensical. Further, the existence of witchcraft was very real to them. For every disease or tragedy, often a spiritual cause was suspected and very often that cause was believed to be the work of a witch. Witches, magic, and religion operated within the same system; humans, divine beings, spirits, and ancestors, while in different stages of existence, interacted and engaged in the same realm and often through ritual.

Thus, magic has been a component of religious practice (and vice versa) for millennia. However, a number of new religious movements have emerged over the previous centuries that build on this lineage, some more self-consciously than others.

MAGIC AS RELIGION

Most of the traditions that arose among slaves in the Afro-Caribbean and southern U.S. contexts were syncretic in nature, combining African religious practices with Christianity and indigenous religions. What was often cast as "mere" witch-craft by slaveowners was employed by slaves to take a modicum of control in terrible circumstances. Hoodoo, also known as conjure or rootwork, was an outgrowth of these traditions, while also transgressing traditional religious lines. Created by the low country Gullah people in the southern United States, Hoodoo employs a variety of herbs and substances often coupled with Christian religious forms like the Bible to divine the future, protect, heal, and, if needed, harm. Clients seek out Hoodoo workers (many of whom are women) for a variety of reasons, often while belonging to other religious traditions. For Hoodoo to work, the client must have faith in its efficacy.

Not all adaptations of magical practice and knowledge were endemic to a particular people, however. In the late nineteenth and early twentieth century, the practice of magic was very consciously adopted by British occultists like Aleister Crowley (1875–1947), Gerald Gardner (1884–1964), and Dion Fortune (1890–1946), who are often viewed as progenitors of various strands of Neopaganism. Crowley, who began participating in occult religious circles during his travels, began experiencing visions, wherein he was visited by divine messengers who dictated to him principles that would ground his magico-religious system, Thelema. Thelema employed magical and mystical practices to attain access to higher, esoteric knowledge found on the spiritual plane. It is presumed to be Crowley who began spelling magic as "magick" in occult circles, which was reflective of a more ancient spelling. Crowley is also known for his practice and advocacy of "sex magick" during Thelemic rituals. Sex was a powerful source of magical power and energy—in fact, Crowley considered the act itself (or the fluids that accompany it) to be sacramental.

Often viewed as the modern founder of Wicca (though he, like many Neopagans, maintained that his practice was the continuation of an ancient tradition), Gardner, like Crowley, dabbled in several different occult circles, accruing religious and magical knowledge along the way, which he merged into his own practice, often referred to as "Gardnerian Wicca." Fortune found her way to magical religious practice and Neopaganism via her experiences as a medium, while a member of the Theosophical Society. While participating in "trance mediumship"—where she would seemingly enter an altered state of consciousness—she found herself able to understand and perform magical ritual. She wrote prolifically of her experiences and gained a significant following.

Unlike various Neopagan traditions that claim to build on something ancient and universal, Chaos Magick is a magico-religious movement that reflects New Age spirituality, which emphasizes individual and eclectic spirituality. Often called "results-based magic," Chaos Magick emerged in the 1970s, when founders Peter J. Carroll (1953–) and Ray Sherwin (1952–) challenged what they saw as the too-exclusive and doctrinaire culture of British Wicca. They argued that religious systems should be tailor-made for each practitioner and focused on achieving desired this and next-worldly results. The use of the term "chaos" reflects the idea that each person has the right to order the universe's chaos in whatever way he or she deems necessary; it is from the universe that each individual draws magical power—a source that may or may not be divine in nature. Given the individualistic nature of Chaos Magick, there is no singular institution, and Chaos magicians are left to their own devices to determine what sources and practices work for them. However, some within Chaos circles have begun to challenge the idea that the magic performed should have no guidelines or parameters, arguing (similar to Neopagans) that tying practices to historical, religious lineages will help to connect practitioners as a community and to streamline rogue practices.

BLACK AND WHITE

In popular culture, "black" and "white" magic are carefully distinguished; black magic involves invoking harm against another person, whereas white magic entailed helping oneself or another. One of the primary ways that "white magic" is believed to operate is through healing. Numerous new religious movements employ rituals of healing, though quite often the practices and beliefs invoked distance themselves from magical connotations, which is reflective of the persistence of the belief that magic and religion are separate entities. For example, Pentecostals believe that the ability to heal comes via the Holy Spirit, and practitioners of Christian Science believe that healing comes through right thinking. In other words, there is a fine line between magical and miraculous healing; how an event is labeled varies by tradition, even if the claims and results are quite similar.

In general, there are very few instances where new religious movements were touted for performing white magic, but there have been instances where particular religions were assailed for practicing black magic. Satanism, generally, and the Church of Satan (CoS), specifically, have been accused of performing black magic, often through blood sacrifice, and occasionally involving children. Many, if not all of these fears—referred to as the Satanic Panic of the 1980s and 1990s—were overblown. The CoS employs the idea of "black magic," but in a satirical sense; all rituals are intended to spur practitioners toward optimizing their power and potential. In CoS's seminal text, *The Satanic Bible* (1969), causing harm to another human being is explicitly prohibited. The Black Mass described in the text employs a variety of magical techniques and ideas, including seeming references to Crowley's sex magick. However, the Black Mass, though a satiric, inversion of the traditional Catholic Mass, was always focused on actualizing individual potential, not on causing harm.

Despite the stigma associated with being a new religious movement, those that employ magical practice, either as an organic part of a religious system or as a deliberately cultivated set of practices, continue to practice and to emerge. Magic or magick, while still conjuring images of children's birthday parties for many, is a viable religion for some.

See also: Chaos Magick; Church of Satan, The; Crowley, Aleister (1875–1947); Fortune, Dion (1890–1946); Gardner, Gerald (1884–1964); Healing, Health, and New Religious Movements; Hoodoo; Mediums; Neopaganism; New Age, The; Occultism and Esotericism; Pentecostalism; Satanic Panic; Satanism; Sex, Sexuality, and New Religious Movements; Thelema; Theosophical Society, The; Wicca.

Further Reading

Butler, Alison. 2011. *Victorian Occultism and the Making of Modern Magic: Invoking Tradition*. New York: Palgrave MacMillan.

Davis, Owen. 2017. *The Oxford Illustrated History of Witchcraft and Magic*. New York: Oxford University Press.

Granholm, Kennet. 2014. *Dark Enlightenment: The Historical, Sociological, and Discursive Contexts of Contemporary Esoteric Magic*. Leiden: Brill.

Urban, Hugh. 2004. "The Beast with Two Backs: Aleister Crowley, Sex Magic and the Exhaustion of Modernity." *Nova Religio* 7, no. 3: 7–25.

Malcolm X (1925–1965)

Malcolm X became a central figure in American political life in the second half of the twentieth century. Born in Omaha, Nebraska, in 1925, Malcolm Little moved with his family to several different cities in the Midwest. Malcolm's father, Earl, was an outspoken proponent of the Black Nationalist ideas of Marcus Garvey (1887–1940). After Earl was likely murdered by a white supremacist group, the Black Legion, in Lansing, Michigan in 1931, Malcolm's family disintegrated.

In his teens, Malcolm moved to Boston to live with his sister Ella and quickly got involved in an escalating series of criminal actions. In 1946, he was convicted of burglary and spent the next seven years in prison.

CONVERSION

Into his twenties, Malcolm professed little interest in religion. In prison, he railed against Christianity frequently enough to have earned the nickname "Satan." Things began to change, however, when early in 1948 he received a letter from his brother Philbert informing him that he and other family members had converted to Islam. A letter from his brother Reginald admonished Malcolm not to eat any pork or smoke cigarettes and promised to show him how to get out of prison. Malcolm soon found himself in the cafeteria declining an offer of meat by saying that he didn't eat pork. In his autobiography, he recalls that gesture as his first step toward Allah. Attracted by its message of black dignity and self-determination, Malcolm quickly became interested in learning more about the group his siblings had joined, the Nation of Islam. He even initiated a correspondence with the group's leader, Elijah Muhammad.

INTO AND OUT OF THE NATION OF ISLAM

After his release from prison in May of 1953, Malcolm began to study directly under Elijah Muhammad in Chicago. He dropped the "slave name" of Little and became Malcolm X. That summer he became an assistant minister at Temple No. 1 in Detroit. A successful recruiter, he was soon dispatched to cities on the east coast to build temples. By then Malcolm was an enthusiastic proponent of the Nation's distinctive form of Islam. He affirmed that Elijah Muhammad had encountered Allah in the person of W. D. Fard in the early 1930s and that Fard had appointed Elijah as his Messenger. He also embraced the millennialist position of the Nation that the fall of America was imminent and that people of African descent could anticipate a better world to take its place.

Malcolm's rapid rise in the Nation provoked some friction with other ministers, particularly those close to Elijah Muhammad at the Chicago headquarters. As he became more of a public figure, he also encountered Muslims from around the world who questioned the orthodoxy of Elijah Muhammad's Islam. In addition, Malcolm became embroiled in the discussions of civil rights that came to the fore in the late 1950s and early 1960s. He clashed frequently with both black and white leaders who favored integration and stuck to the Nation's ideas of black separatism and self-determination. Over time, Malcolm moved toward greater black activism in politics, which fostered deepening suspicions of his motives among those at the Chicago headquarters who were already worried that he had been positioning himself as the likely successor to Elijah Muhammad.

Born Malcolm Little, Malcolm X became the most famous spokesperson and preacher for the Nation of Islam during its mid-twentieth-century heyday. He was the pastor of Temple no. 7 in New York until he formally broke with the movement and converted to Sunni Islam, ultimately taking the name El-Hajj Malik El-Shabazz. He was assassinated by Nation of Islam members on February 21, 1965. (Library of Congress)

Relations between Malcolm and his critics were exacerbated when Malcolm learned that Elijah Muhammad had fathered multiple children through affairs with his secretaries. In December of 1963, Nation of Islam's headquarters capitalized on Malcolm's comment that the violence of John F. Kennedy's assassination represented "the chickens come home to roost" by silencing and suspending him. By March of 1964, Malcolm had formally left the Nation. Twelve days later, he founded the Muslim Mosque Incorporated, which attracted a core of former members of the Nation.

The next, unfulfilled stage of Malcolm's life was energized by his decision to make the pilgrimage to Mecca. His experience on the hajj led him to both a reappraisal of Islam and of his attitude toward white people. On his return, he cofounded the Organization of African American Unity as a secular vehicle for promoting closer relations between American and African blacks.

Malcolm's new plans were abruptly terminated when he was assassinated by members of the Nation of Islam on February 25, 1965. But he left a powerful legacy that remains influential in American religion and politics.

See also: Muhammad, Elijah (1897–1975); Nation of Islam, The.

Further Reading
Marable, Manning. 2011. *Malcolm X: A Life of Reinvention.* New York: Penguin Books.
Malcolm X with Alex Haley. 1965. *The Autobiography of Malcolm X.* New York: Ballantine Books.

Marian Apparitions

Mary, who is a pivotal figure for all Christians, but particularly for Roman Catholics (and, to a slightly lesser degree, by Orthodox Christians), has become a supernatural and powerful figure in her own right as the Blessed Virgin. As the mother of Jesus Christ, she is closer to him than all other figures in the Bible and throughout history. Thus, her miraculous appearance, when it occurs, is interpreted as an event of theological and practical significance.

Though Marian apparitions, or the appearance of the Blessed Virgin, have been occurring throughout Christian history, they seemed to pick up speed in the nineteenth and twentieth centuries, initiating what many theologians and scholars alike have referred to as "the Marian Age," touched off by her multiple appearances at Lourdes. Between February and July of 1858, fourteen-year-old

The Chapel of the Apparitions is located at the site of a famous Marian apparition in Fatima, Portugal, in 1917. Marian apparitions occur worldwide and often become pilgrimage sites, with those who attend hoping to benefit from the presence of the Virgin or petition her for help or healing. (Zts/Dreamstime.com)

Bernadette Soubirous (later Saint Bernadette; 1844–1879) was visited eighteen times by the Virgin Mary in Lourdes. It is the very public and persistent nature of these appearances that have set Lourdes and the Marian Age apart. Those who subscribe to the idea of a Marian Age often attach apocalyptic meaning to her appearance, believing it means that the Second Coming of Christ is near. The fact that Mary often brings prophetic or apocalyptic messages to those who see her seems to confirm this eschatological timeframe.

MARIAN DEVOTIONAL CULTURE

For a Marian apparition to be confirmed, it must be authenticated by the Vatican. It must be deemed "worthy of belief," meaning that the message itself, the messenger, and the various events that surround it, such as miraculous healings, are determined to be true—though it is unclear precisely what the process of determining such truth is.

Often Mary has appeared to children—many of whom are girls who are often illiterate—such as at Lourdes in 1858 or Fatima, Portugal, in 1917 when Mary appeared to three "shepherd children." Children's innocence and credulity translate to a certain openness to miracles. Nonetheless, Mary has also appeared to adults, often women, many of whom have experienced some kind of suffering in their lives. Very often a particular Marian apparition becomes affiliated with a person. Marian "visionaries" are those to whom Mary appears, who often gather followings of their own, based on the fact that Mary continues appearing to them and delivering messages. Or Mary may become tied to a particular place, such as in Guadalupe, Mexico, where the shrine to Our Lady of Guadalupe has become a popular pilgrimage site.

Besides acting as a harbinger (or precipitant) of Christ's arrival, Mary often brings messages focused on preparing the soul and body for such an event. Very often, she comes to reinforce traditional values; this was the case for the Virgin of Bayside (Long Island, New York), who appeared to Veronica Leuken for nearly thirty years and often condemned the hypersexualized culture that surrounded her. Such messages speak to the broader, more subtle impact of Marian apparitions: the reawakening of faith. Though many (if not most Catholics) do not believe in Marian apparitions (nor are they required to by the Church), for those who do, it may reinvigorate their commitment to their faith.

Mary's appearances also seem to coincide with major world events, generally during times of crisis. The appearance of Mary at Fatima, for example, coincided with World War I. Mary reportedly revealed several secrets to the three children, one of which was that only a return to devotion of the Immaculate Heart of Mary would bring about the end of bloodshed. Additionally, Mary recommended consecrating Russia to the Immaculate Heart, which would usher in an era of peace and prosperity. In the twenty-first century, Estela Ruiz (1936–), a Mexican American visionary from Arizona, began to see frequent visions of Mary during her early fifties. Though she initially associated it with her personal suffering at the time (e.g., her son was suffering from a cocaine addiction), her visions began to take on broader

366 Marriage and Relationships in New Religious Movements

significance given the ongoing crisis at the Southern border and questions of citizenship in the United States, which was often a cauldron of bigotry toward Latinx people.

MARY IN A MODERN AGE

Though its most famous instances are historical in nature, Marian devotional culture has exploded with the help of the internet. Virtual devotional groups have formed to spread Mary's message, leading to a seeming spike in Marian apparitions (or at least the reporting thereof). Very few of these apparitions have been approved by the Vatican, however (at the end of the twentieth century, 8 out of 386 achieved that distinction). This has not diminished belief that such occurrences are real as much as it has shown the extension of Marian devotional culture as a new religious movement that exists both inside and outside of the Catholic Church. Understandably, the Catholic Church officially eschews devotion to such apparitions because the fervor with which they are embraced weakens the official power of the Church and because they have not been authenticated and could very likely be fraudulent. Yet, for those who believe they have seen Mary, the internet has empowered them to share their experiences.

It is unclear how many new Marian apparitions will achieve the vaunted status of Vatican-confirmed authenticity. Yet, Mary shows no signs of stopping, continuing to act as source of comfort, direction, and, increasingly, religious innovation for those open enough to perceive her and receive her message.

See also: Children and New Religious Movements; New Religions on/and the Internet.

Further Reading

Apolito, Paolo. 2005. *The Internet and the Madonna: Religious Visionary Experience on the Web*, trans. Antony Shugaar. Chicago: Chicago University Press.

Bromley, David G., & Rachel S. Bobbitt. 2011. "Visions of the Virgin Mary: The organizational Development of Marian Apparitional Movements." *Nova Religio* 14, no. 3: 5–41.

Cuneo, Michael W. 1997. *The Smoke of Satan: Conservative and Traditionalist Dissent in Contemporary American Catholicism*. New York: Oxford University Press.

Laycock, Joseph P. 2015. *The Seer of Bayside: Veronica Lueken & the Struggle to Define Catholicism*. New York: Oxford University Press.

Marriage and Relationships in New Religious Movements

Religions have a stake in marriages and relationships. At base a civil institution—two people connected legally in the eyes of the state—marriage has taken on religious, even salvific, significance.

HOLY MATRIMONY

For some new religions, marriage is central to their plans of salvation or millennialist expectation. Often, though not always, normative marital structures (heterosexual and monogamous pairings) are challenged by these new systems, where particular theologies necessitate such social deviation. For example, Latter-day Saints believe that the more souls born on earth, the more quickly Christ will return and the more people will have the opportunity to become "exalted" to the highest, celestial heaven. These theological factors set the stage for the Mormon system of plural marriage. In the late 1830s, Joseph Smith (1805–1844), founder of the Church of Jesus Christ of Latter-day Saints, began initiating the members of his inner circle into the practice of plural or "celestial" marriage, an ordinance that had been revealed to him by God some years earlier. Entering into plural marriages—whereby a man was "sealed" for eternity to multiple women—became the new mark of the covenant, or the sign of their chosenness in the sight of God, as well as the primary means of achieving exaltation.

Plural marriage was controversial from the start, and even at the height of its practice in Utah between 1852 and 1890, only a small fraction of Latter-day Saints engaged in it. Nonetheless, the vast majority of Mormon men and women defended its necessity, even if they remained in monogamous relationships. The practice was formally discontinued in 1890 following significant pressure from the U.S. government and a revelation to Mormon President Wilford Woodruff (1807–1898). This led to a schism within the Church; over time, many who viewed the decision to cease the practice as a sign of apostasy left the Church to continue the practice and are referred to, broadly, as Fundamentalist Mormons. Fundamentalist Mormon marital practices vary. There are sects that resemble the mainstream Mormon Church in all but name to those, like the Fundamentalist Church of Latter-day Saints (FLDS), led by currently imprisoned prophet, Warren Jeffs (1955–), which practice arranged plural marriages, often between older men and girls as young as twelve.

Also born in the nineteenth century was the Oneida Community, whose system of complex marriage both mirrored and diverged from the Mormons. Following a realization that Christ had returned in AD 70 and that the Kingdom of God was already here, John Humphrey Noyes (1811–1886) insisted that human beings begin living "perfectly." Part of this perfection meant relinquishing any selfish ties to a single person, which distracted from complete love and obedience to God. At his utopian religious community in Oneida, New York, Noyes implemented complex marriage, whereby every member was effectively married to every other member. Men and women engaged in sexual relationships, arranged by Noyes, but the aim was not pleasure but the expression of love of God (men, e.g., were required to practice "continence," meaning they could not ejaculate, which was a selfish, imperfect act). This focus on obedience over enjoyment challenged critiques that those in the community engaged in "free love." Children were born, but procreation was also regulated; mates were chosen by Noyes and children, called "stirpicults," were raised by the community, not by their biological parents exclusively. The practice ultimately faltered as Noyes aged, coupled with the fact that an increasing number of younger or second-generation members desired monogamous partnerships. The religious arm of the community dissolved in 1881.

In the twentieth century, the International Society for Krishna Consciousness (ISKCON or the Hare Krishna movement) advocated for marriage between men and women as a tool of spiritual progression. The movement was critiqued for its potentially retrogressive marital practices, which affirmed the wife's submission to her husband—by no means did all Hare Krishna women engage in these marital traditions. Perhaps no new religious movement during this century is better known for its focus on the sacredness of marriage than the Unification Church. Its founder, Rev. Sun Myung Moon (1920–2012), proposed an alternative to traditional Christian theology and biblical history: *both* Adam and Eve *and* Jesus had failed in their primary mission, which was to create a perfect, sinless family. Adam and Eve failed through their commission of sexual sin prior to having their union blessed and Jesus failed by neglecting to marry and procreate. Moon ultimately revealed that he and his wife, Hak Ja Han (1943–) were the True Parents of humanity and, through them, perfect families would be created who would usher in the Kingdom of God. The ritual outgrowth of this belief system is the Blessing Ceremony, which often occurs en masse (thousands are married at once). Very often couples have never met and most marriages are arranged, thereby negating selfish attachment, allowing the couple to love one another by loving God and enabling the creation of perfect, sinless children. The significant number of conversions by young people to the Unification Church, as well as media coverage of the mass weddings, made the religion vulnerable to accusations of "brainwashing"; and a popular target of the anticult movement.

BREAKING THE MARITAL BONDS

In contrast to those new religions that see marriage as a boon, there are those who view it as a bane. Some argue that marriage is simply an obstacle to spiritual progress, whereas others view it, and very often the sexual relationships that accompany it, as sinful. Among the latter group fall the Shakers. Originally from England, the Shakers migrated across the Atlantic at the time that the United States emerged as a new republic—thereby benefiting from the new constitutional protections of religious practice. The Shakers settled in New York, living communally, but celibately and as singles. This was because the Shakers' former leader, (Mother) Ann Lee (1736–1784), had experienced a revelation that sex was the root of sin—and marriage, as the practice that sacralized sex, was itself a condemnable institution. In preparation for the Second Coming of Christ, Mother Ann dissolved her own marriage, as did her fellow Shakers. Shaker celibacy continues today, though without an influx of new members, there were only two Shakers remaining in 2019.

Many twentieth-century new religions, particularly those born out of the counterculture of the 1960s, eschewed marriage but also celibacy, arguing instead for sacred forms of free love. Various sects of Neopaganism advocated for total sexual freedom and became renowned for their acceptance of the LGBTQ+ individuals (in some instances, such as among Dianic Wiccans, same-sex relationships among women were particularly celebrated and encouraged as a celebration of the divine feminine). The Family International (also known as the Children of God), a millennialist Christian sect, came to notoriety for their communitarian ethos as well as their advocacy of free love as an expression of God's love. Though married couples did join and remain married, very often they explored sexual partnerships with others. Children were also raised communally, though, unlike the Oneida Community, parents were not admonished to avoid special affection or attention toward their biological children. For a time, sex was also employed as a proselytizing tool, which earned the censure of external critics and concerned parents who feared their college-age children (who made up a good proportion of the Family's membership) had been initiated into a dangerous "cult." The 2010 "Reboot" ended the communal lifestyle of the Family and its alternative marital and sexual methods.

For a brief period during the 1980s, the Osho Movement established its own city, Rajneeshpuram, in Oregon, where its members could proceed along the path of spiritual elevation as directed by its leader, Shree Bhagwan Rajneesh or "Osho" (1931–1990). As an advanced spiritual teacher, Osho was believed to have progressed beyond the need for human institutions, such as marriage; social constructs, such as gender; and even human needs, such as sex. Marriage and procreation were discouraged, since they distracted partners and parents from their spiritual needs; this was particularly true for women, whom Osho ranked as more advanced in a spiritual sense, but whose traditional roles of wife and mother often encumbered them unnecessarily. Free love was welcomed as an alternative to monogamous, marital relationships, so long as it did not distract from necessary spiritual work.

The latter half of the twentieth century also witnessed the rise of various UFO religions, several of which concerned themselves with marital practices and the ordering of human relationships. Raëlians, founded by Claude Vorilhon, or Raël (1946–), are those who believe that human beings were created in a lab by extraterrestrial beings, the Elohim (one of the names for God in the Hebrew Bible). Raëlians encourage all forms of sexuality and have advocated for same-sex marriage; marriage as a means for procreation, while not forbidden, is viewed as a secondary measure behind the more important work of cloning. On the opposite side of the spectrum was Heaven's Gate, which discouraged all marital and sexual relationships among its members in preparation for their elevation to The Evolutionary Level Above Human.

CONCERNS OVER REGULATING RELATIONSHIPS

A consistent refrain of critics regarding new religious movements is that either the leaders or institutions seek to control their members. The notion that members must give up practices or rights they might have had in their previous lives is viewed as a dangerous signs that the religion is a "cult." This is particularly true when the relationships of followers are heavily regulated, particularly those of women, who are perceived as vulnerable to sexual predation by their involvement in such groups. Often these accusations are overblown (and exhibit a certain historical myopia given that many major religions have and continue to regulate the sexual relationships of their members, both laity and clergy). Most marriages and relationships that occur in new religious movements involve consenting adults. But nearly all of the new religious movements described above have been, at one time or another, the subject of scrutiny or even legal action because of their marital or relational practices.

However, there are instances where such concerns prove to be valid, such as the systemic statutory and marital rape occurring in Warren Jeff's FLDS. In the case of the Branch Davidians, suspicions of marital and sexual impropriety led to tragedy. Leader of the Branch Davidians, David Koresh (1959–1993), announced to those present with him at Mount Carmel Center in Waco, Texas, that their marriages were dissolved and all sexual practices were to cease. According to a prophecy, only he would be allowed to marry (ultimately taking multiple wives, some underage) and produce children, as his progeny would rule in heaven. Concerns over Koresh's relationships coupled with other accusations (most of which were later disproven) led to a raid by the Bureau of Alcohol, Tobacco, and Firearms and the Federal Bureau of Investigation, resulting in a devastating fire that killed over seventy-five people, including Koresh.

See also: Anticult Movement, The; Brainwashing; Branch Davidians; Children and New Religious Movements; Children of God (The Family International); Church of Jesus Christ of Latter-day Saints, The; Cult; Fundamentalist Mormons; Heaven's Gate; International Society for Krishna Consciousness (ISKCON); Koresh, David (1959–1993); Lee, (Mother) Ann (1736–1784); Millennialism; Moon, Rev. Sun Myung (1920–2012); Neopaganism; Noyes, John Humphrey (1811–1886); Oneida Community, The; Raëlians; Rajneesh, Shree Bhagwan/Osho (1931–1990); Rajneesh/Osho Movement, The; Sex, Sexuality, and New Religious Movements; Shakers, The; Smith, Joseph (1805–1844); UFO Religions; Unification Church, The; Utopianism in New Religious Movements; Vorilhon, Claude (Raël) (1946–); Wicca; Women in New Religious Movements.

Further Reading

Baker, Don. 2007. "Rites of Passage in the Unification Church." In *Religions of Korea in Practice.* Princeton: Princeton University Press.

Daynes, Kathryn M. 2008. *More Wives than One: Transformation of the Mormon Marriage System, 1840–1910.* Champaign: University of Illinois Press.

Elisha, Omri. 2002. "Sustaining Charisma: Mormon Sectarian Culture and the Struggle for Public Marriage, 1852–1890." *Nova Religio* 6, no. 1: 45–63.

Foster, Lawrence. 1984. *Religion and Sexuality: The Shakers, the Mormons, and the Oneida Community.* Urbana: University of Illinois Press.

Lewis, James, & Henrik Bogdan, eds. 2014. *Sexuality and New Religious Movements.* London: Palgrave MacMillan.

Mathers, Samuel Liddell (1854–1918)

The Western esoteric tradition draws on many resources, including Ancient Egyptian myths, Greco-Roman mystery religions, gnostic Christianity, Rosicrucianism, and Freemasonry, among other things. Occultists search for esoteric wisdom and often for practical rituals that can aid their spiritual evolution. Late-nineteenth and early-twentieth-century England saw a surge of interest in the occult and the development of several organizations devoted to occult pursuits. Among them was the Hermetic Order of the Golden Dawn, one of whose founders was Samuel Liddell Mathers, who early in life also took the surname MacGregor in a fictitious claim to Scottish ancestry.

Mathers's career shows the intersection of many lines of occult thought and practice. In 1877, he was initiated into Freemasonry; five years later he joined the "Societas Rosicruciana in Anglia." He was also familiar with Theosophy, irrespective of whether his claims of interaction with Helena Petrovna Blavatsky (1831–1891) were true. Mathers, however, was more interested in Western sources of ancient wisdom than the Eastern sources which Theosophy favored. Mathers even produced the first translation of parts of the *Zohar*, a key Kabbalistic text, even though he was translating from a German text and not the original language. Another mark of Mather's wide-ranging appetite for occult wisdom was his short pamphlet on tarot cards, published in 1888.

Also in 1888 Mathers was one of the founders of the Hermetic Order of the Golden Dawn, along with William Robert Woodman (1828–1891) and William Lynn Westcott (1848–1925). Westcott was the most influential of the founders; he claimed to have found among the papers of another occultist a "cipher manuscript" that outlined the rituals of a non-Masonic initiatory order. Although the claim later proved to be fictitious, the manuscript became central to the new group. Mathers's blend of Freemasonry with the secret wisdom attributed to the ancient Greco-Egyptian "thrice-greatest" deity Hermes also made a strong impact on the new group.

The Hermetic Order of the Golden Dawn, however, did not last long in its original form. Westcott left the Order because his position in it conflicted with his duties as a coroner. Mathers moved to Paris and claimed that he was the only one who had ever been in contact with the "Secret Chiefs," the analogue of Theosophy's Mahatmas. The group soon divided into competing factions, with Aleister Crowley (1875–1947) among those who sided with Mathers. The other faction expelled Mathers from the London temple, but Mathers and, after his death his wife Moina Mathers (née Mina Bergson, 1865–1928), kept the group going under the title Alpha and Omega. A contemporary group in that lineage keeps an archive of Mathers's writings (www.golden-dawn.com).

See also: Crowley, Aleister (1875–1947); Freemasonry; Hermetic Order of the Golden Dawn, The; Kabbalah; Occultism and Esotericism; Rosicrucianism; Waite, Arthur Edward (1857–1942).

Further Reading

Mathers, S. L. Macgregor. 1888. *The Tarot*. Available at: https://www.sacred-texts.com/tarot/mathers/index.htm.

Mathers, S. L. Macgregor, trans. 1912. *The Kabbalah Unveiled*; available at https://www.sacred-texts.com/jud/tku/index.htm.

Silva, Francisco Santos. 2015. "Samuel Liddell Mathers." In Christopher Partridge, ed., *The Occult World*, pp. 247–249. New York: Routledge.

Media and New Religious Movements

The news and entertainment media powerfully shape the ways in which individuals, social movements, and issues are understood by readers and viewers. Despite the professed diversity of viewpoints in the media, with few exceptions, media sources have presented an overwhelmingly one-sided and negative portrait of new religions. Media stories have frequently espoused the anticult position that virtually all new or alternative religions constitute "dangerous cults" that use processes of brainwashing to dupe their members. Those stories have raised alarms about the harm that individuals apparently inevitably suffer in new religions and, especially after the deaths at the Peoples Temple Agricultural Mission in Jonestown, Guyana in 1978, about the broader harm that new religions can do to society.

Media accounts, presumably in the search for more spectacular and engaging stories of rescue and redemption, have typically filtered out stories about individuals who are satisfied with their participation in new religions or who have left such groups quietly. Correspondingly, they have amplified the voices of a relatively few "noisy apostates" who have made strong claims about the malfeasance of their former groups.

Memoirs of disgruntled members of new religions constitute a cottage industry that is continually replenished. The titles of publications from disaffected members of various groups both express and reinforce the public understanding of "dangerous cults." A small sample includes *Crazy for God: The Nightmare of Cult Life* (1979) about the Unification Church; *Seductive Poison: A Jonestown's Survivor's Story of Life and Death in the Peoples Temple* (1998), and *Troublemaker: Surviving Hollywood and Scientology* (2015). Such stories provide fodder for TV movies and other programs that reinforce the stereotypical image of "cults." The actress Leah Remini (1970–), for example, has leveraged her memoir into a documentary series *Leah Remini: Scientology and the Aftermath*, which by 2019 had run for three seasons. *People* has run a series of articles and sponsored a documentary miniseries on "cults" as well.

Media reports have fueled the negative social perception of new religions and broad pleas to "do something" about "cults." That has prompted government inquiries into the "cult problem" in the United States, Europe, Australia, and elsewhere. Media accounts have also been used to justify government actions against groups, including the 1993 siege of the Branch Davidians and international raids against the communal homes of the Children of God. The media helps drive a mutually supporting feedback loop involving activist former members of new religions, the anticult movement, sympathetic journalists who at least implicitly claim the ability to discriminate between legitimate and illegitimate religions, and a public eager for stories that confirm the virtues of the religious status quo and demonize those who depart from it. The resulting image has had real consequences for new religions.

It has been difficult for new religions to alter their public perception and diminish the tensions that they experience in their social environments. One example is the conflation of various forms of contemporary Paganism with

Media and New Religious Movements

Satanism. Satanism elicits shock, revulsion, and fear in the general populace. That, of course, delighted Anton LaVey (1930–1997), the provocateur who founded the Church of Satan. In several instances when Pagan festivals were scheduled to be held in certain locales, local news stories capitalized on residents' fears by linking festivals with vaguely defined, but definitely frightening, Satanic rituals.

Once applied, elements of the media's cult stereotype are very sticky and hard to remove. One group that has made intensive efforts in that direction, though, is the Church of Scientology. From early in its history, for example, Scientology has made a concerted effort to attract high profile members. Individuals like Tom Cruise (1962–) and John Travolta (1954–) enjoy worldwide celebrity because of their appearances in popular films. Scientology both touts their membership and sometimes uses them to present its public face. Scientology also publishes *Celebrity* magazine, which features profiles of celebrity Scientologists in each issue.

Scientology has also striven to burnish its public image by developing a robust presence on the internet and has even started the Scientology channel, its own TV network. Visitors to www.scientology.org, for example, can view a variety of professionally produced videos on topics ranging from the life and work of the founder, L. Ron Hubbard (1911–1986), to the latest voyage of the *Freewinds*, Scientology's floating classroom. Visitors can also view filmed testimonials from people who claim that Scientology has dramatically improved their lives, a direct counter to the statements of critical former members. A similar series of testimonials, produced by the Church of Jesus Christ of Latter-day Saints, appears on YouTube under the general heading, "I'm a Mormon."

The battle between new religions and their opponents will continue to be played out in the print, video, and electronic media for the foreseeable future.

See also: Anticult Movement, The; Brainwashing; Branch Davidians; Children of God (The Family International); Church of Jesus Christ of Latter-day Saints, The; Deprogramming; Disaffiliation and Ex-membership in New Religious Movements; LaVey, Anton Szandor (1930–1997); Neopaganism; Peoples Temple; Satanism; Scientology; Unification Church, The.

Further Reading

Doherty, Bernard. 2014. "Sensational Scientology!: The Church of Scientology and Australian Tabloid Television." *Nova Religio* 17: 38–63.

McCloud, Sean. 2004. *Making the American Religious Fringe: Exotics, Subversives, and Journalists, 1955–1993.* Chapel Hill: The University of North Carolina Press.

Neal, Lynn S. 2011. "'They're Freaks'!: The Cult Stereotype in Fictional Television Shows, 1958–2008." *Nova Religio* 14: 81–107.

Richardson, James T. 1995. "Manufacturing Consent about Koresh: A Structural Analysis of the Role of Media in the Waco Tragedy." In Stuart A. Wright, ed., *Armageddon in Waco: Critical Perspectives on the Branch Davidian Conflict*, pp. 153–176. Chicago: The University of Chicago Press.

Ruskell, Nicole S., & James R. Lewis 2016. "Cult Journalism." In James R. Lewis & Inga B. Tøllefsen, eds., *The Oxford Handbook of New Religious Movements*, Vol. II, 2nd ed., pp. 222–233. New York: Oxford University Press.

Schorey, Shannon Prosper. 2016. "Media, Technology, and New Religious Movements: A Review of the Field." In James R. Lewis & Inga B. Tøllefsen, eds., *The Oxford Handbook of New Religious Movements*, Vol. II, 2nd ed., pp. 264–277. New York: Oxford University Press.

Mediums

Mediums have often served as a source of fascination, particularly among a modern, Western cultural audience who clamors for access to these individuals even as its members are skeptical of the veracity of their claims. And though the basic concept of mediumship is relatively stable—an individual serves as a temporary conduit for a spirit or supernatural entity—the varieties of practice, belief, and tradition that have arisen from the practice are myriad.

Many trace the modern phenomenon of mediumship to the nineteenth century, specifically to Spiritualism. Kate (1837–1892) and Margaret Fox (1833–1893) caused a stir in the late 1840s when they began experiencing "rappings" in their New York home. It was soon discovered that the two were mediums capable of summoning and becoming possessed by departed spirits; they began holding séances and embarked on a tour where they exhibited their abilities for packed audiences. Other mediums and offshoot movements would follow. Some extended the type of supernatural visitor to divine beings whose mission was not only to communicate with bereaved loved ones but to communicate sacred truths to the world. Helena Petrovna Blavatsky (1831–1891), founder of Theosophy and its institutional vehicle, the Theosophical Society, began her career as a Spiritualist medium, but soon found that a set of divine entities, the Great Masters, had much to tell her about the nature of reality, history, and sacred truth.

Each medium's experience varies over time and in comparison to others. Though most mediums forge connections with the spirit realm while in a trance, or even asleep (as was the case of Edgar Cayce [1877–1945], "The Sleeping Prophet"), some mediums experience physical changes, such as a change in voice, altered or enhanced physical abilities, bodily contortions, or according to some accounts, the ability to levitate while being possessed by a spirit. Some mediums experience telekinesis and telepathy while channeling a spirit; others engage in automatic writing, where they would write sacred tomes while entranced and without any memory of having done so after the fact. Some would not exhibit any outward phenomena, but would awake and communicate messages from the spirit world to those present. In the twentieth century, the practice of Channeling, popularized by teacher JZ Knight (1946–), became synonymous with religious mediumship, often attracting a wealthy clientele (actress Shirley MacLaine [1934–] is a famous pupil of Knight's).

Many, if not most, mediums were and are women. Historically, women are conceived as being closer to the spiritual realm than men and, therefore, more susceptible to supernatural influence, for good or ill. However, women who claimed such connections were often suspected rather than praised. At the height of the Spiritualist frenzy in the nineteenth century, many mediums became engaged in women's rights activism. Serving as mediums enabled women a degree of professional success and notoriety not typically permitted by conventional gender roles. Thus, mediumship was a subversive means to assert women's power and ability, which had effects reaching beyond séance circles and into the twentieth century, where women made strides in political and social spheres.

Despite its popularity, as long as there have been claims of mediumship there have been accusations of fraud. Beginning with the Fox sisters, who later admitted to manufacturing much of the famed "phenomena," many mediums have been suspected, accused, and occasionally admitted to fraud. Among those mediums genuinely desirous of speaking to the beyond were certainly a few interested in making money. Further, the practice of mediumship has a long history and extends far past the European-American context. Mediumship in the form of Espiritismo (Kardecism) abounds in the Caribbean and South America, and even earlier traditions of mediumship are rooted in Southeast Asia and Africa. Though it was the Western mystics who captivated and perplexed European society, mediumship predates these people, a fact that highlights the hegemony of white, European history as it does the indebtedness of these Western "esoteric" religions to continents of the Southern and Eastern Hemispheres.

See also: Blavatsky, Helena Petrovna (1831–1891); Cayce, Edgar (1877–1945); Channeling; Fox, Kate (1837–1892), and Margaret (1833–1893); Fraud and Deception in New Religions; Ghosts, the Paranormal, and New Religious Movements; Kardecism (Spiritism); Knight, JZ (Ramtha) (1946–); Occultism and Esotericism; Spiritualism; Theosophical Society, The; Theosophy; Women in New Religious Movements.

Further Reading

Espirito Santo, Diana. 2015. *Developing the Dead: Mediumship and Selfhood in Cuban Espiritismo.* Gainesville: University of Florida Press.

Kuzmeskus, Elaine. 2012. *The Art of Mediumship: Psychic Investigation, Clairvoyance, and Channeling.* Atglen, PA: Schiffer Publishing.

Owen, Alex. 2004. *The Darkened Room: Women, Power, and Spiritualism in Late Victorian England.* Chicago: University of Chicago Press.

Membership and New Religious Movements

Why join a religion? This question can be answered in infinite ways. A life-changing experience that prompts conversion, marriage to someone who is devout, feeling drawn to the community proffered by religion, or connection with a particular belief system—all number among the possible responses. However, when the religion one joins is classified as a "cult," the assumptions about the reasons behind and the requirements for membership often reflect the generally negative opinion of such groups. Stereotypes abound that members of new religions are "brainwashed," isolated and stripped of their autonomy and identity and then ascribed new ones, and that the religions themselves are controlling, manipulative, and sinister in intention. The perception persists that members are trapped in such religions, making disaffiliation nearly impossible without outside intervention. The notion that members of new religious movements are conscious agents in their choice to become members of these groups is ignored.

In reality, the process of membership in new religious movements is far more various than these perceptions allow. While there *are* new religions that require a great deal of their members, including isolation from family and friends, this is certainly not the case for all. Degrees of commitment vary just as they do for more established traditions. Nor, in the cases of religions that are more exclusive and demanding, is it a given that members are duped and forced into participation. In the majority of cases, members join such movements because, not in spite, of these very aspects and the desire to give themselves holistically to a spiritual cause. Issues may arise for children born into these traditions, who, like all children raised in a particular religion, may absorb the beliefs of their parents without question—or whose own interest may wane, leading to disaffiliation. In such a way, new religions are equivalent to established traditions in that the ability to sustain membership, whether by recruitment or across generations, is crucial to their survival and may ultimately shape the requirements for members.

VARIETIES OF MEMBERSHIP IN NEW RELIGIONS

In the internet age in particular, it is far easier to be a dabbler in a religious culture or as a virtual member only. Such is the case for religions such as Vampirism, whose members gather primarily via online forums and who may never actually meet. Little is required of members apart from conscious identification as a Vampire and members may determine their own level of commitment. There are also numerous new religions where those interested may participate in workshops or courses, but whose practice is primarily undertaken privately. This is the case for Transcendental Meditation or the Self-Realization Fellowship, for example. Religious communities such as the Federation of Damanhur offer different pathways of membership from those who live communally onsite in Italy to those who visit occasionally for group worship to those who are casual visitors to its famous Temples of Humankind.

Not all new religions are so open and flexible with their beliefs, practices, and institutions. As with many religions, the ability to participate in or gain access to these systems requires initiation into the religion itself. Some of the perception of new religious movements as dangerous comes from the fact that membership protocols may be carried out in secret or that knowledge of the institution or its beliefs come only when a member has fully invested in the faith. For example, the Church of Jesus Christ of Latter-day Saints, which was historically persecuted, is protective of their rituals, and only initiated (or "endowed") members know their precise nature. Membership is also stringently regulated: to participate in the most sacred Temple rituals, members must produce a "recommend card," which proves they remain a member in good standing of the Church. Other new religious movements, such as Freemasonry, protect both their rituals and its membership, and one may not know who is a member and who is not. This has led to vast conspiracy theories regarding the involvement of Freemasons in major world events.

Though less secretive regarding membership rolls, the Church of Scientology requires members to progress exceedingly far in the spiritual process before they are given key theological information—a process that may take years (or successive lifetimes).

There are new religions where total commitment is required, sometimes, though not always, accompanied with a divestment from one's previous life, interpersonal relationships, and identity. This is often the case for millennialist groups or traditions that believe that external events will soon usher in a new world order—or that this new world has already arrived. For the Shakers, who are best known for their communal, celibate living arrangements, members abstain from sex, familial relationships, and personal ownership of all kinds. The members of Heaven's Gate were also required to live communally and celibately, in addition to being asked to cut ties with the outside world, to take on new names and identities, and to prepare their bodies for advancement to The Evolutionary Level Above Human. The ritual suicide of the members of Heaven's Gate had the unfortunate side-effect of confirming the worst fears of membership in new religious movements: that it is ultimately fatal. This, however, is the exception, not the rule.

See also: Brainwashing; Children of God (The Family International); Church of Jesus Christ of Latter-day Saints, The; Conversion; Cult; Damanhur; Disaffiliation and Ex-Membership in New Religious Movements; Freemasonry; Heaven's Gate; Millennialism; Scientology; Seekers; Self-Realization Fellowship (Yogananda); Shakers, The; Transcendental Meditation; Vampirism.

Further Reading

Coates, Dominiek D. 2014. "New Religious Movement Membership and the Importance of Stable 'Others' for the Making of Selves." *Journal of Religion and Health* 53: 1300–1316.

Dawson, Lorne L. 2003. "Joining New Religions." In *Cults and New Religious Movements: A Reader.* London: Wiley-Blackwell.

Dawson, Lorne L. 2006. "Who Joins New Religious Movements and Why?" In *Comprehending Cults: The Sociology of New Religious Movements.* New York: Oxford University Press.

Murken, Sebastian, & Sussan Namini. 2007. "Childhood Familial Experiences as Antecedents of Adult Membership in New Religious Movements: A Literature Review." *Nova Religio* 10, no. 4: 17–37.

Mesmerism

From one vantage point, the verb "to mesmerize," meaning to entrance or hypnotize, is the only lasting contribution of the movement known as Mesmerism. Viewed another way, Mesmerism lives on in multiple alternative healing and spiritual practices, from chiropractic to homeopathy to Christian Science to the modern wellness movement. Thus, while the actual practice of Mesmerism may have died out, its undergirding belief that people could manipulate their physical surroundings and selves with methods outside of Western medicine and religion persists.

Created by Franz Mesmer, Mesmerism was premised on the theory of animal magnetism, or the notion that there is a universal fluid that permeates all life, which can be manipulated through specific methods (including hypnotism) to promote health and well-being. Mesmeric therapy often involved the use of magnets to manipulate fluid in the body, thus healing bodily ailments; above is depicted a form of ophthalmic mesmeric therapy. (Wellcome Library)

ORIGINS AND FOUNDER

Franz Anton Mesmer (1734–1815) was a German physician who began to experiment with alternative methods of treatment with his patients. Proceeding on a belief that there existed an invisible magnetic connection within and between all living beings (including human beings) Mesmer began to employ magnets in his practice around 1774. In his experiments, he would have the patient swallow a solution that contained iron, after which he would hold magnets at the afflicted points in the body. Many patients reported sensations of fluid rushing through them, accompanied by a relenting of their symptoms.

As a result of his experiments, Mesmer concluded that the mysterious fluid was animal magnetism, which could be manipulated through various means to heal, among other things. Eventually, Mesmer stopped using magnets in his practice, opting for more direct methods: using his hands to place pressure on various points of the body (sometimes for hours) or simply passing his hands over the troubled area. Mesmer grew convinced that healing occurred through the invisible, fluid connection between himself and the patient; the only cure one needed was already present in oneself and the natural world.

Mesmer's practices were met with praise in some quarters and censure in others. After Mesmer moved to France in the late 1770s, the French scientific and medical community fell in the latter category. Try as he might to make animal magnetism a viable scientific method, only a few willingly designated it as such. Only Charles d'Eslon, who coauthored Mesmer's seminal text, *Mémoire sur la découverte du magnétisme animal* (1779; in English, *The Discovery of Animal Magnetism*), would count as a physician of any significant clout. Though Mesmer did continue to gain some disciples, the large-scale rejection of his work on animal magnetism would eventually compel him to leave Paris. He died in relative obscurity in Germany in 1815, though he continued to teach about animal magnetism until his death. By the 1840s, animal magnetism was called *mesmerism*, reflecting the popular focus on Mesmer's methods for healing rather than his discoveries about a universal, invisible fluid.

FROM ANIMAL MAGNETISM TO MESMERISM

In the years following Mesmer's death, animal magnetism continued to attract a following, prompting an investigation by the French Royal Academy of Medicine in 1826 (a similar investigation of 1774 had panned Mesmer and the practice). While refusing to comment on the existence of any magnetic fluid, the investigators acknowledged that the effects of magnetism were real, even recommending that the practice be awarded a place in medicine. A similar evolution would occur as animal magnetism evolved into mesmerism. Not all mesmerists subscribed to the belief that a universal, invisible fluid connected and flowed through all life, but they did believe in the efficacy of the methods Mesmer created or inspired to heal and enact change.

The practice with which mesmerism has become most associated, hypnotism, gained ascendance in the 1840s, although Mesmer had practiced hypnosis during his life. Abbé Faria (1756–1819), a disciple of Mesmer's and a proponent of modern hypnotism, had argued that no special methods were needed to heal someone and that the cure, which he believed was found inside every patient, could be coaxed through the power of suggestion. The mind and nervous system were most suggestible in a hypnotic state. A number of methods were used to hypnotize patients, including music (a favorite of Mesmer's). Once hypnotized, a patient would be able to access knowledge about the illness that could not be accessed while fully awake. In other words, patients were able to diagnose themselves.

Mesmer had often demonstrated his techniques in front of audiences and had been known for his showmanship, but it was "stage hypnotism" that drew the largest audiences. Stage hypnotists still perform today, though they are generally engaged in the practice for entertainment purposes or comic relief, rather than to demonstrate miraculous healing. However, mesmerism should not be conflated with hypnotism; hypnotism is one method among several employed by Mesmer and mesmerists.

OFFSHOOTS AND CULTURAL SIGNIFICANCE

Though created by a scientist and presented as a scientific practice, mesmerism was adapted by those with specifically religious interests. Mary Baker Eddy (1821–1910), the founder of Christian Science, came to Mesmerist and founder of the Mind Cure movement, Phineas Quimby (1802–1866), for healing when Western medicine had failed her. Quimby introduced Eddy to the idea that healing was simply the result of right thinking. After a nearly fatal fall in 1866, Eddy realized that her illness was the result of "sin" or wrong thinking; through prayer and reliance on God, she was healed—a practice she called "Divine Science."

Relics of mesmerism and animal magnetism can also be found in contemporary wellness culture. For example, acupressure—the name one might give Mesmer's pressure technique—is sought by those seeking relief from various ailments. Additionally, hypnosis has become a common practice (called hypnotheraphy) among therapists to treat addiction in mental and physical health issues. Perhaps mesmerism's greatest influence is the belief that healing is—and should be—found outside of Western medicine. It should be no surprise, then, that mesmerism has merged with spiritual healing practices and a broader religious seeker culture that privileged practices outside of established institutions.

See also: Christian Science; Eddy, Mary Baker (1821–1910); Healing, Health, and New Religious Movements; New Thought; Quimby, Phineas (1802–1866).

Further Reading

Darnton, Robert. 1986. *Mesmerism and the End of the Enlightenment in France.* Cambridge, MA: Harvard University Press.

Mesmer, Franz. 2016; 1779. *Mesmerism: The Discovery of Animal Magnetism.* Amazon Digital Services LLC.

Ogden, Emily. 2018. *Credulity: A Cultural History of US Mesmerism.* Chicago: University of Chicago Press.

Messianic Judaism

In the sense that Jews anticipate their Messiah (which means "anointed one" in Hebrew), Judaism can be considered a Messianic religion. However, most Jews reject any connection with the movement known broadly as "Messianic Judaism," which they identify as a branch of evangelical Christianity. Messianic Jews believe, like Christians, that the Messiah arrived in the person of Jesus of Nazareth. What differentiates them from Christians is their practice of traditional Jewish rites and ceremonies. In this way, Messianic Judaism can be said to straddle both Judaism and Christianity, though members of both traditions refuse to claim Messianic Jews as their own.

ORIGINS

In certain books of the Hebrew Bible, notably Isaiah and Daniel, a Messiah is predicted who will deliver the chosen people, known as Israel, from suffering and lead them to the promised land where they will enjoy an eternity of peace and prosperity. During the first century CE, a group of Jews came to believe that Jesus of Nazareth was this Messiah. However, unlike the prophetic texts where all of Israel chose to follow the Messiah, in reality, not all Jews were so convinced. Thus, efforts to convert Jews to Christianity began as soon as something like Christianity took shape and are recorded in the New Testament, with the Apostle Paul being perhaps the most famous Jewish convert (see Gal. 1:11–16; Acts 9:1–18; 22:3–16; 26:4–23). Proselytization of Jews continued in various forms, in varying levels of intensity, and with varying degrees of success from that point onward.

Not until the nineteenth century, however, did a group of Jewish converts to Christianity move to create their own movement, apart from both Judaism and Christianity, while still claiming linkages to both. This movement, known as the Hebrew Christian movement, began in the United Kingdom, when several Hebrew Christian "churches" arose in London; the Hebrew Christian Alliance was founded in 1860. During the latter half of the nineteenth century, Hebrew Christian denominations appeared in New York City. In the early twentieth century, the Hebrew Christian Alliance of America (HCAA) was formed, whose job was to organize the disparate movement as well as to assure their evangelical Christian peers that they were simply their missionary arm that targeted the Jews.

In the mid-twentieth century, Messianic Judaism experienced a boom, particularly following the founding of Israel (1948) and the Six-Day War (1967), both of which seemed to bring to fruition the biblical notion that Israel was the sacred home of the Jews. Further, the return of the Jews to Israel aligned with certain fundamentalist and millennialist interpretations of the Bible, particularly the Book of Revelation, which tied the homecoming of the Jews to the Second Coming of Christ. Prior to Christ's return, a large number of Jews would convert to Christianity and prophesy on behalf of Christ. Though Messianic Jews are millennialist in orientation—they see the events occurring in the Middle East as signs of a new age and the coming of Christ—they often refer to the world to come as "the age of Israel," where Israel (the people) will be seen in their full glory.

In addition to changes occurring in the Middle East during that time, the 1960s in the United States were a period of great religious innovation and fervor. This led to an influx of Jewish converts to the HCAA. Many of these converts were young, born of the counterculture of the 1960s; they would form the Youth Hebrew Christian Alliance. Distinctive Messianic Jewish sects also formed during this time, most notably Jews for Jesus. Founded by Martin "Moishe" Rosen (1932–2010) as Hineni (meaning "Here I Am") Ministries in 1970, then Jews for Jesus in 1973, Jews for Jesus is arguably the most well-known and the most prolific Messianic Jewish denomination. Like other Messianic Jewish groups, it is a proselytizing movement that focuses on the conversion of Jews to Christianity. However, reflective of modern Messianic Jewish groups, Jews for Jesus are conscious of cultivating a distinctive Jewish identity and praxis, over against earlier Hebrew Christian movements, which often faded into "gentile" Christianity.

BELIEFS AND PRACTICES

Though variants of Messianic Judaism may differ on small points of doctrine, all share a common character: they are Christian in belief and (qualified) Jewish in practice. Central to Messianic Jewish belief is that Jesus (often referred to by his Hebrew name, Yeshua) is the Messiah. Jesus is believed to be both God and human and his death enabled the salvation of all. Salvation is available, however, only to those who believe Christ to be the Messiah and savior. They are trinitarian, meaning that they believe God, Jesus, and the Holy Spirit make up equal parts of the "Godhead." All Messianic Jews believe that both the Hebrew Bible and the New Testament are divinely inspired texts, maintaining that the former seamlessly transitions to the latter in terms of narrative. Most Messianic Jews argue that the New Testament is a definitively Jewish text. Opinion varies, however, on the viability of the "Oral Torah," including the Talmud and other rabbinic commentaries. Unlike Orthodox Jewish denominations that often treat the Torah and Talmud as equal partners, Messianic Jews invariably elevate the Torah above the Talmud as a binding and authoritative text.

Though some Messianic Jewish groups still refer to their places of worship as "churches," many opt for the traditionally Jewish synagogue or, more neutrally, congregations. It is in these sites of worship that the syncretism of Judaism and Christianity is most clear. For example, displayed in worship sites and on missionary materials, the Messianic Jewish "seal" includes a menorah, star of David, and fish or "ichthys," an ancient symbol of Christianity. Unlike both Jewish and Christian denominations, Messianic Jewish groups often allow both Jewish and non-Jewish members to join and participate.

Drawing from Judaism, Messianic Jews observe Shabbat, which begins on sundown on Friday and lasts through sundown on Saturday. Weekly and annual services feature readings from both Jewish and Christian scriptures, with a focus on Jesus as the Jewish Messiah, as well as traditional Jewish prayers, songs, and practices. Holidays such as Yom Kippur and Passover are observed, in addition to Christian holidays such as Easter and Christmas. Additionally, the Christian rite of baptism is performed, though it is referred to as "mikveh," or immersion in the traditional Jewish bath. Messianic Jews also have Bar/Bat Mitzvahs, the Jewish service that introduces a young man and woman into the Jewish community; those ceremonies feature readings from both the Hebrew Bible and New Testament.

Messianic Jews are tasked with proselytizing, specifically to Jews, though they believe their message should be spread to everyone. Jews are traditionally non-proselytizing, thus the missionary impulse of Messianic Jews is a decidedly Christian innovation. Spreading literature, such as pamphlets and books, is the primary means through which their message is spread.

CRITIQUE AND CONTEMPORARY CULTURE

Messianic Jews experience critique from many quarters, most notably from Jewish denominations. Most Jews object to the self-designation of Messianic Jews as "Jewish," since they accept Christ as their savior, a doctrine that seemingly disqualifies them. Further, Jews from all of the major denominations have argued that groups like Jews for Jesus are thinly veiled evangelical or Fundamentalist Christian sects, using Judaism disingenuously to "lure" Jews to Christianity.

Christians have both supported and criticized Messianic Judaism. Supporters view the movement as a viable means of bringing more people to the Gospel. Often groups with more millennialist views are supportive of Messianic Jews. Those Christians who are more critical often fall into two categories: those who feel the movement is a Christian movement and should simply be called such and those who dislike the infringement on Jewish people.

In November 2018, a Messianic Jewish rabbi made headlines when Vice President Mike Pence invited him to lead a service in honor of the slain members of the Tree of Life synagogue, who were gunned down in late October of that year. Many were highly critical of the choice, given the fact that most Jews do not consider Messianic Judaism to be a viable Jewish denomination.

However, with membership in the tens to hundreds of thousands by some estimates, to say that Messianic Judaism is controversial does not mean that it does not represent a vital and significant new religious movement—even as its members would claim to be an "ancient religion."

See also: Jews for Jesus; Messianism and New Religious Movements; Millennialism; Sect.

Further Reading

Ariel, Yaakov. 2006. "Judaism and Christianity Unite! The Unique Culture of Messianic Judaism." In Eugene V. Gallagher & Michael W. Ashcraft, eds., *Introduction to New and Alternative Religions in America.* Westport, CT: Greenwood Press.

Ariel, Yaakov. 2016. "Theological and Liturgical Coming of Age: New Developments in the Relationship between Messianic Judaism and Evangelical Christianity." *Hebrew Studies* 57, no. 1: 381–391.

Cohn-Sherbok, Dan. 2000. *Messianic Judaism.* New York: Cassell Publishers.

Harris-Shapiro, Carol. 1999. *Messianic Judaism: A Rabbi's Journey through Religious Change in America.* Boston: Beacon Press.

Stern, David H. 2010. *Restoring the Jewishness of the Gospel: A Message for Christians Condensed from Messianic Judaism.* Clarksville, MD: Messianic Jewish Publishers.

Messianism and New Religious Movements

In the Hebrew Bible/Old Testament the term from which "messiah" is derived refers to someone or something that is anointed. Typically used with reference to high priests and kings, the term has even been applied to the Persian king Cyrus (c. 600–530 BCE) whom the Bible records as having issued an edict permitting Jews held captive in Babylonia to return home (see Isa. 45:1). The term also referred to a future king in the Davidic line who would reunite the twelve tribes and rebuild the temple in Jerusalem. Many early Christians took the messianic prophecies of the Hebrew Bible to refer to Jesus, describing him as having the singular status of the Christos ("anointed one" in Greek). In the wake of Jesus's crucifixion, Christians developed the expectation that he would return sometime in the future to establish the righteous messianic Kingdom of God.

The concept of a Messiah, then, is intimately connected with notions of prophecy, millennialism, and a coming judgment. In Islam, Jesus the human prophet is expected by some to return with the Mahdi ("the rightly guided one") just before the Last Judgment to establish a just society. The Ahmadiyya Muslim Community identifies its founder, Mizra Ghulam Ahmad (1835–1944) as both the Mahdi and the Messiah, but some Muslims accuse the Ahmadis of illegitimate doctrinal innovations and brand them as heretics.

The future orientation of messianic thought, along with the general acknowledgment that Jesus has not yet returned to complete his messianic mission, has led to two thousand years of speculation about precisely when such events might happen and who will fulfill the role of the Messiah. The conviction that the Messiah has returned or is about to return has been a driving force in many new religious movements. As with the concept of the imminent millennium, however, the search for a Messiah has been endlessly frustrated. Claims have been made, candidates have been announced, and individuals have been recognized as messiahs, but salvation from the world's imperfections and wickedness that a messiah will bring has remained tantalizingly out of reach.

MESSIAHS IN NEW RELIGIONS

In the United States one of the earliest messiahs put forward was identified by the Shakers, formally known as the United Society of Believers in Christ's Second Appearing. They came to see Mother Ann Lee (1736–1784) as the female incarnation of Christ and therefore the herald of the imminent transformation of the world. That conviction lent their missionary efforts a special urgency and provided a rationale for the celibate, communal way of life that the Shakers adopted. But Mother Ann's death also created the need for rationalizations about why salvation had not yet occurred.

Elaborate justifications of the messianic status of individuals have been developed in many new religions. David Koresh (1959–1993), for example, supported his claim to be Christ for the present time with both an appeal to his own religious experience and an elaborate interpretation of the Bible. Koresh sometimes alluded to but never gave a full account of having experienced an ascent into the heavens while in Jerusalem in 1985. Koresh was not alone in such claims since Muhammad made his Night Journey from Jerusalem (See Qur'an 17:1) and the early Christian apostle Paul appears to have made a similar claim. In each instance, the ascent invested the individual with divinely sanctioned authority.

In Koresh's case, his ascent led him to identify himself as the Lamb of God mentioned in Revelation 5 who was the only one capable of opening the scroll sealed with seven seals. Koresh taught his followers that as each seal was opened not only would the events be interpreted but they would also be enacted. Thus, he informed his Bible students that during the Federal Bureau of Investigation siege of the Mount Carmel Center that they were now "in the sixth seal" and

Messianism and New Religious Movements

385

consequently very close to the end. Koresh's death on April 19, 1993, virtually wiped out the Branch Davidian community, but others have arisen to claim a similar status among the few remaining faithful.

The contemporary Chabad movement, an orthodox, Hasidic form of Judaism that focuses outreach efforts to unaffiliated Jews, has also produced two candidates for the status of Messiah. Menachem Mendel Schneerson (1902–1994), the seventh Rebbe or spiritual leader of the group, endorsed the messianic claims made for his predecessor and father-in-law Yosef Yitzchak Schneerson (1880–1950). Later, many of Menachem Mendel's followers believed that he was the Messiah, though his position on the question remained unsettled at his death. Such claims, however, can maintain the intense commitments of followers and direct their energies to the propagation of the movement.

Interpretation of biblical sources can push the concept of the Messiah into unforeseen directions. The Unification Church is founded on the Rev. Sun Myung Moon's (1920–2012) experience of revelation on Easter morning in 1936 , which led Moon to offer a thoroughgoing reinterpretation of the Christian scriptures, first published as *Divine Principle* in 1952. That text told the story of the failure of Adam and Eve, and then Jesus himself, to establish a perfect loving family as God intended. Consequently, the world has stood in need of a third Adam and a second advent of the Messiah. Moon hinted at his own status for some time and excited the interest of his followers. Finally, in the 1990s and 2000s, Moon stated unequivocally that he and his wife, Hak Ja Han (1943–), were indeed the True Parents of humankind. Together, they occupied the redemptive position of the Lord of the Second Advent or the Messiah. The evident inadequacies of some of Moon's children and the development of schismatic groups after his death have, among some, cast such claims into doubt, though the consequences of Moon's passing are still being played out.

The line between someone serving as a prophetic herald of a coming millennial transformation and actually serving as the personal savior for a religious community can be very thin. It is clear that Ann Lee, David Koresh, and Sun Myung Moon either claimed or had attributed to them messianic status. They were the ones who could accomplish the transformation of society and not merely envisage it.

But in other cases, charismatic leaders seem to have stopped short of making the transition between prophet and messiah. In the Ghost Dance in the late-nineteenth-century United States, it was clear that Christianity had shaped the expectation for American Indians of the coming age of well-being, even though the mechanism of bringing about the revivification of native culture is the adaptation of a traditional dance. The Prophet Wovoka (1856–1932) envisioned the removal of the white man from native lands and the return of plenty but reserved for "Grandfather" or the Messiah the role of bringing that about. Similarly, in Heaven's Gate, Marshall Applewhite ("Do," 1932–1997) was the only source of accurate information about the "Next Level," but it was the Next Level, and not Applewhite, that would accomplish the imminent transformation of the earth.

In some instances, messianic claims can be made about someone even though that person rejects them. For many, Haile Selassie I of Ethiopia is a divine and messianic figure. Selassie's explicit rejection of such a status did little to deter Rastafari from imagining him as the one who would help them chant down Babylon and establish the messianic kingdom of Zion. The more distant Selassie remained from the Rastafari, the more they have been able to project their hopes upon him.

Some scholars have endeavored to extend the category of messianism beyond the Jewish and Christian traditions. They point, for example, to the concept of the future Buddha, Maitreya, as a messianic concept in Buddhism. Some Buddhist traditions expect the appearance of the bodhisattva Maitreya in the future, when knowledge of the true teaching of Buddhism has been all but lost. Maitreya will then communicate the pure dharma. In his complex mix of Christian and Buddhist ideas, Shoko Asahara (1955–2018), the founder of Aum Shinrikyō, identified himself not only as the Christ but as Maitreya. Asahara's messianic aspirations were undone, however, by his efforts to hasten the arrival of the millennial kingdom of Shambala through Aum's violent attack on the Tokyo subway in 1995.

However they are defined, the search for messianic figures has been an important part of many new religious movements. Such figures can crystalize the hopes and dreams of an audience and identify how they can be made real.

See also: Asahara, Shoko (1955–2018); Charisma and Leadership in New Religious Movements; Ghost Dance Movement (Wovoka); Koresh, David (1959–1993); Messianic Judaism; Millennialism; Moon, Rev. Sun Myung (1920–2012); Rastafari; Shakers, The.

Further Reading
Lantenari, Vittorio. 1963. *The Religions of the Oppressed: A Study of Modern Messianic Cults.* New York: Knopf.

Robbins, Thomas, & Susan Jean Palmer, eds. 1997. *Millennium, Messiahs, and Mayhem: Contemporary Apocalyptic Movements.* New York: Routledge.

Schäfer, Peter, & Mark R. Cohen, eds. 1998. *Toward the Millennium: Messianic Movements from the Bible to Waco.* Leiden: E. J. Brill.

Millennialism

Not to be confused with "millennial," the term now associated with a particular generation that came of age around the turn of the twenty-first century, millennialism is a concept most commonly affiliated with a particular mindset within Christianity generally dated to the first century of the Common Era. However, millennialism extends beyond Christianity in time—one could look to the Book of Daniel, a prophetic book of the Hebrew Bible, for evidence of millennialist tendencies—and in tradition, applying to groups outside of the Christian fold who, even if they are not awaiting the return of Christ, await a new world order and a seismic supernatural event. To be "millennialist," in other words, implies a worldview more than a particular religious affiliation, a fact that, ironically, has spurred the growth of countless religious groups who claim to be millennialist religions.

CONCEPT AND ORIGINS

The term "millennium" translates to "one thousand years." For Christians, however, *the* millennium refers to the return of Christ and his one-thousand-year reign as predicted in the biblical Book of Revelation (see Revelation 20). The expectation of this event is known as millennialism. The expectation of Christ's return was present immediately following Christ's crucifixion (evidently the Apostle Paul believed Christ would return in his lifetime). So, technically, all Christians are millennialists, as Christ's return was built into the very fabric of earliest Christianity.

Over time, the term "millennialism" has come to refer to movements or groups who actively await or even try to bring about the return of Christ (referred to as "Second Advent") or some equivalent religious event; the expectation of various, often catastrophic, events that will accompany this awaited moment; and the belief in the total transformation of the world, which will be enjoyed by the faithful. Such vital anticipation manifests in any number of ways from reading Scripture to trying to predict the "signs" of the coming events, mandating particular practices to prepare the body and soul for Christ's return, "date-setting" or the prediction of various events for particular dates, or engaging in actions believed to precipitate the events themselves.

GENERAL PATTERNS OF MILLENNIALIST BELIEF

The most common varieties of millennialism are pre and postmillennialism, whose practitioners are concerned with one particular event known as "the Rapture." The Rapture refers to the moment when all true believers (both living and dead) will be lifted from earth, where they will meet Christ in the clouds, thus avoiding all of the terrible tribulations about to take place on earth (see 1 Thess. 4:13–17). Premillennialism (often parallel to "catastrophic millennialism" for those who share certain characteristics of this worldview, but who are not Christian) refers to the belief that the Rapture will occur *pre*millennium. Premillennialists typically take a more pessimistic view of the world. They believe that there is little hope for humanity and that the Christian message cannot be spread without heavenly help. Thus, the only recourse is for Christ to remove all Christians and purify a corrupt world. Premillennialists are also among the groups most likely to engage in anticipatory and occasionally defensive or violent action as a result of their belief that the end of the world is imminent. And while all millennialists expect the coming apocalypse (which simply translates to "revelation of something hidden"), the term "apocalypticism" is often mapped onto those of a premillennialist mindset. Those who subscribe to an apocalyptic outlook perceive imminent catastrophe, which, for Christians, will play out in the events described by the Book of Revelation or, for non-Christians or secular millennialists (often awarded the title of "doomsday" thinkers), in accordance with other sacred texts or theories.

Postmillennialists, on the other hand, are those who believe the rapture will occur *post*millennium. Unsurprisingly, they take a more optimistic point of view, believing that the world will continue to improve and that Christianity will spread across the globe, so much so that Christ will return to earth to reign for a thousand years over a pure and holy kingdom. Once the millennium is up, the Rapture will occur and the final Battle between Christ and Satan will ensue (though almost no people will remain during Armageddon). A parallel, though not entirely synonymous phenomenon to postmillennialism, is that of progressive millennialism. Many New Age teachers, for example, are progressive millennialists.

As in postmillennialism, progressive millennialists believe that the world will become increasingly pure, culminating in the collective salvation of all. Postmillennialism, as a Christian system, however, diverges from progressive millennialism in a few key aspects. First, unlike postmillennialists who still believe that the apocalyptic events of the Bible will occur—just after the awaited millennium—progressive millennialists do not insist that any world-ending trauma needs occur to bring the progress of the world to fruition. Additionally, where postmillennialists see themselves as fulfilling some godly ordained plan, progressive millennialists may be secular in their understanding of such providential fulfillment (Nazi National Socialism is a tragic example of progressive millennialism gone wrong, as they sought to purify the world through the extermination of those they deemed impure). Progressive millennialists also do not perceive progress as linear, but expect setbacks, which may mean they will not see the awaited millennium in their lifetimes. Postmillennialists align more closely to premillennialists in the respect that they view history through the lens of steadier (if not completely steady) progress, believing that the current age is definitively better or worse than the last.

There are also those considered amillennialist who reject the notion that Christ will have a literal, physical one-thousand-year reign on earth. In fact, they argue that the millennium is coterminous with what is often called "the church age," or the history of the Church since Christ. Amillennial groups like the short-lived Oneida Community of the nineteenth century, for example, may advocate for alternative or "heavenly" forms of living (which can include communitarian living) since the millennium has already arrived.

Though there are countless millennialist groups, many do share certain notable features. More often than not, some form of scripture or text is at the center of millennialist belief. Generally, millennialists employ a sacred text such as the Bible for the Millerites and the Jehovah's Witnesses, or the Qur'an, in the case of ISIS. However, white supremacist or nativist forms of millennialism, like Christian Identity, may use sources like *The Turner Diaries* from which to derive millennialist beliefs, practices, and prophecy. Sacred texts provide a lens through which to understand events occurring in the world, as well as a map for how to prepare or respond to them. Other millennialist groups, such as Rastafari and the Seventh-day Adventists, have produced their own scriptures as supplements to a main sacred text or as standalone texts, which clarify the specific millennialist message of the group.

Though by no means a requirement, millennialist groups often have a leader whose interpretations of the text (occasionally informed by claims of direct revelation from a higher power) serve as a basis for a given group's beliefs and whose charisma attracts members to one particular message. Classic examples of such

Millennialism   389

charismatic leadership can be seen in millennialist groups like Aum Shinrikyō, the Ghost Dance Movement, and the Shakers. And while certainly not the case for all millennialist groups, very often the leaders and members of certain groups will engage in prophecy, ranging from the general ("Christ's return is imminent") to the specific ("the Rapture will occur on October 22, 1844"). Failed prophecy is a relatively common element of millennialist groups, though rarely does it have the devastating effects people might assume. While members of millennialist groups who experience a failed prophecy may undergo some cognitive dissonance, often those involved can quickly regroup and find a rationale for why the prediction failed.

HISTORICAL AND MODERN VARIETIES

Parsing these categories even further, scholars have argued for designating particular groups or movements according to particular characteristics. For example, "assaulted millennial groups" are those groups, for example, the Branch Davidians, who may be pushed to defensive, militant, or violent action by events or the actions of those outside. The Branch Davidians believed that they would be persecuted by the U.S. government (or "Babylon") as part of a larger, providential series of events that ultimately lead to Christ's return. Thus, when the U.S. Bureau of Alcohol, Tobacco, and Firearms came to the Branch Davidians' base of operation, the Mount Carmel Center in Waco, Texas, to issue a warrant, the Branch Davidians saw this gesture and an ensuing firefight as the fulfillment of prophecy. "Fragile millennial groups," such as Peoples Temple, are similar to assaulted millennial groups, in that external pressure may push the group to pursue their millennialist goals directly. However, a threat need not necessarily come from the outside to push the group to such action or, as was the case of Peoples Temple, internal fragility coupled with the mere perception of a particular action as a threat may provide the necessary nudge. When Congressman Leo Ryan came to visit Jonestown, Guyana in 1978, his presence was enough to set off a series of events that would lead to the mass revolutionary suicide of over nine hundred members of Peoples Temple.

Bridging the gap between New Age and Christian forms of millennialism is Heaven's Gate. Heaven's Gate members believed that they would shed their earthly bodies and ascend to The Evolutionary Level Above Human. Though similar to Christian millennial beliefs in many ways, Heaven's Gate differed in their belief that UFOs and extraterrestrials would bring about the expected change. They viewed the appearance of the Hale-Bopp Comet as a sign of this event, prompting them to "graduate" (or commit ritual suicide) in March of 1997. Though violence, both self-inflicted and externally directed, are not the norm for millennialist groups, it can occur, particularly when those inside the group feel their actions will initiate some awaited for end (like Heaven's Gate) or when they feel provoked from the outside (like Peoples Temple). Heaven's Gate also qualifies for the label of "fragile millennial group," as scholars argue that the death of one of its founders fundamentally changed its outlook and moved the group toward the outcome of suicide.

On the opposite side of the spectrum from these more catastrophic versions of millennialism is the Church of Jesus Christ of Latter-day Saints, or the Mormon Church. As their name suggests, Latter-day Saints believe that they are living in the last days and that the Christ's return is imminent. However, given their extensive missionary program and steady growth in membership, they subscribe to a progressive or postmillennial worldview. Expanding in a different way, by territory rather than converts, ISIS believes that the recreation of the Islamic caliphate will help to bring about apocalyptic events predicted in certain prophetic suras of the Qur'an. Though one would hesitate to qualify them as postmillennial, since they believe that those outside of the caliphate, or infidels, will be killed and condemned during these events, they do believe that steady gains in territory will occur at their hand, aligning them with some interpretations of progressive millennialism.

These are just some of the examples of millenialist groups and movements. Countless groups have lived and been forgotten, multiple such groups abound today, and, undoubtedly, more will come, ready to cast the events of the world as "signs" of a great, anticipated transformational event.

See also: Aum Shinrikyō; Branch Davidians; Charisma and Leadership in New Religious Movements; Christian Identity; Church of Jesus Christ of Latter-day Saints, The; Ghost Dance Movement (Wovoka); Heaven's Gate; ISIS; Millerites, The; Oneida Community, The; Order of the Solar Temple, The; Peoples Temple; Rastafari; Seventh-day Adventism; Shakers, The; Unification Church, The; Watchtower Bible and Tract Society, The (Jehovah's Witnesses).

Further Reading
Landes, Richard. 2011. *Heaven on Earth: The Varieties of Millennial Experience*. Oxford; New York: Oxford University Press.

Robbins, Thomas, & Susan J. Palmer. 1997. *Millennialism, Messiahs, and Mayhew: Contemporary Apocalyptic Movements*. Abingdon, UK; New York: Routledge Press.

Wessinger, Catherine, ed. 2000. *Millennialism, Persecution, & Violence: Historical Cases*. Syracuse University Press.

Wessinger, Catherine, ed. 2011. *The Oxford Handbook of Millennialism*. Oxford; New York: Oxford University Press.

Miller, William (1782–1849)
EARLY HISTORY

Predicting the end of the world and the events that accompany it, including the Second Coming of Christ, is a practice common in the history of Christianity (e.g., the Apostle Paul believed Christ would return in his lifetime; 1 Thess. 4:15–17). However, the methods by which one predicts and prepares for the end vary from mere assent to the idea that Christ's return is imminent to the far riskier practice of "date-setting," whereby precise dates are affixed to biblical events. In the American context, perhaps no one is better known for this riskiest of endeavors than William Miller (1782–1849).

Born in Massachusetts in 1782, but raised in upstate New York, Miller was the precocious child of Baptist parents. After marrying Lucy Smith in 1803, he settled in Poultney, New York, where he enjoyed a rather comfortable existence as a farmer. He was clearly well respected in his community as he was elected to several positions of local governance and law enforcement, including town constable, deputy sheriff, and justice of the peace. By the time he moved to Poultney, he had rejected his Baptist heritage and become a Deist. Ever the voracious reader, he read heavily in the writings of Thomas Paine and David Hume, who convinced him that the historical God of the Bible was fallacious. However, following his service during the War of 1812 as a captain of the thirtieth infantry division, Miller felt his survival (and total lack of injury) was miraculous, thus undermining the impersonal God of his deistical beliefs.

Following the war, Miller entered a period of spiritual turmoil and grappling, where he mused constantly on the state of his soul and his own mortality. This led him to return to the Baptist church of his youth, but this time, he was determined to ascertain the truth of its doctrines by a close and meticulous reading of the Bible.

SETTING THE DATE FOR THE END OF THE WORLD

The result of Miller's close study of the Bible was a firm belief that the prophetic books of the Bible, particularly the Book of Daniel, revealed the precise time of Christ's return. In fact, through an elaborate set of calculations based on determining the date of certain biblical events and extracting passages where certain lengths of time were mentioned, by 1818, Miller believed he had determined the year of Christ's return: 1843. Central to his scriptural mathematics was Daniel 8:14 ("Unto two thousand and three hundred days; then shall the sanctuary be cleansed"), from which he determined that Christ's return would occur approximately twenty-three hundred years from 457 BCE, which was the year that Persian emperor, Artaxerxes I, had promised to rebuild Jerusalem.

By the 1830s, Miller had publicized these views, most notably in his book, *Evidence from Scripture and History of the Second Coming of Christ about the Year 1843: Exhibited in a Course of Lectures.* In the text, Miller took his readers methodically through his process of date-setting. By the 1840s, Miller had sparked a national religious movement, with his followers known as "Millerites," helped in great part by the establishment of the newspaper, *Signs of the Times.* At one point, Miller estimated that between fifty thousand and one hundred thousand people subscribed to his views.

Miller, who had been quite reticent to set an exact date for Christ's return (also known as His "Second Advent"), ultimately decided to do so—the result of mounting pressure from his growing following. He said that Christ would return between March 21, 1843, and March 21, 1844. When March 21, 1844, came and went, Miller conceded that he had erred in determining the correct date, but not in his conviction that Christ's return was imminent. He reset the date for the Second

Advent for October 22, 1844, which was reportedly corroborated by Samuel S. Snow, a Millerite, at a separate revival meeting.

AFTER "THE GREAT DISAPPOINTMENT"

When October 22, 1844, came and Christ did not return, the Millerite movement effectively shattered. The event came to be known as "The Great Disappointment" and was described as the moment of great mourning for all who, expecting Christ to return and their human suffering to end, found themselves still earthbound. Most abandoned Miller and his belief system, returning to their initial denominational homes; the last general conference for the Millerites met in April 1845.

However, there were several movements that arose from the Great Disappointment and simply adapted Miller's prophecy in new ways. The most famous and successful movement in terms of sustainability was the Seventh-day Adventist denomination. Some of Miller's followers, including Hiram Edson, determined that Miller's calculations had been correct, but he had wrongly predicted the event that would occur on October 22, 1844. Christ had not returned to earth but instead had moved into the holiest sanctuary in heaven, marking the beginning of judgment and the end of the probationary period (where people's sins were not marked against them in a permanent sense). The movement would retain the millennialist orientation of William Miller, while avoiding the risk of date-setting. Though there other, smaller Adventist movements that arose from the Millerites, the two that have enjoyed the greatest growth and longevity are the Seventh-day Adventist Church, which now boasts around twenty million members worldwide as of 2015, and the Watchtower Bible and Tract Society (better known as the Jehovah's Witnesses), which in a 2017 study, reportedly had approximately nine million members.

As for Miller, he never gave up on his belief in the imminent return of Christ. He maintained that even though his own human foibles may have caused an error in his biblical calculations that the answer was in the text. However, he would not live long enough to find it, dying on December 20, 1849.

See also: Millennialism; Seventh-day Adventism; Watchtower Bible and Tract Society, The (Jehovah's Witnesses).

Further Reading

Miller, William. 1842. *Evidence from Scripture and History of the Second Coming of Christ about the Year 1843: Exhibited in a Course of Lectures.* Boston: Joshua V. Himes.

Rowe, David L. 2008. *God's Strange Work: William Miller and the End of the World.* Library of Religious Biography. Grand Rapids, MI: Wm. B. Eerdmans Publishing Co.

Millerites, The

ORIGINS AND BELIEFS

During the 1830s, William Miller (1782–1849) publicized his belief that Christ's return (Second Advent) would take place in 1843. Using a complicated set

Though not the only millennialist Christian group of the nineteenth century, the Millerites were perhaps the most famous because their leader, William Miller, predicted the precise date of the Rapture. The movement came to both prominence and ridicule, the latter being depicted in the caricature above. In this picture, a Millerite sits in a fireproof "salamander safe," with various supplies prepared for the world to end. (Library of Congress)

of calculations, Miller had mined the Bible for key dates and numbers that would enable him to make such a prediction—a feat that he published in his book, *Evidence from Scripture and History of the Second Coming of Christ about the Year 1843: Exhibited in a Course of Lectures.* Though slowly at first, his teachings would eventually earn him a substantial and national following. The movement was bolstered by Millerite and publisher Joshua Himes, who was responsible for disseminating Miller's prophecies in print.

During their heyday in the early 1840s, the Millerites were scattered throughout the country, with the largest group hailing from New York and the New England states. However, Miller's writings reached a global (primarily English-speaking) audience, from England to Australia. Though often separated by geography, what connected all Millerites was their belief that Christ would return very soon. Those who did have direct contact with William Miller, either in person or through correspondence, nudged him to set a precise date for the Second Advent. Miller had been historically reticent to name a precise date, given the risk of a failed prediction. However, he eventually relented and said that Christ's Second Advent would occur sometime between March 21, 1843, and March 21, 1844. When these dates passed, Miller announced, following further calculations, that Christ would appear on October 22, 1844.

THE GREAT DISAPPOINTMENT AND BEYOND

On that date in October, the Millerite movement culminated (and effectively ended) in an event later known as "The Great Disappointment." Many Millerites would return to their home denominations after the prophecy failed; still, some would linger, forming separate Millerite factions according to their interpretation of the nonevent. When Miller died in 1849, it appeared that a united Millerite movement had lost the initiative.

Though the Millerites would seem to be a blip on the millennialist Christian scene, the group would put a lasting imprint on the religious landscape in America. Born from the remaining Millerites were such established millennialist Christian groups as the Seventh-day Adventists and the Watch Tower Bible and Tract Society (better known as the Jehovah's Witnesses), which have birthed additional sects in turn. And while the Millerites are perhaps best known for a failed prophecy, they are also evidence of the resilience of millennialist hope and the adaptability of faith.

See also: Branch Davidians; Millennialism; Miller, William (1782–1849); Prophecy in New Religious Movements; Seventh-day Adventism; Watch Tower Bible and Tract Society (Jehovah's Witnesses).

Further Reading

Connors, Richard, & Andrew Colin Gow, eds. 2004. *Anglo-American Millennialism, From Milton to the Millerites.* Leiden; Boston: Brill.

Miller, William. 1842. *Evidence from Scripture and History of the Second Coming of Christ about the Year 1843: Exhibited in a Course of Lectures.* Boston: Joshua V. Himes.

Wessinger, Catherine, ed. 2011. *The Oxford Handbook of Millennialism.* Oxford; New York: Oxford University Press.

PRIMARY SOURCE DOCUMENT

Excerpts from William Miller, *Evidence from Scripture and History of the Second Coming of Christ* (1842)

William Miller was a nineteenth-century preacher who believed, and convinced countless others to believe, that Jesus would return in 1844. After fighting in the War of 1812, Miller became consumed by the idea that the Bible pointed to the world ending imminently. In 1932, he published his beliefs in Evidence from Scripture and History of the Second Coming of Christ. *Excerpts from this text follow below.*

IN presenting these Lectures to the public, the writer is only complying with the solicitations of some of his friends, who have requested that his views on the Prophecies of Daniel and John might be made public. The reader is therefore requested to give the subject a careful and candid perusal, and compare every part with the standard of Divine Truth; for if the explanation the writer has given to the scriptures under consideration should prove correct, the reader will readily perceive that it concerns us all, and becomes doubly important to us, because we live on the eve of one of the most important events ever revealed to man by the wisdom of God—the judgment of the great day. . . .

There are two important points to which all prophecy seems to centre, like a cluster of grapes upon its stem—the first and second coming of Christ; the first coming to proclaim the gospel, set up his kingdom, suffer for sinners, and bring in an everlasting righteousness. His second coming, to which the ardent faith and pious hope of the tried and tempted child of God centres, is for complete redemption from sin, for the justification and glorification promised to all those who look for his appearing, the destruction of the wicked and mystical Babylon, the abomination of the whole earth. . . .

If I have erred in my exposition of the prophecies, the time, being so near at hand, will soon expose my folly; but if I have the truth on the subjects treated on in these pages, how important the era in which we live! What vast and important events must soon be realized! and how necessary that every individual be prepared that that day may not come upon them unawares, while they are surfeited with the cares and riches of this life, and the day overtake them as a thief! "But ye, brethren, are not in darkness, that that day should overtake you as a thief," 1 Thess. v. 4. In studying these prophecies, I have endeavored to divest myself of all prepossessed opinions, not warranted by the word of God, and to weigh well all the objections that might be raised from the Scriptures; and after fourteen years' study of the prophecies and other parts of the Bible, I have come to the following conclusions, and do now commit myself into the hands of God as my Judge, in giving publicity to the sentiments herein contained, conscientiously desiring that this little book may be the means to incite others to study the Scriptures, and to see whether these things be so, and that some minds may be led to believe in the word of God, and find an interest in the offering and sacrifice of the Lamb of God, that their sins might be forgiven them through the blood of the atonement, "when the refreshing shall come from the presence of the Lord, and from the glory of his power," "when he comes to be admired in all them that believe in that day." (From the Introduction) . . .

The Jews had twenty-one signs in the Scriptures given them of the first coming and person of Jesus Christ; yet many rejected him as an impostor. You say, if you had lived in that day, you would have believed; and you in your hearts condemn them as a hardened race of unbelievers; and notwithstanding their great pretence to piety, you say they were justly denounced by our Savior as a generation of vipers and a band of hypocrites. But, my hearers, be careful your own hearts do not condemn you for your unbelief in the signs which the prophets, Christ, and the apostles have given you as tokens of his second coming and the judgment day. I have brought from the word of God twenty-five signs of his second coming, end of the world, and judgment day, and all apparently fulfilled within the age of many present, or fulfilling now before your eyes. And do you believe? Many of you profess to be pious; many of you say, Lord, Lord! But do you believe his word? Are you willing to risk your life, your character, your all, on his word? or are you fearful and unbelieving? Now is the time to try men's souls. Now, if you wish to be sure, examine closely, and see whether your faith will stand in the day of trial which is coming; yes, has already come, in a thousand ways, to draw you from the gospel of Christ to another *new* gospel, which is not the gospel of God. "Can ye not discern the signs of the times?" Let me give you one rule by which you may know a false doctrine. They may have many good things in their creeds, they may be very plausible in their arguments, and after all deceive you. But examine them closely, and you will find they will deny, ridicule, or try to do away some prominent doctrine of the Bible, such as the divinity of Christ, his second coming, office of the Holy Spirit, eternal punishment, doctrine of grace, election, conviction for sin, regeneration, repentance, or faith. And when you hear or see them make light or scoff at any thing of this kind in the word of God, go not after them, nor bid them God speed. "Can ye not discern the signs of the times?"

And to you, impenitent friend, God has at all times given you warning of his approaching judgments. If you repent, believe his word, and break off your sins by righteousness, he is faithful and just to forgive you your sins. Why not take warning by the past? Is there no example for you? Look at the antediluvian world, Sodom and Gomorrah, Nineveh, Babylon, Jerusalem, and the once enlightened Asia, now worse than in heathenish darkness. Will God punish nations, and not individuals? This cannot be, for nations are composed of individuals; and God is just, for he hath appointed a day in which he will judge the world in righteousness. "Can ye not discern the signs of the times?" Will God's word fail of being accomplished? Can you show a single instance? Why not listen, then, to the warnings and admonitions, to the calls and invitations, to the examples and precepts contained therein? "Can ye not discern the signs of the times?" Will God cut off the unbelieving Pharisee for not discerning the signs of the times, and let you, with twofold more light, go free? No: how can ye escape, if you neglect this great salvation? Watch, then," the signs of the times." I say, Watch. (From Lecture XIX)

> **Source:** Miller, William. *Evidence from Scripture and History of the Second Coming of Christ.* Boston: Moses A. Dow, 1842.

Moon, Rev. Sun Myung (1920–2012)

During the 1970s, the founder of the Unification Church, Rev. Sun Myung Moon, became widely recognized as the epitome of the suspicious cult leader. Moon had founded his Church in Korea in 1954, and the first missionaries came to the United States at the end of that decade. Their efforts began to bear substantial fruit in the later 1960s and Rev. Moon himself moved to the United States in 1971, giving the country a pivotal role in his version of salvation history.

For many, Moon's appeal was baffling. He inspired extraordinary devotion among his American acolytes even though he did not speak English well at all. His sober and conservative focus on family and marriage seemed antithetical to the enthusiasms of the counterculture. And his dramatic reinterpretation of central biblical narratives was religiously shocking. Nonetheless, Moon and his church became prominent in the American media.

MOON'S PROPHETIC PERSONA

Moon's appeal relied on the prophetic persona that he had cultivated for himself. His claims were grounded in a transformative experience that occurred on Easter morning in 1936 when the sixteen-year-old had a vision of Jesus. Like many before him, Moon understood that encounter as a call and commission to undertake God's work. In particular, Moon came to understand his task as preaching the restoration of humans to the status that God had originally intended for them before Eve and Adam were expelled from the Garden of Eden.

In Moon's interpretation, not only had Eve and Adam failed in their task of establishing a perfect, loving family dedicated to God but Jesus, too, had failed in a similar mission. Moon thus proclaimed the need for a third Adam and a Second Advent of the Messiah to reestablish the world as God intended. Over time, Moon became more forthcoming about his own role in that scenario, eventually identifying himself and his second wife, Hak Ja Han (1943–), as the True Parents of humankind and himself as the anticipated Messiah.

Moon's inspired teachings were compiled in the *Divine Principle*, a correction of and supplement to the Bible that he first recorded in 1952. Among Unificationists that text holds scriptural status since it expresses both God's plans for the world and Moon's role in those plans. Eventually, a collection of Moon's speeches was elevated to canonical status alongside the *Divine Principle*. Those texts mediate Moon's presence to those who cannot encounter him directly. Stories from

LEADERSHIP AND TRANSITION

converts, for example, confirm the powerful impact that learning the teachings of the *Divine Principle* can have on individuals.

Moon led the Unificationist movement for nearly sixty years. He supervised its global expansion, directed its diversification into an array of related organizations, and oversaw its expansive business interests. But most importantly he served as teacher, prophet, and Lord of the Second Advent. Moon functions as both an ethical and exemplary prophet. His teachings outline the proper way of life for individuals at the same time that he was held to embody those ideals in his own life. In the view of salvation that he elaborated, Moon and his second wife, Hak Ja Han, serve as the True Parents of humankind. Their family provides a living example of the True Family that God desires for all humans.

Since Moon emphasized that he and his family personified the virtues that were so essential to the Unificationist Church and the movement, he was vulnerable to criticism when any of them appeared to fall short of those lofty standards. For example, Moon's conviction and imprisonment for tax evasion in 1983–1984 reinforced the general public's impression that "cult" leaders were interested only in personal gain, despite the support that Moon received from many mainstream religious leaders.

More damaging were the revelations in the memoir published by Nansook Hong (1966–), the former wife of Moon's eldest son, Hyo Jin (1962–2008). In Hong's recollection, her husband was a dissolute, violently abusive, and thoroughly inattentive husband who was hardly qualified to succeed his father; Hyo Jin's mother was primarily interested in shopping and enjoying luxuries, and Rev. Moon himself was a duplicitous fraud. Even though such revelations reinforced the dominant public narrative about the evils of "cults" even more strongly than the many regretful tales of former members that were published, Moon was not dislodged from his central position within Unificationism and continued in his role until his death.

Although Moon attempted to establish a plan for succession, he was not able to forestall the contention that often accompanies the death of a charismatic leader. As Nansook Hong detailed, Moon's eldest son, Hyo Jin, was in no way fit to succeed him. Moon's second eldest son, Heung Jin (1966–1984) died in a car accident at seventeen. Other siblings, making various claims to authority and operating from different bases of power within the movement, positioned themselves as successors to their father. In addition, Moon's widow, drawing on Korean sources of charismatic legitimation, has also laid claim to leadership. The dispute over leadership continues to play out, with different groups claiming to represent the true intentions of the founder.

The long career of Rev. Moon shows how charismatic leadership can be claimed, extended, undermined, defended, and, potentially, passed on to a second generation. Moon's ability to persevere through organized opposition, legal troubles, and embarrassing revelations show how charismatic authority is able to remain durable, with sufficient support from followers.

See also: Anticult Movement, The; Charisma and Leadership in New Religious Movements; *Divine Principle*; Unification Church, The.

Further Reading

Chryssides, George D. 1991. *The Advent of Sun Myung Moon: The Origins, Beliefs and Practices of the Unification Church*. London: Macmillan.

Hong, Nansook. 1998. *In the Shadow of the Moons: My Life in the Reverend Sun Myung Moon's Family*. New York: Little, Brown.

Mickler, Michael L. 2013. "The Post-Sun Myung Unification Church." In Eileen Barker, ed., *Revisionism and Diversification in New Religious Movements*, pp. 47–65. Burlington, VT: Ashgate.

Moon, Sun Myung. 2009. *As a Peace-Loving Global Citizen*. Washington, DC: The Washington Times Foundation.

Moorish Science Temple of America, The

During the late nineteenth and early twentieth centuries, multiple religious groups attempted to address the enduring effects of slavery and colonialism on Americans of African descent. They sought in various ways to connect African Americans to an ancient and noble identity. Some of the movements featured individuals who claimed at least prophetic authority, if not some form of divinity. For some, a perceived connection to Islam enabled them to bypass the complicity of Christianity with their oppression. The Moorish Science Temple was one of those movements.

ORIGINS

The Temple was founded by Noble Drew Ali (1886–1929). Born in North Carolina in 1886 as Timothy Drew, he claimed a colorful past, including a trip to Egypt in his late teens during which he was initiated into an ancient cult and received his new name. Although the Moorish Science Temple was only officially incorporated in Chicago in 1928, Drew Ali was active as a religious teacher before that. Around 1913, he founded a Canaanite Temple in Newark, New Jersey. By 1925, he had moved to Chicago and begun to attract a substantial number of followers.

BELIEFS AND PRACTICES

Drew Ali taught that African Americans were not "Negroes" but rather "Moors." They descended from the ancient Asiatic settlers of Africa, the Moabites, who had come from the biblical land of Canaan. They constituted a nation unto themselves and their true religion was Islam. He offered self-knowledge and salvation to what he saw as "fallen humanity." The Islam that Drew Ali taught, however, was not orthodox. He was strongly influenced by Freemasonry and other esoteric systems of thought. He likely drew Islamic symbols, including the distinctive fez worn by members, from black Shriners, particularly The Ancient Egyptian Arabic Order, Nobles of the Mystic Shrine.

Drew Ali's eclectic beliefs animate the central text of the movement, *The Holy Koran of the Moorish Science Temple of America*, known colloquially as the "Circle 7 Koran" because of its cover illustration of a red number seven surrounded by a blue circle. Readings from the *Holy Koran* and discussions of it were a central part of Temple religious ceremonies. Although the text is presented as having been "divinely prepared" by Drew Ali, it is in fact built substantially on two previous publications. Chapters two through nineteen draw extensively on an esoteric text first published in 1907 by Levi H. Dowling, *The Aquarian Gospel of Jesus the Christ*. Drew Ali follows his source exactly, deviating only to identify God as "Allah" and Jesus as "Isa." In addition, Chapters twenty through forty-four draw equally heavily on *Unto Thee I Grant*, a Rosicrucian work attributed to Sri Ramatherio and originally published in 1925. Only some prefatory material, chapter one, and chapters forty-five through forty-eight may come from Drew Ali himself.

The message of the text reflects its source material. For example, in a parallel to the hagiographical account of Drew Ali's early life, Jesus and his family are depicted as learning in an Egyptian mystery school that Allah and man are one. That empowering notion, along with the promise that the *Holy Koran* revealed other esoteric knowledge that had previously been kept from the world, was attractive to Drew Ali's audience. The Temple's eclectic theology is hinted at in the "passport" that was issued to members. It states that the Temple honors all the prophets of God and mentions specifically Jesus, Muhammad, Buddha, and Confucius. Beyond that, there is some indication that Drew Ali presented himself as the reincarnation of both Jesus and Muhammad, among other prophetic figures.

Drew Ali did not ignore practical matters. In addition to the *Circle 7 Koran*, the Temple published its own collections of hadith, the *Divine Constitution and By-Laws*, and its own newspaper, the *Moorish Guide*. Members of the Temple were to adopt new surnames of Bey or El. Drew Ali counseled a strict morality and enjoined his followers to avoid meat, eggs, and alcohol. Members of the Temple were also to be scrupulous in their cleanliness and reject hair straightening. In addition, they were to pray three times a day and attend the Temple on Friday. Temple members were encouraged to establish economic independence. The Moorish Manufacturing Corporation offered the faithful many useful products, from herbal remedies for common ailments to clothing and other household items. The Temple's theology and focus on black self-sufficiency may have influenced the similar practices of the Nation of Islam.

DREW ALI'S DEATH AND ITS AFTERMATH

By 1929, the Temple had gained a following in the tens of thousands. That success, possibly coupled with a millennialist prophecy that saw the imminent destruction of the status quo, emboldened some of the Moors to confront white people, despite Drew Ali's counsel to obey the law. External conflicts were compounded by internal ones, with Drew Ali's authority being challenged and criticisms of his financial stewardship being made. At one point, Sheik Claude D. Greene, thinking that he had sufficient support, attempted to usurp Drew Ali's position. When Greene was murdered soon after, Drew Ali and nine other Temple members were arrested. After being released on bail, however, Drew Ali soon died under uncertain circumstances. Although Kirkman Bey was appointed to succeed Drew Ali, others claimed that the prophet had been reincarnated in them. The Temple then fragmented into factions, many of which continue to this day (see www.moorishsciencetempleofamerica.org).

See also: Ali, Noble Drew (1886–1929); Freemasonry; Millennialism; Nation of Islam, The; Race and New Religious Movements.

Further Reading

Curtis, Edward E., IV. 2002. *Islam in Black America: Identity, Liberation, and Difference in African-American Islamic Thought.* Albany: State University of New York Press.

Department of Supreme Wisdom, The. 2009. *The Foundations of a Nation, Volume One: The Circle 7 Holy Koran: Noble Drew Ali & The Moorish Science Temple of America.* No publication data.

Dorman, Jacob. 2020. *The Princess and the Prophet: The Secret History of Magic, Race, and Moorish Muslims in America.* Boston: Beacon Press.

Gomez, Michael A. 2005. *Black Crescent: The Experience and Legacy of African Muslims in the Americas.* Cambridge: Cambridge University Press.

Wilson, Peter Lamborn. 1993. *Sacred Drift: Essays on the Margins of Islam.* San Francisco: City Lights Books.

PRIMARY SOURCE DOCUMENT

Excerpt from *The Holy Koran of the Moorish Science Temple*

The Holy Koran of the Moorish Science Temple of America *(also known as The Circle 7 Koran) is a religious text that teaches that all black people have Moorish origins and have been stripped of their Muslim identity as a result of slavery and racism. Drew Ali, the movement's Prophet Noble, called for a return to Islam as practiced by Moorish ancestors. His hope was that this dedication to past religious practices would lead to a reclamation of spiritual heritage. An excerpt from the Moorish Science Temple's primary text, a new version of The Holy Koran, follows below.*

Chapter XLVII
  Egypt, the Capital Empire of the Dominion of Africa

  1. The inhabitants of Africa are the descendants of the ancient Canaanites from the land of Canaan.

2. Old man Cush and his family are the first inhabitants of Africa who came from the land of Canaan.
3. His father Ham and his family were second. Then came the word Ethiopia, which means the demarcation line of the dominion of Amexem, the first true and divine name of Africa. The dividing of the land between the father and the son.
4. The dominion of Cush, North-East and South-East Africa and North-West and South-West was his father's dominion of Africa.
5. In later years many of their bretheren from Asia and the Holy Lands joined them.
6. The Moabites from the land of Moab who received permission from the Pharaohs of Egypt to settle and inhabit North-West Africa; they were the founders and are the true possessors of the present Moroccan Empire. With their Canaanite, Hittite, and Amorite bretheren who sojourned from the land of Canaan seeking new homes.
7. Their dominion and inhabitation extended from North-East and South-West Africa, across great Atlantis even unto the present North, South, and Central America and also Mexico and the Atlantis Islands; before the great earthquake, which caused the great Atlantic Ocean.
8. The River Nile was dredged and made by the ancient Pharaohs of Egypt, in order to trade with the surrounding kingdoms. Also the Niger river was dredged by the great Pharaoh of Egypt in those ancient days for trade, and it extends eastward from the River Nile, westward across the great Atlantic. It was used for trade and transportation.
9. According to all true and divine records of the human race there is no negro, black, or colored race attached to the human family, because all the inhabitants of Africa were and are of the human race, descendants of the ancient Canaanite nation from the holy land of Canaan.
10. What your ancient forefathers were, you are today without doubt or contradiction.
11. There is no one who is able to change man from the descendant nature of his forefathers; unless his power extends beyond the great universal Creator Allah Himself.
12. These holy and divine laws are from the Prophet, Noble Drew Ali, the founder of the uniting of the Moorish Science Temple of America.
13. These laws are to be strictly preserved by the members of all the Temples, of the Moorish Science Temple of America. That they will learn to open their meeting and guide it according to the principles of Love, Truth, Peace, Freedom and Justice.

Moorish Science Temple of America, The

14. Every subordinate Temple of the Grand-Major Temple is to form under the covenant of Love, Truth, Peace, Freedom and Justice; and to create their own laws and customs, in conjunction with the laws of the Holy Prophet and the Grand Temple. I, the Prophet, Noble Drew Ali, was sent by the great God, Allah, to warn all Asiatics of America to repent from their sinful ways; before that great and awful day that is sure to come.

15. The time has come when every nation must worship under its own vine and fig tree, and every tongue must confess his own.

16. Through sin and disobedience every nation has suffered slavery, due to the fact that they honored not the creed and principles of their forefathers.

17. That is why the nationality of the Moors was taken away from them in 1774 and the word negro, black and colored, was given to the Asiatics of America who were of Moorish descent, because they honored not the principles of their mother and father, and strayed after the gods of Europe of whom they knew nothing.

Chapter XLVIII
The End of Time and the Fulfilling of the Prophesies

1. The last Prophet in these days is Noble Drew Ali, who was prepared divinely in due time by Allah to redeem men from their sinful ways; and to warn them of the great wrath which is sure to come upon the earth.

2. John the Baptist was the forerunner of Jesus in those days, to warn and stir up the nation and prepare them to receive the divine creed which was to be taught by Jesus.

3. In these modern days there came a forerunner of Jesus, who was divinely prepared by the great God-Allah and his name is Marcus Garvey, who did teach and warn the nations of the earth to prepare to meet the coming Prophet; who was to bring the true and divine Creed of Islam, and his name is Noble Drew Ali who was prepared and sent to this earth by Allah, to teach the oldtime religion and the everlasting gospel to the sons of men. That every nation shall and must worship under their own vine and fig tree, and return to their own and be one with their Father God-Allah.

4. The Moorish Science Temple of America is a lawfully chartered and incorporated organization. Any subordinate Temple that desires to receive a charter; the prophet has them to issue to every state throughout the United States, etc.

5. That the world may hear and know the truth, that among the descendants of Africa there is still much wisdom to be learned in these days for the redemption of the sons of men under Love, Truth, Peace, Freedom, and Justice.

6. We, as a clean and pure nation descended from the inhabitants of Africa, do not desire to amalgamate or marry into the families of the pale skin nations of Europe. Neither serve the gods of their religion, because our forefathers are the true and divine founders of the first religious creed, for the redemption and salvation of mankind on earth.

7. Therefore we are returning the Church and Christianity back to the European Nations, as it was prepared by their forefathers for their earthly salvation.

8. While we, the Moorish Americans are returning to Islam, which was founded by our forefathers for our earthly and divine salvation.

9. The covenant of the great God-Allah: "Honor they father and they mother that thy days may be longer upon the earth land, which the Lord thy God, Allah hath given thee!"

10. Come all ye Asiatics of America and hear the truth about your nationality and birthrights, because you are not negroes. Learn of your forefathers ancient and divine Creed. That you will learn to love instead of hate.

11. We are trying to uplift fallen humanity. Come and link yourselves with the families of nations. We honor all the true and divine prophets.

Source: Ali, Drew. *The Holy Koran of the Moorish Science Temple*, Chapters 47–48. Library of Congress, African and Middle East Division, Omar Ibn Said Collection.

Movement for the Restoration of the Ten Commandments of God, The

Among the violent incidents involving new or alternative religions that took place at the end of the twentieth century was one that involved a sectarian Roman Catholic group in rural southwest Uganda near the border with Rwanda. When news of the tragic loss of nearly eight hundred lives that took place in March 2000 finally reached Europe and North America, it was quickly assimilated by journalists and anticult activists to a model that had been developed on the examples of Jonestown, Waco, Aum Shinrikyō, and The Order of the Solar Temple. Such homogenizing instant analysis, however, missed many of the details of the particular incident and ignored what was, and to some extent still is, unknown about the group.

The millennialist group known as the Movement for the Restoration of the Ten Commandments of God (MRTCG) had its origins in the visionary experiences of a small set of individuals, several of whom were from the same family. Credonia

Mwerinde (1952–2000) was one of the most important contributors to the thought of the MRTCG. She claimed to have beheld many visions of the Virgin Mary and Jesus, beginning in 1981. For nine years she kept her experiences to herself, but in 1990, she was directed by another vision to make them public to everyone, regardless of religious affiliation, race, or any other characteristic. Mwerinde's father, Paul Kashako (1890–1991) had preceded her in receiving visions and her sister Angelina Migisha (1947–2000) and Angelina's daughter, Ursula Komuhangi (1962–2000), also became visionaries. In 1989, Mwerinde met Joseph Kibwetere (1932–2000) who had also begun to receive visions in 1984. Many of those visions are recorded in the group's text, *A Timely Message from Heaven: The End of the Present Times*, first published in 1991.

Mwerinde and Kibwetere quickly joined forces and moved with followers to a property owned by Kibwetere. Dominic Kataribaabo (1932–2000), a Roman Catholic priest who had fallen out with his bishop, joined the movement in 1989 or 1990. He became part of the leadership group and served as the author of many of its communications. The group appointed a group of twelve apostles, six male and six female, to help with the administration of daily affairs.

From the beginning, MRTCG was insistent that they were not beginning a new religion. Instead, they were trying to bring humans back to the observation of the Ten Commandments, which had long been ignored. The group considered itself part of the Roman Catholic Church, acknowledged the authority of the Pope, and followed the Catholic liturgy. Their Catholicism was generally conservative and selectively blended some pre-Vatican II practices, such as saying Mass in Latin, with post-Vatican II ones. As their emphasis on observing the commandments indicates, MRTCG promoted a sober, even monastic, morality and closely monitored the behavior of its members.

MRTCG was distinctive in their conviction that both Jesus and Mary were speaking to some individuals in the present. The group was influenced not only by Marian apparitions that had been reported in nearby Rwanda in the 1980s but also by a worldwide network of Marian visionaries, some of whose literature reached Uganda. In the seers' understanding, the last judgment was imminent. Only through the tearful intercession of Mary and her Son had God agreed to offer humans one final chance at repentance. Humanity had departed so far from the ethical prescriptions of the Ten Commandments that God did not anticipate that many would be saved.

Although the information is somewhat ambiguous, it appears that MRTCG anticipated that the new heaven and new earth mentioned in Revelation 21 would be established immediately after the year 2000. Their literature refers frequently to 2001 as "year one" of the new era.

Tensions with Kibwetere's family had forced the group to relocate to the village of Kanungu in 1992. The group also experienced some tension with the Roman Catholic hierarchy and also with people in the Kanungu area, but there appears to have been no sustained serious opposition. In Kanungu and other areas, the group continued to practice with few disturbances. The Kanungu community was depicted as an ark of safety from the catastrophes of the end-times or a "Rescue Place for the Virgin Mary."

406   **Movement of Spiritual Inner Awareness**

But the prophecy that the end was near, as it has with other groups, kept people edgily expectant. There is some evidence, though the statements in *A Timely Message from Heaven* can support multiple interpretations, that the end had been predicted for earlier times in the 1990s. Some members of the group, which may have numbered as many as five thousand participants at its height, were getting restless in Kanungu. In March of 2000, members of MRTCG began to spread the word that they expected another, decisive encounter with Mary very soon. Members sold their possessions for very little and implored relatives and former members to join them in Kanungu. Kibwetere deposited important MRTCG documents with the local police.

On March 17, 2000, more than five hundred members of MRTCG died when a fire ripped through their church in Kanungu. Later, the graves of more than two hundred more were discovered. Some clearly died by suicide, others may have entered the church not knowing how they would make the transition to the new world, and still others were likely murdered. Multiple explanations have been proposed, but none has been decisive.

See also: Aum Shinrikyō; Branch Davidians; Marian Apparitions; Millennialism; Order of the Solar Temple, The; Peoples Temple; Violence and New Religious Movements.

Further Reading

Anon. 1996. *A Timely Message from Heaven: The End of the Present Times*, 3rd ed. Rukungiri-Bushenyi, Uganda: Movement for the Restoration of the Ten Commandments of God.

Mayer, Jean-François. 2001. "The Movement for the Restoration of the Ten Commandments of God." *Nova Religio* 5: 203–210.

Vokes, Richard. 2009. *Ghosts of Kanungu: Fertility, Secrecy, and Exchange in the Great Lakes of East Africa*. Woodbridge, Suffolk, UK: James Currey.

Wallis, John. 2005. "Making Sense of the Movement for the Restoration of the Ten Commandments of God." *Nova Religio* 9: 49–66.

Movement of Spiritual Inner Awareness

Movement of Spiritual Inner Awareness or MSIA, which is pronounced "Messiah," arose at the height of New Age. Its influences and origins were various and its founder John-Roger Hinkins's (1934–2014) charismatic entrée onto the packed religious landscape of the 1960s attracted droves of members and critics alike. The movement, like many New Age traditions, promises individual spiritual awakening and progress for the devotee, known as the path of "Soul Transcendence," which its website (www.msia.org) explains as "becoming aware of oneself as a soul and as one with God, not as a theory but as a living reality."

FOUNDER AND ORIGINS

John-Roger Hinkins (referred to simply as John-Roger by members of MSIA) was raised in the Church of Jesus Christ of Latter-day Saints, though according to

MSIA, he was a spiritual seeker from a very young age. He pursued a psychology degree at the University of Utah and had plans to become a secondary school teacher, before a near-death experience compelled him to change course. Following surgery for removal of a kidney stone in 1963, Rogers fell into a coma that lasted nine days, during which another spiritual consciousness, referred to as the "Mystical Traveler," merged with his, giving him the "keys" to guide others to this state of spiritual awakening.

By 1968, John-Roger had organized a series of seminars, and ultimately published their content as *Soul Awareness Discourse*. By 1971, he had formally incorporated MSIA as the Church of Movement of Inner Spiritual Awareness and founded the magazine *On the Light Side* (later *The New Day Herald*, which is still a primary vehicle for MSIA's teachings). In 1974, he purchased property in Los Angeles that served as his and, at its height, 130 MSIA members' home; the property was called *Prana* meaning "wisdom" or "breath of life" in Sanskrit. As a mechanism for spreading his teachings, John-Roger established the Prana Theological Seminary, which provided more intensive spiritual training to those interested, and Koh-e-nor University, which offered graduate degrees in the area of spiritual psychology. MSIA also founded its own publishing house, humanitarian institute, and television studio. Throughout the 1970s, the movement spread across continents, aided by John-Roger's broadcasting of his seminars and publication of his writings. John-Roger continued to take members on spiritual retreats, lecture, and write until his death in 2014. He was succeeded by John Morton (1951–) who, as of 2020, serves as spiritual director of MSIA.

BELIEFS, PRACTICES, AND ORGANIZATION

MSIA derives beliefs and practices from ancient religious traditions, such as Hinduism and Buddhism, and newer religious traditions, such as Rosicrucianism, the Hindu Radhasoami sect, and Eckankar. John-Roger studied widely in religious traditions and texts, while maintaining that MSIA arose autonomously through his own realization of the Mystical Traveler Consciousness. In fact, he argues, religious leaders across many world traditions have been revealing the truth of MSIA for millennia, with Jesus Christ acting as the true head of the Mystic Traveler Consciousness. Equipped with the true knowledge of spiritual reality, John-Roger as the "way-shower" can align all religious traditions under the broader umbrella of MSIA. Nonetheless, plagiarism accusations have arisen in regards to similarities between MSIA and Eckankar, though John-Roger denied initiation into the tradition.

Realization of the Mystic Traveler Consciousness is a crucial step toward the ultimate goal of Soul Transcendence, whereby people realize that they, and all creation, emanate directly from God. In fact, physical existence is an illusion and is simply the form adopted by individuals to house their souls through successive life cycles. Through these life cycles (which map onto the Hindu system of karma and samskara), the soul either progresses toward or regresses from greater spiritual knowledge. Ultimately (and seemingly conversely), soul transcendence will also bear practical, thisworldly effects, such as health, happiness, even wealth. This message has appealed to those without specifically spiritual interests, prompting John-Roger's publication of his best-seller *Do It! Get Off Your Butts* (1992), a staple of so-called self-help culture.

For those with religious aims, John-Roger identified several practices or "keys" to soul transcendence. For example, realization of the "sound current," which is audible energy that derives directly from God, occurs when individuals are able to consistently focus their attention; once they have heard it, they "can never live without [it]" (www.msia.org). MSIA practitioners proceed through six levels of initiation, referred to as the physical (which takes place at the time of birth), astral (which occurs while asleep and deals with the imagination), causal (located in the emotions), mental (which deals with the mind), etheric (which operates in the unconscious), and the soul (referred to as the "true self"). Most initiations occur through the chanting of mantras (specifically, "Hu" or "Ani Hu"), studying of John-Roger's teachings, and meditation.

Today, membership is not considered formal and precise numbers are unknown. Most members of MSIA participate in short-term seminars and online courses; very few live onsite at Prana, which continues to serve as MSIA's headquarters. Despite its loose membership protocols, MSIA has been profiled as a "cult" based around the persona of John-Roger, rather than a genuine religion. The movement has also weathered critique for its seeming dance between secular psychology and self-help culture and religious practice. Nonetheless, people continue to stream John-Roger's seminars, and his books, though no longer atop best-seller lists, maintain a steady readership.

See also: Charisma and Leadership in New Religious Movements; Church of Jesus Christ of Latter-day Saints, The; Eckankar; New Age, The; Rosicrucianism; Seekers.

Further Reading

Hinkins, John-Roger. 1997. *Inner Worlds of Meditation.* Los Angeles: Mandeville Press.

Lewis, James R. 1998. *Seeking the Light: Revealing the Truth About the MSIA and its Founder, John-Roger.* Los Angeles: Mandeville Press.

Tumminia, Diana G. 2005. "Heart and Soul: A Qualitative Look at the Ethos of the Movement of Spiritual Inner Awareness." In James R. Lewis & Jesper Aagaard, eds., *Controversial New Religions.* New York: Oxford University Press.

Tumminia, Diana G., & James R. Lewis. 2013. *A Study of the Movement of Spiritual Inner Awareness: Religious Innovation and Cultural Change.* New York: Palgrave Macmillan.

Muhammad, Elijah (1897–1975)

As part of the Great Migration of African Americans from the rural south to urban areas of the Northeast, Midwest, and West, Elijah Poole left his birthplace in Sandersville, Georgia, and moved to Detroit in 1923. In 1931, he met a mysterious peddler known as W. D. Fard or Farad Muhammad (1877–?). Out of that encounter developed the Nation of Islam, a religious movement that continues to attract African Americans in the twenty-first century.

Elijah Muhammad (né Poole) was the prophet and founder of the Nation of Islam. Muhammad decried the erasure of African American identity by white supremacy, arguing that to be black was to be Muslim and offering a new sacred history wherein black people were the true chosen people of God. (Library of Congress)

THE MAKING OF A MESSENGER

Little is known about Fard, but his followers attributed to him an exotic background. They claimed he was born in Mecca and descended from the same tribe, the Quraysh, as the prophet Muhammad. Fard exhorted his audience to live hardworking, sober lives and promised them that salvation was coming. He claimed the status of a prophet and asserted that he knew the true identity of African Americans. They were, he asserted, not "Negroes" but rather members of the lost tribe of Shabazz, who had been stolen from the city of Mecca in the past. Consequently, their true religion was Islam and the knowledge of their true origins and culture had been hidden from them.

Fard quickly attracted an audience in the black neighborhoods of Detroit, and his most significant recruit was Elijah Poole. By the second time he encountered Fard, in August 1931, Poole was convinced that he had discerned Fard's true identity. In a widely reported conversation, Poole told Fard that he believed that he was God himself, but Fard cautioned him that it was not the time to disclose that truth. In that brief exchange was the germ of the distinctive theology of the Nation of Islam. In strong contrast to mainstream forms of Islam, the Nation would continue to hold that God had appeared in the human form of Fard and that Fard had chosen Poole, who would eventually become known as Elijah Muhammad, the Messenger of Allah.

By many accounts, Poole did not possess the personal characteristics that would make him an obvious candidate for such a role, but Fard nonetheless granted him substantial responsibilities and gave him a new name, Elijah Karriem (Noble). Poole's elevated status was a source of contention among Fard's followers. Fard left Detroit in May 1933 and then in 1934 disappeared as mysteriously as he had appeared. Elijah soon decamped to Chicago. Even there, however, his authority was contested.

In the decade after Fard's disappearance, Elijah encountered multiple difficulties. Many of the original members of the Nation defected to other groups or simply faded away. Then, in 1942, Elijah was arrested for failing to register for the military draft. Convicted, he remained in prison until August 1946. During that period, Elijah's wife Clara (1899–1972) helped to keep the movement functioning, and Elijah communicated with his followers through letters. After Elijah returned to Chicago, the Nation of Islam began a rapid expansion.

TEACHINGS

At the core of Elijah's teachings was an assertion about the true identity of the "so-called Negroes." He preached that their sufferings under slavery and colonialism were in fact a reversal of their original status. Despite the appearances of Caucasian domination over other races, blacks were the original inhabitants of the planet. Their true God was Allah and their true religion was Islam.

The nature of the disastrous reversal of fortune for black people is vividly expressed in the narrative about a "big head scientist" named Yacub. Around six thousand years ago, the story goes, Yacub, an extremely intelligent but dissident member of the tribe of Shabazz, began an experiment in eugenics on the island of Patmos in the Aegean Sea, where he had been exiled with his followers. He resolved, out of bitterness toward Allah, to create a new race that would bedevil black people. After hundreds of years, Yacub and his successors eventually produced a race of blond, pale-skinned people. After another six hundred years those white people moved to the mainland and began to turn blacks against each other. They were captured and removed to Europe, where they only increased their savagery. It was prophesied that they would rule the world for some six thousand years.

Since the story of Yacub set a fixed span for the global domination of whites, it anticipated a restoration of blacks to their former status. Elijah taught that the end of white ascendancy and the "fall of America" were at hand. Black Americans, he argued, needed to abandon Christianity, which was the religion that sanctioned their second-class status, and return to the natural, original religion of black people, Islam. Soon, he preached, the Great Wheel or Mother Plane, the largest man-made mechanical object in the sky (see Ezekiel 1: 15–18), would initiate the final battle between the partisans of Allah and the white devils.

Although Elijah quoted as freely from the Qur'an as from the Bible, his understanding of Islam was distinctive. Although Elijah's theology was not orthodox, it still appealed to an audience deeply familiar with generations of suffering.

Elijah did not ignore more prosaic issues. While they were waiting for a country of their own and for Armageddon, he counseled his followers to remove themselves as much as possible from the taint and dangers of white society. Self-determination for members of the Nation included founding and patronizing their own businesses and attending their own schools. Elijah even counseled them on a healthy diet.

At his death, Elijah was succeeded by his son Wallace Dean Muhammad, who soon moved the Nation toward mainstream Sunni Islam. In 1981, Louis Farrakhan (1933–) began to reestablish the Nation on the basis of Elijah's teachings.

See also: Malcolm X (1925–1965); Nation of Gods and Earths, The (The Five Percent Nation); Nation of Islam, The.

Further Reading

Clegg, Claude Andrew, III. 1997. *An Original Man: The Life and Times of Elijah Muhammad.* New York: St. Martin's Press.

Evanzz, Karl. 1999. *The Messenger: The Rise and Fall of Elijah Muhammad.* New York: Vintage Books.

Muhammad, Elijah. 1965. *Message to the Blackman in America.* Atlanta, GA: Messenger Elijah Muhammad Propagation Society.

Mungiki

Members of the Kenyan Mungiki movement describe it as a "chameleon." Many descriptions from inside Kenya and most from outside, however, describe it as a violent gang that has been involved in multiple violent incidents. In fact, Mungiki now serves as an umbrella term that unites rural and urban members, violent and nonviolent actors, and individuals with a range of religious, economic, and political goals.

There are multiple stories about the origins of Mungiki, all of which date it to the late 1980s. Maina Njenga (1969–) and his cousin Ndura Waruinge (1973–) were among those involved. Some accounts describe Njenga receiving a call from the God of the Kikuyu tribe, Ngai, which would commission him to restore his people to their traditional religious and cultural roots. Taking the Mau Mau opponents to British colonialism as a model, Mungiki has opposed Westernization, modernization, Christianity, and globalization, especially as they have negatively impacted the Kikuyu, whether at the hands of a rapacious central government or other tribal groups.

Mungiki aims to free the Kikuyu from oppression, whatever its sources. The group has recruited both in the more rural African Rift Valley area and in cities like Nairobi. Especially in Nairobi, the movement attracted many street youths. While Mungiki claimed that, through things like its takeover of the minibus taxi service, it was delivering necessary social services to an ignored population, the government accused it of extortion, corruption, and acts of violence. That perception of the group as violent was supported when individuals associated with Mungiki participated in massacres in 2002 and 2009.

Among the religious practices of Mungiki are an initiation that moves the individual through water and then smoke as a means of purification, prayer facing in the direction of Mount Kenya (Kirinyaga) where Ngai resides, and traditional animal sacrifices. More evidence of the chameleon-like character of the movement came in 2000 when some of its leaders and a larger group of followers converted to Islam. In 2009, Njenga converted to a Pentecostal church after his release from prison.

Mungiki provides a strong example of the different motivations held within a single movement and of the radically different ways in which a group can be perceived by its members and outsiders.

See also: African New Religious Movements; Charisma and Leadership in New Religious Movements; Violence and New Religious Movements.

Further Reading

Kagwanja, Peter Mwangi. 2003. "Facing Mount Kenya or Facing Mecca? The Mungiki, Ethnic Violence, and the Politics of the Moi Succession in Kenya, 1987–2002." *African Affairs* 102: 25–49.

Rasmussen, Jacob. 2014. "'We Are the True Blood of the Mau Mau': The Mungiki Movement in Kenya." In Jannifer M. Hazen & Dennis Rodgers, eds., *Global Gangs: Street Violence across the World*, pp. 213–236. Minneapolis: University of Minnesota Press.

Wamue-Ngare, Grace Nyatugah. 2012. "The Mungiki Movement: A Source of Religio-Political Conflict in Kenya." In James Howard Smith & Rosalind I. J. Hackett, eds., *Displacing the State: Religion and Conflict in Neoliberal Africa*, pp. 85–111. South Bend, IN: University of Notre Dame Press.

Music and New Religious Movements

Few would deny that music can be transportive. Hearing a particular song or composition might bring back a particular memory, move a person to tears, or remove a person, if not bodily then emotionally, from a particular time and place into a state that feels timeless and universal. For many religious traditions, however, music is not only capable of such feats for aesthetic reasons but because it is inherently divine. Numerous sacred texts employ the language of music rather than prose when describing the spiritual or supernatural. The Upanishads, a major Hindu text, for example, is translated as "The Last Song," and in the scriptures of ancient Aztecs, it is written that God "sang" the world into being.

New religious movements, like major world religions, have employed music in various ways: as a component of religious practice, as a tool of proselytization and prophecy, and as a means of gathering a holy community.

MUSIC AS SACRED PRACTICE

Paramahansa Yogananda (1893–1952), founder of the Hindu new religious movement, the Self-Realization Fellowship, wrote in his autobiography that music could lead an individual to God-consciousness; that in fact, sound, was perhaps the most potent force for achieving enlightenment. In practice, this translated to the repetitive chanting of the word "aum," which represented the divine presence and enabled practitioners to clear their minds and focus on their oneness with God. In

Music and New Religious Movements 413

other words, by drawing out the "aum," rather than simply speaking it, the practitioner vibrates with the universe. Similarly, members of Soka Gakkai, a Japanese new religious movement, repeatedly chant the *Daimoku*—"Nam-myoho-reenge-kyo" (translated as "Glory to the Sutra of the Lotus of the Supreme Law")—which they believe will ultimately bring about change, not only in their lives, but in the world around them, by releasing the underlying forces of the universe.

Akin to these Asian religious traditions, German doctor Franz Anton Mesmer (1734–1815) believed that a particular force or substance, known as animal magnetism, united all reality. By manipulating this substance in specific ways, one could heal ailments without Western medicine. To perform such feats of healing, a patient was often hypnotized. One of the primary means of bringing a patient into a hypnotic state was music, which relaxed patients bodily and mentally, bringing them into a state of suggestibility and susceptibility to Mesmerist methods.

The notion that music can relax the mind and senses and open an individual up to revelation or spiritual transformation is common to traditions that have an esoteric bent. G. I. Gurdjieff (1866–1949), creator of the Fourth Way—a religious tradition that focused on self-development through a combination of practices focused on bettering a person bodily, intellectually, and emotionally—was also a composer. He employed music—very often of his own composition—to help his students hone their burgeoning abilities. At Damanhur, an intentional religious community in the foothills near Turin, Italy, music represents one of the "pathways" to spiritual growth and enlightenment. Members of Damanhur believe that a divine spark exists in every human being, but that it has been lost. To renew one's divinity, then, cultivation of human abilities, including of the musical sort, become central to spiritual practice.

Many Afro-Caribbean and African American traditions that emerged during the era of slavery established music as a predominant ritual element. Enslaved Africans brought with them the traditions of their home continent and combined them with Christian and indigenous traditions, including the use of drums, song, and dance to join the practitioners together and to invoke divine and spiritual beings. In Candomblé, an African Brazilian tradition, for example, all practice involves facilitating relationships with orixás (deities), whose patronage will help the community, either by ensuring its health and prosperity or by defending it against external (or internal) enemies. Mediums are connected to individual orixás; each must learn a prescribed set of songs, dances, and musical themes, which are to be performed to invoke and appease a particular orixá, often while in a trance-like state.

Music employed in worship services is nothing new, particularly for groups that have emerged out of Christianity. The Exclusive (Plymouth) Brethren employ music during every "Meeting," all of which is drawn from a particular hymnbook created by the movement's founder, John Nelson Darby (1800–1882). The hymnbook reflects the millennialist message of the group and the particular theology of Darby. Though the focus and nature of worship is quite opposite to the Brethren, the Church of Satan employs music in its own rituals that are also specifically tailored to its message: the realization of each individual's power and potential to do and accomplish whatever he or she desires. Though somewhat satirical in nature, the specified chants and musical style play up the hedonistic nature of the Church's worship. Founder Anton LaVey (1930–1997), who wrote much of the liturgical music, was a musician by training and played the calliope.

Neopaganism, as a broad tradition encompassing much of modern religious witchcraft, has employed music in a number of ways. Annual gatherings or festivals of Neopagans often employ music as a central ritual element; rarely does a ritual not have some form of music, even if it comes in the form of rhythmic chants. Not only that, but a number of Neopagans have enjoyed successful musical careers, often through the creation of "Pagan Pop," or popular music that engages with religious ideas central to Neopagan practice.

MUSIC AS A TOOL

Some leaders of new religious movements have parlayed their musical ability into their efforts to draw and retain members, to disseminate their message, and to maintain their authority in various ways.

David Koresh (1959–1993), before he assumed leadership of the Branch Davidians in the 1980s, played guitar and sang in church services at the movement's base, the Mount Carmel Center, in Waco, Texas. He was also a member of a band that played locally. After ascending to leadership, his musical aspirations did not cease; he produced several albums that conveyed his particular prophetic message. Not only the means of sharing his prophecy, music played a role in the prophecies themselves. During the siege of Mount Carmel by the Bureau of Alcohol Tobacco and Firearms and the Federal Bureau of Investigation, which would ultimately claim his life and that of over eighty Branch Davidians, Koresh reportedly received a sign from God, which indicated to him that he must complete a particular task and then turn himself in. The sign was a cloud shaped like a guitar.

Likely few would claim to have been introduced to David Koresh and the Branch Davidians through the former's music; the same cannot be said for Bob Marley (1945–1981) and Rastafari. A syncretic religion that combined Judeo-Christianity, African religion, and Jamaican culture, Rastafari emerged in the early twentieth century as a religion of resistance for black Jamaicans against "Babylon," or the white, European institutions that systematically suppressed them. Rastas believed that the 1930 coronation of Ethiopian Emperor Haile Selassie I (born Ras Tafari Makkonen) was a millennial event, signifying the advent of the Messiah who would redeem all black people and enable their return to Africa. Though the movement ultimately reshaped itself once a return to Africa seemed less feasible, its themes of resistance, self-empowerment, and racial pride persisted. For a great many people, their primary and perhaps only introduction to Rastafari thought and practice came through a particular style of music synonymous with the religion, Reggae, and through a particular musical artist, Bob Marley and the Wailers. Marley's many songs, like "Exodus" and "Babylon System," were explicitly Rasta in nature.

More recently, rapper Snoop Dogg (born Calvin Broadus; 1971–) chronicled his conversion to Rastafari via film, including his (brief) change of name to Snoop Lion, in honor of Haile Selassie, whose symbol was the lion. Rap and hip-hop have increasingly become vehicles for new religious movements, such as Public Enemy's invocation of the Nation of Islam and the influence of the Nation of Gods and Earths (Five Percent Nation) on Jay-Z, Common, and the Wu Tang Clan, among others. Very often these artists engage with notions of blackness as divine and resistance to white supremacy as a sacred act.

Though the use and style of music varies by new religious movement and often by practitioner, music functions as a major source of practice and identity for these traditions—and new musical styles have and will continue to emerge out of them.

See also: Branch Davidians; Candomblé; Church of Satan, The; Damanhur; Exclusive (Plymouth) Brethren; Fourth Way, The; Gurdjieff, G. I. (1866–1949); Koresh, David (1959–1993); Lavey, Anton Szandor (1930–1997); Mesmerism; Millennialism; Nation of Gods and Earths, The (The Five Percent Nation); Nation of Islam, The; Neopaganism; Occultism and Esotericism; Race and New Religious Movements; Rastafari; Self-Realization Fellowship (Yogananda); Soka Gakkai.

Further Reading

Coggins, Owen. 2019. *Mysticism, Ritual and Religion in Drone Metal.* London: Bloomsbury Publishing.

McLaughlin, Levi. 2003. "Faith and Practice: Bringing Religion, Music, and Beethoven to Life in Soka Gakkai." *Social Science Japan Journal* 6, no. 2: 161–179.

Till, Rupert. 2010. *Pop Cult Religion and Popular Music.* New York: Continuum Press.

Weston, Donna, & Andy Bennett, eds. 2014. *Pop Pagans: Paganism and Popular Music.* Durham, UK: Acumen Publishing.

Mysticism

Like many aspects of religion, mysticism can be understood as both a scholarly category and a religious practice or belief system. Some scholars argue that the concept of mysticism has no life outside of the academy, that it is strictly a helpful comparative term when examining multiple religions, and that religions partaking of "mystical" practice do not use such terminology, but refer to it by other names. In other words, mysticism, like religion, predates the language used to describe it. However, various new religious movements have self-consciously appropriated mysticism as both a label and a distinct theological or practical system.

At its base, mysticism refers to individuals' (and occasionally community's) communion with the divine or sacred. Most religions bear elements of mystical practices and, therefore, mysticism manifests in a number of different ways. For example, in Judaism, mystics are those with the ability to understand sacred texts in a way that the average person cannot. Privy not only to higher meaning but to certain privileged texts such as the Zohar, those who have completed certain levels of rabbinic training engage in mystical interpretive practices. In Sufism, the mystical branch of Islam, practitioners engage in rites that turn their focus inward, seeking communion with God through their own souls. Often Sufis are ascetic, stripping themselves of worldly wants to clarify their focus on God. Christian Gnostics (*gnosis* means "knowledge") are replete throughout Christian history and exhibit a variety of mystical practices: asceticism, spiritual interpretation of texts, and often immediate revelatory experience of the divine.

Thus, there is no one way of practicing mysticism or being a mystic. In fact, mysticism lends itself to variation not only between traditions but between individuals. Each mystic may practice or experience the sacred differently. Ironically, as is the case for many new religious movements that draw upon or claim to be mystical in nature, mystics often believe that they are tapping into something universal and eternal, even as they experience it as something singular and definitively located in their time and place.

CONTEMPORARY MYSTICAL MOVEMENTS

Some historians locate the origins of modern mysticism in nineteenth-century Transcendentalism, a predominantly American movement that combined various intellectual strains, eschewed institutional control, and located the divine in the self. Transcendentalists like Ralph Waldo Emerson (1803–1882) argued for a return to nature whereby people could see their own divinity reflected in the created world. He famously described this experience in his book *Nature* (1836) as becoming a "transparent eyeball," with all matter dissolved and only consciousness remaining. Emerson and other Transcendentalists were influenced by a number of sources, including Asian religions such as Hinduism and Buddhism, and the writings of Emmanuel Swedenborg (1688–1772). Swedenborg was a Swedish scientist who suddenly began experiencing visions and contact with spiritual beings who revealed to him the hidden meaning of the Bible. They influenced his theory of correspondence or the idea that for every natural or human fact, there was a corresponding divine reality. The New Church arose from Swedenborg's ideas, including the belief that humanity had entered its "fifth age" of spiritual evolution, which would usher in a time of great progress characterized by greater trust in individuals' mystical abilities.

There are also a number of new religious movements that claim a lineage from more established mystical traditions. There are Neo-Sufi movements, which have arisen around various spiritual guides or *shaykhs* since the twelfth century (certain scholars argue that Sufism, as a whole, is a new religious movement, since it emerged from a major religion—Islam—and is constantly creating new branches as new mystical leaders arise). Subud, though it does not claim to be a subsect of Sufism, arose from the teachings of Muslim mystic Pak Subuh (1901–1987) and can be likened to Neo-Sufi traditions. Additionally, Kabbalah, which is the name for the branch of Jewish mysticism in traditional Judaism, has been remade as a modern new religion open to all and not only those with years of schooling in a yeshiva (a traditional rabbinical school). Typically Jewish kabbalists are exclusively men and rabbis by trade, however, celebrities such as Madonna (1958–) have taken up the practice under new guise. The Kabbalah Centre, founded by Philip Berg (1927–2013) and Yehuda Tzvi Brandwein (1904–1969) in 1965, claims

Mysticism

to descend from traditional Kabbalah and to base its teachings on the mystical readings of the Zohar, while also promoting itself as a New Age "spirituality for the modern world" (see www.kabbalah.com).

New Age Gnostic movements also exist, which according to scholars include the Unification Church, known for its belief that Rev. Sun Myung Moon (1920–2012) and his wife Hak Ja Han (1943–) were the True Parents of humanity—a conclusion based on Moon's many revelatory and visionary experiences. The founders of Heaven's Gate, a Christian UFO group, Marshall Applewhite (1931–1997) and Bonnie Lu Nettles (1927–1985) combined Christian apocalypticism, New Age spirituality, and mysticism into a religious movement that promised its members that they would be elevated to The Evolutionary Level Above Human. Not only were Applewhite and Nettles privy to special knowledge and access to higher, alien beings, but they claimed to be these very beings, incarnated in human form to help humanity in its spiritual progress.

Beyond these various movements, mystical traditions will continue to emerge as they have for centuries, highlighting the desire for people to access and even merge with the divine and to know things only a rare few seem to know.

See also: Applewhite, Marshall (1932–1997), and Bonnie Lu Nettles (1927–1985); Gnostic Groups; Heaven's Gate; Kabbalah; Moon, Rev. Sun Myung (1920–2012); New Age, The; New Church, The; Subud; Sufi New Religious Movements; Swedenborg, Emanuel (1688–1772); Transcendentalism; UFO Religions; Unification Church, The.

Further Reading

Cupitt, Don. 1998. *Mysticism after Modernity*. Oxford: Blackwell Publishing.

Kripal, Jeffrey J. 2006. "Mysticism." In Robert A. Segal, ed., *The Blackwell Companion to the Study of Religion*. Oxford: Blackwell Publishing.

Schmidt, Leigh Eric. 2003. "The Making of Modern 'Mysticism.'" *The Journal of the American Academy of Religion* 71: 273–302.

Woods, Richard, ed. 1980. *Understanding Mysticism*. New York: Doubleday.

Nation of Gods and Earths, The (The Five Percent Nation)

In 1963, Clarence 13X Smith (1928–1969) left the Nation of Islam. He had studied with Malcolm X (1925–1965) at Harlem's Mosque No. 7, but questioned whether only W. D. Fard (1877–?) could be considered God in the flesh. Smith concluded that every "Asiatic Black Man" (with the strong focus on males) was inherently God. He spread his ideas on the streets of Harlem and found success primarily among teenagers in the underclass. As he gathered more students, Smith became known as Father Allah and his movement became known as the Nation of Gods and Earths, in which males were identified as Gods and females as Earths.

The other designation for Father Allah's followers derived from the Nation of Islam's contention that 85 percent of the population lived in ignorance, 10 percent knew the truth but used their knowledge to exploit the others, and only 5 percent knew the truth and were willing to use it to raise up others. Father Allah and his disciples derived their teachings from the Nation of Islam. But they supplemented the 120 Supreme Wisdom lessons with what they called Supreme Mathematics (in which single numbers stood for specific concepts, e.g., 1 for knowledge) and the Supreme Alphabet (which associated all twenty-six letters with concepts). The resulting ideology was a complex blend of Islamic ideas as mediated by the Nation, numerology, speculative philosophy, and Black Nationalism. As that system developed, it moved away from identifying itself with any form of Islam, although the Nation of Gods and Earth still maintains cordial relations with the Nation of Islam led by Louis Farrakhan.

Especially since it emphasizes that each (male) person is God, the Nation of Gods and Earths has never been highly organized. After Father Allah's murder in 1969, multiple figures claimed to teach his principles but no central figure has emerged. Individual members are supposed to devote themselves to personal study, "building" or reasoning with other Gods, and to attend periodic Universal Parliaments.

Throughout their history, the Five Percenters have flourished in prison. Law enforcement agencies have kept them under nearly constant surveillance and have often encountered difficulty in determining whether they were criminals, sincere religious people, or both.

The broadest influence of Fiver Percenters on the larger culture has come through hip hop, with artists such as Rakim, Big Daddy Kane, members of the Wu Tang Clan, and Erykah Badu, among others, weaving Father Allah's messages into their music. Even as they wrestle with issues concerning patriarchal attitudes

420 Nation of Islam, The

(which make female Earths subservient to male Gods) and race (including whether white people can be Gods), the Five Percenters continue to attract members.

See also: Nation of Islam, The; Malcolm X (1925–1965).

Further Reading

Allah, God Supreme. 1993. *Supreme Lessons of the Gods and Earths: A Guide for Five Percenters to Follow as Taught by Clarence 13 X Allah.* NP: African American Bookstore.

Knight, Michael Muhammad. 2007. *The Five Percenters: Islam, Hip Hop and the Gods of New York.* London: Oneworld Publications.

Nation of Islam, The

Muslims originally came to the Americas through the slave trade. Although there is no demonstrable continuity between those early Muslims and contemporary Muslims of African descent, various configurations of Islam, both imported from abroad and devised in the United States, have exerted a powerful attraction on African Americans in the twentieth and twenty-first centuries.

Beginning in the 1920s, for example, missionaries from the Ahmadiyya movement founded in nineteenth-century India made African American converts. A decade earlier, Noble Drew Ali (1886–1929) established the first location of the Moorish Science Temple of America in Newark in 1913. The Moorish Science Temple had its own "Holy Koran" and collection of hadith, though neither of them resembled the Qur'an and hadith of Sunni Islam. Of all the religious movements that focused on black dignity and identity in the early twentieth century, however, none had the impact of the Nation of Islam.

ORIGINS

The Nation of Islam originated in the encounter between Elijah Poole (1897–1975) and the mysterious figure known as W. D. Fard and Farad Muhammad (1877–?). Poole had moved from his birthplace of Sandersville, Georgia, to Detroit in 1923. Fard appeared in Detroit in 1930, preaching his distinctive message. He claimed that African Americans were not "Negroes" but rather members of the "Lost-Found Tribe of Shabazz" whose ancestors had been forcibly removed from their homes in Mecca nearly four hundred years ago. Their true identities and their true religion of Islam had been hidden from them by the devilish white people to dominate them. Fard's message aimed to liberate black people from the continuing effects of slavery and colonialism and restore their dignity and sense of self-worth.

Fard's public ministry only lasted a few years. By 1933, he had left Detroit and there are no traces of him after 1934. But he had quickly decided that Elijah Poole would become his messenger and after his disappearance, Poole, originally known as Elijah Karriem ("Noble") and then as Elijah Muhammad, became the leader of the movement based on Fard's teachings.

Nation of Islam, The

Elijah's status as leader of the new group was contested and he eventually departed for Chicago, which became the headquarters of the fledgling Nation of Islam. Efforts at growth were hindered when Elijah was convicted of failing to register for the draft in 1942. Only after his release in 1946 did the Nation begin to see a dramatic increase in membership. By the early 1960s, it counted between fifty and seventy-five thousand members.

The core doctrines of the Nation are expressed in a widely reported story known as "Yacub's History." It tells how the original, black inhabitants of earth fell under the sway of a race of white devils who were created through the eugenics experiments conducted by the "big head scientist" Yacub, a renegade member of the tribe of Shabazz. As a result, the white race would dominate the world for six thousand years. The Nation taught that the era of white supremacy was coming to an end, that blacks could recover their lost identities, and that the fall of America would result in blacks resuming their original status as Allah's favored race.

The Nation urged black self-determination in all areas. It advised its members to build up and patronize their own businesses and to establish and send their children to their own schools. It counseled members to live diligent and sober lives and to adopt a healthy diet that avoided pork, many kinds of fish, alcohol, and canned foods, among other things. The Nation's emphasis on self-determination and separatism set it at odds with integrationist movements and leaders, such as Martin Luther King Jr.

The Nation's message had deep resonance for African Americans who had suffered under slavery and its aftermath, experienced social and economic discrimination, and frequently faced prejudicial actions by law enforcement. The mission of the Nation intersected with those of other movements in the 1950s and 1960s that acted for black civil rights and power, even as Elijah stuck to a pronounced nonpolitical stance.

One of those attracted to the Nation was Malcolm Little (1925–1965). While he was serving a prison term for burglary, Malcolm learned that several members of his family had converted to Islam. His interest was piqued when one of his brothers informed him that he knew how Malcolm could get out of prison. Malcolm's conversion began when he refused an offer of pork in the prison cafeteria. His connection to the Nation deepened as he embarked on a correspondence with Elijah. He soon adopted X to replace his "slave name" of Little.

When Malcolm was released from prison, he began to study Islam directly with Elijah. Soon, he was a rising figure in the Nation, tasked with expanding the membership of Temples throughout the Northeast. Largely self-taught while in prison, Malcolm became a mesmerizing speaker and he was frequently invited to universities and other public forums. As a result, he eventually became recognized as the public face of the Nation, even more so than Elijah himself. Malcolm's swift ascent, however, created tension with other members of the Nation's hierarchy. In the early 1960s, his relations with the Chicago headquarters and Elijah himself became progressively tenser. When Malcolm remarked that the violent assassination of John F. Kennedy showed that the "chickens were coming home to roost," Malcolm's enemies within the movement capitalized on the opportunity and Elijah suspended Malcolm from the Nation in December of 1963.

Nation of Islam, The

By March of 1964, Malcolm had formally left the Nation. His subsequent pilgrimage to Mecca drew him closer to orthodox Islam even as he became more politically active. With Malcolm gone, Elijah and his lieutenants at the Chicago headquarters consolidated their power. Elijah continued to lead the Nation for another decade and prepared his son, Wallace Dean (1933–2008), to take over for him.

TRANSITIONS

When Elijah died on February 25, 1975, Wallace Dean became the leader of the Nation of Islam. Like many other members of the Nation, he had become aware of the idiosyncratic nature of the Nation's theology. Soon after he replaced his father, Wallace Dean began to dismantle the distinctive teachings that Elijah and Fard had developed. He dissolved the Nation of Islam in 1976. He taught that whites would no longer be identified as devils nor would blacks be identified as gods. Both Fard and Elijah were demoted to the status of ordinary Muslim teachers. Those changes smoothed the way for a rapprochement with orthodox, Sunni Islam.

Although many members of the Nation followed Wallace (later, Warith) Dean into Sunni Islam, some saw his changes as a betrayal of his father's teachings. In 1978, Minister Louis Farrakhan (1933–) formally parted ways with Wallace Dean to found his own organization that would remain true to Elijah's original teachings. By 1981, he had reclaimed the Nation of Islam as the name for his group. Farrakhan, who early on had served as assistant minister at the Harlem temple led by Malcolm X and had succeeded him in 1964, justified his position on the basis of his closeness to Elijah Muhammad, who had frequently expressed his approval of him. Indeed, some within the Nation had seen him as a likely successor to Elijah.

Farrakhan also claimed supernatural approval for his leadership. Most notably, he claimed to have seen in a vision that Elijah was, in fact, not dead. Later, in 1985, Farrakhan claimed to have been taken aboard the Mother Ship or Mother Wheel (see Ezekiel 1: 15–18) where he received a verbal commission directly from Elijah himself and also received a scroll filled with Allah's message to humanity.

With Farrakhan's assertion of charismatic authority, the Nation of Islam returned to its roots in the relationship between Elijah and W. D. Fard. In direct contrast to Wallace Dean's leadership, Farrakhan both maintained and extended the teachings that separated the Nation from the rest of Islam. The directions taken by the two major factions after the death of Elijah represent two very different conceptions of what it means to be a Muslim. Both groups remain active. The group led by Wallace Dean is now known as the American Society of Muslims. Farrakhan continues to lead the reinvigorated Nation of Islam.

See also: Ahmadiyya Movement, The; Ali, Noble Drew (1886–1929); Charisma and Leadership in New Religious Movements; Moorish Science Temple of America, The; Malcolm X (1925–1965); Muhammad, Elijah (1897–1975); Nation of Gods and Earths, The (The Five Percent Nation).

Further Reading

Curtis, Edward E., IV. 2006. *Black Muslim Religion in the Nation of Islam, 1960–1975*. Chapel Hill: University of North Carolina Press.

Gardell, Mattias. 1996. *In the Name of Elijah Muhammad: Louis Farrakhan and the Nation of Islam*. Durham, NC: Duke University Press.

Gomez, Michael A. 2005. *Black Crescent: The Experience and Legacy of African Muslims in the Americas*. Cambridge: Cambridge University Press.

Marable, Manning. 2011. *Malcolm X: A Life of Reinvention*. New York: Vintage Books.

Muhammad, Elijah. 1965. *Message to the Blackman in America*. Atlanta, GA: Messenger Elijah Muhammad Propagation Society.

Nation of Yahweh, The

In the twentieth century, many new religious movements sought to provide people in the African diaspora with an identity and history not determined by the "white" Christianity that had been imposed on them by slave holders and other colonialists. In the United States, some of those groups, such as the Moorish Science Temple and the Nation of Islam, found inspiration in forms of Islam, even though they departed from orthodox Sunni Islam. Other groups focused on connecting contemporary people of African descent to the ancient Israelites or Hebrews and adopted the Jewish ritual calendar and various ritual practices. Often, the groups drew on other sources, including various esoteric traditions and even lore about UFOs. The Nation of Yahweh or Temple of Love is generally identified as a Black Hebrew Israelite group.

Founded in 1979 and headquartered in Miami, the Nation of Yahweh was led by an individual who identified himself as Yahweh ben Yahweh (Yahweh, son of Yahweh, né Hulon Mitchell Jr., 1935–2007), the son of God. Before he founded his own group, Mitchell had been active in the Black cultic milieu, having been a member of the Nation of Islam in the 1960s and then operating as an independent faith healer under the name of "Father Mitchell."

The teachings of the Nation of Yahweh bear resemblances to both the Nation of Islam and to Black Hebrew Israelite groups. The Nation is distinctive in the emphasis that it puts on the New Testament, however. It takes the life of Jesus as a paradigm for understanding the career of Yahweh ben Yahweh, for example. Like other groups associated with Black Judaism and Black Islam, the Nation asserts that both the ancient Hebrew Prophets and Jesus were black. Unfortunately, contemporary African Americans are lost and ignorant of their own connections to that history. They need to be awakened, set free from misguided perceptions, and to acquire right knowledge by heeding the teachings of Yahweh ben Yahweh. The Nation enjoins its followers to follow the Jewish ritual calendar and dietary laws. It also tightly governs the daily schedules of its members, requiring them to dress in white robes and also regulating their sex lives.

There is some urgency to the Nation's mission, because as the September 2015 issue of the Nation's magazine *The Good News of Yahweh* put it, the second coming of Yahweh ben Yahweh would happen in 2019. He is depicted as having ascended to heaven after his death and his return was eagerly awaited.

In Miami, the Nation of Yahweh initially received positive recognition for its efforts in establishing businesses such as grocery stores in poor neighborhoods such as Liberty City. One observer remarked that the Nation had "turned the ghetto beautiful." The group quickly became an economic juggernaut, and expanded from its Miami base to other U.S. cities and some sixteen foreign countries. It all unraveled, however, in the early 1990s. Robert Rozier (1955–), one of Yahweh ben Yahweh's followers pleaded guilty to having committed seven murders, purportedly at the direction of Yahweh ben Yahweh. The religious leader and several followers were eventually convicted under the federal Racketeer Influenced and Corrupt Organizations Act of conspiracy for their roles in more than a dozen murders. From 1990 to 2001, Yahweh ben Yahweh served eleven years of an eighteen-year prison term. On his release he was prohibited from having any contact with his congregation. The conviction of their leader cost the Nation dearly, with followers split between those who continued to maintain his innocence and those who left the group in disillusionment. In 2006, Yahweh ben Yahweh was released from parole but he died the next year.

Since his death a successor, claiming to be Yahweh ben Yahweh ben Yahweh, has arisen and the group continues to publicize the founder's teachings through its website (www.yahwehbenyahweh.com). Yahweh ben Yahweh has also had an afterlife as a prime example of the harm that "cult" leaders can do, with a profile in *People* magazine in 2018 and a dramatic documentary on the Oxygen television network in 2019.

See also: Black Judaism; Millennialism; Moorish Science Temple of America, The; Nation of Islam, The; Race and New Religious Movements; UFO Religions.

Further Reading

Freedberg, Sydney J. 1994. *Brother Love: Money, Murder, and a Messiah.* New York: Pantheon Books.

Mock, Brentin. 2007. "Nation of Yahweh Mourns Death of Leader, Shows Signs of New Life." *Intelligence Report*, Southern Poverty Law Center, October, 2007. Available at: https://www.splcenter.org/fighting-hate/intelligence-report/2007/nation-yahweh -mourns-loss-leader-shows-signs-new-life.

"Uncovered: The Cult of Yahweh ben Yahweh." 2019. Oxygen Network.

Native American Church, The

Now the largest indigenous American religious movement, the Native American Church (NAC) emerged from a variety of influences in the context of U.S. imperialism in the Western states and territories during the nineteenth century. During this period, white settlers moved westward bringing their concept of civilization to bear on the indigenous peoples already inhabiting the land. And Christianization went hand in hand with civilization. Thus, at the same time that Native Americans were being stripped of their lands, cultures, names, and traditions, they were being forcibly introduced to Christian theological ideas and institutions. The effect was not what the white settlers expected.

Instead of accepting Christianity wholesale—or rejecting it outright—Native Americans often adapted Christian ideas and practices for their own uses. Often these religious systems became movements of millennial resistance, as seen in the Ghost Dance Movement of the 1890s. They were always created out of a desire for cultural preservation. At the same time that white Christian settlers sought to spread their religion in the Great Plains region, the use of peyote (a cactus, from which the psychedelic drug mescaline is derived) grew in prominence, introduced by immigration from Mexico. Soon it was being employed in religious rituals. Beginning in Oklahoma in the mid-nineteenth century among the Comanche and Kiowa tribes, Native Americans began to combine peyote practice with Christian and indigenous religious ideas. From this was born the NAC, also known as Peyotism or Peyote Religion. Though there is no one known founder, Quanah Parker (c. 1845–1911), a Comanche warrior, is often credited as the progenitor of the NAC; the Church was formally incorporated in 1918. The religion spread quickly after that creating a pantribal unity against the encroaching forces of white civilization.

BELIEFS AND PRACTICES

The practices of the NAC are not monolithic and reflect the particular tribal and geographical origins of areas in which it exists. However, there are certain beliefs and practices that the various chapters of the NAC share in common. Members share a belief in a supreme God known as the Great Spirit, reflecting their Christian roots, as well as in a variety of lesser deities or spirits that interact with people on earth and through ritual, reflecting their native religious roots. Jesus appears in the pantheon of divine beings, though he is either conceived as a heroic human or as the healing and powerful "Peyote Spirit" invoked during most rituals. These spirits are invoked in ritual to petition their aid, give them thanks, and, occasionally, inhabit participants or for participants to be inhabited by them.

Central to all NAC practice is the use of peyote as a sacrament (though other hallucinogenic substances, such as cannabis, have been used in its place). Peyote is imbibed to communicate with God, spirits, and deceased ancestors, who provide a source of sacred knowledge and power, which manifests in prophecy, spiritual guidance, and healing, among other things. Church services often take all night (as a sacrifice to God) and take place in tipis. Typically, participants will have taken a bath ahead of time; similar to Christian baptism, the NAC believes that one must be purified to take the sacrament. Besides peyote, participants eat four other sacramental foods, including water, beef, corn mush, and berries, which some argue were added later to balance the bitter taste of peyote knobs. Accompanying consumption, the priest, chief, or "Roadman" also leads those present in Bible readings, prayer, and singing. Those present usually partake of a breakfast the following morning. Unlike traditional Christianity, services are not a weekly occurrence. Instead, peyote rites are performed upon request—for healing or celebration—or to acknowledge various rites of passage.

IN CONTEMPORARY SOCIETY

Much of the criticism of the NAC involves the use of peyote. NAC members maintain that all growing substances are "naturally prepared by the Creator" and therefore good to use (https://nativeamericanchurches.org). Though some have raised concerns over its effect on the body, studies have reported that there is little long-term harm caused by peyote. The American Indian Religious Freedom Act (1978) protects the use of peyote, but its consumption is still illegal outside of the NAC, a distinction that has created a legal gray area.

The Church and ritual peyote use made national headlines in 1990 when the Supreme Court ruled on the case, *Employment Division v. Smith.* Two members of the NAC, Galen Black and Alfred Leo Smith, were fired from their positions at a state-run drug rehabilitation clinic for ingesting peyote during religious ceremonies. They were also denied unemployment benefits, since they were fired for the use of an illegal substance. Black and Smith appealed their termination on First Amendment grounds. In a 6–3 ruling, the Supreme Court decided against the plaintiffs, arguing that the state had grounds to fire Black and Smith and deny them unemployment benefits. The decision was controversial, and the dissenting opinion written by Justice Henry Blackmun expressed concern that it would now be easier to discriminate against minority religions.

Despite this setback, the NAC has remained relatively steady in membership (around 275,000 in 1977 and 250,000 today)—a feat for any new religion. Today, the Church welcomes members of all ethnicities and races, specifically those with ecological leanings. Born of earth-centered indigenous religious practices, the Church emphasizes environmental and spiritual concerns as well as its more well-known ritual use of psychedelic substances. Though some Native Americans critique the NAC for its blurring of tribal lines in favor of a pan-Indian movement, its continued presence stands as a sharp rebuke to the cultural annihilation of Western imperialism and shows the resilience of indigenous religious practices.

See also: Courts and New Religious Movements; Ghost Dance Movement (Wovoka).

Further Reading

Calabrese, Joseph D. 2013. *A Different Medicine: Postcolonial Healing in the Native American Church.* New York: Oxford University Press.

Maroukis, Thomas Constantine. 2010. *The Peyote Road: Religious Freedom and the Native American Church.* Norman: University of Oklahoma Press.

White, Phillip M. 2000. *Peyotism and the Native American Church: An Annotated Bibliography.* Westport, CT: Greenwood Press.

Neopaganism

Although the Latin term "paganus" originally referred to someone who lived in the countryside, it was taken over by early Christians in the fourth century to refer pejoratively to various non-Christian religions. Over time, it acquired a wider reach as a description of all non-Christian religions while retaining its negative inflection. But there never really was a single religious system known as Paganism. Nonetheless, the religions of ancient Greece and Rome continued to exert an

Neopaganism is an umbrella term for a number of religions that coalesced around the worship and communion with nature, the use of magic and witchcraft, and often feminist and LGBTQ+ activism. Numerous traditions characterize themselves as descended from or related to Neopaganism, including Wicca. The above depicts a Wiccan handfasting ritual, which is typically performed during marriage ceremonies and involves the binding of wrists with ribbon to symbolize the couple's connection to each other. (Heather Cornelius)

attraction particularly in eighteenth and nineteenth-century Romanticism and in the creation of mythologies for modern nation-states.

Paganism always retained the character of being an alternative to Christianity. That status became an important element in the contemporary development of the diverse array of traditions subsumed under the umbrella category of Neopaganism, Contemporary Paganism, or Modern Paganism. Various forms of paganism appeal to individuals who are seeking an alternative to dominant monotheistic traditions. Although accurate numbers are difficult to establish, there may be as many as one million self-professed Pagans throughout the world in the early twenty-first century.

ORIGINS AND DEVELOPMENT

Although it has roots in Romanticism, various national folklores, and also the work of the British occultist Aleister Crowley (1875–1947), modern Paganism in the United Kingdom and the United States, at least, can trace its origins to the British colonial administrator Gerald Gardner (1884–1964). Gardner claimed that in 1939 he had been initiated into the "old religion" that had survived all Christian attempts to eradicate it. Gardner's account gave further impetus to the theory of Margaret Murray (1862–1963), who argued in *The Witch-Cult in Western Europe* (1921) that pre-Christian witchcraft had been the religion of much of Europe and actually had survived underground throughout the centuries of Christian domination. Murray's and Gardner's claims would inspire other contemporary Pagans to revive what they saw as long suppressed practices. Relatively quickly, however, the "myth of Wicca" came under sustained scrutiny from both scholars and practitioners. They concluded that the idea of an unbroken tradition from pre-Christian times to the present could not be upheld.

Nonetheless, Gardner inspired a prominent tradition of contemporary Paganism. Raymond Buckland (1934–2017), for example, claimed to have introduced Gardnerian Wicca to the United States, and other prominent figures can trace their initiatory lineage to Gardner. Gardner's *Book of Shadows* (c. late 1940s; see https://www.sacred-texts.com/pag/gbos/index.htm), a compendium of ritual directions and magical lore designed to be customized by individual practitioners, originally circulated privately and was only formally published in 1971. It has been used and adapted by many Pagans, both within and beyond the Gardnerian tradition.

In other areas, particularly Slavic countries, contemporary Paganism had multiple points of origin, with many individuals claiming to recover ancient practices. In 1964, in Canada, the Ukrainian Lev Sylenko (1921–) was the first to use the term "Native Faith" to describe a reconstruction of ancient pre-Christian Ukrainian religion. Variations of the term "Rodnovery" (roughly "Native Faith") became widely used among Slavic peoples despite differences among groups, with six Russian organizations formally agreeing in 2002 to use that term as the primary name for Slavic forms of Paganism. The Slavic examples show that contemporary Paganism is an expansive umbrella category under which a diverse array of groups, individuals, and movements can be organized.

Particularly in the United States, the development of Paganism intersected with the development of various kinds of feminist religion and spirituality, including worship of the Goddess or various goddesses. Finding the patriarchy of world religions like Christianity irredeemable, some feminists sought female images of the divine in pre-Christian or non-Christian religions. Some of those women became active in Paganism. Z Budapest (née Zsuzsanna Emese Mokcsay, 1940–), for example, established the Susan B. Anthony Coven #1 in 1971 in Southern California. She founded the Dianic form of Wicca, which, in contrast to the Gardnerian, focuses on the duality of the male god and goddess and concentrates on the Goddess, who is perceived to encompass all female deities. Her Dianic coven admits only women. Budapest's *The Feminist Book of Lights and Shadows* (1976) remains an influential text.

The Reclaiming tradition of Paganism grew out of the teaching and ritual work of Starhawk (née Miriam Simos, 1951–) and others in the San Francisco Bay area in 1980 (see www.reclaiming.org). While not limiting participation to women, Reclaiming blends strong emphases on feminism and political activism with its Paganism. Starhawk remains Reclaiming's most influential teacher and her first book, *The Spiral Dance* (1979), which has gone through multiple editions, is the single most influential statement of contemporary Paganism. In fact, Starhawk's writings are part of a large and ever-expanding collection of written texts that have sustained and spread contemporary Paganism. They offer both inspiration to those who participate at least in worship with other Pagans and sustenance to many solitary practitioners. Many trace their moment of realization that they were Pagans to reading a particular text.

Another important contemporary Pagan group in the United States was founded by Tim Zell (1942–) and another student while they attended Fulton College in Missouri in the late 1960s. The Church of All Worlds (see www.caw.org), inspired by the fiction of Robert Heinlein (1907–1988), was incorporated in 1968 and recognized by the Internal Revenue Service as a religion in 1970. Although Zell's relationship with the Church went through ups and downs, he has remained an important proponent of contemporary Paganism for half a century, emphasizing the divinity inherent in every individual, care for the living being of the earth (known as Gaea), and an open approach to sexuality.

Other forms of Paganism that have political emphases include the various movements that connect particular religious practices and beliefs with ethnicities. For example, some strands of Odinism and Ásatrú (see www.asatru.org and asatrufolkassembly.org), the worship of the pre-Christian Norse Gods, have made common cause with white nationalist movements. At least some of the various Rodnovery (or Slavic Native Faith) movements have also championed ethnic purity, white superiority, and even embraced anti-semitism. Though the emphasis on following a religious path connected to a particular ethnicity can lead not only to the celebration of that ethnic group but also the denigration of others as inferior, that is not necessarily the case with all ethnic forms of Paganism.

BELIEFS AND PRACTICES

Given the rich diversity of contemporary Paganism, it is difficult to identify beliefs and practices that Neopagans have in common. Compounding that difficulty is the overall lack of organization in contemporary Paganism. Although individual groups may have their own structures, there is no overarching body that governs all Pagan groups. In fact, the freedom to improvise and exercise individual creativity has attracted many to Neopaganism. Moreover, very few Pagans indulge in systematization of their religious convictions, preferring instead to focus on more immediate experiences of the God or Goddess. Finally, in many forms of Paganism, there are individual practitioners who have no substantial ties to any particular group. Often inspired by books, such as Silver Ravenwolf's *Solitary Witch: The Ultimate Book of Shadows for the New Generation* (2003), they frequently have their own eclectic mixes of practices and beliefs. The rise of the internet has made it much easier for isolated individuals to gain access to Pagan materials and construct their own versions of Pagan practice even as it has promoted the formation of some Pagan virtual communities.

Contemporary Pagans can be found all along a continuum that runs from rich eclecticism on one side to reconstruction on the other. Eclectic Pagans borrow images, ideas, and practices from multiple cultures and devise others from their own imaginations to produce individually satisfying forms of practice. Reconstructionists, to varying degrees, aim to put into practice what they see as particular ancient, pre-Christian rites. Nova Roma, for example, intends to restore ancient Roman Paganism as faithfully as possible (see www.novaroma.org).

Despite the extraordinary diversity of contemporary Paganism, some commonalities can be identified. As Margot Adler generalized with appropriate hesitation, Pagans see the natural world itself as holy, the body and sexuality as holy, and the imagination as holy. The divine is immanent in nature and can be found both within and outside of individuals (see Adler 1986). Pagans also generally recognize multiple gods, even when they focus on a single one. Pagan ritual cycles are typically aligned with the seasons. Relations between the earth and the sun and moon drive the ritual calendar. The Pagan year often starts with Samhain, on the evening of October 31, which roughly coincides with the onset of winter in the Northern Hemisphere. Observations of the winter, spring, and summer solstices are also held. Beltane, for example, begins on the evening before May 1 and welcomes summer and the fertility of both the earth and humans. Rituals keyed to the appearance of the new moon also frequently occur. But other public and home rituals can occur at any time. Many Pagans also observe rituals based on the life cycle; a wiccaning introduces a young child to the parents' Pagan community but does not commit the child to following a Pagan path and a handfasting joins two Pagans together in marriage, for example.

Pagans rarely build specific edifices for their religious practices, preferring instead to perform rituals either in their homes or outside. In such cases, the ritual space has to be constituted anew by casting a circle. The circle puts the participants in direct contact with each other and becomes the locus for generating a heightened awareness of the divine presence. Officiants, who may be any member of the assembled group, can begin by acknowledging the cardinal directions and may recite the "charge of the Goddess" to summon her presence. The energy generated in a Pagan circle can be used to perform magic, understood as the ability to change reality or personal consciousness in accordance with the Will.

Pagan ethics center on the maxim known as the Wiccan Rede, "An [if] it harm none, do what thou wilt." The first clause of that statement puts an important check on the second. Many Pagans also believe that their actions in the world are subject to the "Law of Threefold Return," which stipulates that whatever good or evil one does returns in triplicate. Although Pagan ethical reflection generally lags behind reflection on ritual and symbolism, some Pagan teachers are striving to uncover the implications of their principles. T. Thorn Coyle (1965–), for example, presses the idea that the assertion "Thou Art Goddess" implies compassion for everyone, including those with whom one disagrees. Starhawk, building on the idea that the earth is a living organism, endorses an "ethic of interconnection," which views individuals as cells in a larger being.

Contemporary Paganism constitutes a diverse and vibrant family of religious practices that will likely continue to attract practitioners, develop, and mutate.

See also: Ásatrú; Church of all Worlds, The; Crowley, Aleister (1875–1947); Druidry; Eco-Paganism; Odinism; Starhawk (1951–); Wicca; Women in New Religious Movements.

Further Reading

Adler, Margot. 1986. *Drawing Down the Moon: Witches, Druids, Goddess-Worshippers, and Other Pagans in America*, rev. ed. Boston: Beacon Press.

Aitamurto, Kaarina, & Scott Simpson, eds. 2013. *Modern Pagan and Native Faith Movements in Central and Eastern Europe*. Durham, UK: Acumen Press.

Berger, Helen A. 1999. *A Community of Witches: Contemporary Neo-Paganism and Witchcraft in the United States*. Columbia: University of South Carolina Press.

Clifton, Chas. 2006. *Her Hidden Children: The Rise of Wicca and Paganism in America*. Lanhan, MD: AltaMira Press.

Cowan, Douglas E. 2005. *Cyberhenge: Modern Pagans on the Internet*. New York: Routledge.

Doyle White, Ethan. 2016. *Wicca: History, Belief, and Community in Modern Pagan Witchcraft*. Chicago: Sussex Academic Press.

Gardell, Mattias. 2003. *Gods of the Blood: The Pagan Revival and White Separatism*. Durham, NC: Duke University Press.

Hutton, Ronald. 1999. *The Triumph of the Moon: A History of Modern Pagan Witchcraft*. New York: Oxford University Press.

Pike, Sarah M. 2004. *New Age and Neopagan Religions in America*. New York: Columbia University Press.

Salomonsen, Jone. 2002. *Enchanted Feminism: The Reclaiming Witches of San Francisco*. New York: Routledge.

Strmiska, Michael, ed. 2005. *Modern Paganism in World Cultures: Comparative Perspectives*. Santa Barbara, CA: ABC-CLIO.

PRIMARY SOURCE DOCUMENT

Starhawk, "Religion from Nature, Not Archaeology" Response to *Atlantic Monthly* (2001)

Starhawk is a vocal activist of earth-based spirituality and ecofeminism. In 2001, she wrote an open letter to the editor of Atlantic Monthly, *addressing inaccuracies she noticed in Charlotte Allen's article "The Scholars and the Goddess" (January 2001). The text of that letter, meant to legitimize and support Goddess religion, is as follows.*

Goddess religion is not based on belief, in history, in archaeology, in any Great Goddess past or present. Our spirituality is based on experience, on a direct relationship with the cycles of birth, growth, death and regeneration in nature and in human lives. We see the complex interwoven web of life as sacred, which is to say, real and important, worth protecting, worth taking a stand for. At a time when every major ecosystem on the planet is under assault, calling nature sacred is a radical act because it threatens the overriding value of profit that allows us to despoil the basic life support systems of the earth. And at a time when women still live with the daily threat of violence and the realities of inequality and abuse, it is an equally radical act to envision deity as female and assert the sacred nature of female (and male) sexuality and bodies. . . .

To us, Goddesses, Gods, and for that matter, archaeological theories are not something to believe in, nor are they merely metaphors. An image of deity, a symbol on a pot, a cave painting, a liturgy are more like portals to particular states of consciousness and constellations of energies. Meditate on them, contemplate them, and they take you someplace, generally into some aspect of those cycles of death and regeneration. The heart of my connection to the Goddess has less to do with what I believe happened five thousand years ago or five hundred years ago, and much more to do with what I notice when I step outside my door: that oak leaves fall to the ground, decay and make fertile soil. Calling that process sacred means that I approach this everyday miracle with a sense of awe and wonder and gratitude, and that in very practical terms, I compost my own garbage.

> **Source:** Starhawk. "Religion from Nature, Not Archaeology: Starhawk Responds to the Atlantic Monthly." January 5, 2001. Available at: https://starhawk.org/Goddess-Pagan/Religion%20From%20Nature%20Not%20Archaeology%20Starhawk%20Responds%20to%20the%20Atlantic%20Monthly.pdf.

New Age, The

Although the "New Age movement" emerged in public consciousness in the 1970s as an identifiable phenomenon, the term itself is misleading in several ways. What has counted as New Age typically differs from one observer to another. There has been no single organization and certainly no founder or widely recognized leadership structure, and the term "movement" implies more coherence than actually has existed. Some scholars have also contended that the term "New Age" was not even widely used by those identified by others as New Agers. Although celebrities like Shirley Maclaine (1934–), in her autobiographical *Out on a Limb* (1983) and other writings, did much to popularize the term and the practices and beliefs associated with it, precisely what it refers to remains fuzzy.

The term "New Age" does point toward a cultic milieu that is focused on the transformation of both self and society. It also points to an audience that is eager for spiritual wisdom and ready to take it from any number of sources outside mainstream religions. Such "seekers" move fluidly and often frequently from one teacher or experience to another. They tend to vest authority not in any external organization or authoritative figure but rather in themselves as they cobble together idiosyncratic worldviews and activities that make sense to them as individuals. Their associations with other seekers tend to be fleeting and exist in constantly changing patterns.

The characteristics of New Age teachers are similarly diverse. Many New Age teachers have been aware of others making similar claims and some have affirmed multiple sources of transformative wisdom, but others have emphasized the distinctiveness or even exclusiveness of the particular knowledge that they offer. Individual teachers thus can be viewed as nodes in a shifting network of providers and consumers of transformative wisdom. Even when teachers stress the exclusiveness of what they teach, they generally cannot control whether their disciples or clients seek wisdom elsewhere.

ROOTS

Scholars have cautioned that there is actually little new about the New Age. The general desire for a total, imminent, collective transformation of the world as we know it through supernatural means is a widespread pattern of religious thought and action. Such millennialism takes two typical forms—a catastrophic destruction of this world and its replacement by a "new heaven and new earth" (see Rev. 21:1) or a gradual progression toward the new world through cumulative human effort—whether guided by supernatural entities or not. Both types of millennialism are evident in New Age thinking, though the second, progressive type predominates. Of course, the announcement of the approach of a new age is in itself a millennialist concept. The New Age focuses on the imminent transformation of the world through the cumulative transformation of individuals. It is preeminently a form of "self-religion" with comparatively little emphasis, save for a few exceptions, on forming lasting communities.

The contemporary New Age has roots in various currents of Western esotericism, including Spiritualism, Theosophy, and New Thought, and also has been influenced by beliefs in UFOs and extraterrestrials, the human potential movement, and the counterculture of the 1960s. But the most direct antecedent for the term, at least, may be found in the writings of the Theosophist Alice Bailey (1880–1949), who used it frequently. For Bailey, the New Age was interchangeable with the Aquarian Age, which was in the process of replacing the emphasis on authority and belief of the Piscean or Christian Age with an emphasis on individual understanding and direct knowledge. Marilyn Ferguson (1938–2008) also used the astrological system of ages in *The Aquarian Conspiracy: Personal and Social Transformation in the 1980s* (1980), which drew a large audience. But the broadest public impact of the concept of a new, Aquarian age came from the song "Aquarius" from the musical *Hair* (1967).

EMERGENCE

In the early 1960s, a small group of religious seekers began to coalesce in the unlikely location of a caravan, or trailer, park near the village of Findhorn and the Moray Firth in Northeast Scotland. The focal point of the group was Eileen Caddy (1917–2006) who began to receive communications from God in 1953. She initially shared them with her husband Peter (1917–1994) and a few intimates but they gradually reached a broader audience, especially when she first published *God Spoke to Me* in 1967. The Findhorn community also became well known for its extremely productive garden. Dorothy Maclean, a cofounder with the Caddys, traced its abundance to the cooperation of the nature spirits, or *devas*.

As the fame of Findhorn increased, so did its role in the international network of New Age practitioners. One example of the international exchange of New Age ideas is the American New Age thinker David Spangler's (1945–) residence at Findhorn from 1970 to 1973. For a time Spangler codirected Findhorn with Peter Caddy. When he left, along with Dorothy Maclean, he established the Lorian Association (www.lorian.org), which now devotes itself to promoting "incarnational spirituality." Even though Spangler quickly left behind the label of New Age, his activities show not only the influence of Findhorn but also the shifting alliances and constantly mutating ideas that characterize the New Age milieu.

Around the time that the Findhorn colony took shape, an array of teachers in the United States began to attract both clients and general notoriety. Among the earliest and most influential was Jane Roberts (1929–1984). Though she had no prior interest in the occult or paranormal, Roberts had an extraordinary experience in December 1963. While using an Ouija board with her husband, Robert Butts (1919–2008), they began to receive messages from a distinct male personality who identified himself as Seth and who identified Roberts as the channel through whom he would communicate with humanity. Soon, Roberts began to hear Seth's messages without the aid of the Ouija board and she began to dictate what she heard from him, and sometimes from others, including the philosopher William James and the painter Paul Cézanne. Roberts would eventually produce many volumes of "Seth material" and sell more than seven million copies. Seth's teachings continue to be promulgated by the Seth Learning Center (http://sethlearningcenter.org/), which presents Seth as the teacher who launched the New Age, particularly because he coined the phrase that has pervaded the New Age milieu: "You create your own reality."

In fact, the channeling undertaken by Roberts had several antecedents, such as the "sleeping prophet" Edgar Cayce (1877–1945), who received communications while in a trance state, and the Spiritualists of the nineteenth century. The familiar phenomenon only began to be called channeling, however, in the 1960s and 1970s in New Age circles. Roberts was soon joined by many others who claimed to be receiving messages from a different realm. Some performed what they called conscious channeling, while others, like Cayce, channeled while in some form of trance state. For example, Kevin Ryerson (1951–) claims to be a trance channel in the tradition of Edgar Cayce and Jane Roberts. Ryerson channels several entities, including a contemporary of Jesus named John. Ryerson achieved widespread recognition when he was mentioned favorably in actress Shirley MacLaine's autobiographical account of her spiritual searching, *Out on a Limb* (1983). On his website, www.kevinryerson.com, Ryerson continues his work and advertises, "tele-readings" over the phone, which consist of both conversation and channeling.

In published forms, channeled wisdom, such as Roberts's Seth materials, has achieved broadly authoritative status in New Age subcultures. No text has been as influential as *A Course in Miracles*, which was received by Helen Schucman (1909–1981) over seven years and published in 1976 in three volumes. As with the published messages received by Eileen Caddy and other channels, the *Course* has achieved scriptural status for some audiences.

Among the many other notable channels are JZ Knight (1946–), who channels a thirty-five-thousand-year-old warrior from Atlantis named Ramtha, and Jach Pursel (1947–), who channels Lazaris, a formless spark of consciousness. Some teachers emphasize that any individual can learn to channel wisdom from realms beyond the human, but the most well-known channels enforce orthodoxy by claiming a monopoly on the entities with whom they are in communication.

Though the sources to which they are attributed vary widely, the messages conveyed by their channels have significant overlap. Since channels are purportedly connected with a wide array of figures from other realms, they also bring to the attention of their audiences a variety of concepts from many religious traditions, including karma, reincarnation, yoga, the power of crystals, and the use of Tarot cards, among other things. Channeled messages definitely aim to empower those who hear them, as in Seth's statement that "you create your own reality."

Beyond that, channeled teachings frequently elevate the status of all individuals. The vocabulary varies, but many channels and their New Age audiences often speak of a "higher self" or even a "Christ self" that is the essence of each individual. The positing of such a connection links the New Age to a gnostic tradition that stretches from Late Antiquity to the present. Like the ancient gnostics who saw a spark of the divine in every individual, contemporary New Agers emphasize the extraordinary abilities that individuals can access if they only awaken to their inherent divinity. It is because of their true identities that individuals are actually able to create their own realities.

DIFFUSION

Although few claim the label of New Age today, the influence of New Age ideas and practices is internationally pervasive. It can be seen, for example, in various forms of holistic healing, including Reiki and homeopathy, diverse festivals, conferences, and expos devoted to lifestyles focused on health and spirituality, and in some ecological concerns, particularly when they conceive of the earth as a single living entity (often called Gaea). In addition, many channels continue to find interested audiences and their books continue to sell at a brisk pace. Specifically, New Age ideas and practices have not so much disappeared as they have diffused throughout the contemporary cultic milieu, the continuing fund of practices and ideas that inspire individual spiritual quests and fuel the development of new groups.

CONTROVERSY

New Age teachers have fallen prey to some of the same accusations that have dogged other leaders of alternative or new religions. JZ Knight, for example, has been accused of exploiting her followers for personal financial gain. As with any other person who claims to be in touch with entities from another realm, individuals purporting to be channels have been dismissed as charlatans striving to hoodwink the gullible. The marketing of consultations, workshops, and courses by various New Age teachers has also been criticized as a naked grab for cash; Ryerson's tele-readings, for example, cost $275 for ninety minutes. In response, both providers and consumers of New Age services argue that it is appropriate to pay for such valuable guidance. Finally, some observers have critiqued the intense New Age focus on the individual self, arguing that it leads to an indulgent self-absorption that ignores social problems. Such critiques, however, have done little to deter determined seekers and convinced providers of transformational wisdom from continuing their individual efforts to bring about a New Age.

See also: Caddy, Eileen (1917–2006); Cayce, Edgar (1877–1945); Channeling; *Course in Miracles, A*; Crystals; Findhorn Foundation, The; Knight, JZ (Ramtha) (1946–); Millennialism; New Thought; Pursel, Jach (Lazaris) (1947–); Seekers; Spiritualism; Theosophy.

Further Reading

Brown, Michael F. 1997. *The Channeling Zone: American Spirituality in an Anxious Age.* Cambridge, MA: Harvard University Press.

Guittierez, Cathy, ed. 2015. *Handbook of Spiritualism and Channeling.* Leiden: E. J. Brill.

Hanegraff, Wouter J. 1996. *New Age Religion and Western Culture: Esotericism in the Mirror of Secular Thought.* Leiden: E. J. Brill.

Heelas, Paul. 1996. *The New Age Movement: Celebrating the Self and the Sacralization of Modernity.* Oxford: Blackwell.

Kemp, Daren, & James R. Lewis, eds. 2007. *Handbook of New Age.* Leiden: E. J. Brill.

Lewis, James R., & J. Gordon Melton, eds. 1992. *Perspectives on the New Age.* Albany: SUNY Press.

Sutcliffe, Steven J. 2003. *Children of the New Age: A History of Spiritual Practices.* New York: Routledge.

New Cathar Church, The

In their medieval context, the Cathars (from the Greek *katheroi*, "pure or perfect ones") were a sectarian new religious movement that emerged in the eleventh century and persisted until the fourteenth. The origins of the movement are unclear, but it is generally supposed to have come from the Byzantine empire. Although beliefs varied among Cathar groups, they most often were dualist, affirming the existence of both a good and evil deity, possibly influenced by the Manichaeans.

The good God was identified as the God of the New Testament, while the evil God was either the creator God of the Old Testament or Satan himself. The Cathars were also gnostics, believing in the inherent divinity of the human spirit, which through Satan's efforts had become trapped in the material world. They rejected Baptism and the Eucharist (denying that the host could possibly be the body of Jesus) and practiced instead the ritual of *Consolamentum*, which elevated the participant to perfection. The Cathars were bitterly opposed by representatives of Catholic orthodoxy, including Pope Innocent III (1160/61–1216) who declared a crusade against the Cathars in 1208.

The medieval Cathars faded away, or at least went underground, in the fourteenth century. But their critical stance against orthodoxy and their dualism continued to stimulate the imagination of participants in the Western esoteric tradition. In the late nineteenth century, Napoléon Peyrat (1809–1881) helped to popularize the Cathars again, and in *fin-de-siècle* Paris, Cathars began to show up as spirits in séances and other gatherings of esotericists. After World War I, British spiritualists also became interested in the supposedly secret lore of the Cathars. In 1933, Otto Rahn (1904–1939), a German medievalist and SS member, connected the Cathars to the legend of the Holy Grail. That association would also appear in *Holy Blood, Holy Grail* (1982), one of many attempts at an alternative history of Jesus. In that case he married Mary Magdalene and moved to the south of France. The Languedoc region, a medieval Cathar stronghold, also became a site for countercultural tourists in the 1960s and 1970s.

Mythological embellishments of the original Cathars also found their way into the thinking of both the Order of the Solar Temple and Heaven's Gate. It is not surprising, then, that they also appealed to a Russian religious dissident who began his prophetic career receiving visions and communications from the Virgin Mary.

Veniamin Iakovlevich Bereslavskii (1946–), later known as the Blessed John of the Holy Grail and John Bogomil, received his first revelation from Mary in 1984. By then he had already become deeply involved in Russian Orthodoxy and adopted an ascetic way of life. Dissatisfied with Orthodoxy under the Soviet regime, by 1985, Bereslavskii was ordained as a priest and monk in the underground True Orthodox Church. In 1990, he became bishop of his own Russian Autocephalous Orthodox Church, which soon became the Church of the Mother of God. At Mary's prompting, Bereslavskii added elements to the Russian Orthodox liturgy, including musical prayers that he composed. He also integrated himself into the worldwide network of Marian visionaries.

The shifting attitudes of the Russian parliament in the 1990s toward freedom of religion made it difficult for Bereslavskii to stay in his homeland. During a visit in 2005 to the traditional site of Mary's last days in Turkey, he received revelations that turned his movement in a new direction. Sharply critical of established forms of Christianity, Mary informed Bereslavskii that Christianity had reached a dead end. He turned instead to the Cathars, a peaceful, loving society that had been brutally repressed by the Catholic Church. Bereslavskii's new goal was to restore divine dignity to humankind and spread a universal spirituality (see www.cathar.org). He adopted the Cathars' gnostic view of human perfectability and established The New Cathar Church as the inheritor of the teachings of the medieval Cathars. He adopted the name John Bogomil, referring to the Cathars' predecessor, a Christian sectarian group from Bulgaria, the Bogomils ("Friends of God").

See also: Charisma and Leadership in New Religious Movements; Gnostic Groups; Heaven's Gate; Marian Apparitions; Occultism and Esotericism; Order of the Solar Temple, The.

Further Reading

Clay, J. Eugene. 2013. "The Orthodox Church of the Sovereign Mother of God/The New Cathar Church." In Eileen Barker, ed., *Revisionism and Diversification in New Religious Movements*, pp. 93–113. Burlington, VT: Ashgate Publishing Company.

O'Shea, Stephen. 2000. *The Perfect Heresy: The Revolutionary Life and Death of the Medieval Cathars*. New York: Walker and Company.

O'Shea, Stephen. 2000. "Raiders of the Lost Faith." *The Guardian*, October 6. Available at: https://www.theguardian.com/books/2000/oct/07/books.guardianreview.

New Church, The

In *True Christianity* (1771), Emmanuel Swedenborg (1688–1772) laid the groundwork for a "new church," one that would usher in the "fifth age" of humanity's spiritual evolution. This age would be characterized by a trust of intuitive and mystical knowledge and a sunsetting of traditional sacred texts and doctrines. Despite this prognostications, Swedenborg evidently never intended to create an actual "new church": he wrote his treatise in response to the ban of his works by Swedish authorities and as a check on the power of the Swedish Lutheran Church.

Nonetheless, The New Church (also called the Swedenborgian Church) was born—founded in England a decade after Swedenborg's death, rather than in Sweden, where his works were still banned.

The New Church bases its beliefs on the work and revelations of Swedenborg. Beginning in the 1740s, Swedenborg experienced visions, in which he came into contact with divine beings that revealed to him, among other things, the true meaning of the Bible. Defying tendencies to read the Bible as the literal word of God, Swedenborg argued that its meaning could only be discerned by heeding the intuited, spiritual message appearing in the reader's mind. Every word or fact of the Bible corresponded to a spiritual or mystical truth (better known as Swedenborg's theory of "correspondence"). Still, Swedenborg was not the only influence; the New Church's theology blends elements of traditional Christianity with a burgeoning nineteenth-century interest in occult knowledge, particularly the idea that the divine may appear in different aspects to every believer and that ultimate truth can be variously interpreted and found in a variety of (often hidden) places.

Primary among the doctrines of the New Church is the belief in one, visible God: the Lord Jesus Christ. Jesus is God incarnate, not (as certain interpretations of the traditional Christian trinity contend) an emanation of the Godhead. The trinity, in fact, refers to Jesus's soul, body, and spirit—meaning that the trinity is also present in every person, thus enabling the individual connection between the human and the divine realms. Similar to traditional Christian doctrine, faith in Jesus and adherence to his commandments are essential for salvation. However, since faith in Jesus is ultimately faith in humanity—since Jesus was a man—then true faith means the belief that God dwells within. Such faith must be accompanied with good works, particularly charity toward others (since God dwells in them as well). As for salvation, New Church concepts of heaven and hell are also Swedenborgian in nature; heaven and hell are not physical destinations but manifestations of the individual soul. For the person who lives a good life with faith in the indwelling-God, heaven will emanate from that state of being; hell, conversely, represents a person's lack of spiritual progress and is ultimately defined by a lack of desire to do good for him or herself or humanity as a whole. In this way, God neither condemns nor saves, since it is the realization and adherence to God in the soul that determines one's eternal condition.

The Bible is the central religious text for the New Church, though it parses which books are spiritually necessary (and divinely inspired) and those that are valued as important, but not sacred scripture. The former includes the Gospels and the Book of Revelation in the New Testament, the five books of the Torah (Genesis, Exodus Leviticus, Numbers, Deuteronomy), and a number of Prophetic books, such as Isaiah and Daniel. Despite this spiritual emphasis on books that are often considered eschatological, or dealing with the end of time, the New Church does not believe in an apocalyptic end of the world. According to Swedenborg, each previous age ended with a Divine Judgment (the last Judgment occurred at the dawn of the fifth age in the late eighteenth century) and that the establishment of a "new church" would represent the Christ's Second Coming (in lieu of Christ's physical reappearance).

Today, the New Church exists predominantly in the United States and Europe, counting around ten thousand members worldwide. It is congregational in structure with authority granted to individual congregations to elect ministers and send delegates to conventions.

See also: Mysticism; Occultism and Esotericism; Swedenborg, Emanuel (1688–1772).

Further Reading

Rose, Jonathan S., Stuart Shotwell, & Mary Lou Bertucci. 2005. *Scribe of Heaven: Swedenborg's Life, Work, and Impact.* West Chester, PA: Swedenborg Foundation Publishers.

Swedenborg, Emanuel. 2012. *The Divine Revelation of the New Jerusalem.* Three Volumes. New York: Houghton Mifflin.

New Religions on/and the Internet

In December 2012, the Pope tweeted for the first time. In many ways, the moment represented a natural step: the internet was the means by which people across the world communicated with each other; thus, the Pope's twitter account was a feature of the modern age. Particularly for an institution that had faced backlash for its lack of transparency in recent decades, a tweeting Pope felt less removed from the rank and file. For some the move might seem obvious or even slow given that it has become an expectation that religions engage with the digital realm. It is rare that an established religion will not have an official website, with some now employing marketing and social media content management teams the size of entire parishes. There are religious groups that purposefully avoid the virtual realm for theological or practical reasons, such as the Amish, but they are the exception. Whether with the times or behind them, what the Pope's twitter account reveals is that religion exists firmly in a digital age.

Some scholars argue that new religious movements, perhaps due to their newness and innovation, have been quick to incorporate the internet into their religious systems and institutions. For most, this has meant a means of recruiting potential members, promoting their particular brand of faith, and providing information (sometimes information gotten without their consent). Some groups, however, could be called "virtual religions," but for the internet it is unlikely that these religions would even exist.

RELIGIOUS INNOVATION AND THE INTERNET

First and foremost, what the internet has done is to catalyze the process of globalization. Via the internet people are exposed to a much greater number of ideas, peoples, institutions, and events than they were prior to its invention. New religious movements have simultaneously benefited and suffered from such processes of globalization. One the one hand, niche movements of twenty followers might accrue a more robust online following, thus bolstering their membership and even their financial stability. The internet has also made marketing new religions, particularly those with significant resources, far easier—look no further than the "I'm a Mormon" campaign produced by the Church of Jesus Christ of Latter-day Saints. And for those who identify as spiritual or as seekers, the internet has brought them into contact with numerous religious groups, making it possible for them to find the religion that fits them best or to embark on a "conversion career," testing many religions over a lifetime. On the other hand, the internet has also enabled the spread of misinformation. New religions, which are already historically maligned and marginalized groups, cannot control their portrayal as readily as they would in more traditional worship settings. For critics of new religions, the internet might confirm their worst fears about new religions. Perhaps worse are those who might seek to defraud credulous seekers, creating false websites and fronts—a fact that further exacerbates the scrutiny of new religious movements in general.

The internet has offered a powerful means of recruiting new members. At the strike of a few keys, a seeking individual can learn about a religion and even "chat" with members of the religion. On the website for the Church of Jesus Christ of Latter-day Saints, a message often appears asking if the visitor would like to ask any questions. Social media sites, in particular, have served as online vehicles for recruitment, a fact that came to light in the media when it was discovered that ISIS was using Facebook to recruit potential members.

The creation of sacred space in cyberspace has reshaped processes such as conversion and membership in various religious groups. If a religion exists primarily online or if all of its practices and beliefs can be undertaken in the privacy of one's home, then one could convert to a religion without undertaking a single ritual in a designated, physical worship site or proving one's knowledge of a particular faith. Being a member might also look quite different. Particularly with streaming services, many people in even the more mainstream religions can participate in worship without leaving the comfort of their couch. One may never actually meet another member of one's religion in person. With the rising rate of those who are unaffiliated, increasing a religion's online presence could be perceived as a means of drawing people back in by bringing religion *to* them. Critics, however, might perceive such a move as a dilution of traditional religion and the effective death of traditional membership. Additionally, this makes it difficult to know how many members actually comprise a given religion, since many may identify as such, but without ever setting foot in a place of worship.

VIRTUAL RELIGIONS

In 1997, Heaven's Gate, a millennialist UFO religion, made headlines because of the ritual suicide (or "graduation") of thirty-nine members around the time of the Hale-Bopp Comet's appearance. They believed that by shedding their mortal bodies, they would ascend to The Evolutionary Level Above Human. Members of Heaven's Gate believed that the world was going to be "recycled" in an imminent, apocalyptic event, but that an advanced race of alien beings would save those who had accepted the truth and sought to prepare themselves, bodily and spiritually. Before, during, and after this event, the group was notable for its avid use of the internet in the explanation of its rationale for graduation, the spread of its ideals, and the recruitment of members. The founders of Heaven's Gate, Marshall Herff Applewhite (1931–1997) and Bonnie Lu Nettles (1927–1985) claimed to be aliens themselves, a fact that helps to explain, in part, their early employment of the internet since they were a technologically advanced species. To this day, their website is still functional—even though it has not been updated since 1997—one can read the sacred texts written by Applewhite and Nettles, watch videos made by Applewhite, and read testimony of members. At the top of the page, the phrase "Red Alert" blinks, a reminder that the world as we know it will cease to exist soon (http://www.heavensgate.com). The website's continued maintenance by former members highlights its graduated members' realization that a virtual presence would be necessary to remain relevant, even after they were gone.

Unlike Heaven's Gate, which had a sustaining group of members who worshipped and lived together, the internet has enabled religions to spread, in which members gather around common interests or beliefs, but who rarely, if ever, meet. Jediism, or the religion of the *Star Wars* characters, the Jedi, seemingly arose as a spoof in 2001, when a number of people prompted by an online, grassroots campaign recorded their religion as "Jedi" on census forms. Since that time, however, Jediism has emerged as a vibrant, primarily virtual, religion. Its members adhere to a common set of philosophical principles, set out as the Jedi Code, which can be found online (https://nzjedi.org/the-jedi-code.php). It is difficult to know how many members there actually are; nonetheless, petitions to build temples and seek legal protections in various countries, including the United States, reveal that the movement may in fact move from the realm of the virtual to the real.

Religions based around the existence of mythical or supernatural creatures, such as Otherkin and Vampirism, are also predominantly internet phenomena. Otherkin, or those who identify as part human and part "something else," first emerged as a concept in the 1990s in online community forums that connected elven and faery folk. Those who identify as Otherkin often reject the label of religion, primarily because being Otherkin is a state of being more than a theological or practical system but also because its members interact almost exclusively on the internet. Those who identify as Vampires are often considered to be Otherkin, though they maintain that they are a distinctive group in their own right. While Vampirism is more a subculture than a singular movement, the Temple of the Vampire is the community's most established group and exists almost entirely online. Via its website (www.templeofthevampire.com), members or interested parties can browse *The Vampire Bible* (1989) and connect to other vampires. Critics might view the online presence of these groups as proof that its members' powers are fantastical; this is belied by the fact that there are instances (though not often) where members have met and by the nature of these groups themselves, which highlight the individual and often isolated existence of beings with extraordinary powers.

Given these religions that seem to exist primarily or even entirely on the internet, it is unsurprising that a religion "of the internet" has emerged. Derived from the phrase "copy me," Kopimism is a religious movement whose fundamental belief is the freedom of information and whose fundamental practice is that sharing information is a sacred act. The movement, founded in Sweden, has an almost exclusively virtual presence, though Kopimist priests or "ops" do exist, whose primary function is to protect the identity of members, to combat copyrights (or heretical bans against copying), and, occasionally, to perform weddings.

RELIGIOUS CONTROVERSIES OF THE DIGITAL FRONTIER

The internet has been a bane as well as a boon to certain new religious movements. The Church of Scientology, for example, which has a pronounced online presence—its website is state-of-the-art—has struggled with critiques and copyright issues as a result. In the age of clickbait, stories about celebrity defections from Scientology are proven to receive high internet traffic. Stories spread about Scientology with little input from the Church itself either sought or heard over the din of cultural backlash. More serious, however, has been the Church's battle to contain the spread of theological doctrines that are only available to those who have achieved the level of Operating Thetan 3 in spiritual development. These doctrines, believed to be too sacred to reveal to those who are spiritually unprepared, have spread online, leading to further critique of Scientology and accusations that it is a "cult." The Church has retaliated with lawsuits, but with the information readily available, it is difficult to stem its spread outside of the institution.

Issues have also arisen, when multiple online versions of a particular religion exist, under slightly different domain names, all claiming lineage to the same group. Such was the case of the Hermetic Order of the Golden Dawn, a magico-religious group that arose in the early twentieth century. The Authentic Hermetic Order of the Golden Dawn (www.golden-dawn.com), the Hermetic Order of the Morning Star International (www.golden-dawn.org), and the Hermetic Order of the Golden Dawn (www.hermeticgoldendawn.org) all claim to be the authentic continuation of the original institution. So, who is right? It depends upon who one asks. And since the internet is a place where options are endless, such debates show no sign of ending soon.

See also: Amish, The; Church of Jesus Christ of Latter-day Saints, The; Conversion; Fraud and New Religious Movements; Globalization and New Religious Movements; Heaven's Gate; Hermetic Order of the Golden Dawn, The; ISIS; Jediism; Kopimism; Media and New Religious Movements; Membership and New Religious Movements; Otherkin; Science, Technology, and New Religious Movements; Scientology; Seekers; Spiritual but Not Religious; UFO Religions; Vampirism.

Further Reading

Cowan, Douglas E. 2004. *Cyberhenge: Modern Pagans on the Internet.* London: Routledge Press.

Cowan, Douglas E., & Jeffrey K. Hadden. 2008. "Virtually Religious: New Religious Movements and the World Wide Web." In James R. Lewis, ed., *The Oxford Handbook of New Religious Movements.* Oxford: Oxford University Press.

Dawson, Lorne L., & Jennifer Hennebry. 1999. "New Religions and the Internet: Recruiting in a New Public Space." *Journal of Contemporary Religion* 14, no. 1: 17–39.

Hadden, Jeffrey K., & Douglas E. Cowan, eds. 2000. *Religion on the Internet: Research Prospects and Promises.* London: JAI/Elsevier Science.

Mayer, Jean-François Mayer. 2014. "The Role of the Internet." In George D. Chryssides & Benjamin E. Zeller, eds., *The Bloomsbury Companion to New Religious Movements.* London: Bloomsbury Academic.

Urban, Hugh B. 2000. "The Devil at Heaven's Gate: Rethinking the Study of Religion in the Age of Cyber-Space." *Nova Religio* 3, no. 2: 269–302.

New Scriptures and New Religious Movements

To attract attention, approval, and adherents, new religious movements need to establish their legitimacy in the contexts in which they take shape. But they also need to temper their claims to novelty with equally important claims to familiarity. In other words, they need to establish a measure of continuity with the cultures in which they develop so that they appear innovative enough to be intriguing but recognizable enough to be attractive. They frequently do that by linking themselves to a past widely acknowledged to be authoritative. New religions constantly adapt and reuse elements of established religious histories at the same time as they claim to be delivering unprecedented religious messages. One prominent way in which they claim and adapt an authoritative past is by both offering novel interpretations of revered scriptures and producing new holy books of their own that claim a status equal to or greater than scriptures widely accepted as authoritative. The Church of Jesus Christ of Latter-day Saints, for example, describes *The Book of Mormon* as "another testament of Jesus Christ."

The production, use, interpretation, and revision of sacred texts is as central to new religions as it is to other, more established ones. In their own holy books, new religions express their self-understanding, situate themselves in relation to competing groups, prescribe appropriate conduct for their adherents, and communicate a shared vocabulary, common set of narratives, and images of exemplary figures that help to form and maintain a corporate identity. Although many scholars have observed that it is later generations that elevate certain texts to scriptural status, new religions cannot afford that luxury because they urgently need to establish legitimacy. Consequently, their texts frequently include a variety of strategies designed to establish their authoritative status. For example, *The Twelve Blessings*, a central text of the Aetherius Society, not only claims that it was delivered to George King by Jesus but also includes a scene in which Jesus himself blesses the book.

CLAIMING AUTHORITY

The production of sacred texts in new religions is frequently linked to the extraordinary experiences of their founders. In January 1985, for example, Vernon Howell had a profound religious experience while visiting Jerusalem. He would subsequently report that he underwent something like an ascent into the heavens, during which he received a full understanding of the scroll sealed with seven seals mentioned in Revelation 5. Howell would later change his name to David Koresh to reflect his messianic claims, and assume the leadership of a group of Bible students at the Mount Carmel Center outside Waco, Texas. There, Koresh spent most of his time explaining his interpretation of the seven seals and spreading his message by sending audio cassettes to potentially interested parties. When the Mount Carmel Center was stormed by members of the U.S. Bureau of Alcohol, Tobacco and Firearms on February 28, 1993, a fifty-one-day siege ensued. During that time, Koresh began to write down his explanation of Revelation's seven seals. When a fire consumed the Mount Carmel Center on April 19, 1993, one of the nine survivors escaped with the disk containing Koresh's partial manuscript. Koresh clearly intended the text to constitute his authoritative interpretation of Revelation, buttressed by his status as the Lamb of God (see Rev. 5) who was the only one who could open the sealed scroll.

Similarly, the *Divine Principle*, the central text of the Unificationist movement, anchors its authority in the religious experience of the Rev. Sun Myung Moon. Moon recounts that on Easter morning in 1936 Jesus appeared to him and informed him that he had a special mission to perform God's work on earth. The religious message that Moon developed is detailed in the *Divine Principle*. The text presents itself as both a correction of and supplement to the Christian Bible.

It predicts the imminent Second Advent and asserts that it contains God's latest message that will establish the new heaven and new earth mentioned in Revelation 21:1. The *Divine Principle* offers both an innovative interpretation of the story of the Fall in Genesis and a reconsideration of the purpose of the life of Jesus, both of which hinge on Moon's conviction that God does not want humans to suffer but wants them to live in the peaceful and happy world that He originally created. Moon's mission is to restore humankind to the state that God intended for it. From its completion in 1952, the *Divine Principle* held canonical status for Moon's followers. In 2002, Unificationists completed their canon by issuing an authoritative set of Moon's teachings, thus establishing the canon of the Completed Testament Age.

MAKING INTERPRETATIONS

New religions frequently offer novel interpretations of established sacred texts. Focusing on such texts enables new religions to borrow their widely acknowledged authority at the same time that they subvert it by casting an old text in a thoroughly new light.

The story of Claude Vorilhon's first encounter with an extraterrestrial provides a good example. Vorhilon's meeting occurred on December 13, 1973, when he was hiking alone in a dormant volcano near Clermont-Ferrand, France. Much to his surprise, he saw a spaceship and then met its occupant. The extraterrestrial instructed Vorilhon to return the next day with his Bible and to be ready to take notes. During a week of intensive study, Vorilhon's otherworldly visitor guided him through the proper understanding of selected passages from the Bible and even some of the Apocrypha. Vorilhon learned, for example, that the "Elohim" who created humans are actually a race of technologically advanced beings from worlds beyond the earth. Throughout his interactions with his new teacher, Vorilhon was never led to doubt the central authority of the Bible, but only to its accurate interpretation. Over the course of his multiple interactions with his extraterrestrial guide, Vorilhon acquired a new identity as the Messianic prophet Raël, a new direction for his life as the earthly ambassador of the Elohim, and a new doctrine that would serve as the intellectual foundation of a new religious movement. But despite his innovations, throughout *Intelligent Design: Message from the Designers*, Raël never abandons the conviction that the Bible is the authoritative source for learning about who humans are and who their creators are.

The presentation of the ancient Hindu *Bhagavad-gītā* by the founder of the International Society for Krishna Consciousness, A. C. Bhaktivedanta Swami Prabhupada, reveals a very different interpretive strategy. The title of the movement's central text, *The Bhagavad-Gītā As It Is*, directly renounces any attempts at interpretation. Prabhupada simply intends to "re-present" with complete fidelity ancient wisdom that comes straight to the deity. Of course, any assertion that a text "speaks for itself" actually constitutes an interpretive choice, no matter how strong the disclaimers.

The dramatic reimagining of the meaning of the Bible by Raël and the steadfast refusal by Prabhupada to offer any overt interpretation of the *Bhagavad-gītā* actually indicate the poles of a continuum of interpretations. Between them, there are multiple possibilities for determining the contemporary relevance of ancient scriptural texts. The interpretive processes and strategies adopted by new religions really do not differ from the processes employed by more established religions, even when their results appear to undermine long-held understandings of what the texts mean.

MAKING SCRIPTURES

Both David Koresh's commentary on the seven seals and Raël's rereading of the Bible show how interpretive texts can achieve authoritative status within a group. *Intelligent Design* functions for the Raëlian movement both as a clarification of what the Bible really means and a scriptural text in its own right, along with Raël's other writings. The death of David Koresh and the destruction of the Branch Davidian community cut short the history of reception of his commentary on the seven seals, but it is clear that he intended it to be the authoritative statement of his views.

In other cases, however, texts are produced that directly claim the status of a "new Bible." In 1882, for example, John Ballou Newbrough published *Oahspe Bible: A New Bible in the Words of Jehovih and His Angel Embassadors*. Newbrough's idiosyncratic spelling hinted at his innovative message. He had been immersed in the Spiritualist milieu of the late nineteenth century but had become dissatisfied with the messages received from the spirits. In response, Newbrough undertook a six-year period of bodily purification that prepared him to receive from an intelligence other than his own a new Bible. In half-hour early morning sessions over a fifty-week period, Newbrough produced his extensive text through a process of automatic writing. Like other scriptures, *Oahspe* aims to provide a comprehensive account of the universe and of the place of human beings within it. It identifies the creator God as both masculine and feminine and promotes a complex cyclic view of human history.

Similarly, in 1924, Robert Athlyi Rogers published *The Holy Piby*. Like Raël's *Intelligent Design*, Roger's text blended interpretations of the Bible with scenes of his own prophetic call and commissioning. Like *Oahspe*, *The Holy Piby* claims to deliver a new religion suited to the current time. In particular, *The Holy Piby* addresses people of African descent both at home and in diaspora. It assures them that God has heard their pleas and provides them with a set of twelve commandments (only one of which replicates one of the biblical ten) to regulate their behavior. Although Rogers's Afro Athlican Constructive Church was short lived, *The Holy Piby* was influential in the founding of the Rastafari movement and has been hailed as "the Blackman's Bible."

OPPOSITION TO NEW SCRIPTURES

Despite their efforts to establish their authority through appeals to the extraordinary experiences of their authors or the uncanny means of their production, the sacred texts of new religions have frequently been met with derision and incredulity. A passage in II Nephi of *The Book of Mormon*, for example, refers to the claim of non-Mormons that they already have a Bible and that there is therefore no need for a new one. More recently, Martin Gardner published a book-length broadside against *The Urantia Book* that expressed a similar sentiment. Such entrenched resistance to the idea that there could be any new scriptures has made it incumbent for new religions to make the case for their new bibles as strongly as possible.

Cultural opposition, however, has done little to stanch the flow of new scriptures. The Church of Scientology, for example, asserts that all of the teachings of its founder, L. Ron Hubbard, have the status of scripture. Scientology has accordingly made exceptional efforts to make sure that Hubbard's teachings are preserved in their original form and promulgated in uniform editions. In contrast, collections of authoritative texts have also been subject to revisions as the central teachings of religious groups have changed over time. For example, in the Children of God (later the Family of Love and the Family International), the "Mo Letters" written by the founder David Brandt Berg have been supplemented after his death by letters written by his successor and former wife. In effect, therefore, the Family International has an open canon, which admits the possibility of continuing revelation after the time of the founder. The Mormons have a similarly open canon, which now includes revelations received by presidents of the church in both 1890 (against plural marriage) and 1978 (allowing men of African descent to enter the priesthood).

Like other religions, new religions produced sacred texts that they accept as authoritative. Despite social opposition to new scriptures, new religions will continue to produce them and argue passionately for their acceptance.

See also: Aetherius Society, The; Church of Jesus Christ of Latter-day Saints, The; *Divine Principle*; *Holy Piby, The*; International Society for Krishna Consciousness (ISKCON); Koresh, David (1959–1993); Millennialism; *Oahspe*; Scientology; Unification Church, The; *Urantia Book, The*.

Further Reading
Gallagher, Eugene V. 2014. *Reading and Writing Scripture in New Religious Movements: New Bibles and New Revelations*. New York: Palgrave/Macmillan.

Hammer, Olav, & Mikael Rothstein. 2012. "Canonical and Extracanonical Texts in New Religions." In Olav Hammer & Mikael Rothstein, eds., *The Cambridge Companion to New Religious Movements*, pp. 113–129. Cambridge: Cambridge University Press.

Tabor, James D., & Eugene V. Gallagher. 1995. *Why Waco? Cults and the Battle for Religious Freedom in America*. Berkeley: University of California Press.

New Thought

On her talkshow in 2008, Oprah Winfrey (1954–) told her audience of a book called *The Secret*, by Rhonda Byrne (1945–). Byrne posited the "Law of Attraction," which is the idea that concentrating one's thoughts on a particular desire or outcome will bring it to pass. These ideas were and are reflected in "prosperity" churches, where sharply dressed pastors with dazzling smiles promise that wealth, health, and victory are guaranteed to those who believe in the power of Christ to make all things possible; "name it and claim it" they announce! In the mid-twentieth century, pastor Norman Vincent Peale's (1898–1993) book *The Power of Positive Thinking* became a best-seller. These and many more movements are the product of New Thought, a nineteenth-century new religious movement rooted in the idea that obstacles to salvation, of both earthly and heavenly varieties, and wellness, of both body and psyche, are rooted in the mind and soul. In other words, human beings are capable of willing their sinful and diseased natures away by the power of thought.

BEGINNINGS

Historians attribute some of the ideology of New Thought to Swedish philosopher Emmanuel Swedenborg (1688–1772). Swedenborg posited an inner "Spiritual sense," which revealed ultimate and divine truth. The human mind, in this way, "corresponded" to the Divine mind; this was the basis for the eponymous religious movement, Swedenborgianism. Transcendentalist Ralph Waldo Emerson (1803–1882) is also commonly cited as a proponent of New Thought ideas, before there was a formal movement of which to speak. Emerson, like other Transcendentalists, was influenced by Swedenborg, Romanticism, and German Idealism, all of which located divinity in the mind. Emerson's writings reflected the idea that the mind, and the mind alone, was real, and all truth sprang from it intuitively.

Though Swedenborg and Emerson may have been intellectual forebears of New Thought, most historians cite Phineas Parkhurst Quimby (1802–1866) as the creator of New Thought. His work prompted the creation of New Thought groups. Quimby was a Mesmerist or one who believed that there was a substance called "animal magnetism" that permeated everything in the world, including human beings. Mesmerists believed that the substance could be manipulated through the use of magnets to heal maladies. In his experiments with Mesmerism, Quimby made a fascinating discovery. He realized that the ability to cure patients depended invariably on their state of mind; if they believed they would be cured, then they would be. This was the origin of "Mind Cure," which posited that the mind was the source of all cures.

Soon, Quimby's theories began to gain attention, as his patients claimed to be cured of whatever malady they had previously suffered. He began to attract students, including Mary Baker Eddy (1821–1910). Eddy was historically plagued by illness and had no success with Western medicine. After seeking healing and later apprenticing under Quimby, Eddy experienced a debilitating fall in 1866. Near death, Eddy turned to the Bible where she meditated on Christ's miraculous healings. Three days later, she rose from her bed, completely healed. This healing inspired the creation of "Divine Science," later Christian Science, which posited that through prayer and right thinking, disease—even death—could be conquered.

Quimby and Eddy would diverge in their attribution of these healings to a divine cause; while Eddy maintained that it was faith in God that healed, Quimby equivocated on whether there was a supernatural or natural cause of bodily cures. Though Eddy's Christian Science was not its progenitor, due to Eddy's relationship with Quimby, her religion can be seen as a parallel tradition to that of the broader religious movement known as New Thought.

BELIEFS, PRACTICES, AND VARIETIES

Since New Thought is a diffuse movement rather than a single institution, there are many traditions that fall under its umbrella. Nonetheless, most share certain beliefs in common. First and foremost is the idea that there is God—sometimes referred to as Infinite Intelligence or Ultimate Reality—who is benevolent, eternal, and universal. From God, all things derive and all created beings are echoes of God. For this reason, most New Thought practitioners argue that each individual is divine or bears the divine "spark" within. Often this spark goes unnoticed, meaning that individuals do not or cannot tap into their full potential, which can include power over their physical body. Thus, it behooves each individual to learn how to channel and control this power through proper focusing of the mind.

Warren Felt Evans (1817–1889), also a student of Quimby's, took New Thought in a different direction than his fellow student, Mary Baker Eddy. Though he believed, like Eddy, that the mind was immaterial, he argued that the body did exist. Positing the existence of a "spiritual body," which linked immaterial mind and physical body, he argued that words could affect material change and heal the body. Unlike Christian Scientists, who believed that healing ailments through right thinking ultimately proved the spiritual nature of all matter, including the body, Evans believed that matter was inherently good and could be manipulated to benefit humanity. Evans was arguably the most prolific author among nineteenth-century proponents of New Thought, functioning as the movement's evangelist, to Quimby's founder. His books *The Mental Cure (Illustrating the Influence of the Mind on the Body, Both in Health and Disease, and the Psychological Method of Treatment)* and *The Divine Law of Cure* (1884), among others, served as foundational texts for New Thought practitioners.

Those involved in the earliest stages of New Thought formed a rather diffuse network of groups and practitioners. Nonetheless, by the late 1890s, an attempt at formalizing these connections began with the inaugural convention of The Metaphysical Club (1895). This was one of the first religious organizations to claim the name "New Thought" as a religious affiliation. It was replaced the next year by the International Metaphysical League; briefly it was also known as the International New Thought Convention. In 1914, the name was settled as the International New Thought Alliance (INTA), which is the name that the organization still bears. The INTA has its own periodical—*New Thought Magazine*—and holds annual "congresses" that bring together New Thought practitioners and groups from around the world.

However, the iterations of New Thought were not limited to those involved with the Metaphysical Club or the INTA. The most well-known, offshoot of New Thought is Christian Science. Eddy's Christian Science builds on all of traditional New Thought principles, but reads them through its particular, distinctively Christian lens. For example, Christian Scientists maintain that Spirit is the only reality and that not only matter but also sin are functions of the mind. Sin is simply "wrong thinking." Thus, the realization that all is Spirit and that everything derives from God enables one to see that learning to think correctly will awaken untapped divine ability. Christ, in this way, is a savior because he models right thinking and the ability of human beings to heal themselves through belief.

MODERN ITERATIONS AND CULTURAL LEGACY

Among the second generation of New Thought figures were Charles (1854–1948) and Myrtle Fillmore (1845–1931), the founders of the Unity School of Christianity or "Unity Church." Charles and Myrtle shared a common history with other New Thought founders Quimby—Charles suffered from physical maladies from an early age (his acquired by an ice skating accident) and Myrtle suffered from chronic tuberculosis. After Western medicine failed, they found New Thought and attributed their recoveries to mind cure, prayer, and positive thinking. Charles, who had been a religious seeker and dabbler throughout his life, and Myrtle began to publish on the subject of New Thought in the late 1880s. This evolved into a prayer group called Silent Unity, which in turn led to the founding of *Unity Magazine*. Though initially hesitant to found a religious institution, those who subscribed to *Unity Magazine* or attended the prayer group called for something more formal; this led to the founding of the Unity School of Christianity in 1906. Unity identifies as "Christian New Thought," and teaches standard New Thought principles—the reality of God as the source of all spirit and humanity's internal divine spark—while also maintaining that "affirmative prayer" and actively living one's spiritual principles are necessary for health, wellness, and an intimate connection with God. According to Unity theology, God is unlimited energy, rather than an anthropomorphized figure, and Christ is divine, but only insofar as all human beings are divine.

The prospertiy gospel and its vehicle, prosperity churches were a derivative of New Thought and a definitively Christian movement. The prosperity gospel began in the early twentieth century and preached the idea that one's faith was measured by one's success in health. If a person was healthy, then it was due to their faith in Christ; conversely, if a person was sick, this was a sign of the lack of faith. Similar to Christian Science, which posits a spiritual cause for all physical ailments, the prosperity gospel argues that through prayer and genuine belief, health can be achieved. Unlike Christian Scientists, however, those who subscribe to the prosperity gospel often employ Western medicine; they simply believe that it will not be effective unless faith is involved. The same would go for wealth and all achievements, which were the product of "right thinking" or the belief that Christ would provide.

In the latter twentieth and twenty-first centuries, New Thought has experienced alignment with both secular and religious (or "spiritual") movements. New Thought and modern "Self-Help" culture have also found each other as bedfellows. Self-help, or the notion that people can through their own efforts manage their physical and mental well-being. Often seen as an effect of modern psychology, Self-Help culture posits that humans can will themselves into mental or physical well-being. The book *The Secret* is a more popular, and purposefully metaphysical, example of Self-Help culture, which, as noted earlier, argues for the Law of Attraction or the idea that "whatever you believe will be." Additionally, New Thought has dovetailed with the modern wellness movement, which merges nutrition, visualization or positive thinking, and, often, Asian religious practices, such as meditation or traditional healing, in a program that promises to yield physical, emotional, and spiritual fulfillment.

Along its long history, New Thought has received its fair share of criticism, particularly from the scientific community that cast Mind Cure and other such alternative healing practices as potentially dangerous pseudoscience.

Also in some extreme instances, Christian Scientists have found themselves in court for child negligence or negligent homicide when a child in their care died due to lack of medical treatment. Prosperity churches also come under fire from Christians and non-Christians alike who feel their doctrine of material wealth defies Christ's spiritual message.

New Thought has witnessed an evolution from scientific experiment in new methods of healing, to Christian systems based on Mind Cure and positive faith, to secular movements built on the idea that the human mind has extraordinary potential to shape one's reality. Built upon the notion that the human mind is capable of knowing and doing more than people can imagine, New Thought as a movement will continue to push practitioners, of both religious and secular varieties, to change their realities and to make their dreams come true.

See also: Christian Science; Eddy, Mary Baker (1821–1910); Healing, Health, and New Religious Movements; Mesmerism; Pentecostalism; Quimby, Phineas (1802–1866); Swedenborg, Emanuel (1688–1772); Transcendentalism; Unity School of Christianity.

Further Reading

Albanese, Catherine. 2007. *A Republic of Mind and Spirit: A Cultural History of American Metaphysical Religion.* New Haven, CT: Yale University Press.

Albanese, Catherine, & Warren Felt Evans. 2016. *The Spiritual Journals of Warren Felt Evans: From Methodism to Mind Cure.* Bloomington: Indiana University Press.

Anderson, Alan, & Deb Whitehouse. 2003. *New Thought: A Practical American Spirituality.* Bloomington, IN: AuthorHouse.

Bowler, Kate. 2013. *Blessed: A History of the American Prosperity Gospel.* Oxford: Oxford University Press.

Evans, Warren Felt. 1884. *The Divine Law of Cure.* Boston: H.H. Carter & Co.

Fillmore, Charles. 2010 [1930]. *The Twelve Powers of Man.* Whitefish, MT: Kessinger Publishing, LLC.

PRIMARY SOURCE DOCUMENT

Excerpt from Charles Fillmore's *Talks on Truth* (1926)

Charles Fillmore and Myrtle Page Fillmore founded Unity Church, an off-shoot of the New Thought movement, in the late 1880s. Published in 1926, Fillmore's Talks on Truth *set forth the basic principles of Unity Church. An excerpt follows below.*

Lesson I
Reform Your God Thought

This is distinctly the age of reforms. Never before have there been such widespread and persistent efforts by both men and women to right the wrongs of religion, society, and politics.

2. From the hearts and the souls of millions goes up the cry, "Set us free from our burdens!" Every imaginable scheme of release is proposed, and each advocate of a panacea for the people's ills stoutly affirms his to be the only remedy that has virtue. It is observed that the majority of these reformers are clamorous that laws be enacted to force their theories upon the people. In this they are following the same methods to cure the ills of the body politic that they have followed in curing the body physical, and the results will surely be of like impotency.

3. Laws, whether natural or artificial, are but the evidence of an unseen power. They are simply effects, and effects have no power in themselves. When man looks to them for help in any condition of inharmony, he is departing from a universally recognized principle of sequence. God, Spirit or Mind—whatever you choose to name it—is the supreme dictator, and thought is its only mode of manifestation. Mind generates thought perpetually; all the harmonious and permanent affairs of men, and the innumerable systems of the infinite cosmos, are moved in majestic measures by its steady flow.

4. All power has its birth in the silence. There is no exception to this rule in all the evidence of life. Noise is the dying vibration of a spent force. All the clatter of visibility, from the harangue of the ward politician to the thunder's roar, is but evidence of exhausted power. As well try to control the lightning's flash by wrapping the thunder about it, as attempt to regulate mind by statutory enactments.

5. All reforms must begin with their cause. Their cause is mind, and mind does all its work in the realm of silence, which in reality is the only realm where sound and power go hand in hand. The visible outer world, with all its social, religious, and political laws,

customs, and ceremonies, is but the flimsy screen upon which mind throws its incongruous opinions. God's thought is love, the inherent potentiality of the God man, which knows neither persons nor things, mine nor thine, but a universal brotherhood in which perfect equity and justice reign in joint supremacy. All philosophers and sages have recognized this silent cause, this perpetual outflow from center to circumference. Emerson says of Plato: "He was born to behold the self-evolving power of Spirit, endless generator of new ends; a power which is the key at once to the centrality and the evanescence of things." Jesus Christ said: "The kingdom of God is within you." "Seek ye first his kingdom, and his righteousness; and all these things shall be added unto you." Elijah found God, not in the whirlwind, or the earthquake, or the fire, but in the "still small voice."

6. All men who have moved the world to better things have received their inspiration from the Spirit within and have always looked to it for instruction. God is not a person who has set creation in motion and gone away and left it to run down like a clock. God is Spirit, infinite Mind, the immanent force and intelligence everywhere manifest in nature. God is the silent voice that speaks into visibility all the life there is. This power builds with hands deft beyond the comprehension of man and keeps going, with all its intricate machinery, universe upon universe, one within another, yet never conflicting. All its building is from center to circumference. The evidence for this runs from the molecule and the atom of the physicist to the mighty swing of a universe of planets around their central sun. . . .

11. God is your higher self and is in constant waiting upon you. He loves to serve, and will attend faithfully to the most minute details of your daily life. If you are a man of the world, ask Him to help you to success in any line that you may choose, and He will show you what true success is. Use Him every hour of the day. If you are in doubt about a business move, no matter how trivial, close your eyes for an instant and ask the silent one within yourself what to do, just as you would send a mental message to one whom you know and who could catch your thought. The answer may not come instantly; it may come when you least think of it, and you will find yourself moved to do just the right thing. Never be formal with God. He cares no more for forms and ceremonies than do the principles of mathematics for fine figures or elaborate blackboards.

12. You cannot use God too often. He loves to be used, and the more you use Him the more easily you use Him and the more pleasant His help becomes. If you want a dress, a car, a house, or if you are

thinking of driving a sharp bargain with your neighbor, going on a journey, giving a friend a present, running for office, or reforming a nation, ask God for guidance, in a moment of silent soul desire.

13. Nothing is too wicked or unholy to ask God about. . . .

15. God's kingdom of love and unity is now being set up in the earth. His hand will guide the only ship that will ever sail into the Arcadian port, and the contented, peaceful, and happy people that throng its decks will sing with one voice: "Glory to God in the highest."

Source: Fillmore, Charles. *Talks on Truth*. Kansas City, MO: Unity School of Christianity, 1926.

Noyes, John Humphrey (1811–1886)

HISTORY AND REVELATION

As is often the case with founders of new religious movements, John Humphrey Noyes has been read through a rather narrow, psychoanalytical lens, which typically locates the impetus for his creation of a utopian religious community in his own sexual frustrations. But this misses the fact that Noyes built this community on biblical and Christian millennialist premises; sex, revelation, and the coming of Kingdom of God all informed Noyes's vision.

Born in Vermont in 1811, Noyes was the fourth of nine siblings born to John and Polly Noyes. His parents were Christian, though it was not until 1831 that Noyes experienced a religious conversion at a revival, prompting him to seek a ministerial degree at Yale Theological Seminary. His career as a seminary student was marked by a deepening desire to understand the true meaning of the Bible—a vocation that led him to a seminal discovery. Plagued by anxiety about his own salvation, Noyes came to the conclusion that only the perfect person could be saved. The impossibility of achieving such perfection was mitigated, however, when in 1834, he came to the realization that the Kingdom of God had already arrived (long ago in AD 70). Since the Kingdom had arrived, earthly perfection, he believed, was now possible.

Over the next few years, Noyes tried in earnest to spread his message, ultimately losing his ministerial license as a result. However, he persisted and sharpened his message of how Christians could live "perfectly" on earth. Increasingly, his understanding of perfectionist living became tied to alternative conceptions of familial and sexual relationships. Noyes inherited a painful shyness around women from his father and uncles—all of whom married cousins, who obviously already existed in their circle of acquaintance. For his part, Noyes had an early marriage proposal rejected and began to view marriage as increasingly transactional and romance as spiritual or intellectual; his eventual marriage to Harriet

Holton is often characterized in this way. His wife's difficult experiences with childbirth and the loss of four out of five infants also contributed to his belief that romantic and sexual attraction were an obstacle to true Christian perfection. Following his discovery of 1834, Noyes applied biblical conceptions of heaven, wherein there was no marriage, no procreation, nor any clear distinctions between genders, to his growing vision of a utopian community devoid of traditional marital and sexual conventions.

ONEIDA

Following a few years spent gathering converts near his hometown of Putney, Vermont, Noyes and his burgeoning band moved to Oneida, New York, where they officially founded the Oneida Community in 1848. It was there that Noyes would implement his vision of Christian perfection. Among his innovations, Noyes dissolved the concept of gender roles, calling for total equality of the sexes in thought and in role; created an equalitarian form of marriage known as "complex marriage," where everyone was married to everyone else; and instituted the practice of male continence, whereby men were instructed not to orgasm to make the sexual act about God and not their individual desire. He did this while setting himself up as the final authority on all matters, including choices of sexual partners. The Oneida Community's tenure was defined by this tension between equalitarian relationships among its members and total devotion to Noyes, who watchfully guarded and ran the practices of the community.

Unsurprisingly, the perception that Oneidans were practicing "free love" under the instruction of their authoritarian leader led to increased scrutiny on the community and on Noyes. This scrutiny prompted formal accusations in June 1879, when Noyes learned he would be arrested for statutory rape. (As a feature of Oneidan initiation practices, young members were initiated by older, more experienced

John Humphrey Noyes was a Christian perfectionist and millennialist who, following his realization that the Kingdom of God had already arrived, determined to create a religious community that lived accordingly. Noyes founded the Oneida Community where, among other things, he implemented the practice of "complex marriage," whereby all members of the community were married to each other. (Oneida Ltd.)

members, meaning that young women were initiated by older men and vice versa). Noyes fled to Ontario, Canada and in January of 1881 formally dissolved the religious community. His influence remained among his followers, some of whom came to live near him near Niagara Falls. He died in April of 1886; his body was returned to Oneida and buried in a cemetery among his fellow Oneidans.

See also: Oneida Community, The; Utopianism in New Religious Movements.

Further Reading

Noyes, George, & Lawrence Foster. 2001. *Free Love in Utopia: John Humphrey Noyes and the Origin of the Oneida Community.* Chicago: University of Illinois.

Noyes, John. 1870. *History of American Socialisms.* Philadelphia: J.B. Lippincott & Co.

Noyes, John. 1877. *Male Continence: On Lovemaking without Ejaculation.* Oneida, NY: Office of Oneida Circular.

NXIVM

NXIVM is not the first, nor will it be the last, new religious movement to crash on the shoals of public notoriety. Though some question its classification as "religious," none question its outward and fundamentally New Age aims of advancing human beings to their full potential. The question remains for many as to whether these aims were authentic or a front for something much more sinister: a sex "cult" as it was portrayed in popular venues like *People* magazine and *The New York Times.*

A founder of multiple businesses, Keith Raniere (1960–) started NXIVM (pronounced Nex-i-em) in 1998 outside of Albany, New York. The group maintained chapters throughout the country as well as in Canada and Mexico. He marketed NXIVM as a set of techniques, rolled out in curriculum, for people seeking self-improvement. Drawing from New Thought beliefs that the means of improvement lie within and New Age eclecticism, NXIVM, particularly through its "Executive Success Programs" attracted those seeking advancement of all kinds—professional, social, and spiritual. For those who attend seminars, Raniere is known as "Vanguard." Celebrities such as Richard Branson and actress Grace Park attended seminars on Executive Success Programs. And though the content of the seminars, termed "Rational Inquiry," is trademarked and kept secret (those who partake are bound by nondisclosure agreements), leaks of seminar techniques have occurred, causing backlash for NXIVM and for the leaker.

During its two decade existence, NXIVM was hounded by bad press and accusations of "brainwashing" and sexual deviance, the result of persistent leaks and a growing number of ex-members with stories to tell. Revelations of the alleged sexual misconduct, unlawful imprisonment, and terrorization of NXIVM members came to light in 2017 when *The New York Times* published an exposé on the group. The article's subject, Sarah Edmondson, described her recruitment as an NXIVM member and subsequent initiation process where she was stripped and branded. These rituals were elements of a secret movement within NXIVM known as "The Vow." Once initiated, Edmondson and fellow recruits were referred to as "slaves" and compelled to partake in sexual acts with Raniere or coveted NXIVM clients. If they refused, sexually explicit photos could be employed to blackmail them. Soon, other news networks followed, catapulting an elite, but little-known, movement into the spotlight.

In early 2018, Raniere was indicted and arrested on charges of sex trafficking and enforced enslavement. His associate, former actress Allison Mack (1982–), and various executives within NXIVM were arrested on similar charges. In April 2019, Mack pled guilty to racketeering. In June 2019, Raniere was convicted of racketeering and sex trafficking, and in October 2020, he was sentenced to 120 years in prison.

See also: Brainwashing; Courts and New Religious Movements; Cult; Disaffiliation and Ex-Membership in New Religious Movements; Media and New Religious Movements; New Age, The; New Thought; Sex, Sexuality, and New Religious Movements.

Further Reading

Meier, Barry. "Inside a Secret Group Where Women Are Branded." *The New York Times*, October 17, 2017. Available at: https://www.nytimes.com/2017/10/17/nyregion/nxivm-women-branded-albany.html.

"NXIVM." Available at: www.nxivm.com.

Oahspe

The Spiritualist movement that began in the mid-nineteenth century offered individuals the attractive possibility of communicating with people who had already died. For some, such contact proved to be emotionally moving and deeply comforting. For others, however, the messages that came from beyond the veil that separated the living and the dead turned out to be pedestrian and uninspiring. The American dentist John Ballou Newbrough (1828–1891) was among that latter group. Newbrough had participated in Spiritualism, but became dissatisfied with the messages typically received from the spirits. He eventually produced his own scriptural text, *Oahspe: A Kosmon Bible in the Words of Jehovih and His Angel Embassadors* (the title varies slightly in different presentations of the text). Despite Newbrough's idiosyncratic spelling, his message is clear. The new Bible comes directly from God, rather than ordinary spirits; its authority is therefore unimpeachable.

Newbrough initially published *Oahspe* (the term refers to earth, sky, and spirit; see *Oahspe* 1:20) in 1882 with no mention of the process by which it originated. In 1883, at the editor's request, he provided an account to the Spiritualist newspaper, *The Banner of Light*. In that letter, Newbrough details his prior experience with Spiritualist séances, highlighting his facility at "automatic writing" during which his hands would involuntarily transcribe messages. He would also occasionally experience alterations in his speech, sight, and hearing. Newbrough was sufficiently impressed by his experiences that he embarked on an extensive investigation of Spiritualism, including conversations with more than two hundred mediums.

But Newbrough was not satisfied with messages from deceased friends and relatives. He yearned to learn the wisdom of the angels. To prepare himself for such a possibility, he undertook a rigorous six-year program of physical discipline and bodily purification. The initial communications that Newbrough received from the angels perplexed him, but after two years, he perceived a change in the angels' guidance. Every morning he found his hands directed to the typewriter (a new invention at the time), where he would record his inspiration without editing or revision. That process occurred over a half-hour every day for fifty weeks. At the end, Newbrough was directed to read and publish *Oahspe* and to add the many drawings that he received in a similar fashion.

The resulting book is complex and extensive, running to nearly nine hundred pages. It is about twice the length of *The Book of Mormon* and around 80 percent the length of the Christian scriptures. The layout of the text recalls the more familiar Christian scriptures; it is divided into books, which are further subdivided into chapters and verses. *Oahspe* opens with an account of the creation of humans and sets human history within a sequence of three-thousand-year cycles, encompassing all ancient civilizations and continuing to the present. Jehovih is identified as the creator of this world and humankind and as being both male and female.

Oahspe draws particular attention to the division of the world among four major religions, what it calls the Brahmins, Buddhists, Christians, and Mohammedans. Their influence, however, is depicted as negative. Each of them is portrayed as commanding its own army and, collectively, they are responsible for the corruption of humans. But the text anticipates that a seventh era is at hand during which humans, led by the revelations contained in *Oahspe*, will come to know their creator and return to their original peaceful ways, vegetarian diet, cultivation of virtue, and service to others. Those who do not will remain under the dominion of the four-headed beast that signifies the four predominant religions; they will be known as "UZIANS" or destroyers. Those who attend to the Creator's voice, however, will be known as "FAITHISTS" and will help to inaugurate the new KOSMON era.

Like the scriptures of other new religions, *Oahspe* renders a negative judgment on the current state of the world and holds out the tantalizing hope for a new, better world for those who follow its guidance.

See also: Millennialism; New Scriptures and New Religious Movements; Spiritualism.

Further Reading

Anonymous, 1882. *Oahspe: A Kosmon Bible in the Words of Jehovih and His Angel Embassadors*. New York: Oahspe Publishing Association. Available at: http://www.sacred-texts.com/oah/index.htm.

Gallagher, Eugene V. 2014. *Reading and Writing Scripture in New Religious Movements: New Bibles and New Revelations*. New York: Palgrave/Macmillan.

Hammer, Olav, & Mikael Rothstein. 2012. "Canonical and Extracanonical Texts in New Religions." In Olav Hammer & Mikael Rothstein, eds., *The Cambridge Companion to New Religious Movements*, pp. 113–129. Cambridge: Cambridge University Press.

Newbrough, John Ballou. 1883. "The Origin of Oahspe." In *The Banner of Light*. Available at: http://www.sacred-texts.com/oah/pamphlet.htm.

PRIMARY SOURCE DOCUMENT

Chapter 1 of *Oahspe: A Kosmon Bible in the Words of Jehovih and His Angel Embassadors* (1882)

Though published anonymously, it was John Ballou Newbrough, an American dentist who claimed the book was a product of automatic writing, who brought Oahspe to the public. It was first published in 1882, and set forth "new revelations." The text was written down by John Ballou Newbrough, an American dentist who claimed that the book was a product of automatic writing. An excerpt is as follows.

1. AFTER the creation of man, the Creator, Jehovih, said unto him: That thou shalt know thou art the work of My hand, I have given thee capacity for knowledge, power and dominion. This was the first era.

2. But man was helpless, crawling on his belly, and he understood not the voice of the Almighty. And Jehovih called his angels, who were older than the earth, and he said unto them: Go ye, raise man upright, and teach him to understand.

3. And the angels of heaven descended to the earth and raised man upright. And man wandered about on the earth. This was the second era.

4. Jehovih said to the angels that were with man: Behold, man hath multiplied on the earth. Bring ye them together; teach them to dwell in cities and nations.

5. And the angels of Jehovih taught the peoples of the earth to dwell together in cities and nations. This was the third era.

6. And in that same time the Beast (self) rose up before man and spake to him, saying: Possess thou whatsoever thou wilt, for all things are thine, and are good for thee.

7. And man obeyed the Beast; and war came into the world. This was the fourth era.

8. And man was sick at heart, and he called out to the Beast, saying: Thou saidst: Possess thyself of all things, for they are good for thee. Now, behold, war and death have encompassed me about on all sides. I pray thee, therefore, teach me peace!

9. But the Beast said: Think not I am come to send peace on the earth; I come not to send peace, but a sword. I come to set man at variance against his father; and a daughter against her mother. Whatsoever thou findest to eat, be it fish or flesh, eat thou thereof, taking no thought of to-morrow.

10. And man ate fish and flesh, becoming carnivorous, and darkness came upon him, and he no more heard the voice of Jehovih, or believed in Him. This was the fifth era.

11. And the Beast divided itself into four great heads, and possessed the earth about; and man fell down and worshipped them.

12. And the names of the heads of the Beast were BRAHMIN, BUDDHIST, CHRISTIAN and MOHAMMEDAN. And they divided the earth, and apportioned it between themselves, choosing soldiers and standing armies for the maintenance of their earthly aggrandizement.

13. And the Brahmins had seven million soldiers; the Buddhists twenty millions; the Christians seven millions; and the Mohammedans two millions, whose trade was killing man. And man, in service of the Beast, gave one-sixth of his life and his labor to war and standing armies; and one-third of his life he gave to dissipation and drunkenness. This was the sixth era.

14. Jehovih called out to man to desist from evil; but man heard Him not. For the cunning of the Beast had changed man's flesh, so that his soul was hid as if in a cloud, and he loved sin.

15. Jehovih called unto His angels in heaven, saying: Go ye down to the earth once more, to man, whom I created to inhabit the earth and enjoy it, and say ye to man: Thus saith Jehovih:

16. Behold, the seventh era is at hand. Thy Creator commandeth thy change from a carnivorous man of contention to an herbivorous man of peace. The four heads of the Beast shall be put away; and war shall be no more on the earth.

17. Thy armies shall be disbanded. And, from this time forth, whosoever desireth not to war, thou shall not impress; for it is the commandment of thy Creator.

18. Neither shalt thou have any God, nor Lord, nor Savior, but only thy Creator, Jehovih! Him only shalt thou worship henceforth forever. I am sufficient unto Mine own creations.

19. And to as many as separate themselves from the dominion of the Beast, making these covenants unto Me, have I given the foundation of My kingdom on earth.

20. And all such shall be My chosen: By their covenants and by their works shall they be known henceforth on the earth as Mine, and shall be called FAITHISTS.

21. But to as many as will not make these covenants, have I given the numbers of the Beast, and they shall be called UZIANS, signifying destroyers. And these shall be henceforth the two kinds of people on earth, FAITHISTS and UZIANS.

22. And the angels of heaven descended to the earth, to man, and appeared before him face to face, hundreds of thousands of them, speaking as man speaketh, and writing as man writeth, teaching these things of Jehovih and His works.

23. And in the thirty-third year thereof, the Embassadors of the angel hosts of heaven prepared and revealed unto man in the name of Jehovih, His heavenly kingdoms; and have thus herein made known the plan of his delightful creations, for the resurrection of the peoples of the earth.

24. Not immaculate in this Book, OAHSPE; but to teach mortals HOW TO ATTAIN TO HEAR THE CREATOR'S VOICE, and to SEE HIS HEAVENS, in full consciousness, whilst still living on the

earth; and to know of a truth the place and condition awaiting them after death.

25. Neither are, nor were, the revelations within this OAHSPE wholly new to mortals. The same things have been revealed at the same time unto many, who live at remote distances from one another, but who were not in correspondence till afterward.

26. Because this light is thus comprehensive, embracing corporeal and spiritual things, it is called the beginning of the KOSMON ERA. And because it relates to earth, sky and spirit, it is called OAHSPE.

Source: Newbrough, John Ballou. *Oahspe: A New Bible of the Words of Jehovih and His Angel Embassadors.* New York: Oahspe Publishing Association, 1882, chapter 1.

Occultism and Esotericism

In common parlance, the words "occult" and "esoteric" are often used pejoratively to mean, respectively, "demonic" and "obscure." These definitions are problematic for their narrowness; in reality, the two terms are far more complex, particularly when religion is involved, and scholars have struggled to land on a singular definition, often denying that there is one. Nonetheless, there are numerous new religious movements that self-describe as esoteric and/or occult, which means that for those involved in such traditions, the terms do have bearing on how members self-identify and even on why they founded or joined these religions in the first place.

Esoteric is a term that has been in use for centuries to describe knowledge that is privy to only a select few. However, the concept of "esotericism," as a tradition, came into vogue during the nineteenth century, popularized by white religious figures such as Éliphas Lévi (1810–1875) to describe new traditions then arising, which considered themselves keepers of specialized knowledge (often gleaned from allegedly ancient sources), and older traditions, often from Asia, that were ascribed the label by foreigners (such as "Esoteric Buddhism"). Similarly, occult, which means "hidden" or "secret," came to be associated with mysterious, magical, or supernatural powers and practices around the same period. Those considered "occultists" could also be classified as esotericists, believing that they derived special knowledge from magical practices (and vice versa), which they employed to create their own religious traditions.

THE NINETEENTH CENTURY: WESTERN ESOTERICISM IN ASIA

Much of what is considered the "Western esoteric tradition" grew from the process of globalization, spurred by the European colonial enterprise to Asia. The

464   **Occultism and Esotericism**

fascination with the "exotic East," besides highlighting European orientalism, spurred interest in Asian religious and philosophical traditions particularly during the nineteenth and twentieth centuries. Europeans and Americans clamored for knowledge and texts from Asia, which often predated their own religions by millennia and provided different answers to age-old religious questions.

A belief prevailed that Asia was a treasure trove of esoteric knowledge waiting to be uncovered (often with little awareness by white Westerners doing the "uncovering" that they were appropriating and often divorcing this knowledge from historical, theological, and cultural lineages of South and East Asian people). For example, Pierre Bernard (1875–1955) traveled to India at the turn of the twentieth century where he claimed initiation into secret, Tantric (a form of Tibetan Buddhism) circles. He returned to the United States and soon founded the Tantrik Order in New York, which became famous for its belief that sex was a necessary and liberative practice at the heart of spiritual advancement. In Tibetan Buddhism, the purpose of all practices is to obtain "shakti," or creative power, thus sexual release is eschewed; not so, however, in the Tantrik Order, which emphasized that sexual arousal and orgasm could evoke magical powers for the practitioner.

Theosophy and its institutional body the Theosophical Society combined a fascination with Asian, esoteric knowledge with Spiritualist practice. Spiritualism was a nineteenth-century movement founded on the idea that communication with the spiritual realm was possible. Helena Petrovna Blavatsky (1831–1891) was a Spiritualist medium who was contacted by several individuals claiming to be Great Masters, or advanced individuals, who had been sent to earth throughout history to guide human beings in their spiritual evolution. Prior to her entrée into Spiritualist circles, she traveled extensively in India and Tibet, where she was educated in ancient and esoteric Hindu and Buddhist knowledge. She would eventually record her encounters with many of these Masters in a variety of publications that served as sacred texts for Theosophists. It was Blavatsky's partnership with Henry Steel Olcott (1832–1907), also a Spiritualist, that would bring the association of Theosophy with Asian religious traditions full circle. In 1878, Blavatsky and Olcott traveled to India where they established the international center of the Theosophical Society. Olcott would remain there for the duration of his life, eventually taking Buddhist vows and writing numerous Theosophical texts that bore a distinctively Buddhist bent.

From the Theosophical tradition emerged a host of esoteric new religious groups. Anthroposophy, founded by Rudolf Steiner (1861–1925), adapted Theosophical belief in Ascended Masters, while eschewing the Asian religious bent of Theosophy's claim to special knowledge. Steiner emphasized the idea that human beings possessed secret, sacred knowledge, which they had lost over time; the ability to reclaim this knowledge began with belief in Jesus Christ. The Fourth Way, founded by G. I. Gurdjieff (1866–1949) and adapted by P. D. Ouspensky (1878–1947), built on the Theosophical belief that all human beings were capable of learning great, universal truths through their own efforts by combining the focused work of the body, emotions, and mind. Other Theosophical traditions, such as the I AM Activity and the Church Universal and Triumphant, were based on the interactions of their respective founders with specific Ascended Masters,

THE TWENTIETH CENTURY AND THE OCCULT IN ENGLAND

The early to mid-twentieth century witnessed a wave of interest in occult religion, particularly in England, where numerous magic-based traditions were born. Several major British occultists came to the practice via the Hermetic Order of the Golden Dawn, a tradition founded on the practices of Freemasonry (a global secret society) and Rosicrucianism (an esoteric tradition claiming privileged knowledge of Judeo-Christianity), including British poet Arthur Edward Waite (1857–1942), Dion Fortune (1890–1946), and Aleister Crowley (1875–1947), who is often viewed as the father of modern occultism. Crowley had also been a member of Ordo Templi Orientis, an occult religious tradition founded in Germany in Austria in the early twentieth century, before establishing his own religious tradition known as Thelema based on communications he received from the Egyptian God, Horus. Thelemic principles and texts found their way across the globe, influencing those like American astrophysicist John Whiteside Parsons (1914–1952), who would combine his magical, occult practices with his work on rocket propulsion.

Numerous Neopagan traditions were born during these moments of peak interest in the occult, the secret, and the magical. The "father" of modern witchcraft, Gerald Gardner (1884–1964) maintained, similar to those who traveled to Asia seeking timeless wisdom, that he was simply reintroducing an ancient religious system to a modern audience. After a period of membership in occult groups, Gardner founded the New Forest Coven and began to practice Wicca, putting his own stamp on it in the process, including an increasing focus on worship of the "Goddess" as well as the male "Horned God." Not all Neopagan traditions view what they do as ancient, however. Many branches took inspiration from eclectic sources, including feminism and environmentalism, even absorbing characteristics of New Age religion, which forwarded the idea that universal, eternal wisdom could be shaped and adapted to individualized spirituality.

Often mistakenly conflated with Neopaganism, Satanism is another diverse occult tradition that arose during the twentieth century. The most famous Satanic sect is the Church of Satan, which is focused on actualizing one's full potential through magical ritual and takes a certain satiric, hedonistic view of religious practice. The Temple of Set, known in the twenty-first century for its public battle for First Amendment rights, is an occult religious group that often denies the label of Satanism, though it adopts Set, an ancient Egyptian God of chaos and mischief as the central focus of worship. Rituals such as initiation are fiercely guarded secrets, since each comes with a different degree of magical expertise and power.

Interest in the occult and the esoteric has not waned in the twenty-first century by any means nor is it exclusive to Asian or British lineages. Religions such as

Heaven's Gate and Scientology in the United States or Kardecism in South America developed their own theologies based on the belief in secret, often magical, knowledge reserved for those willing to access it.

See also: Anthroposophy; Blavatsky, Helena Petrovna (1831–1891); Church of Satan, The; Church Universal and Triumphant, The; Crowley, Aleister (1875–1947); Freemasonry; Fortune, Dion (1890–1946); Fourth Way, The; Gardner, Gerald (1884–1964); Globalization and New Religious Movements; Gurdjieff, G. I. (1866–1949); Heaven's Gate; Hermetic Order of the Golden Dawn, The; I AM Activity, The; Kardecism (Spiritism); Lévi, Éliphas (1810–1875); Magic and New Religious Movements; Mediums; Neopaganism; New Age, The; Olcott, Henry Steel (1832–1907); Ordo Templi Orientis; Ouspensky, P. D. (1878–1947); Parsons, John Whiteside (1914–1952); Rosicrucianism; Satanism; Scientology; Spiritualism; Steiner, Rudolf (1861–1925); Tantrik Order, The; Temple of Set, The; Thelema; Theosophical Society, The; Theosophy; Waite, Arthur Edward (1857–1942); Wicca.

Further Reading

Djurdjevic, Gordan. 2014. *India and the Occult: The Influence of South Asian Spirituality on Modern Western Occultism.* London: Palgrave Macmillan.

Faivre, Antoine, & Jacob Needleman, ed. 1995. *Modern Esoteric Spirituality.* Edinburgh, UK: Alban Books.

Franklin, J. Jeffrey. 2018. *Spirit Matters: Occult Beliefs, Alternative Religions, and the Crisis of Faith in Victorian Britain.* Ithaca, NY: Cornell University Press.

Granholm, Kennet. 2014. "Researching Esoteric Groups." In George D. Chryssides & Benjamin E. Zeller, eds., *The Bloomsbury Companion to New Religious Movements.* London: Bloomsbury Publishing.

Hammer, Olav. 2004. "Esotericism in New Religious Movements." In James R. Lewis, ed., *The Oxford Handbook of New Religious Movements.* New York: Oxford.

Odinism

Overlapping with Ásatrú, Heathenry, and other forms of contemporary Norse and Germanic Paganism, Odinism refers to the worship of the pre-Christian Norse gods, in particular Odin, who is a complex figure associated with war, sovereignty, wisdom, shamanism, and the dead, among other things. Odinists frequently emphasize that theirs is a "warrior religion," which has appealed to individuals who seek a dramatic, even violent, change in the status quo. It remains challenging to separate various strands of Odinism and Ásatrú, particularly on the basis of the racial attitudes they espouse. Some are universalist or even explicitly antiracist, others emphasize the "folkish" connection between ancestry or bloodlines and the worship of certain gods, and a small but significant group makes common cause with various forms of white supremacism and anti-semitism.

The reconstruction and reinvention of the ancient northern European Pagan religion flourished in the 1970s as part of the general interest in forming new Pagan religions. A distinctive feature of Odinism and related religions is the conviction that there is an essential link between one's ancestry and the deities one should worship. Accordingly, those of northern European ancestry should worship the old Norse and Germanic gods; others should worship the gods of their own ancestors. The universalism of Christianity is rejected in favor of a focus on ethnic connections to the gods and among worshippers.

The career of the founder of the first Odinist group in the United States, the Odinist Fellowship, shows the dominant role that the intertwining of race and religion has taken in Odinism as opposed to the more diverse understandings of the connections between race and religion in other forms of Norse Paganism, such as Ásatrú.

Else Christensen (1913–2005) was born in Denmark where she later became a member of the National Socialist Workers' Party of Denmark and married a fellow Danish Nazi in 1937. Christensen was influenced by the writings of the Australian Alexander Rud Mills (1885–1964), who had founded an Odinist group in Melbourne in 1936 and who was also a Nazi sympathizer and anti-semite. Mills focused on the "British race" and argued that Odinism rather than Christianity was native to people of that racial group. Although Christensen differed with Mills on some points, she embraced the anti-semitic conspiracy theory that Jews controlled the Western world and the attendant racialist understanding of Odinism as the appropriate religion for those of northern European ancestry. From 1971 to 1992, Christensen published a ten-page newsletter, *The Odinist*, examples of which are archived on the website of The Odinist Fellowship (see www.odinistfellowship.com). Christensen continues to be hailed as the "Grandmother" of racially focused Odinism, particularly in North America. Her development of an Odinist prison ministry in the 1980s helped the religion engage recruits behind bars, where it remains popular.

Independent of Christensen's influence Stephen McNallen (1948–) found the gods of the Vikings while he was in college in the late 1960s. He founded the Ásatrú Free Assembly in 1969; it dissolved in 1987 and was reestablished in 1996 as the Ásatrú Folk Assembly. Despite claims that his ethnic version of Nordic Paganism ultimately differs little from Christensen's forthright endorsements of white supremacy and anti-semitism, McNallen has rejected both neo-Nazis and National Socialism.

Probably the most virulent expression of racialist Odinism is Wotansfolk, cofounded by David Lane (1938–2007), his wife Katja, and Ron McVan (1950–) in 1995. In his understanding, Wotan was not only another name for Odin but also stood for "Will of the Aryan Nation." Lane had been a member of the domestic terrorist group, The Order or The Silent Brotherhood, in the 1980s and is revered in white supremacist circles for coining the "Fourteen Words" ("We must secure the existence of our people and a future for white children"). Lane saw the worship of the ancient Norse gods as an essential element in the survival of the white race and like others on the Euro-American radical right looked forward to a coming Racial Holy War ("RaHoWa").

See also: Ásatrú; Neopaganism; Race and New Religious Movements.

Further Reading

Berry, Damon T. 2017. *Blood and Faith: Christianity in American White Nationalism.* Syracuse, NY: Syracuse University Press.

Gardell, Mattias. 2003. *Gods of the Blood: The Pagan Revival and White Separatism.* Durham, NC: Duke University Press.

Gardell, Mattias. 2015. "Wolf Age Pagans." In James R. Lewis & Jesper Aa. Petersen, eds., *Controversial New Religions*, 2nd ed. New York: Oxford University Press.

Kaplan, Jeffrey. 1997. *Radical Religion in America: Millenarian Movements from the Far Right to the Children of Noah*. Syracuse, NY: Syracuse University Press.

Olcott, Henry Steel (1832–1907)

EARLY LIFE

Unlike his counterpart in the Theosophical Society, Helena Petrovna Blavatsky (1831–1891), Henry Steel Olcott's early life is well documented, though by no means conventional. Olcott was born in New Jersey in 1832 to Presbyterian parents. During his formative years, he traded time between work on his father's farm and elite education at established New York institutions like Columbia University. Well before he was recognized as a Western occultist and religious leader, Olcott earned acclaim for his agricultural savvy and had his pick of job opportunities, ultimately determining to serve as Agricultural Editor of the *New York Tribune* in 1857. While serving as editor he was briefly arrested for suspicion of his involvement with abolitionist John Brown and the Harper's Ferry Raid.

Olcott married Mary Epplee Morgan in 1860 with whom he had four children (two of which died in infancy). Shortly thereafter, Olcott joined the Union Army, ultimately ascending to the rank of Colonel. Following the war, Olcott worked for the New York Mustering and Discharging Office as Investigator. He was ultimately admitted to the New York bar 1868, pursuing private practice until he began to privilege more spiritual pursuits.

THE THEOSOPHICAL SOCIETY AND THE MOVE "EASTWARD"

Olcott had an interest in Spiritualism for much of his life. Spiritualism, or the belief that human beings are capable of contacting the deceased who exist on another plane, had taken the country by a storm since the 1840s. In 1874, he traveled to Chittenden, Vermont, to report on the psychic phenomena he saw; there, he met Blavatsky. Their spiritual connection was swift, forging a bond that would lead to the establishment of the Theosophical Society only a year later, for which Olcott was elected president.

Traditional views of the pair paint Blavatasky as the religious genius to Olcott's administrator. There is some truth to this. It was Blavatsky who first experienced contact with the Great Masters and recorded their revelations in best-selling books such as *Isis Unveiled*. And Olcott was the natural administrator of the two, given his professional skillset. However, this view belies Olcott's own intellectual influence on the group, particularly as he became increasingly immersed in Hindu and Buddhist religious thought. In 1878, Blavatsky and Olcott moved their nascent movement to India, where they established the international base of the Theosophical Society in Adyar.

Though he would continue to travel in order to spread Theosophy—the religious system at the base of the Society—it was his travels within India that were the most formative and helped to give Theosophy, and his writings on the subject, a particularly Asian bent. In 1880, he would take lay Buddhist vows and be instrumental in uniting various sects of Buddhism in a coalition to promote Buddhism. Theosophical principles maintained that one could be a Theosophist and maintain affiliation with another religion; Olcott had not defected from the Society. However, his Theosophical writings were quite often Buddhist in content—*A Buddhist Catechism*, for example—as were the encounters he reported having with the Mahatmas (intellectually advanced beings, often deceased, who guide humanity toward spiritual progress and universal brotherhood).

LEGACY

Through the years, the Theosophical Society was plagued with scandal, mostly surrounding Blavatsky, who was the more visible and flamboyant of the two. Nonetheless, her death in 1891 was a devastating blow to Olcott, who had to lead the Society, even as it began to fracture in the wake of her passing. Olcott was soon joined in leadership by Annie Besant, who would helm the Society after he died.

Olcott was a fixture on the Indian religious scene. He worked consistently to promote Buddhist and Hindu principles, schools, and texts as well as those of other religious traditions, such as Zoroastrianism, until the end of his life. After experiencing a fall aboard a steamer ship returning him from a lecture tour in the United States in October 1906, Olcott was hospitalized in Italy. He never recovered from his injuries and died in February 1907 in Adyar. His farewell letter bidding goodbye to those he left behind and hello to those he would meet on higher planes.

See also: Blavatsky, Helena Petrovna (1831–1891); I AM Activity, The; Occultism and Esotericism; Spiritualism; Theosophical Society, The; Theosophy.

Further Reading

Olcott, Henry Steel. 1881 [1908]. *A Buddhist Catechism*. London; Benares: The Theosophical Publishing Society.

Olcott, Henry Steel. 1885. *Theosophy, Religion, and Occult Science*. London: George Redway.

Prothero, Stephen. 2010. *The White Buddhist: The Asian Odyssey of Henry Steel Olcott*. Religion in North America. Bloomington: Indiana University Press.

Oneida Community, The

HISTORY

Utopian communities were common during the nineteenth century, but perhaps none were so scrutinized as the Oneida Community. Founded by John Humphrey Noyes in 1848, Oneida became the site of great religious and social

The Oneida Community was a utopian religious community famous for their, by nineteenth-century standards, unconventional approach to marriage and sexuality. The community lasted from 1848 to 1881; however, its primary dwelling, Mansion House (depicted here) in Oneida, New York, still exists and operates as a tourist site. Its architecture reflects the communal living promoted by the Oneidans. (Library of Congress)

experimentation, where Christian perfectionism met alternative familial, economic, and sexual structures and practices.

Noyes (1811–1886) felt called to the ministry at a very young age and experienced a religious conversion at the age of twenty, which confirmed for him that the millennium (Christ's reign of one thousand years) was near. Yet, it was in 1834 while seeking a ministerial degree at Yale Theological Seminary and avidly studying the Bible that he came to a momentous discovery: Christ's second coming, the event that preceded the millennium, had already occurred in AD 70 (the year that the Romans destroyed the Second Temple in Jerusalem). The millennium, in other words, was already here.

Given the arrival of God's Kingdom, Noyes began to preach that it was essential and possible for humans to live lives free of sin—a doctrine known as "perfectionism," or the notion that to be truly Christian was to be "perfect" or sinless. For his views, Yale's administration stripped Noyes of his newly awarded preaching license. In the ensuing years, he married Harriet Holton (even though he would later undermine the very nature of that institution) and returned to his birthplace, Putney, Vermont. From 1841 to 1846, he grew his religious vision among his family and a growing band of interested seekers. In 1847, he laid down his views in

The Berean (a biblical reference to Acts 17:11). These beliefs would be formally implemented into a set of practices when he founded the Oneida Community (Oneida, New York) in 1848—the realization of his vision for a "perfect" model of Christian utopia.

BELIEFS AND PRACTICES

Out of the paradigm-shifting revelation that the millennium was at hand and that Christians could (and must be) perfect arose Noyes's belief that human relationships must be restructured. Though married himself, he came to believe that marriage and monogamy were a form of spiritual slavery—placing selfish love of an individual ahead of love of God and His creation. Since there would be no marriage in the Kingdom of Heaven (see Matt. 22:30), marriage was an unnecessary institution. Noyes dissolved all marriages in favor of "complex marriage." Those who entered the community were instantly married to everyone else (including men to men and women to women) and lived communally.

These universal marital bonds extended themselves into sexual relationships among members: members were "initiated" through sex with a current member of the opposite sex. Noyes generally arranged sexual partners for everyone himself to avoid selfish romantic attachments from forming. Thus, the common contemporary critique of the group was that it was a proponent of "free love"—profligate, random sex with multiple partners. Rather, at Oneida, sex factored into the system of perfectionism Noyes envisioned in several ways. One of the products of a living in God's kingdom was perfect, unselfish love for all of God's creatures, particularly fellow human beings, because God loved them. Sex was seen as the best, most intimate means of expressing this love for all of creation, and therefore for God. However, to avoid making sex a selfish act, male Oneida members were advised to practice "male continence"—the avoidance of orgasm. Such avoidance, besides making the act about an expression of love for God, also avoided procreation—which Noyes argued was not the point of sex in the Kingdom. However, Noyes instituted the practice of "stirpiculture," or spiritual eugenics. To create "stirpicults," Noyes would match two individuals whose qualities, he believed, would marry to create perfect children. These children were then raised by the community, not their biological parents, thus creating a generation who were already accepting of Oneida's perfectionist practices.

The focus on total equality and equanimity in relationships manifested in several other practices among the Oneidans, most notably in the practice of mutual criticism and a system of total gender equality. Mutual criticism entailed an open evaluation of an individual who, seated at the center of a circle, would hear about ways she or he could improve. This suppressed the ego and ensured that members were focused on God, not themselves. And not only was marriage dissolved in heaven: gender was as well and so were gender roles. The traditional division of labor between women's and men's work was eradicated in favor of a system where tasks were distributed regardless of gender. For this reason, Oneidan women adopted a particular uniform, including pants (worn under a skirt), to ensure their readiness for tasks that involved more heavy lifting.

LEGACY

As is understandable, the group experienced a tremendous amount of critique. From their sexual practices to Noyes's message of perfectionism to their gender-bending clothing line, Oneidans defied Victorian mores of respectability. The group weathered the criticism fairly well, but began to founder when members of the group (particularly younger members who had arrived with their more committed parents) expressed desires for monogamous relationships. By 1881, Noyes was too frail to run the community as he once had; facing mounting opposition from within, he formally dissolved Oneida as a religious utopian society. He died five years later in the "Mansion House," the main building of the Oneida compound.

To sustain itself during its heyday, the community had started a surprisingly successful cutlery and silver brand. When the religious component of the community dissolved, many remained to continue to run the business, named "Oneida Limited," which still exists today.

See also: Noyes, John Humphrey (1811–1886); Utopianism in New Religious Movements.

Further Reading

Carden, Maren Lockwood. 1971. *Oneida: Utopian Community to Modern Corporation.* New York: Harper & Row.

Foster, Lawrence. 1984. *Religion and Sexuality: The Shakers, the Mormons, and the Oneida Community.* Oxford: Oxford University Press.

Noyes, John Humphrey. 1847. *The Berean: A Manual for Those Who Seek the Faith of the Primitive Church.* Putney, VT: Published at the Office of the Spiritual Magazine.

Order of the Solar Temple, The

During the 1990s, several incidents involving new or alternative religions and violence claimed public attention. In 1993, nearly eighty people died at the Branch Davidians' Mount Carmel Center. The Japanese group, Aum Shrinkyō, killed a dozen after it released sarin gas in the Tokyo subway. In 1997, a collective suicide claimed the lives of thirty-nine members of Heaven's Gate, a UFO religious group. In 1994, Swiss law enforcement officials found the bodies of fifty-three members of the Order of the Solar Temple in several locations; those deaths, some by murder and others by suicide, were followed by more in 1995 and 1997.

Although the shocking cases were quickly homogenized by journalists and anticult activists, each group and the violence it experienced had a distinctive character. The Solar Temple, for example, grew out of the Western esoteric cultic milieu. Its founder, Joseph Di Mambro (1924–1994) was a member of the Rosicrucian Order, AMORC, from 1956 to 1969. During the 1970s, he operated as an independent New Age teacher. In 1973, he founded the Center for the Preparation of the New Age in France near the border with Switzerland. Later, in 1976, he founded a communal group, Le Pyramide, in Geneva; it was followed in 1978 by The Golden Way Foundation. Golden Way gave birth to The International Chivalric Organization of the Solar Tradition or

Order of the Solar Temple in 1984. In the early 1980s, Di Mambro met the homeopathic doctor and New Age teacher Luc Jouret (1947–1994), who had traveled in some of the same esoteric circles. Jouret joined Di Mambro in establishing the Solar Temple as an initiatory secret society and thereafter served as its primary public representative. The group quickly established a center in Quebec as well as in Switzerland. It had some 442 members at the peak of its membership in 1989.

As its full name suggests, the Solar Temple located itself within the tradition of the medieval Knights Templar. The original Templar group was founded at the beginning of the twelfth century and its members participated in the Crusades to recapture the Holy Land. Multiple contemporary neo-Templar groups trace their lineages back to the medieval period, but their claims cannot be substantiated. Nonetheless, neo-Templar groups have flourished since the nineteenth century as secret societies that blended occult elements, ceremonial magic, theosophical concepts, and Rosicrucian ideas. Di Mambro was also influenced by French esotericists Jacques Breyer (1922–1996), who founded the Sovereign Order of the Solar Temple in 1952 after having mystical experiences, and Julien Origas (1920–1983), who founded the Renewed Order of the Temple in 1968 in a schism from Breyer's group.

Di Mambro presented himself as the only prophetic messenger who was bringing the message of the Great White Brotherhood to humanity at a time of crisis. He also claimed to be the reincarnation of ancient Gods like Osiris and famous historical persons. Di Mambro also saw the Order as producing "cosmic children," most importantly his daughter Emmanuelle, who would rebuild the ancient Temple and prevent the apocalypse. When members of the group named their own child Christopher Emmanuel, however, it contributed to friction that eventually contributed to the deaths in 1994, 1995, and 1997.

In ritual settings, such as initiations into the secret society, Di Mambro claimed that the Cosmic Masters manifested themselves. Defectors from the group, however, exposed Di Mambro's claims as common trickery. Di Mambro initially taught a form of progressive millennialism that anticipated a transformation of consciousness as the world moved from the Age of Pisces to the Age of Aquarius. One of the Order's rituals used the Great Invocation developed by theosophist Alice Bailey (1880–1949) in 1937. It asks that the light in God's mind enter the minds of humans and anticipates the return of Christ as the Buddha Maitreya and the dawn of life in accordance with God's plan.

Di Mambro may always have anticipated a "transit" of his followers to a higher plane, mentioning before 1990 the possibility that flying saucers would take his followers to another world. But the growing fragility of the group due to internal criticism and defections, the perception external opposition sparked by investigations of the Order in Quebec, and Di Mambro's failing health led the Order's understanding of the coming transition to take a pessimistic turn in the early 1990s. By 1993, members had heard enough about the concept of a transit back to the Father or a return to unity with the Divine that they were prepared for its eventuality even if they were not entirely clear about the means by which it would be achieved. Added to that was the concept that the "Elder Brothers of the Rosy

Cross" had already departed the earth at the beginning of January 1994 so that the members of the Order could soon follow them.

Those developments in Di Mambro's theology paved the way for events later in 1994. In early October in Morin Heights, Quebec and two small towns in Switzerland, fifty-three bodies of Order members were found. Some clearly had been murdered, some may have willingly sought help with their transits, and others committed suicide. The power of the notion of a transit was proven in 1995 when another sixteen members died in France and again in 1997 when five more died in Quebec.

See also: Aum Shinrikyō; Branch Davidians; Heaven's Gate; Millennialism; Rosicrucianism; Theosophy; UFO Religions; Violence and New Religious Movements.

Further Reading

Introvigne, Massimo. 1995. "Ordeal by Fire: The Tragedy of the Solar Temple." *Religion* 25: 267–283.

Introvigne, Massimo, & Jean-François Mayer. 2002. "Occult Masters and the Temple of Doom: The Fiery End of the Solar Temple." In David G. Bromley & J. Gordon Melton, eds., *Cults, Religion, and Violence*, pp. 170–188. Cambridge: Cambridge University Press.

Lewis, James R., ed. 2016 [2006]. *The Order of the Solar Temple: The Temple of Death.* New York: Routledge.

Mayer, Jean-François. 1999. "'Our Terrestrial Journey Is Coming to an End': The Last Voyage of the Solar Temple." *Nova Religio* 2: 172–196.

Ordo Templi Orientis

Like Freemasonry from which it drew inspiration, Ordo Templi Orientis is a new religion that also claims to be very old. Founded at the turn of the twentieth century in Germany and Austria by Carl Kellner (1851–1905) and Thedore Reuss (1855–1923), Ordo Templi Orientis began as an institution designed specifically to confer degrees, which would grant members access to special, secret knowledge held only by those in the order. However, Ordo Templi Orientis's scope of interest expanded into multiple areas of occult knowledge, coinciding with the initiation of British occultist, Aleister Crowley (1875–1947) into its ranks.

Though its members had begun dabbling in Gnostic Catholicism and Western Esotericism prior to Crowley's initiation, it was during his tenure Ordo Templi Orientis acquired many of its distinctive characteristics. Crowley was appointed to oversee the order in Great Britain, prompting the creation of the Mysteria Mystica Maxima, which soon became the official initiatory arm of the order and reflected Crowley's intellectual influence. Crowley, who proclaimed himself the prophet of the new Aeon of Horus, composed *The Book of Law* (1910), which laid out the principles of Thelema. Chief among them was the Law of Thelema: "Do what thou wilt shall be the whole of the Law." Thelemic law and practice soon became standard practice among Ordo Templi Orientis practitioners.

Though many of Ordo Templi Orientis's rituals align with those of Freemasonic groups, the language and symbolism are suffused with Thelemic themes.

Much of the ritual involves initiation into various levels of esoteric knowledge about Thelema, though there are rituals that employ magic, even science, to realize humanity's inherent divine ability. These are reflected most readily in the Gnostic Catholic mass, also created by Crowley, which is the primary rite of the Ecclesia Gnostica Catholica (EGC), the ecclesiastical arm of Ordo Templi Orientis. The liturgy is written around the principles of Thelema and culminates with the consumption of the Eucharist, after which the participants proclaim their own divinity. Though viewed by many as blasphemous, the rite is practiced openly and none who are interested in it are turned away. The EGC also performs baptisms and confirmations.

Following Crowley's death, there was a struggle for power and legitimacy in the order. The various branches (Grand Lodges) of the movement, which are often organized by country, each claimed to be Crowley's true successor. Today, the Ordo Templi Orientis maintains a small, but persistent presence in Europe, Australia, and North America. Organized in "lodges," similar to Freemasonry, members continue to live by the Law of Thelema and to attend secret, often subversive, rites that promise to reveal esoteric knowledge.

See also: Crowley, Aleister (1875–1947); Freemasonry; Gardner, Gerald (1884–1964); Gnostic Groups; Magic and New Religious Movements; Occultism and Esotericism.

Further Reading

Bogdan, Henrik, & Martin P. Starr, ed. 2012. *Aleister Crowley and Western Esotericism.* Oxford: Oxford University Press.

Crowley, Aleister. 1938. *Book of the Law.* Samuel Weiser, Incorporated. Originally published in 1904.

Straude, Clyde. 2015. *Ordo Templi Orientis.* Scotts Valley, CA: CreateSpace Independent Publishing Platform.

Otherkin

Otherkin is a religious subculture comprising those who believe they are not completely human, but are part animal, mythological creature such as a vampire or shapeshifter, angel, alien, or faery, among other possibilities. The identification of individuals as "Otherkin" began in the 1990s, though claims to be something other than human have a long history. During the nineteenth century, Spiritualist mediums served as hosts for other, spiritual beings; though these beings were often human, it opened the door to the idea that humans could contain multiple entities, sometimes called "walk-ins," including those that were supernatural or nonhuman. New Age religions, such as Channeling and some branches of Neopaganism, brought these beliefs into vogue during the late twentieth century. Some associate the recent rise of a diffuse, but stalwart, Otherkin community with the profusion of elven and faery communities in the Western United States, while others attribute its rise to the internet, specifically online community forums where the word Otherkin first appeared.

Many Otherkin have resisted the label of "religion," a fact seemingly confirmed by their lack of institutional structure, formal liturgical or theological system, and a definitive set of practices. There is no "Otherkinism." Nonetheless, many of their beliefs can be seen as fundamentally religious and metaphysical in nature, even if they are diverse and not universally held by all Otherkin. For example, some Otherkin believe that they were born this way and are "awoken" to this fact, an event that maps onto the experience of conversion for its suddenness. Many believe their current state is the result of reincarnation and is evidence that their souls have progressed in their spiritual evolution. Otherkin of various ilks cite different origin stories, though most are mythological in character and often rooted in folklore and even fiction (such as J. R. R. Tolkien's *Lord of the Rings* trilogy); these stories become sacred in nature, representing the creation narratives of Otherkin. Some Otherkin believe in a concept known as "The Veil," which posits that there exists a barrier between the natural and supernatural realms, which will be broken open at some point, thus allowing for the spread and practice of magic and supernatural abilities throughout the world. On its own, the belief that one is Otherkin constitutes a worldview that replaces religion, since it helps individuals who identify as such to explain the world around them and their place in it.

Most Otherkin claim unique physical characteristics or abilities, such as heightened senses, either high or low body temperature, unique eye color, or traits that might be considered physical deformities but are also signs of their nonhuman side. Those who identify as Vampires seemingly fall under the umbrella of Otherkin, however, they remain relatively separate from other varieties of Otherkin and do not often self-identify as such. Otherkin may meet in person, though their primary contact is often through the internet. It is through the support of this community, however scattered, that Otherkin exhibits their clearest religious dimension, namely, that of acting the part of a religious institution, which provides support, legitimacy, and information regarding their experiences and lives as Otherkin.

Otherkin have experienced criticism from those who perceive the religion as fetishistic and related to the fulfilling of sexual fantasies, thus confusing Otherkin with "Plushy" and "Furry" subcultures. Some view the belief of Otherkin that they are part animal as evidence of psychological illness, rather than true belief. Others reject the idea that this constitutes a religion (including some Otherkin) since it exists primarily online. Even some fellow new religionists, such as Neopagans, critique Otherkin for taking mythological lore out of context and interpreting it to fit an individual's religious desire. Otherkin take these critiques in their stride, believing that they cannot live but as their true, not entirely human, selves.

See also: Mediums; Neopaganism; New Age, The; New Religions on/and the Internet; Spiritualism; Vampirism.

Further Reading

Dawson, Lorne, & Jenna Hennebry. 2004. "New Religions and the Internet: Recruiting in a New Public Space." In Lorne L. Dawson & Douglas E. Cowan, eds., *Religion Online: Finding Faith on the Internet*. New York: Routledge Press.

Kirby, Danielle. 2009. "From Pulp Fiction to Revealed Text: A Study of the Role of the Text in the Otherkin Community." In Christopher Deacy & Elisabeth Arweck, eds., *Exploring Religion and the Sacred in a Media Age*. Burlington, VT: Ashgate Publishing.

Laycock, Joseph P. 2012. "'We Are Spirits of Another Sort': Ontological Rebellion and Religious Dimensions of the Otherkin Community." *Nova Religio* 15, no. 3: 65–90.

Ouspensky, P. D. (1878–1947)

Though overshadowed by his teacher G. I. Gurdjieff (c. 1866–1949) and his more flamboyant countrywoman and founder of Theosophy, Helena Petrovna Blavatsky (1831–1891), Pyotr Demianovich (P. D.) Ouspenskii (spelled Ouspensky on most published materials) made contributions to the world of occult religion that would continue to highlight Russia's prominence in Western esotericism. Ouspensky was born in Moscow. Following his expulsion from school, he began working as a journalist and he discovered Theosophy. In 1913, he traveled to Adyar, India, the Eastern center of the Theosophical Society. It was there that he met Gurdjieff, with whom he would study from 1915 to 1918.

Ouspensky had been publishing his own esoteric writings prior to meeting Gurdjieff, including *Tertium Organum* (1912), a book that sought to align scientific discovery with religious knowledge. As a result of his relationship to Gurdjieff, he reworked and republished his earlier ideas to reflect those of his mentor. As in Theosophy, Ouspensky proposed that human beings had the ability to know great, universal truths through their mind (a feature of what he called the "psychological method."). He believed that what little human beings knew of these great truths represented not the beginning of knowledge, but its deterioration. Over many lifetimes, human knowledge had depreciated in the soul and only through active discipline of the mind could one gain back the knowledge lost concerning metaphysics and ultimate meaning.

Soon, Ouspensky's ideas found an audience in Great Britain and the United States when *Tertium Organum* was translated from Russian to English. He began a lecture tour, landing in London, where occult ideas held a certain cachet among the literary and cultural elite (supposedly, T. S. Eliot [1888–1965] was a fan of Ouspensky's work and may have attended his lectures). Particularly attractive were Ouspensky's ideas of a "fourth dimension" that existed beyond time and space and out of which all life emerged and would return in a series of eternal cycles.

Eventually, Ouspensky would part ways with Gurdjieff, finding that his own interpretation of the ideas of his mentor had diverged enough to warrant teaching his own version of Gurdjieff's method, known as "The Fourth Way." According to Gurdjieff and later Ouspensky, the ultimate goal of human existence is "self-development." Self-development occurs in many ways and through various paths. The first path, the Way of Fakir, focuses on development of the physical body; the second path, the Way of the Monk, emphasizes controlling and harnessing emotions; and the third path, the Way of the Yogi, seeks to master the mind and improve mental habits (and, ultimately, capabilities). The Fourth Way represented a combination of all three paths and proceeded on the belief that each person was best attuned to spiritual, mental, and physical betterment when all components of the person were focused and engaged. Ouspensky would still represent his teaching of the Fourth Way as derived from Gurdjieff (hence the title of his book, published posthumously, *The Fourth Way: A Record of Talks and Answers Based on the Teachings of G. I. Gurdjieff*), his inclusion of theories on the fourth dimension, and his uses of modern psychology.

Ouspensky would also teach and practice Gurdjieff's method known as "self-remembering," which involved a deep state of meditation (even sleep) where one was aware not only of what was going on but of one's *awareness* of being aware. In other words, a person who was self-remembering would be able to report on what he or she had learned in this deep state of meditation and the experience of this state and the revelation of knowledge. Ouspensky expressed personal difficulty at both practicing and teaching this method, believing that it was exceedingly difficult to achieve such total, consuming awareness. Nonetheless, Ouspensky emphasized the absolute importance of cultivating self-awareness, believing that self-knowledge was the ultimate intellectual and spiritual aim for all life.

Ouspensky died in 1947, leaving behind a corpus of influential writings on metaphysics and occult knowledge, even if his name was often relegated to a secondary role in the world of Western religious esotericism.

See also: Blavatsky, Helena Petrovna (1831–1891); Fourth Way, The; Gurdjieff, G. I. (c. 1866–1949); Occultism and Esotericism; Theosophical Society, The; Theosophy.

Further Reading
Lachman, Gary. 2004. *In Search of P. D. Ouspensky: The Genius in the Shadow of Gurdjieff.* Wheaton, IL: Quest Books.

Ouspensky, P. D. 1920 [1912]. *Tertium Organum: The Third Canon of Thought, a Key to the Enigmas of the World.* New York: Manas Press.

Ouspensky, P. D. 1957. *The Fourth Way: A Record of Talks and Answers Based on the Teachings of G. I. Gurdjieff.* New York: Knopf Press.

P

Parsons, John Whiteside (1914–1952)

At the same time that he was making important contributions to the development of rocket technology in association with the California Institute of Technology and what became the Jet Propulsion Lab, Jack Parsons was deeply involved with the occult.

In 1939, Parsons became a devotee of Aleister Crowley's (1875–1947) magickal system of Thelema. Parsons saw his scientific career and his devotion to esoteric wisdom as complementary. After he was initiated into the Agape Lodge of the Ordo Templi Orientis (OTO) in the Los Angeles area, he quickly became an influential participant and rose to a position of leadership. In 1941, Parsons joined with other occultists to live communally in a large estate in Pasadena, which also served as the headquarters of the OTO. There he would continue his excursions into the occult in the company of a diverse array of bohemians, science fiction writers, and scientists.

In 1945, Parsons met a newly discharged naval officer, L. Ron Hubbard (1911–1986), and began a friendship, even though Parsons's girlfriend at the time soon took up with Hubbard. Parsons believed that Hubbard possessed substantial magickal talents and enlisted him as a ritual partner. Following Crowley's teaching and using the practices of Enochian magic, Parsons undertook a series of ritual actions designed to invoke the Thelemic goddess Babalon, which though present in everyone, could manifest in a specific woman. Parsons understood his "Babalon Working" as nothing less than an attempt to turn the world away from its domination by a malevolent force and toward love, understanding, and freedom.

From January 4 to 15, 1946, Parsons performed various rituals in the Mojave desert, with, he claimed, Hubbard serving as his "scribe." When Parsons returned home he met for the first time Marjorie Cameron (1922–1995), whom he identified as the manifestation of Babalon. They quickly fell into an intense sexual relationship, understood by Parsons to be an effort to produce a "moonchild" who would possess extraordinary knowledge and power. The ritual activities continued into March and Parsons related his extraordinary experience to a bewildered Crowley.

Parsons's "Babalon Working" both provides a glimpse into the practice of Crowleyan magick in the United States and raises questions about Parsons's possible influences on Hubbard's system of Dianetics, which would be announced to the world in 1950. While the Church of Scientology has disavowed any connections between Dianetics and Scientology and Parsons's occultism, some scholars have argued that Parsons may have constituted one of the many influences that Hubbard assimilated and transformed as he worked out his own therapeutic and religious system.

See also: Crowley, Aleister (1875–1947); Dianetics; Hubbard, L. Ron (1911–1986); Magic and New Religious Movements; Ordo Templi Orientis; Scientology.

Further Reading

Bogdan, Henrik. 2016. "The Babalon Working 1946: L. Ron Hubbard, John Whiteside Parsons, and the Practice of Enochian Magic." *Numen* 63: 12–32.

Carter, John. 2004. *Sex and Rockets: The Occult World of Jack Parsons*. Fort Townsend, WA: Feral House.

Pendle, George. 2005. *Strange Angel: The Otherworldly Life of Rocket Scientist John Whiteside Parsons*. New York: Harcourt.

Pastafarianism (The Church of the Flying Spaghetti Monster)

Pastafarianism (or the Church of the Flying Spaghetti Monster), which began as an internet spoof in 2005 (www.venganza.org), has emerged as a religious movement that continues to test the boundaries of religious freedom and the definition of religion itself. In response to the Kansas State Board of Education's decision to devote equal time teaching intelligent design and evolutionary theory in science classrooms, Bobby Henderson (1980–) sent the Board a letter satirizing creationism. A physics graduate of Oregon State University, Henderson posited that since proponents of intelligent design employ ambiguous language about the "creator" of the universe, it was just as feasible that this creator was actually a supernatural being who resembled a bowl of spaghetti and meatballs. The exchange that followed, which Henderson posted to his website, became an internet phenomenon, garnering equally positive and negative responses.

The beliefs of Pastafarians can best be understood as inversions or parodies of traditional Christian beliefs. Pastafarians argue that the Flying Spaghetti Monster created the universe after a night of heavy drinking, which helps to explain the world's "fallen" state. Given the fallen state of the world, human beings need someone to lead them away from sin and toward salvation—which is typically the role Jesus plays having "died for our sins." However, in Pastafarian belief, it is the Flying Spaghetti Monster himself who will intervene, since "he boiled for our sins." Those who are saved will ascend to a heaven that includes a "beer volcano" and a stripper factory. Hell is a lesser version of heaven—no fire and brimstone, but the beer is stale and the strippers have sexually transmitted diseases. Additionally, Pastafarians maintain that pirates were the original Pastafarians. Their reputations have been maligned by other religious institutions, but they were in fact a peace-loving bunch, whose mission was to spread joy (and candy) around the world.

Shortly after issuing his letter to the Kansas Board of Education, Henderson published *The Gospel of the Flying Spaghetti Monster*, which employs humor to "debunk" evolutionary theory and to propose the proper Pastafarian way of life. Accompanying their own sacred canon is a Pastafarian liturgical calendar, with

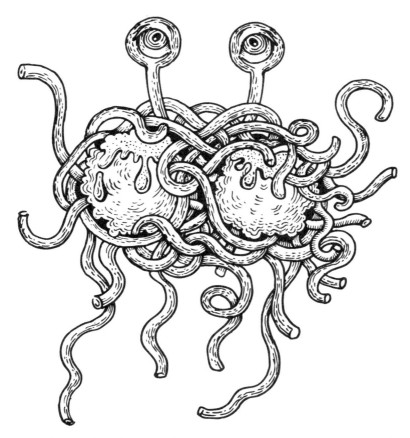

Unlike some religions, Pastafarianism has no strictures against depicting the deity, in this case an amalgam of spaghetti strands and meatballs with eyes at the ends of two of the noodles. The image reinforces the church's humorous approach to religious issues. (Alexander Pokusay/Dreamstime.com)

weekly Sabbaths (where every prayer is ended with "Ramen," rather than "Amen") and Pastafarian versions of major holidays from various religions (including Christmas and Passover, which they term "Pastover").

Though Pastafarian beliefs walk a fine line between satire and genuine belief, Pastafarians have made a very real mark on conversations regarding religious freedom in the United States. While a federal judge decided against the protection of the Church under the First Amendment, individual Pastafarians have won the ability to wear the traditional headwear of Pastafarianism—the colander—in legal ID photos. Begun as a spoof, Church of the Flying Spaghetti Monster provides a critical and satirical eye to notions of belief and the rights of those belief systems to exist or to impose on the worldview of others.

Further Reading

Cusack, Carole. 2010. *Invented Religions: Imagination, Fiction and Faith.* New York: Ashgate Publishing.

Henderson, Bobby. 2006. *The Gospel of the Flying Spaghetti Monster.* New York: Villard Books.

Patrick, Ted (1930–)

A chance meeting on the Fourth of July between his son and nephew and emissaries of the Children of God (now The Family) ignited Ted Patrick's interest in groups he identified as "cults." At that time, in the summer of 1971, Patrick was serving as Governor Ronald Reagan's Special Representative for Community Relations in San Diego and Imperial counties in southern California. The Children of God, which had been founded in Huntington Beach, California, were then actively proselytizing among young people. Patrick was appalled by what he saw as instantaneous negative changes in the two teenagers and began to learn more about the group.

Soon after that initial encounter, a woman came to Patrick's office concerned about the disappearance of her own son on the same day. It turned out that he had gone off with the Children of God. Patrick determined that he had a problem on his hands. Concluding that the issue fell within the responsibilities of his office, he began to research the Children of God and was soon in contact with scores of families whose children had joined. By the Fall, Patrick had resigned from his job to tackle the problem of cults full-time.

Patrick quickly concluded that the dramatic changes experienced by young members of the Children of God had an equally dramatic explanation. He believed that the group practiced "on-the-spot hypnosis" that effectively programmed or reprogrammed their recruits. To extricate them from the group, he asserted, they needed to be "deprogrammed." Patrick thus introduced the concept of deprogramming into the contemporary battle against new religions.

Patrick's deprogramming was a crude tool. Avowing that neither the law nor any form of counseling could prevail against cults, he took matters into his own hands. His form of deprogramming involved kidnapping individuals against their will, holding them captive in remote locations, and haranguing them until they gave up their new beliefs. Though Patrick denied that he was in it for the money and simply wanted to free individuals from the cultic constraints to which they had been subjected, he managed to turn deprogramming into a well-paid career for a time.

Patrick joined forces with a group of parents whose children had joined the Children of God and in 1972 was instrumental in founding FREECOG (Free the Children of God), the original, contemporary anticult group in the United States. Eventually, the violent excesses of Patrick's form of deprogramming caught up with him, and he was convicted on charges of kidnapping in 1980. Beginning in the 1980s, the anticult movement began to turn away from involuntary deprogrammings toward ostensibly more therapeutic forms of removing individuals from stigmatized religious groups, called exit counseling.

See also: Anticult Movement, The; Brainwashing; Cult; Deprogramming; Exit Counseling; FREECOG (Free the Children of God); Love Israel Family, The.

Further Reading

Patrick, Ted, & Tom Dulack. 1976. *Let Our Children Go!* New York: E. P. Dutton.

Shupe, Anson D., & David G. Bromley. 1980. *The New Vigilantes: Deprogrammers, Anti-Cultists, and the New Religions*. Beverly Hills, CA: Sage.

Pentecostalism

For many in the United States, the news that Pentecostalism counts around a quarter of a billion believers worldwide will come as a shock. Many have not heard of Pentecostalism or have reduced its adherents to those who "speak in tongues." The gift of tongues exists, certainly, but it represents one tiny facet of a variegated, global Christian phenomenon. Born of nineteenth-century American holiness movements, shaped by overt Biblicism, millennialism, and a belief in the active working of the Holy Spirit, and tied to both progressive and conservative strains of social and political religiosity, Pentecostalism is a new religious movement that is as hard to definitively categorize as it is easy to miss.

ORIGINS AND EARLY HISTORY

The term Pentecostalism derives from the Christian holiday of Pentecost (which corresponds roughly to the Jewish holiday of Shavuot or the Feast of Weeks and is celebrated fifty days after Easter in the Christian calendar). As related in the second chapter of the Book of Acts, as the Apostles gathered in Jerusalem to celebrate Shavuot, "a violent wind came from heaven and filled the whole house where they were sitting" (Acts 2:2, NIV). With this wind, the Holy Spirit brought to each of them the gift of tongues, enabling them to speak in a variety of new languages for the purpose of bringing the Gospel to the broader, gentile world (Acts 2:3–4). As the Apostles spoke in various tongues, many gathered, each hearing the Gospel spoken in their own language. Though some who gathered were skeptical, Peter confirmed that the gift of tongues was a sign of the "last days" or, as many Pentecostals now argue, evidence of the "latter rain" (Acts 2: 5–17). Though it was tongues addressed in this passage, for Pentecostals, the broader significance of this passage was the appearance of holy gifts as evidence of the Holy Spirit's active work in the world and the fact that the world was nearing its end.

The belief in spiritual gifts associated with the latter rain characterized nineteenth-century Holiness movements. Holiness doctrine arose from Methodism and the Wesleyan (so named for Methodism's founder, John Wesley [1701–1791]) doctrine of sanctification or "second work of grace." Separate from "new birth" (the first work of grace, where the believer is reborn through Christ), sanctification means the transformation of a Christian toward holy living and holy "being," which may even result in perfection—a phenomenon known as Christian perfectionism.

Charles Fox Parham (1873–1929), who is touted as a progenitor of Pentecostalism, was a Methodist and Holiness preacher. After a miraculous recovery from illness, which he attributed to divine intervention, he began preaching on the power of divine healing. After traveling to hear other Holiness preachers and founding his own school, Bethel Bible College, Parham began instructing his ministerial students that true baptism implied a fuller experience of the Holy Spirit than allowed by current Christian denominations. Reportedly, as a

Pentecostalism was a charismatic Christian movement that emerged in the early twentieth century. Characterized by ecstatic experience, including the ability to speak in tongues and prophecy, it ultimately grew exponentially (and continues to grow, particularly in the global south), producing numerous denominations. Pentecostalism was also home to a number of religious celebrities, including Aimee Semple McPherson (depicted here), whose charismatic and spirit-driven performances allowed her to traverse the traditional gender boundaries of the twentieth century. (Aimee Semple McPherson. *This is That*. Los Angeles: Echo Park Evangelistic Association, 1923)

preacher, he witnessed parishioners speak in tongues and even healed a few. Parham's ministry came to be known as the "Apostolic Faith movement." Then, in 1903, Parham met William J. Seymour (1870–1922), a partially blind African American man who felt called to the ministry. Subject to the pervasive racism of his context, Parham did not allow African Americans to enroll at his school; instead, he allowed Seymour to listen to lessons outside of the classroom window. Parham and Seymour did, however, preach alongside each other, due in great part to Seymour's charisma and oratorical ability.

Seymour and Parham parted ways in 1906 when the former accepted a call to serve as a pastor in Los Angeles. Shortly after his arrival at Azusa Street, Seymour built a robust, multiracial congregation. Even before the events that would be known as the "Azusa Street Revival" began, Seymour's congregation experienced steady growth and an outpouring of spiritual gifts. However, when the Revival began in late Spring of 1906, both the congregation and the signs of the Holy Spirit grew exponentially. One of Seymour's parishioners Frank Bartleman (1871–1936) served as a scribe for the Revival and published *How Pentecost Came to Los Angeles* (1925; later, *Azusa Street*). He identified the San Francisco earthquake, which took place on April 18, 1906, as a sign and precipitating event for the Revival, thereby aligning world events with the great experience of the Spirit. Many cite the Asuza Street Revival as the founding moment of modern

Pentecostalism and as foreshadowing of the multiracial, diverse phenomenon it has become.

Since its early-twentieth-century beginnings, Pentecostalism has grown and innovated even as it has experienced schism and critique, particularly in the United States. Many Pentecostals who rejoiced at Azusa Street were averse to the interracial ethos of the Revival, thus breaking off to form all or majority-white denominations. At the same time, women preachers such as Maria Wood-worth-Etter (1844–1924) and Aimee Semple McPherson (1890–1944) opened doors for female leadership among Pentecostals often unheard of in other denominations. Women have played a pivotal role in Pentecostalism from its outset. They comprised a large majority of Pentecostal adherents from the outset, and McPherson is often touted as one of (if not the) first religious celebrity. In terms of their relationship to their peers, while Pentecostals tend to align theologically (and often politically) with conservative Christians, their more established brethren often viewed with disdain their effervescent worship and belief in continuing revelation and spiritual gifts. Following World War II, Pentecostals experienced a modicum of acceptance among their Christian peers, both as the Charismatic movement brought Pentecostal-style worship into the mainstream and as religious "celebrity" preachers like famed healer Oral Roberts (1918–2009) attracted large, often nondenominational audiences to the movement.

BELIEFS AND PRACTICES

Pentecostalism is a variant of Charismatic Christianity. Charismatics are those, generally, who share a belief in spiritual gifts, the possibility of miracles, and who place emphasis on the work of the Holy Spirit in the world. Not all Charismatics are Pentecostals, however. Many Charismatics belong to "mainline" Christian or evangelical denominations; in such cases, either the denomination or the members themselves emphasize spiritual gifts without formally aligning with Pentecostal denominations. Many argue that Pentecostals represented the earliest so-called "wave" of Charismatic Christianity, which saw the creation of independent Pentecostal denominations. In the latter decades of the twentieth century, Charismatics often opted to remain in their original denominations and reform its worship from within. Charismatics often viewed their Pentecostal coreligionists as slightly more conservative, perhaps even "backward" when it came to issues of dress, consumption of alcohol, and gender roles. However, the rise of Charismatic Christianity in the latter half of the twentieth century has evidently had a mitigating effect on Pentecostalism, which generally has become more progressive. Together, Charismatic and Pentecostal Christians make up over a quarter of the world's Christians (around 570 million).

In many fundamental ways, Pentecostals share traditionally Protestant beliefs. Most emphasize the centrality of the Bible as a source of sacred authority, even if they may vary on questions of the Bible's inerrancy and whether its words are verbally inspired by God. Belief that salvation is possible as a result of the death and resurrection of Jesus Christ is standard. Many Pentecostals have absorbed the millennialism that characterized the movement's beginnings, believing that they are living in the last days and that Christ's return will occur in their lifetimes.

Central to Pentecostal belief is Holy Spirit baptism. Often (though not always), the sign of Holy Spirit baptism is the awarding of "spiritual gifts." In the scheme of Pentecostal salvation, baptism of the Holy Spirit is the third work of grace, which equips the believer for spreading the Gospel, in emulation of the Apostles after Pentecost. Not every individual who receives the third work of grace experiences spiritual gifts, but many do. One of the most common spiritual gifts is defined as words of wisdom, which describes revelations by the Holy Spirit that helps the recipient to find in the Bible an answer to a contemporary situation. Words of knowledge, on the other hand, are revelations that inform an individual about what God intends to do in his or her life or in the life of another. Pentecostals are open to such revelations and expect that the Holy Spirit will speak to them at one point or another.

The more outwardly identifiable spiritual gifts include speaking in unknown tongues, translating the message of those who speak in tongues, prophesying, and healing. The gift of tongues can manifest in earthly languages previously unknown to the speaker or can occur in a divine vernacular. Thus, those who are able to translate the message of the earthly or divine speech may be able to provide illumination on anything from a stubborn passage in scripture to a contemporary crisis; occasionally, translators may prophesy future events. Prophesying may also arise unaccompanied by translation. For someone gifted with prophecy, they can discern signs in the surrounding world or in scripture, which often pertain to the approaching millennium and Christ's Second Coming. Finally, healing, which is perhaps the most visible spiritual gift after the ability to speak in tongues, is perhaps the most extraordinary of all. From its early-twentieth-century outset, Pentecostal preachers and laity alike reported miraculous healings.

One of the greatest schisms within Pentecostalism occurred over the nature of the Trinity. The vast majority of Pentecostals are Trinitarian, meaning they maintain a belief that God, Christ, and the Holy Spirit are distinctive, eternal, and divine personalities who exist together as one Godhead. Oneness Pentecostals are those who believe that there is one divine entity and one divine personality, which was Jesus Christ. God the Father and the Holy Spirit were titles assumed by Christ at different times and for different purposes. However, worship and devotion were directed toward Jesus alone, confirmed by the fact that salvation came via Christ. Oneness Pentecostalism arose from the Assemblies of God denomination.

A GLOBAL PHENOMENON

Beyond broad divisions in Trinitarian theology, there are hundreds of different Pentecostal denominations. Among the major denominations is the

Foursquare Gospel Church, which was founded by Aimee Semple McPherson in 1923 and now counts around eight million members worldwide. The Assemblies of God, which encompasses a network of loosely affiliated churches, numbers members around seventy million and is the largest Pentecostal denomination in the world. Assemblies of God arose out of the Church of God in Christ or COGIC, which began as Holiness denomination whose founders attended the Azusa Street Revival and aligned the denomination with the new Pentecostalism shortly thereafter. In 1914, however, due to racial tensions with a rapidly diversifying COGIC, a group of members broke off to form the Assemblies of God. To this day, COGIC remains a predominantly African American Pentecostal denomination, with the greatest concentration of its members (approximately seven million) in the United States. There are also a great number of small and independent Pentecostal churches. As of 1994, the Pentecostal/Charismatic Churches of North America and the Pentecostal World Conference represent formal attempts to align a vast and diverse movement.

The greatest growth in Pentecostalism has occurred in the Global South, particularly in South America and Africa; in fact the majority of Pentecostals live outside of the United States. The interracial character of the movement, its effusive and lively worship style, and its emphasis on gifts of the Holy Spirit have proven incredibly attractive to those outside of the United States.

See also: Gender and New Religious Movements; Globalization and New Religious Movements; Healing, Health, and New Religious Movements; Millennialism; Seymour, William (1870–1922).

Further Reading

Anderson, Allan Heaton. 2013. *To the Ends of the Earth: Pentecostalism and the Transformation of World Christianity.* Oxford: Oxford University Press.

Cox, Harvey. 2001. *Fire from Heaven: The Rise of Pentecostal Spirituality and the Reshaping of Religion in the 21st Century.* Cambridge, MA: De Capo Press.

Espinosa, Gaston. 2014. *William J. Seymour and the Origins of Global Pentecostalism: A Biography and Documentary History.* Durham, NC: Duke University Press.

Payne, Leah. 2015. *Gender and Pentecostal Revivalism: Making a Female Ministry in the Early Twentieth Century.* Basingstoke, UK: Palgrave McMillan.

Wacker, Grant. 2003. *Heaven Below: Early Pentecostals and American Culture.* Cambridge, MA: Harvard University Press.

Peoples Temple

Over the course of its short history, Peoples Temple went through dramatic changes. The group is now indelibly linked with the tragic deaths of more than nine hundred people at the Peoples Temple Agricultural Mission in Jonestown, Guyana on November 17–18, 1978. For many, Peoples Temple has become a primary example of the dangers inherent in cult membership. But the path that brought the interracial congregation under the leadership of the Rev. Jim Jones (1931–1978) to its climax in the Guyanese jungle is less well known.

EARLY YEARS

Founded by Jones in Indianapolis in the mid-1950s, Peoples Temple focused its ministry on promoting racial equality and civil rights for disenfranchised African Americans and working-class whites. In high school, Jones developed an interest in the Christian communism of Acts 2:44 and 4:32, where members of the early Christian community are described as holding all things in common. That understanding of what true Christianity demanded would provide a model for the organization of Peoples Temple throughout its history, even as the group's theology moved further away from Christianity.

When he began Peoples Temple (with no apostrophe to signal that no one owned it), Jones was in his twenties. He had become interested in religion as a youth when he attended services at the Church of the Nazarene with a neighbor, Myrtle Kennedy, in Lynn, Indiana. As he grew older, Jones would preach his message of racial equality informally to African Americans and poor whites in nearby Richmond, Indiana. Jones eventually became a student pastor at Somerset Methodist Church in Indianapolis in 1952. His attendance at revival meetings around the same time gave his developing preaching style a Pentecostal flair. By 1954, he had founded his own Church, Community Unity, which mixed attention to the practical needs of his congregants with faith healing and a message of racial equality. Both Jones's message and his racially mixed congregation seemed radical to many in 1950s Indiana.

Community Unity grew quickly and soon left behind its original name. It was briefly known as Wings of Deliverance and then became Peoples Temple. It then became Peoples Temple Apostolic Church and finally, in 1959, Peoples Temple Christian Church Full Gospel. In 1960, Peoples Temple became part of the Disciples of Christ denomination, an affiliation that it retained to the end. By 1960, Peoples Temple was at least 20 percent African American, and that percentage may have been higher. Jones's experiment in brotherhood and racial equality was taking concrete shape. At the same time, it was also provoking negative reactions from other churches and some citizens of Indianapolis. Jones suffered under the strain of such opposition and eventually left Indianapolis for two years, leaving the Temple in the hands of associate ministers.

When Jones returned at the end of 1963 to Peoples Temple from his sojourn in Belo Horizonte and Rio de Janiero, Brazil, it was on the verge of collapse. Tensions between members who emphasized social activism and those who preferred Pentecostal worship had led to significant departures. Jones himself had become convinced of an impending nuclear war, due in part to a vision he experienced in 1961. He had even discussed moving the Temple before his return from Brazil, since he was convinced that any blast that took out Chicago would destroy Indianapolis as well. Jones's commitment to the sharing of resources for the common good was also increasing. Jones concluded that his congregation needed a safe haven from both the nuclear threat and oppressive discrimination. He was also developing the sense that he was something more than a pastor: he was a prophet with special powers.

FROM INDIANA TO CALIFORNIA

In 1965, the Jones family and some eighty-five members of Peoples Temple moved to Ukiah and Redwood Valley, California. In the new context, the African American members of the Temple were constantly harassed. External hostility led the group to band more closely together and Peoples Temple moved further toward becoming a self-sustaining communal group. In early 1969, Peoples Temple moved to its own church-building in Redwood Valley. By that time, the group also had other businesses that provided income, including ranching and farming. The church also helped its members who were eligible to collect benefits from the social welfare system. Several members of the local Mendocino County welfare office even joined Peoples Temple.

The church's advocacy for the rights of individuals also helped attract new members.

In California, Peoples Temple also attracted young, college-educated white members whose political idealism led them to embrace its racial equality and economic egalitarianism. Some of those members would occupy important leadership roles in the church, and some would eventually play crucial parts in a group formed to combat Peoples Temple, the Concerned Relatives, after they left the church.

The group in Redwood Valley was not wholly self-contained, however. Jones extended his proselytizing efforts throughout the West Coast. The church developed a substantial presence in both the Bay area and Los Angeles. Jones's message continued to move away from mainstream Christianity, though it retained its emphasis on "apostolic social justice."

As it had in Indiana, Peoples Temple became a political force. In Indianapolis, Peoples Temple's outspoken efforts at integration had earned Jones the position of director of the Indianapolis Human Rights Commission in 1961. In San Francisco, the ability of Temple members to mobilize African Americans drew the attention of liberal George Moscone, who was in a tight race for mayor. Temple members were recruited to get out the vote, and when Moscone won the election in 1975, Peoples Temple, and Jones, received some of the credit. Jones was eventually appointed to a seat on the San Francisco Housing Commission. With that success, the Temple increased its focus on political matters.

LIFE IN PEOPLES TEMPLE

The public face of Peoples Temple as a progressive church dedicated to racial equality and serving the least fortunate did not wholly capture what life was like for the members. The church did manage to create a community in which the dignity and contributions of all members, particularly senior citizens, were recognized and celebrated. Through its various enterprises, Peoples Temple provided meaningful work for members as well as income for the group. By providing room, board, and a small allowance for members who donated their paychecks to the church, the Temple reinforced group solidarity. It also kept members busy supporting the proselytizing trips that Jones organized.

Most importantly, however, Peoples Temple gave members a concrete outlet for their idealism. It lifted many of its members out of poverty and assured them that any discrimination that they experienced was unjust and that the work of the Temple could make a positive difference in the world. That reassurance was especially important for those, including the Indiana members who had followed Jones to California, who sacrificed much or all of their previous lives to join the group. Members of Peoples Temple believed that their commitments to social change were both being realized within the Temple community and were serving as a model for everyone else.

But harsher measures were also implemented to ensure that individuals put the needs of the group above their own. Even during the time in Indianapolis, church members were required to participate in "corrective fellowship" sessions in which they would be criticized by fellow members for falling short of expectations. In Redwood Valley, similar meetings were held weekly and individuals were expected to confess publically their shortcomings, which ranged from the mundane to the fantastic. Punishments could include assigned extra work, but corporal punishment was also used on occasion.

Over time, Jones also tried to regulate the sex lives of Peoples Temple members. He matched couples and encouraged some of them to have children and others to remain celibate. More dramatically, Jones encouraged all members, male and female, to confess their sexual interest in him. Despite remaining married to his wife, Marceline, he also initiated affairs with several young women in the Temple. Though they provoked some defections, all of those activities increased Jones's hold over the members who acceded to his desires.

A challenge for those members who thought they had joined a Christian congregation was Jones's growing disenchantment with the Bible. Jones had come to see the Bible, particularly in its King James translation, as providing a charter for racism, sexism, and other problems in society. He questioned whether the Creator God was truly a good God who cared for all humans. In contrast, Jones lauded the principle of "Divine Socialism." He eventually presented himself as the embodiment of that socialism.

Despite the Temple's emphasis on social equality, its membership was also stratified. Though he held ultimate authority, Jones consulted with a planning commission that included around hundred members by 1977. But within that group there were also several inner circles, each of which was privy to at least some of the secrets of the organization. The most powerful inner circle included Marceline, Carolyn Moore Layton, and several men. But Jones kept knowledge about the inner workings of Peoples Temple carefully compartmentalized, even among the inner circle.

FROM CALIFORNIA TO GUYANA

Peoples Temple's rise to prominence in California attracted more scrutiny of the group. Even before the Temple received recognition for its support of Moscone's campaign, in 1972, Lester Kinsolving had published an exposé in the *San*

Peoples Temple

Francisco Examiner that noted, among other things, Jones's contempt for the biblical Creator. But the greatest impact came from a 1977 article in *New West* magazine by Marshall Kilduff and Phil Tracy. Informed by disgruntled members of Peoples Temple, they accused the Temple of financial fraud, physical abuse of members, and harassment of ex-members. Before the article appeared, Jones left California for Guyana.

Peoples Temple had leased three thousand acres from the socialist Guyanese government in 1974, with the intention of establishing a utopian socialist community. By the middle of that year, Temple volunteers were clearing land for the Peoples Temple Agricultural Mission, known as Jonestown. It was not easy work and it became much harder when nearly a thousand members of Peoples Temple followed Jones to Guyana in the summer of 1977. Fending off the encroaching jungle and providing sufficient food for a group that included large numbers of seniors and children severely taxed the able-bodied members.

The community at Jonestown was fragile, and Jones was convinced that external enemies were arrayed against it. In mid-1977, an organized opposition to Peoples Temple had coalesced around a group of former members. Their tales of financial chicanery, being worked to exhaustion, and being physically abused found a sympathetic audience among members of the press. Eventually, the negative press captured the attention of Representative Leo Ryan (D-CA), who resolved to investigate.

Ryan's appearance in Guyana set in motion the demise of Peoples Temple and the deaths of nearly all of its members. When a handful of members expressed their desire to leave Jonestown with Ryan, Jones saw their departure as an extraordinary betrayal. When Temple members murdered Ryan and four others at the nearby Port Kaituma airstrip, Jones anticipated punitive action. In an extraordinary decision, he exhorted the members to follow him in an act of "revolutionary suicide." The decision to die was captured on an audiotape, on which Jones asserts that the only way to preserve the cause of Peoples Temple was to die for it. When one of the residents asked Jones about alternatives, he informed her that there were none and another member encouraged her to die for her ideals. Eventually, more than nine hundred adults and children died at Jonestown, including Jones. The hope that their self-sacrifice would attract the admiration of the world was not realized, however. Instead, for many, Jonestown and Peoples Temple became testimonies to the dangers of charismatic leaders and groups identified as cults.

See also: Jones, Rev. Jim (1931–1978); Millennialism; Violence and New Religious Movements.

Further Reading

Chidester, David. 2003. *Salvation and Suicide: Jim Jones, the Peoples Temple, and Jonestown*, rev. ed. Bloomington: Indiana University Press.

Hall, John R. 1987. *Gone from the Promised Land: Jonestown in American Cultural History*. New Brunswick, NJ: Transaction Publishers.

Moore, Rebecca. 2009. *Understanding Jonestown and Peoples Temple*. Westport, CT: Praeger.

Moore, Rebecca. 2018. "Alternative Considerations of Jonestown and Peoples Temple." April 6, 2018. Available at: https://jonestown.sdsu.edu/.

Prabhupada, A. C. Bhaktivedanta (1896–1977)

Religions from Asia have come to the West through a variety of means. In the United States, the Immigration and Nationality Act of 1965 abolished de facto discrimination against Asians and other groups in immigration. That paved the way for an influx of Asian religious teachers, including A. C. Bhaktivedanta Swami Prabhupada.

Born Abhay Charan De in Calcutta in 1896, Prabhupada worked in pharmaceuticals for most of his life. He was initiated into the Gaudiya (Chaitanya) form of Vaisnavism, which considers Vishnu the supreme God, in 1933. In 1936, he was charged by his spiritual director, Bhaktisiddhanta (1874–1937), to spread Krishna Consciousness in the West. It took time for that charge to come to fruition.

In 1950, Prabhupada left his family and resettled in Vrindavan, the sacred city where Krishna, the eighth avatar of Vishnu, purportedly spent most of his childhood. In 1959, Prabhupada became a monk and spent his time writing and performing devotions. Only in 1965, at the age of sixty-nine, did Prabhupada set sail for the United States. But by 1966, he had formed the International Society for Krishna Consciousness in New York and soon after attracted "Hare Krishnas" throughout North America and Europe, including George Harrison (1943–2001) of the Beatles.

The way in which Prabhupada constituted his authority is distinctive. In his most well-known work, *Bhagavad-Gītā As It Is* (1984), he situates himself as the thirty-second in a "disciplic succession" (*parampara*) that reaches all the way back to Krishna. Chaitnya Mahaprabhu (1486–1534), the founder of Gaudya Vaisnavism, was the twenty-second in that line. Prabhupada emphasized that someone can only properly learn about God through a bona fide guru, who is the absolute authority. That underlined the importance of the unbroken line of succession that he claimed.

It is not the guru's personal qualities, but rather his possession of the correct teaching, that matters. In his introduction to *Bhagavad-Gītā As It Is*, Prabhupada consistently stresses that the text can speak for itself; it needs no human interpretation but only acceptance as the ancient wisdom that it is. Thus, charisma is invested in the ancient texts rather than in the person of the guru. The guru ensures that the message of the ancient texts, which comes directly from the deity, is communicated without alteration. Yet, without Prabhupada, there is no opportunity for others to understand the meaning of, for example, the Bhagavad Gita. What is distinctive about ISKCON, he claims, is that it has appeared at a time when people all over the globe are hungering for religious wisdom.

See also: Charisma and Leadership in New Religious Movements; International Society for Krishna Consciousness (ISKCON); Seekers.

Further Reading

Bryant, Edwin F., & Maria L. Ekstrand, eds. 2004. *The Hare Krishna Movement: The Postcharismatic Fate of a Religious Transplant*. New York: Columbia University Press.

Prabhupāda, A. C. Bhaktivedanta Swami. 1984. *Bhagavad-Gītā As It Is*. Los Angeles: International Society for Krishna Consciousness.

Rochford, E. Burke, Jr. 1985. *Hare Krishna in America*. New Brunswick, NJ: Rutgers University Press.

Prophecy in New Religious Movements

Prophets, prophesying, and prophecy are a common feature of religious traditions, particularly those in the Abrahamic vein (Christianity, Judaism, and Islam). The term "prophet" comes from the Greek term for "spokesman," which, in a religious sense, means a spokesman for God or the divine. Accounts of prophets are replete in texts like the Bible and Qur'an, and generally involve an individual who is contacted by a divine entity for a particular purpose.

Sometimes a prophet's role is foundational, such as the prophet Muhammad, whose encounter with God initiated the religion of Islam; sometimes it is redemptive, as was the case for those like Moses or, for Muslims, Jesus, who led their people to a better future; and sometimes it is forewarning, such as Jeremiah, who foresaw doom for those who failed to obey. Sociologist Max Weber (1864–1920) further nuanced the term by parsing ethical from exemplary prophets: ethical prophets are those who are tasked with spreading a divine message and who command obedience to it whereas exemplary prophets are those who may have no such divine imprimatur, but who live lives that others will seek to emulate.

While many prophets arise to strengthen or renew an established tradition, new religious movements are often created around a particular prophet or upon a particular prophecy. The notion that an individual has special contact with the divine or supernatural can entice seeking individuals to leave their prior religious affiliation. Yet, the risk can often outweigh the reward. Fulfilled prophecies would represent a tremendous boon to a religion and seemingly prove doubters wrong in an instant; however, failure is more likely. New religions or individuals that claim prophetic authority may see their prospects sink when prophecies fail to materialize; it is often the mark of a sustainable new religion when prophets are able to "routinize" their claims to special authority into institutions or theological systems.

CLAIMING PROPHETHOOD

Though many have claimed to be prophets, only a few can boast establishing followings large enough to be considered viable religious movements or institutions. Often the success of a given prophet results from some combination of the personality or charisma of the prophet in question, the context in which the prophet arises or the prophecy occurs, the nature of the prophetic message, and the willingness of believers to accept and disseminate the truth of this message.

Joseph Smith Jr. (1805–1844) combines all of these factors: known for his personal magnetism and conviction, even at the ripe age of fourteen when he learned he was a prophet, Smith rose to prominence during a period of growth and chaos, where competition between sects yielded many who were searching for the "right" religion. Smith and his early band of followers founded the Church of Jesus Christ of Latter-day Saints in 1830, grounding its establishment in Smith's prophetic authority as the person tasked by God to create the true Church on earth. Further, though only the Prophet could receive revelation that could become scripture and act as binding for believers, Smith opened the door for others to receive messages from the divine as well. By tying prophetic authority to the office of the prophet rather than to himself, Smith facilitated the transfer of prophetic power to a successor, which became necessary following his martyrdom in 1844. To this day, the Mormon Church is headed by the Prophet, appointed by the Quorum of Twelve Apostles from among their ranks.

Some prophets and prophecies are tied to particular historical moments, causing them to be rather short lived. The Ghost Dance Movement, a millennialist revitalization movement among American Indians, particularly the Lakota Sioux, grew from the prophecies of Wovoka (né Jack Wilson; 1856–1932), a Pauite Indian. Wovoka received a series of visions promising the imminent return of Christ, which would usher in the end of white European rule in the American west, the resurrection of the ancestors, and the return of the buffalo. To bring this to pass, Wovoka encouraged all tribes to dance the Ghost Dance, a ritual that would last many days and induce trances in those who practiced it. The movement came to a tragic end at Wounded Knee when over two hundred unarmed Lakota were massacred by U.S. soldiers. Though Wovoka was not present at Wounded Knee, the momentum built around his prophetic message fizzled as did his personal claims to prophetic authority.

Though equally tied to its historical context, the Nation of Islam has survived through the years. Inspired by the message of a mysterious man, Wallace D. Fard (c. 1877–c. 1934), who claimed that blacks were the true chosen people and their true religion was Islam, Elijah Poole (1897–1975) sought him out in 1931, telling Fard that he knew him to be Allah. Fard admitted as much but also bestowed upon Poole the title of Prophet—the last prophet. Elijah Poole became Elijah Muhammad, whose prophetic status and message included a rewriting of biblical history in such a way as to cast white people and whiteness as the result of evil experiments and black people as God's chosen from whom everything had been stripped—until then. Muhammad attracted numerous African Americans whose experience in the United States as a maligned and systematically oppressed minority had stripped them of their self-worth; the Nation of Islam gave it back to them. Muhammad, among other things, prophesied a time when blacks would be ascendant in and as their own nation if they would convert to Islam. His death brought the effective end of prophetic authority for the Nation of Islam, though it continued despite the lost direct connection to God.

For some religious traditions, such as Pentecostalism, prophecy was never the purview of one person, but was evidence of a divine gift given to believers. Pentecostalism arose from a series of revivals that occurred at the turn of the twentieth century when numerous people experienced the "latter rain," which gestured to the imminent end of the world and manifested itself in various gifts of the Holy Spirit. Most commonly associated with Pentecostalism is the gift of tongues or the ability to speak in different, most likely divine, languages. However, prophecy is also a gift of the Holy Spirit. Those who are gifted the ability to prophesy rarely attempt major prophecies, such as setting the date for the end of the world, and often stick to generalities. Nonetheless, prophecy is democratized and expected as a feature of a world swiftly coming to a close.

FAILED PROPHECIES AND THEIR CONSEQUENCES

The vast majority of prophecies fail. All prophecies that have predicted the end of the world have failed, for example. Some religions crumble following failed prophecies, others adapt. What would compel someone to remain in a religious tradition following a failed prophecy? When the alternative is a crisis of faith or identity, it makes sense that victims of false prophecy would seek to make sense of the nonevent. Some blame human error and reinvest in the idea that no one can know, truly, how divine events unfold. Others may argue that a particular prophecy did come to pass, but in a different form than originally predicted. Occasionally, new religions are born from the ranks of those left bereft from such failures.

One of the most famous examples of failed prophecy involved the Millerites and their leader, William Miller (1782–1849). Miller made a careful study of the Bible and claimed, through a series of complex calculations, to be able to predict the precise date of Christ's Second Advent. He published his findings and soon garnered a significant following, both near and far. Miller predicted that Christ would return sometime between March 21, 1843, and March 21, 1844. When this time period passed with no event, Miller conceded he had made an error, but claimed to correct it and set a new, definitive date: October 22, 1844. This date would come to be known as "the Great Disappointment" when, again, Christ failed to appear.

Though most Millerites had remained steadfast up to that point, this failure led to a mass defection from Miller. Still, not all rejected completely the idea that Miller's date-setting had merit. A group of former Millerites including Ellen Gould White (1827–1915) argued that Christ's return had been a spiritual one, not a physical one; instead of returning to earth, Christ moved to a different room in heaven where he now sat in judgment of humanity, marking the end of the period of probation for human sinfulness. This group, soon known as the Seventh-day Adventists, were galvanized by White, whose own prophetic abilities guided the movement toward a particularly way of living in constant preparation for the Day of Judgment.

Failed prophecies are by no means a thing of the past with multiple new religious movements and prophetic figures taking the risk to varying effect. The

496   Prophecy in New Religious Movements

Church Universal and Triumphant (CUT) led by Elizabeth Clare Prophet (1939–2009) experienced a sharp drop in membership after Prophet predicted that nuclear war would break out on March 15, 1990. Urging followers to give up their lives and livelihoods and move to Montana to safely await the end of the world, CUT experienced significant backlash when the predicted war did not occur. Despite the immediate loss of members, Prophet adapted by claiming that the efforts of her followers had prevented apocalypse for the time being; CUT, though somewhat diminished, still operates today. Chen Tao, a Taiwanese religious movement, experienced a steady decline following a failed prophecy. Founder Hon-Ming Chen (1955–) predicted that in March 1998, Jesus would appear twice: first on television and then in person in Garland, Texas (where the group had relocated). When Christ failed to appear, Teacher Chen, as he was known, sought to spiritualize Christ's visit like the Seventh-day Adventists had after the Great Disappointment, but to no avail. The movement ultimately foundered a few years later.

On occasion there are movements that must adjust expectations when part of a prophecy fails. Such was the case for Heaven's Gate when one of its leaders, Bonnie Lu Nettles, died in 1985. Prior to her death, Nettles and Applewhite, known as "Ti" and "Do," respectively, predicted that they along with their followers would be transported bodily to The Evolutionary Level Above Human. However, Nettles's death ultimately paved the way to a position that advocated for "graduation" or ritual suicide; now, the bodies of Heaven's Gate members would need to die physically before they could be transported to spaceships where their transformation would take place.

Clearly, becoming a prophet and issuing prophecies is a high-risk, high-reward endeavor depending upon the nature of the prophecy and the commitment of those involved. The appeal of prophecy for many is that, if proven right, their belief may bring reprieve from catastrophe, at the least, and divine reward, at best. Even at the risk of a crisis of faith (which, confoundingly for many on the outside, is not the most likely outcome), people seek prophets for their connection to the divine and prophecies for their mitigation of the unknown.

See also: Applewhite, Marshall (1932–1997), and Bonnie Lu Nettles (1927–1985); Charisma and Leadership in New Religious Movements; Chen Tao; Church of Jesus Christ of Latter-day Saints, The; Church Universal and Triumphant, The; Ghost Dance Movement (Wovoka); Heaven's Gate; Millennialism; Miller, William (1782–1849); Millerites, The; Muhammad, Elijah (1897–1975); Nation of Islam, The; Prophet, Elizabeth Clare (1939–2009); Seventh-day Adventism; Smith, Joseph (1805–1844); White, Ellen G. (1827–1915).

Further Reading

Dawson, Lorne L. 1999. "When Prophecy Fails and Faith Persists: A Theoretical Overview." *Nova Religio* 3, no. 1: 60–82.

Harvey, Sarah. 2014. *Prophecy in the New Millennium: When Prophecies Persist.* Farnham, UK: Ashgate Publishing.

Stone, Jon R. 2000. *Expecting Armageddon: Essential Readings in Failed Prophecy.* London: Routledge.

Stone, Jon R. 2014. "Prophecy." In George D. Chryssides & Benjamine E. Zeller, eds., *The Bloomsbury Companion of New Religious Movements*. London: Bloomsbury Publishing.

Tumminia, Diana G. 2005. *When Prophecy Never Fails: Myth and Reality in a Flying Saucer Group*. Oxford: Oxford University Press.

Tumminia, Diana G., & William H. Swatos, Jr., eds. 2011. *How Prophecy Lives*. Leiden: Brill.

Prophet, Elizabeth Clare (1939–2009)

In 1930, an "Ascended Master," identified as Saint Germain, contacted Guy Ballard (1878–1939) at Mount Shasta in California. Ballard went on to become the founder of the "I AM Activity," which focused on helping individuals realize the true "God Self" or "Christ Self" within. Although Ballard's group was virtually destroyed by an ongoing and unprecedented legal case of mail fraud, where it was accused of sending false teachings through the U.S. Postal Service, it served as an important bridge between its Theosophical predecessors and elements of the later New Age milieu.

As Ballard's movement dwindled due to its legal troubles and external critiques, several offshoots developed. One was the Lighthouse of Freedom, founded in 1958 by former participants in Ballard's movement. The newsletter of the Lighthouse featured further communications from the Ascended Masters, channeled through an anonymous receiver. That contact person turned out to be Mark L. Prophet (1918–1973), who had begun receiving messages from the Master El Morya in 1952. In 1958, Prophet founded the Summit Lighthouse in Washington, D.C. In 1963, Mark married Elizabeth Clare Wulf Ytreberg (1939–2009), whom he had met in 1961, and began to tutor her in his developing theology. Elizabeth had practiced Christian Science in her youth and young adulthood and was also familiar with the Theosophical Society and the I AM Activity.

Elizabeth proved to be an apt pupil and by the late 1960s was serving as a comessenger with her husband. After his sudden death in 1973, she established herself as the unquestioned leader of the Summit Lighthouse, which in 1974 she renamed the Church Universal and Triumphant (CUT). One of her early actions as leader was to declare that her husband, like Guy Ballard, had ascended and become one of the Masters, named Lanello.

Elizabeth saw herself as continuing a tradition that included the Ballards but also drew on many other sources. She emphasized that each individual has a divine potential that, when realized, can lead to ascension and uniting with the "I AM Presence." Prominent ritual actions include spoken affirmations and prayers that promote and reinforce an individual's realization of the "Holy Christ Self."

Like others in the esoteric and New Age milieus Elizabeth claimed to have recovered the lost teachings of Jesus, especially those he developed during his "lost years" in India. From Indian teachers, Jesus learned concepts like karma and reincarnation, which locates CUT's eclectic blend of religious ideas firmly in an authoritative past.

Prophet, Elizabeth Clare

Elizabeth also inherited from Mark a millennialist focus. As early as 1965, Mark Prophet had warned that evil extraterrestrials had long been endeavoring to impede the path to spiritual perfection. When Elizabeth assumed the leadership of the movement, she added her own twist. Although it was not the only focus of her teachings, she repeatedly warned about the possibility of a nuclear conflict. That led to conflicts with law enforcement when the movement was accused of stockpiling weapons.

By the beginning of the 1980s, the church began to purchase parcels of land in an isolated area of Montana adjacent to Yellowstone National Park. A move to the new headquarters took place gradually from 1981 to 1986 as the church acquired more land and established a largely self-sufficient community in the wilderness, known as the Royal Teton Ranch. In late 1985, Saint Germain, through Elizabeth, confirmed the importance of the new location as a spiritual center. The following Thanksgiving Saint Germain directed the members of CUT to prepare for a coming nuclear war by building underground fallout shelters. After some indecision about the date of the impending catastrophe, the church eventually determined that it could be expected on March 15, 1990. When CUT's prediction suffered the same fate as other attempts to set the time of the end, the church lost thousands of members and entered a cycle of ongoing transformations, including a short-lived attempt to integrate into the general New Age movement and recruitment drives outside the United States, particularly in Latin America.

But the most jarring event after the 1990 disconfirmation of prophecy was Elizabeth's own withdrawal from the movement she had led for more than twenty years as the result of Alzheimer's disease. Her declining health forced on the movement the necessity of developing an organizational structure that could persist in her absence of its messenger.

Elizabeth's withdrawal from active leadership of CUT created a leadership vacuum even while she remained alive. She could not establish a leadership transition within the family, similar to her succeeding Mark, because her daughter Erin had resigned from the church in 1993, followed by her son, Sean, in 1994, and daughter Tatiana in 1995. Although different individuals or groups have occupied leadership roles since Elizabeth's withdrawal and death, no new messenger of the Ascended Masters has been recognized. Estimates of the membership of CUT vary widely, but it is clear that it never reached the heights that it had before the failed prophecy in 1990.

Like other new religions the church has experienced both controversies, including allegations of staff misconduct, and schisms (see www.templeofthepresence.org), but it continues an active ministry through its website (www.summitlighthouse.org), groups in some cities, and conferences at the ranch.

See also: I AM Activity, The; Law Enforcement and New Religious Movements; Millennialism; New Age, The; Occultism and Esotericism; Theosophy.

Further Reading
Lewis, James R., & J. Gordon Melton, eds. 1994. *Church Universal and Triumphant in Scholarly Perspective.* Stanford, CA: Center for Academic Publication.

Noonan, John T. 1998. *The Lustre of Our Country: The American Experience of Religious Freedom.* Berkeley: University of California Press.

Prophet, Elizabeth Clare. 2009. *In My Own Words; Memoirs of a Twentieth-Century Mystic.* Gardiner, MT: Summit University Press.

Prophet, Erin. 2009. *Prophet's Daughter: My Life with Elizabeth Clare Prophet Inside the Church Universal and Triumphant.* Guilford, CT: The Globe Pequot Press.

Prophet Erin, & Susan Palmer. 2018. "Church Universal and Triumphant/Summit Lighthouse." *World Religions and Spirituality Project.* Available at: https://wrldrels .org/2018/04/08/church-universal-triumphant-summit-lighthouse/.

Whitsel, Bradley. 2003. *The Church Universal and Triumphant: Elizabeth Clare Prophet's Apocalyptic Movement.* Syracuse, NY: Syracuse University Press.

Pursel, Jach (Lazaris) (1947–)

The development of the New Age religious milieu in the 1960s and 1970s brought with it an array of individuals who claimed to be able to communicate with realms beyond the mundane. Although that phenomenon had significant antecedents in, for example, nineteenth-century Spiritualism, from the 1960s on, it took on a distinctive name, channeling. Individual channels, frequently operating in trance states, broadcast the teachings of a diverse array of deities, deceased individuals, and other disincarnate figures. One of the most popular channels was Jach Pursel (1947–), who continues to be the sole communicator of the teachings of Lazaris, a self-described spark of consciousness without physical form.

Pursel's experience with Lazaris officially began on October 4, 1974, though Lazaris notes that he had been tentatively in touch with Pursel through many prior lifetimes. As with many other events that initiated religious innovations, Pursel's experience was not something that he sought, but rather something that came to him unbidden. He thought that he had fallen asleep while trying to meditate, but two hours later when he apologized to his wife, Peny, she told him that he had been channeling Lazaris the entire time. Lazaris claimed that he had intended to speak only with Peny, but soon agreed to communicate with a broader audience. After a short period of adjustments, a small circle of Pursel's friends began interacting with Lazaris. Pursel got to know him by what his friends reported after he had exited his trance state.

Lazaris's distinctive reason for communicating with those on the physical plane is that he is simply interested in learning about human experience. In turn, he offers both opportunities for humans to see their experience from his perspective and to learn about his own reality. Lazaris emphasizes a mutual exchange with his audience. He rejects the ideas that he is a savior, father figure, or some sort of guru. Instead, he positions himself as a friend who will make suggestions, particularly about how his audience might create a reality that is more congenial to them. But he will never tell them what to do. Lazaris's avuncular presence effectively reassures his audience that they can develop in the ways that they want to, with his gentle guidance.

Lazaris's teachings fit well within the general New Age milieu. His emphasis on individuals' ability to create their own realities echoes a very prominent theme.

Also, his acknowledgment that every human has lived multiple past lives fits with a general emphasis on reincarnation.

Although the official website presents Lazaris's followers as a community, like the audiences for other channels they form a community of a distinct sort. They may come together at workshops and other public events in shifting patterns of participation, but the community is largely maintained online through a forum hosted at the Lazaris website and through an active Facebook group. Lazaris thus has both a clientele that interacts with him through discrete events and a worldwide audience that constitutes a spiritual community without forming a corresponding social group. Thus, the audience for Lazaris echoes other characteristics of the New Age milieu, including its individualism, focus on self-development, and minimal social structures.

Lazaris and Pursel quickly moved from channeling for a small circle of friends and acquaintances to offering more structured workshops. Pursel now offers both live workshops and a variety of pay-per-view events, including archived "legacy" events, that can be accessed through his website (www.lazaris01.worldsecuresystems.com). The site offers a variety of other products for sale, including books, videos, music, and talismans crafted by Pursel under the guidance of Lazaris that individuals can use in their own practice.

Like many other channels, Pursel has been criticized for charging for his services and for claiming a monopoly on the communications from Lazaris. He had organized the Synergy Foundation in 1977 and transformed it into Concept Synergy in 1980, which remains the business entity that organizes all of Pursel's activities on behalf of Lazaris. Comparatively little material from Lazaris, therefore, is available for free in any medium. Pursel's tight hold over the Lazaris material seems to some to be antithetical to the characterization of Lazaris as a concerned friend.

See also: Channeling; Knight, JZ (Ramtha) (1946–); Mediums; New Age, The; Spiritualism.

Further Reading

Brown, Michael F. 1999. *The Channeling Zone: American Spirituality in an Anxious Age.* Cambridge, MA: Harvard University Press.

Lazaris. 1997. *The Sacred Journey: You and Your Higher Self.* Palm Beach, FL: NPN Publishing.

Lazaris. 2017. "Awakening the Love." Available at: https://www.youtube.com/watch?v =_yGaRFXbiSc.

Quimby, Phineas (1802–1866)

Though Mary Baker Eddy (1821–1910), founder of Christian Science, would eclipse her former teacher in renown, she owed a great deal of her religious thought to Phineas Parkhurst Quimby. In fact, the New Thought movement, which ran parallel to Christian Science, grew out of Quimby's discoveries around "Mind Cure," or the power of the mind to remedy all ailments, whether physical, mental, or spiritual.

Born in Lebanon, New Hampshire, Quimby was sickly as a youth. Once prescribed calomel (mercury chloride) by a doctor to cure a bout of tuberculosis, Quimby grew frustrated at traditional medical practices when the calomel began to rot his teeth. He began to experiment with alternative cures, which brought him in the path of Charles Poyen (?–1844), a French mesmerist, who was traveling a lecture circuit in the United States in beginning of 1838.

MESMERISM AND MIND CURE

Mesmerism, or animal magnetism, named for its founder Franz Anton Mesmer (1734–1815), was a theory that posited the existence of an invisible force that permeated all living beings (from plants to humans). This force or substance could be manipulated, often through hypnosis, to alter the physical environment, including healing various ailments. When Quimby first heard Poyen lecture on Mesmerism in 1838, he realized quickly that this was the method for which he had been looking. Though a clockmaker by trade, Quimby left his job to shadow Poyen on his lecture tour and to learn the art of mesmerism.

Returning to New Hampshire in 1840, Quimby began his own mesmerist practice, where he reported numerous successful healings. He also began to adapt mesmerism according to his own discoveries. Over time, Quimby concluded that achieving a successful cure depended more on the patient's state of mind than on the mesmerist methods employed; if people believed they were being cured, they would be cured, or if they believed they could not be cured, they would remain ill. This was the basic premise of his theory of "Mind Cure."

Though Quimby never renounced mesmerism or its methods—employing them throughout his life—he soon attracted students who wished to learn (and be healed by) Mind Cure. Among those students was a perennially ill young woman named Mary Baker (later Eddy), who came to Quimby for healing in 1862. Similar to Quimby, she had been disappointed with Western medicine and sought a different sort of cure. Eddy and Quimby would later diverge in their views: Eddy, following a fateful fall in 1866, attributed her recovery to the Bible and prayer and a new theory she called "Divine Science." Quimby, though never dismissive of a divine cause or source of healing, was reticent to cast his successful healings as "divine" or "miraculous," seeing them as the result of natural practices.

Quimby continued to perform healings and practice Mind Cure until his death in January 1866.

LEGACY

Phineas Parkhurst Quimby was the progenitor of "Mind Cure," a nineteenth-century practice, which posited that many human ailments exist solely in the mind and can be cured by "right thinking." While treating patients using Mesmeric practices, Quimby discovered that those who believed they would be cured ultimately healed more quickly or fared better in general. (Cirker, Hayward and Blanche Cirker, eds. *Dictionary of American Portraits*, 1967)

Many of Quimby's works were published posthumously, content as he had been to maintain a small practice and teach those who came to him. It was through his students that Quimby and Mind Cure rose to fame as the founder and founding method, respectively, of New Thought. Warren Felt Evans (1817–1889) had been healed by Quimby and became his student and an unofficial scribe for the Mind Cure movement. His book *The Mental Cure* was published in 1869. Evans would go on to found his own mind-cure sanitarium in Massachusetts, which became the primary conservator of Quimby's methods, and continued to publish on mind cure and metaphysics.

Eddy distanced herself from Quimby, not only due to differences in thought but because her detractors had accused her of plagiarizing Quimby's ideas in her own theology. Under Eddy, Christian Science would take on its specifically religious cast, namely, by affirming that God was the ultimate reality and that humans were inherently divine. However, Quimby's legacy would live on in the central New Thought belief that a person's mental state was ultimately responsible for their own well-being and that of the world.

See also: Christian Science; Eddy, Mary Baker (1821–1910); Healing, Health, and New Religious Movements; Mesmerism; New Thought.

Further Reading

Evans, Warren Felt. 1886; 1869. *The Mental Cure (Illustrating the Influence of the Mind on the Body, Both in Health and Disease, and the Psychological Method of Treatment)*. Boston: Colby and Rich Publishers.

Hughes, Ronald. 2009. *Phineas Parkhurst Quimby: His Complete Writings and Beyond*. Howard City, MI: Phineas Parkhurst Quimby Resource Center.

Seale, Ervin. 1997. *Mingling Minds: Phineas Parkhurst Quimby's Science of Health and Happiness*. Camarillo, CA: Devorss & Co.

R

Race and New Religious Movements

Religions are meaning-making systems: they construct how people perceive and understand the world around them and their place in it. These meanings are often tied to questions of transcendent truth, salvation, and life after death. Thus, as systems that shape how people understand these matters of ultimate concern, religion has served as a source of solace, agency, and redemption, on the one hand, and disenfranchisement, oppression, and violence, on the other. Similarly, the social category of "race" has become a means by which people understand the world and their place in it. As history has shown, however, race was born from colonialism and conquest as a system of categorizing those who were non-white and, more often than not, justifying their subjugation. When religion and race intersect, particularly in the creation of new religions, the mixture produces both movements devoted to maintaining racial division and hierarchy and movements devoted to healing and empowering people in spite of *or* because of their race. Though there are numerous new religious movements that could be included in this discussion regarding race, this entry examines those that stem from the Judeo-Christian tradition and those that relate to either black or white racial identity.

Religions have also been implicated in the perpetuation of racial categories or even their creation. The Curse of Ham, for example, has been employed by white structures of power to subjugate blacks. Ham, the son of Noah, saw his father drunk and naked, resulting in a curse placed on his offspring, Canaan, and his line. From this story, grew the pseudobiblical myth that the line of Ham was black; thus, to be black was to be cursed. Further, the terms "blackness" and "whiteness" took on theological weight as well: to be "black" of soul meant one was full of sin and bound for hell, whereas if someone's soul were "white," then she or he was likely saved. (Or in the case of American Indians, "redness" or "the red man" was often equated to Satan and the demonic as well).

In the colonial context, specifically the era of slavery, religion served as a source of racial subjugation and redemption. Religion was a tool of the oppressor; slave masters consulted the Bible, and religious institutions blessed the cause of evangelism through enslavement. Many new religions were forged in the crucible of slavery. Most of these religions were creole, meaning a mixture of African, indigenous, and colonial, usually Christian, religions. Examples include Umbanda in Brazil, Santería in Cuba, Vodou in Haiti, and Hoodoo in the southern North American mainland (later United States). These religions acted as sites of resistance for slaves whose actions were often monitored and who could find ways of subverting the system through religious ritual. One need look no further than the

506 Race and New Religious Movements

Haitian Revolution of 1791, which was a successful slave rebellion and began with a Petro Vodou ritual, to see how religion acted as a means of uniting and energizing black slaves.

Religious innovation extended beyond the era of slavery, well into the twenty-first century, with new religions that attempted to create genuine interracial initiatives (with varying degrees of success), movements that empowered a particular race, and religions that sought to place one race over others.

INTERRACIAL UTOPIAS

Today one of the largest global Christian movements is Pentecostalism, which is particularly popular in the global South. Many trace the origins of Pentecostalism to an interracial revival that caught fire in Los Angeles in 1906. William Seymour (1870–1922), a partially blind, black pastor who preached about spiritual "gifts," such as the ability to speak in tongues and heal, presided over the revival, which brought together people of all races. Though white members of the growing denomination of Pentecostalism would split to form their own denomination, the Assemblies of God, the interracial character of Pentecostalism has continued to characterize its modern and global outlook.

Though less far-reaching, Father Divine's (c. 1876–1975) International Peace Mission Movement was intentionally interracial from the start. Divine (né George Baker) was black, yet he encouraged his followers to understand that race was an illusion. His second wife was a white woman, still a scandalous pairing for the early twentieth century, but one that reflected the intentional "color-blindness" of his mission. Divine received criticism, given his commitment to outreach and community unity, for remaining aloof to systemic racism and injustice; eventually, he became more vocal on the subject, supporting social and political efforts at integration.

The most recent famous example of an interracial utopia was Peoples Temple. Founder Jim Jones (1931–1978) had been raised among white supremacists and learned quickly that he wished to break that cycle. After becoming ordained in the Disciples of Christ denomination, he founded his own church, Peoples Temple, wherein he preached a doctrine of racial equality, social justice, and charitable outreach. He attracted a wide and interracial group of followers who were attracted to his message in the context of a U.S. society where racial equality was the exception. Eventually, Jones would declare that as the embodiment of Divine Socialism, he was God and he was black. Following Peoples Temple's move to Jonestown, Guyana, the interracial initiatives became overshadowed in the popular mind by rumors of Jones's paranoia and, eventually, the mass suicide that ended the movement in 1978.

BLACK ETHNIC RELIGIONS

In the twentieth century, the United States witnessed a boom of "black ethnic religions." These religions wove together historical, religious, and racial

Race and New Religious Movements

narratives, which elevate black people to the status of "chosen ones." Enslaved Africans and their descendants had lost a sense of their own history and had been ascribed a new story by white people, one seemingly confirmed by biblical precedent and relegated to a perpetual inferior status. Black ethnic religions not only rejected these whitewashed versions of history, but reworked them to prove the reverse: that black people were the original people and white people were the experiment gone wrong.

One of the first black ethnic religions was Noble Drew Ali's (1886–1929) Moorish Science Temple. Ali taught that all blacks were originally descended from the Moors (Spanish Muslims) and thus were Muslim by descent. He insisted that members of the Temple carry ID that designated their race as "Moor" rather than "Negro," thus defying the racial designations imposed upon them. Building on this idea years later, Dwight York founded the United Nuwaubian Nation of Moors (1945–) as an eclectic mix of black nationalism, Islam, esotericism, and later New Age and Amerindian religions. For black people, Islam posed an attractive alternative to Christianity. Like Christianity, it shared a devotion to a sacred text, claimed descent from Abraham, and enjoyed a vast global community. Unlike Christianity or its Euro-American variety at least, it had not been shaped by white people and through white institutions.

Such thinking was foundational to the Nation of Islam (NOI), founded by W. D. Fard (1877–c. 1934) in 1930s Detroit. Elijah Muhammad (né Poole; 1897–1975) preached the notion that black people were the original, chosen people. In a revision of biblical history, Muhammad revealed that a scientist named Yacub had created white people, a cursed and abominable race who were prophesied to reign over the chosen race for centuries until a chosen time. Muhammad maintained that the time for the return of black people to their rightful status was now. After converting to the NOI while in prison, Malcolm X (né Little; 1925–1965) became its most visible figure during his tenure as the powerful and charismatic preacher of Temple No. 7 in New York City. X spoke often about the belief that "to be black was to be Muslim." Today, Louis Farrakhan (1933–) leads the reborn NOI after a large portion of the group followed Muhammad's son and converted to Sunni Islam; Farrakhan is touted as the keeper of Muhammad's black nationalistic message. The Nation of Gods and Earths (Five Percenters) was born from the NOI, as its founder Clarence 13X Smith (1928–1969), interpreted Muhammad's teachings to mean that, in fact, every "Asiatic Black Man" was god in the flesh.

Just as the NOI had been influenced by Marcus Garvey's (1887–1940) plea for black nationalism and pan-Africanism, Rabbi Wentworth Arthur Matthew (1892–1973) found inspiration in the notion that blacks were joined not just by history, but by blood. He founded the Commandment Keepers in 1919 and reinterpreted biblical history as one that favored blacks as those with a covenant with God. Matthew famously reworked the Curse of Ham narrative to show that even though Ham was black, the descendants of Ham married the descendants of Shem (the progenitors of white people) and it was through them that Abraham descended. Thus, Abraham was black and the Hebrews, the chosen people, were as well. The Nation of Yahweh also self-identifies as a religion of black Jews, with the explicit mission of returning the original Israelites, black people, to Israel.

508   Race and New Religious Movements

This phenomenon was not exclusive to the United States. In Jamaica, Rastafarianism arose as a religion of social protest that celebrated the idea that God was Black. Following the coronation of Ethiopian prince Ras Tafari Makonnen, who took the imperial name, Haile Selassie I, Jamaicans believed that the Messiah (as predicted in the Hebrew Bible) walked the earth. As originally conceived, Rastas believed that the Messiah would lead all black people to Ethiopia. However, when that exodus failed to materialize, Rastas, instead, interpreted Selassie's coronation as a metaphor for the self-determination and agency of black people throughout the diaspora. In their home communities in Jamaica and beyond, Rasta beliefs and rituals are built around principles of black autonomy and empowerment and the avoidance of "Babylon," or white civilization.

RELIGIONS OF WHITE SUPREMACY

Religion has served as a tool of white supremacists since the colonial period, if not earlier. Such theological and symbolic assertion of white superiority did not die when the colonial era or World War II ended, but was reborn in a number of white supremacist religions. Christian Identity (CI) takes a specifically Christian and anti-semitic approach to white supremacist religion. Born in England in the early twentieth century, CI is rooted in devotion to "whiteness" and traces the lineage of Anglo-Saxons to the Israelites. Adherents believe that the "serpent seed of Cain" or the descendants of Eve and Satan (not Eve and Adam) represents the Jews and all those who are non-white. They advocate for a strict form of racial segregation, one that ensures the dominance of the chosen, white people over everybody else. They are premillennial in belief, meaning that they believe that the Second Coming of Christ is imminent and will most likely be ignited by a race war.

Unlike CI, the World Church of the Creator (also called Creativity) is overtly anti-Christian as well as being anti-semitic, Neo-Nazi, and white supremacist. Adherents maintain that their race is their religion and reject all supernatural religious beliefs or explanations for world events. Despite this, they maintain a canon of scriptures, holy days, and practices, while eschewing traditional theology. They believe that, at all times, they are involved in a racial holy war with all non-whites.

Some forms of contemporary Paganism, such as Ásatrú, have also been associated with white supremacist ideas.

See also: Ali, Noble Drew (1886–1929); Ásatrú; Black Judaism; Christian Identity; Farrakhan, Louis (1933–); Father Divine (c. 1876–1965); Hoodoo; International Peace Mission Movement; Jones, Rev. Jim (1931–1978); Malcolm X (1925–1965); Moorish Science Temple of America, The; Muhammad, Elijah (1897–1975); Nation of Gods and Earths, The (The Five Percent Nation); Nation of Islam, The; Nation of Yahweh, The; Pentecostalism; Peoples Temple; Rastafari; Santeriá; Seymour, William (1870–1922); Umbanda; United Nuwaubian Nation of Moors, The; Vodou; World Church of the Creator.

Further Reading
Barkun, Michael. 1997. *Religion and the Racist Right: The Origins of the Christian Identity Movement.* Chapel Hill: University of North Carolina Press.

Clark, Emily Suzanne. 2019. *Race and New Religious Movements in the U.S.A.: A Documentary Reader*. New York: Bloomsbury Academic.

Dallam, Marie. 2016. "Race and Ethnicity." In *The Bloomsbury Companion to New Religious Movements*. New York: Bloomsbury Academic.

Johnson, Sylvester. 2015. *African American Religions, 1500–2000: Colonialism, Democracy, and Freedom*. Cambridge: Cambridge University Press.

Weisenfeld, Judith. 2016. *New World A-Coming: Black Religion and Racial Identity during the Great Migration*. New York: New York University Press.

Raëlians, The

In the second half of the twentieth century several new religions appeared that traced their origins to encounters between humans and alien beings. The aliens were generally portrayed as superior to humans, with advanced wisdom that they desired to bestow on humanity. The Raëlians are one of the more prominent of those groups.

ORIGINS

The International Raëlian movement developed out of the experiences of Claude Vorilhon (1946–), a French motor sports journalist, race car driver, poet, and singer (see www.rael.org). In December 1973, while walking in the mountainous area near Clermont-Ferrand in southern central France, at Puy de Lassolas, Vorilhon quite unexpectedly saw a "flying saucer" and then met its alien occupant, one of the Elohim. That was the beginning of a continuing relationship, rather than a single, fleeting encounter. In a significant gesture, the alien instructed Vorilhon to return the next day with a Bible and to be prepared to take notes. For the next six days, Vorilhon learned a fantastic take on a familiar story, which he recounted in *The Book Which Tells the Truth* (1974, originally published in French).

In his tutorial, the alien worked through a selective interpretation of the Bible, with particular focus on the creation story of Genesis. As Vorilhon reports, he learned that the biblical creation was the work not of God but of a race of advanced beings and that the earth was only one of many worlds with life. Accordingly, in the Bible, "Elohim" (singular: "Eloha") is the term not for God but for our true creators, "those who came from the sky." Vorilhon also learned that only parts of the Bible were worth paying attention to, and the Eloha guided him through those passages during his week-long lesson.

The Elohim created life on earth as part of a vast series of scientific experiments on many different worlds. In the past they have communicated with figures like Moses and many other prophets, but now, with humanity on the verge of a new era, they have communicated through Vorilhon. They contacted Vorilhon at a turning point in human history. Beginning with the bombing of Hiroshima on August 6, 1945, humanity had entered the "Age of Apocalypse." From then on, humans had the capacity to destroy themselves or to usher in a new golden age of

Raëlism is a UFO religion, of which the primary belief is that the world and all of its creatures were developed by heavenly and scientifically advanced beings known as the Elohim. Elohim is a word for "God" in the Hebrew Bible, hence the reappropriation of the Star of David in the Raëlian symbol. This symbol is controversial because of the prominent placement of the swastika at its center. Raëlians are determined to "rehabilitate" the symbol, which is a Sanskritic symbol referring to infinity in time. (Fancyart/Dreamstime.com)

interplanetary civilization. By heeding the teachings of the Elohim communicated through Vorilhon, humans could advance toward a positive future. Raëlians expect the Elohim to return by 2035.

Vorilhon's contact with the Elohim was not limited to that first encounter. In October 1976, he experienced an ascent to the heavens, which took him to the home planet of the Elohim. There he encountered Yahweh, Jesus, Buddha, and Muhammad, among others. He also learned that like Jesus he was the son of Yahweh. During that trip he was given the name Raël, meaning "the one who brings the light" or "the light of the Elohim." Raël published the narrative of his trip in *Extraterrestrials Took Me to Their Planet* (1977, originally in French), which was subsequently published together with his previous book under various titles. Raël's second encounter with the Elohim also expanded the religious repertoire of his movement to include influences from outside the Jewish and Christian traditions. Raël affirms that all religions have truth in them. In keeping with the millennialist emphasis of his movement, he eventually also came to identify himself as the future Buddha, Maitreya.

BELIEFS, PRACTICES, AND ORGANIZATIONS

Science is central to the Raëlian movement, which contends that the goal of human life is to make scientific progress, so much so that Raëlians declare that "science is our religion." But their faith in science is contradicted by the Raëlians' rejection of the theory of evolution, which clashes with their interpretation of the biblical narratives about the creation of humans. The most prominent indication of the Raëlians' faith in science is their endorsement of the cloning of humans. Raëlians founded Clonaid in 1997 to pursue human cloning and in 2002 announced that an American woman had gone through a cloning process that resulted in a human baby named Eve. Despite their claims, however, the Raëlians could not provide evidence that would satisfy either public or scientific curiosity.

Cloning also comes into play with the initiation ceremonies of the Raëlians. Four times a year new members can go through a ritual that focuses on their establishing telepathic contact with the Elohim and acknowledging them as their creators. As an extension of the ceremony, new members are urged to sign contracts with local morticians that will allow them, after Raëlians' deaths, to remove a square centimeter of the frontal bone of members' foreheads. It is to be held in safekeeping so that a Raëlian might be found worthy to be cloned in the future and then live forever on the planet of the Elohim.

That such eternal life is not guaranteed for every Raëlian also shows the pronounced elitism of the movement. Raëlians unabashedly endorse a form of government that they call "geniocracy" in which the most intelligent and accomplished humans will rule over all others. Cultivating geniuses will help humanity close the gaps in intelligence, creativity, and scientific accomplishments between humans and their advanced creators.

The Raëlians anticipate that the Elohim will return to earth by 2035. In the meantime they are to spread the message that Raël received and also build an embassy to welcome our creators on their return. From the beginning, Raël intended the embassy, for which he has concrete plans and scale models, to be built in Israel, because Raëlians view contemporary Jews as the descendants of those who mated with the Elohim, identified as "sons of God" in Genesis 6. But the Israeli government has not been receptive to that desire and the Raëlians have sought alternative locations.

In many ways, the Raëlians are a world-affirming group. They advocate for what they call "sensual education," which aims at developing all the human senses so that individuals can derive enjoyment from the world in which they live. They specifically practice sensual meditation, which was taught to Raël during his visit

512   Raëlians, The

to the planet of the Elohim to experience a heightened connection between themselves and nature. During the process, Raëlians may imagine themselves to be on the planet of the Elohim and in telepathic communication with them.

From the beginning, the prophet Raël has been the unquestioned leader of the movement. But it has gone through different organizational forms. Soon after his first meeting with the Eloha, Vorilhon founded MADECH (a French acronym for the Movement to Welcome the Elohim, Creators of Humanity). It held its first meeting on the anniversary of Vorhilon's initial contact at Puy de Lassolas. By the beginning of 1976, however, MADECH was dissolved, in part due to infighting in its hierarchy. In its place, Vorhilon developed a new structure that divided the membership into a group of Guides, who accept the authority of Raël as the "Guide of Guides," and an outer group of affiliated Raëlians who pay dues and receive the organization's newsletter, *Apocalypse*.

In July 1998, Raël added a distinctive new group to his organization. Tracing its founding to a revelation he had received the previous December on the anniversary of his first contact, Raël established "The Order of Raël's Angels." The new group would be only for women, roughly similar to orders of nuns within the Catholic Church. Raël would train them to be the ones who would personally welcome the extraterrestrials when they returned. They would function as hostesses, companions, and even lovers for the returning creators. Only they would be permitted to enter the embassy and they would serve as liaisons between the Elohim and the rest of the world. The Angels give further evidence of the Raëlians' positive attitude toward sexuality in its myriad forms. The Raëlians advocate for individuals' freedom to love whomever they chose; they do not recommend marriage and members of the inner group rarely have children.

CONTROVERSIES

Despite some of their more innovative practices, the Raëlians have generally maintained a mild level of tension with their social environment. They have, however, been sharply critical of the Catholic Church, particularly in France. And they have been criticized in turn. As with other new religions, some disgruntled former members have banded together as opponents of the movement, with some of their criticisms, including the allegation that Raël plagiarized the teachings that he attributed to the Elohim, are available on the website, www.raelian.com.

See also: Aetherius Society, The; Cult; Millennialism; Sex, Sexuality, and New Religious Movements; Women in New Religious Movements.

Further Reading
Palmer, Susan J. 2004. *Aliens Adored: Raël's UFO Religion.* New Brunswick, NJ: Rutgers University Press.

Partridge, Christopher, ed. 2003. *UFO Religions.* New York: Routledge.

Raël. 2001. *Yes to Human Cloning: Immortality Thanks to Science.* Vaduz, FL: Raelian Foundation.

Raël. 2005. *Intelligent Design: Message from the Designers.* N.p.: Nova Distribution.

Tumminia, Diane G., ed. 2007. *Alien Worlds: Social and Religious Dimensions of Extraterrestrial Contact*. Syracuse, NY: Syracuse University Press.

Rajneesh, Shree Bhagwan/Osho (1931–1990)

During his career as a religious teacher the man born as Mohan Chandra Jain, and nicknamed Rajneesh, took a variety of titles that signaled who he was and the significance of his work. Virtually from the start the future Osho delighted in rebellion, iconoclasm, paradox, and critique. He stood out in school for his willingness to challenge his teachers but nonetheless earned both BA and MA degrees and began to teach philosophy in Indian colleges. His criticism of Indian society's then-socialist economic principles and religious establishment both angered many and earned him a growing group of disciples. He quickly left university teaching and set himself up as an independent guru, taking the title Acharya ("teacher") in 1966.

By 1970, Rajneesh initiated his first followers, identifying them as *sannyasins* (renunciants) or *neo-sannyasins*, indicating that he had begun a new religious movement. The *neo-sannyasins* wore orange robes and necklaces with a locket containing a picture of Rajneesh. Rajneesh's new religion, however, was distinctive in several ways. In marked contrast to the traditional Hindu understanding of renunciation, Rajneesh's followers were told not to reject the world and adopt asceticism but rather to affirm life and embrace the pleasures that it offers. In an eclectic theology that eventually drew upon elements of many world religions, various philosophers, and Western psychoanalysis, Rajneesh taught that we all have the potential to become Buddhas. He eventually described the ideal as "Zorba the Buddha," a reconciliation of the spiritual and the material that would overcome the damaging separation of the soul from the body.

Soon after he initiated his first *sannyasins*, Rajneesh enlarged his self-understanding, calling himself Bhagwan Shree Rajneesh in 1971. "Bhagwan" derives from the Sanskrit and means holy or divine and is a traditional name for God. "Shree" is an honorific title meaning light or radiance. The new title was both a provocation of traditional believers and a crystallization of Rajneesh's contention that everyone is potentially a Buddha.

Rajneesh's teaching career was successful enough that in 1974 he was able, with the support of some wealthy followers, to establish an ashram in the city of Pune (Poona). There he instructed his followers in the basics of his "religionless religion" and began to attract spiritual tourists from all over the world, including Europe and North America.

The central practice for Rajneesh's followers was "dynamic meditation." In contrast to the focused stillness of many other forms of meditation, Rajneesh's style involves vigorous movement over the course of an hour. It begins with unpatterned fast, chaotic breathing designed to bring internal energy to the surface. That is followed by another ten-minute period in which individuals are encouraged to achieve catharsis by whatever means they choose, including dancing, singing, weeping, and jumping, among other methods. That is followed by another ten minutes of leaping up and landing on the balls of one's feet while repeating the Sufi word Hoo (meaning Him, one of God's names in Islam). Only after that is there a period of silence when individuals freeze in whatever position they had ended up. The meditation ends with a period of free-form dance meant to express the bliss experienced in the fourth state.

The Bhagwan's teachings earned him both an international clientele and concerted opposition in India. In response, he made plans to move his center of operations to the United States In 1981, he purchased and began to occupy the Big Muddy Ranch in central Oregon, which was renamed Rajneeshpuram. On arriving, Rajneesh retreated into silence, only gracing those assembled at the utopian experiment with daily glimpses as he paraded slowly by in one of his Rolls-Royces. Efforts to establish political control over that region of Oregon and violent actions against opponents led to the dissolution of the utopian experiment in 1985 and Rajneesh's negotiated departure from the United States.

Rajneesh eventually resettled in India, reestablished the ashram as a healing and meditation center, and took the name Osho (signifying the oceanic feeling of the mystic and the title for a Zen Buddhist priest) in 1989. Osho's teachings are kept in circulation now by the International Osho Foundation and a few splinter groups.

See also: Globalization and New Religious Movements; Rajneesh/Osho Movement, The.

Further Reading

Milne Hugh. 1986 [2015]. *Bhagawan: The God that Failed.* New York: St. Martin's Press.

Osho. 2000. *Autobiography of a Spiritually Incorrect Mystic.* New York: St. Martin's Press.

Urban, Hugh B. 2015. *Zorba the Buddha: Sex, Spirituality, and Capitalism in the Global Osho Movement.* Berkeley: University of California Press.

Rajneesh/Osho Movement, The

Generally best known outside of India for the dramatic rise and fall of its utopian settlement in central Oregon from 1981 to 1985, the Rajneesh/Osho movement has had both a substantial history before that time and a long life after it. Although its founder, known for a long time as Bhagwan Shree Rajneesh (1931–1990), died in 1990, several groups, including the Osho International Foundation (www.osho.com), continue to make his teachings available.

ORIGINS

Born Mohan Chandra Jain and nicknamed Rajneesh, the movement's leader developed a rebellious and iconoclastic attitude at an early age that led him to critique India's educational, economic, and religious systems. After a brief time teaching in two Indian colleges, he established himself as an independent guru and took the title of Acharya (teacher) in 1966. Rajneesh became the central figure of a new religious movement when he initiated his first followers in 1970. Though he identified them as *sannyasins* or *neo-sannyasins*, they did not conform to the traditional Hindu model of ascetic withdrawal from the world.

Rajneesh's eclectic teaching drew on many religious sources, Western philosophers, and psychoanalysis. He wanted individuals to awaken to the knowledge that they are all inherently divine or Buddhas. But the influences of families, society, politics, and religious institutions have made it difficult for anyone to realize that. He strove to preach a "religionless religion," without organized doctrines, creeds, rituals, or priesthood that could help his followers throw off the negative effects of social conditioning and recover their true identities.

In 1971, Rajneesh began to identify himself as Bhagwan Shree Rajneesh, an identity he would keep for the next fifteen years. His new title had roots in Sanskrit terms, Bhagwan is a name for God and Shree refers to light or radiance. He conceived of his new title as a deliberate provocation of Hindus, Christians, and Muslims.

At the center of Rajneesh's practice, which he had devised in 1970, was the process of "dynamic meditation." In comparison to other forms of meditation that require stillness of both body and mind, dynamic meditation involves structured but unpatterned moments of rapid breathing, dramatic physical and emotional expressiveness, dance, and silent contemplation. Like Western "primal scream" therapy, Rajneesh's form of meditation was designed to release individuals from their habitual ways of thinking and acting.

Rajneesh's teachings and practices attracted a growing number of international spiritual tourists and pilgrims. By 1974, with the help of wealthy patrons, he established an ashram in Pune. By 1977, he had some twenty-five thousand followers throughout the world and many more had encountered his teachings. His ideal human, "Zorba the Buddha," which, in contrast to the Hindu ascetic ideal, married spiritual pursuits with delight in the material world, exerted a cross-cultural appeal.

Part of Rajneesh's allure was his frank appreciation of sexual activity. Sex, along with money, was one of the pleasures of this world that he promoted. In doing so, Rajneesh transformed the complex and multifaceted ancient Hindu Tantric tradition into a modernized and streamlined spirituality of sex. Rather than indicting the body and sexuality as hindrances to religious awakening, Rajneesh depicted them as sites of religious experience.

Even as they attracted spiritual adventurers, Rajneesh's teachings, including his frequent criticisms of established Hinduism, offended many in India. In the early 1980s, conservative Hindus mounted opposition to the ashram in Pune and prompted an investigation of its tax-exempt status. Rajneesh's followers attributed fire-bombings of several of their sites to external opponents, but investigators decided that they were perpetrated by insiders to inflame public opinion. At the same time that the climate was becoming more inhospitable in India, the Rajneesh movement was expanding overseas. By 1981, there were 126 Rajneesh centers in Europe and the number kept growing through the mid-1980s.

RAJNEESHPURAM

The combination of opposition in India and an eager audience elsewhere shaped the decision to move the Rajneesh headquarters to the United States. In

1981, Rajneesh and a core group of followers settled into a six-square-mile property in central Oregon to begin a communal utopian experiment. In the early days, Rajneeshpuram flourished, even though Rajneesh had retreated into silence and only appeared to his followers during a daily drive in one of his Rolls-Royces.

Organizational control of Rajneeshpuram reverted to Rajneesh's secretary, Ma Anand Sheela (1949–, neé Sheela Ambalal Patel), and a small coterie of insiders. The movement's purchase of a large parcel of land and attempts to gain political control of their own settlement and the nearby town of Antelope provoked substantial opposition. Sheela, in particular, was vitriolic in response. Escalating tensions eventually resulted in the largest bioterrorist attack on U.S. soil when in 1984 members of the group spread salmonella at eight salad bars in the Wascoe County seat of The Dalles, poisoning 751 people. After that, Rajneeshpuram quickly disintegrated. By September of 1985, with the authorities at their heels, Sheela and a small group fled to Germany. A week later Rajneesh denounced Sheela and accused her of various crimes. She was arrested in Germany on October 28, extradited to the United States, and convicted of multiple crimes. Rajneesh himself was arrested while trying to flee the United States and released after paying $400,000 in a plea bargain agreement.

Despite the implosion of Rajneeshpuram, Rajneesh, who became Osho in 1989, eventually returned to India and reopened his ashram as a luxury retreat and meditation center. It continues to provide services to spiritual pilgrims even as different factions of the movement lay claim to Rajneesh's legacy.

See also: Hindu New Religious Movements; Rajneesh, Shree Bhagwan/Osho (1931–1990); Sex, Sexuality, and New Religious Movements.

Further Reading

Carter, Lewis F. 1990. *Charisma and Control in Rajneeshpuram: The Role of Shared Values in the Creation of a Community.* New York: Cambridge University Press.

Palmer, Susan J., & Arvind Sharma, eds. 1993. *The Rajneesh Papers: Studies in a New Religious Movement.* New Delhi: Motilal Banarsidass.

Urban, Hugh B. 2015. *Zorba the Buddha: Sex, Spirituality, and Capitalism in the Global Osho Movement.* Berkeley: University of California Press.

Way, Chapman, & Maclain Way. 2018. *Wild, Wild Country.* Netflix, 6 episodes.

Ramakrishna Mission

The Ramakrishna Mission follows the pattern of many new religious movements, which is, ironically, to claim that it is really very old. Like many Hindu religions newly "discovered" in the West, the Ramakrishna Mission highlights ancient practices packaged in concepts familiar to its new context. In this way, it purports to be not just an "old" new religion but a universal religion. Unlike some Hindu new religious movements such as the Self-Realization Fellowship, however, its institutional center remains in India rather than the West, which inhibits the global movement from straying from its Hindu origins.

ORIGINS

Gadadhar Chattarjee, who later became Ramakrishna Paramahansa (1836–1886), was a nineteenth-century Indian yogi and Hindu saint. Devotees of the Ramakrishna Mission refer to him as the "Prophet" or "Avatar" of the Modern Age. Prior to his birth, his parents reportedly experienced numerous visions and supernatural events that foreshadowed the birth of an exceptional child. The young Ramakrishna did not disappoint, experiencing spiritual ecstasies where his consciousness was altered and he was transported into higher spiritual realms. As a teenager, he became a priest at a temple of the Hindu deity, Kali, but he soon determined that a monastic life was the path for him. This decision was complicated by the fact that he had recently contracted an arranged marriage. However, his bride was significantly younger (he was twenty-three, and she was five), meaning that the marriage was never consummated and, in fact, his bride, Sarada Devi (1853–1920) became his disciple and a religious figure in her own right. She is called "Holy Mother" by monks of the Ramakrishna Math (the monastic order).

Ramakrishna studied under a variety of teachers, including Bhairavi Brahmani, a Hindu nun, who initiated him into Tantric yoga practice. Tantra focuses on the harnessing of energy in the body, known as Shakti, through a variety of contemplative and physical practices, including sexual intercourse (though contrary to popular portrayals, the aim is control rather than release). Though Ramakrishna did not partake of sex (and discouraged it among his own disciples), he incorporated Tantric efforts to control one's internal cosmic energy as a means of achieving greater spiritual knowledge into his own religious practice. However, it was a monk named Totapuri (?–1884) who introduced Ramakrishna to Vedanta. Vedanta means "end or goal of the Vedas," referring to a set of religious ideas that arose from the Upanishads that emphasize the "oneness" of all reality in Brahman or God.

Over time, Ramakrishna earned the reputation as a spiritual adept and mystic who began to attract disciples of his own. One of these disciples was Swami Vivekananda (1863–1902) who gave the Ramakrishna Mission its missionary focus and nonsectarian religious bent. Prior to his death, Ramakrishna charged Vivekananda with the spiritual and physical care of the monks then studying under him. Following the death of his master in 1886, Vivekananda founded the Ramakrishna Math. Not content to remain stationary, Vivekananda sought to spread the truth of his master's wisdom outside of his monastic order. After traveling for some time in India, Vivekananda turned to the West, where his performance at the 1893 World's Parliament of Religion in Chicago put the teachings of Ramakrishna on the map. As a result of his success, Vivekananda founded the Vedanta Society in New York in 1894 and, on a return trip to India, formally founded the Ramakrishna Mission in Belur (the Math would also be housed there from that point onward).

BELIEFS AND PRACTICES

The religious system of the Ramakrishna Mission is Vedanta, of which the primary goal is the realization of "God-consciousness," or one's unity with

Brahman. Given this unity, the true human self or soul, called "Atman," is actually Brahman; thus, the soul is divine. Most people are ignorant ("maya") of their true nature, which is the cause of suffering and, coupled with the consequences of karma ("action"), ensures continued reincarnation in endless cycles of birth and death. Realization of inner divinity and oneness with Brahman is achieved through four variations of yoga: jnana-yoga, the path of knowledge, emphasizes study of Vedantist texts; bhakti yoga, the path of love, involves devotion or worship ("puja") of a particular deity (or avatar, such as Ramakrishna), often through repetitions of its name; raja-yoga, the path of meditation, focuses on internal practice, often guided by a guru, and contemplation; and karma-yoga, the path of work, espouses charity and service to others. These four yogas are interdependent; no one path will allow a person to achieve enlightenment, whereas practicing all four will yield that result eventually. Though most practice is to be undertaken individually, there are also times of communal prayer, reading, and worship held at Ramakrishna centers.

Due in great part to the work of Vivekananda, the Ramakrishna Mission also emphasizes the essential oneness of all religious systems. The Ramakrishna Mission advertises Vedanta as a creedless, nondogmatic religious system that is united with all religions in the pursuit of eternal truth. Additionally, the Ramakrishna Mission does not recognize caste, a fact that has caused friction with Indian society. The motto of the Ramakrishna Mission is "For one's own salvation and for the welfare of the world" or, more concisely, "renunciation and service." Renunciation refers, broadly to the renunciation of the self in pursuit of oneness with the divine, and specifically to the renunciation of worldly goods and society embraced by monks. Service refers to the belief that service to the poor is an essential function of the religious mission and something, which Ramakrishna had emphasized explicitly.

Though many practitioners of Vedanta are not monks, monastic life is still a central component of the Ramakrishna Mission. A women's monastic order, Sri Sarada Math (named for Sarada Devi) was founded in 1954 as a counterpart to the Ramakrishna Math, which solely comprised men. Monks and nuns are both called "sannyasins," the Hindu word for monastic. Though sannyasins live a typical life of asceticism, mirroring Vivekananda, they are also expected to leave the monastery and serve others, even to travel to spread the message of the Mission.

ORGANIZATION AND LATER HISTORY

Though the two are spiritually aligned, share a president (currently Swami Smarananananda, 1929–), and are both centered in Belur, the Ramakrishna Math and the Ramakrishna Mission are legally separate entities. For example, of the 205 branch centers spread over twenty-two countries around the world, most are extensions of the Ramakrishna Mission (such as Vedanta Societies scattered throughout the United States and Europe) and do not have an accompanying monastery, even though they are most likely run by monks and nuns. The Ramakrishna Mission also houses "affiliated centers," those that are not explicitly spawned from the original religious movement, but which align enough to be included in a network of affiliation. Most sannyasins reside in India and all members of the institutional hierarchy of Math and Mission are monastics, including the president and board of trustees. Thus, even though many practitioners of Vedanta are most likely not monastically inclined, the governing and spiritual heart of the mission is the Math, which seeks to mimic the work of the "Holy Trio": Ramakrishna, Sarada Devi, and Vivekananda. And in line with their emphasis on service, the Mission also maintains a number of hospitals, clinics, universities, and humanitarian aid societies among other institutions and functions. The Math and Mission also own their own publishing house, which focuses primarily on disseminating the work of Ramakrishna and Vivekananda. The religion also has an established virtual presence with an online reading room administered through its website (https://belurmath.org/).

There has been some debate as to whether the Ramakrishna Mission qualifies as a Hindu religious movement, particularly given its ecumenism and westernized branches, such as the Vedanta Society. In the 1980s, in fact, the Ramakrishna Mission petitioned the Indian government to be granted the status of a non-Hindu minority religion. This move arose out of political expediency and fear that the local government would take over its schools, which ultimately came to naught (the government determined that it was a Hindu sect). Today, the Ramakrishna Mission maintains that it is not a purveyor of "occult" knowledge, which was precisely the appeal for many among Vivekananda's initial audience and disciples. The notion that one could have access to secrets known only to the initiated few was (and is) very appealing in the West. Nonetheless, the Mission and Math, today, are quite explicit that their religious views align with Vedanta, which is an established branch of Hinduism, rather than a secret society of esoteric knowledge.

See also: Hindu New Religious Movements; Occultism and Esotericism; Self-Realization Fellowship (Yogananda); Vedanta Society, The; Vivekananda, Swami (1863–1902); World's Parliament of Religion, The; Yoga.

Further Reading
Beckerlegge, Gwilym. 2001. *The Ramakrishna Mission: The Making of a Modern Hindu Movement.* Oxford: Oxford University Press.

Gupta, Mahendranath, & Swami Nikhilananda. 1942. *The Gospel of Sri Ramakrishna.* New York: Ramakrishna-Vivekananda Center.

Kripal, Jeffrey J. 1998. *Kali's Child: The Mystical and the Erotic in the Life and Teachings of Ramakrishna.* Chicago; London: University of Chicago Press.

Ramakrishna Mission. "Belur Math-Ramakrishna Mission." Available at: https://belurmath .org/.

Rastafari

When Africans were wrenched from their homelands and forced to work as slaves in the New World, they struggled to make meaningful lives for themselves in oppressive circumstances. For some, that meant accepting the Christianity of their masters, while for others it meant selectively adapting and supplementing it

520   **Rastafari**

and for others, wholly rejecting it. Several new religious movements developed among the forcibly relocated Africans and their descendants, including Vodou in Haiti, Santería in Cuba, and Candomblé in Brazil. Each of those new religions eventually spread beyond its point of origin. They drew upon actual and imagined elements of African traditions, the Bible, and local religious ideas. Rastafari, which took shape in Jamaica in the early 1930s, was part of that general religious trend.

ORIGINS

Rastafari developed among the Jamaican peasantry and had multiple predecessors. The related native religious complexes of Myal and Revival featured charismatic leaders and promoted direct experience of the spirit, including the Christian Holy Spirit, through ritual possession. One prominent figure, Alexander Bedward (1859–1930), was a successful Revival preacher who attracted as many as thirty thousand followers to the Jamaica Native Free Baptist Church. He established a healing ministry and prophesied that blacks would soon conquer their white oppressors. Bedward aligned his movement with the "Back to Africa" teachings of Marcus Garvey (1887–1940), depicting himself as Aaron and Garvey as Moses. His emphasis on Africa as the source of identity and true home of blacks in the diaspora would become a main theme in Rastafari. A follower of Bedward, Robert Hinds, was one of the first Rasta preachers.

Other currents of thought that idealized Africa also inspired the earliest Rastafari. The redemptive ideology of Ethiopianism, which built on the passage in Psalm 68:31 that "Princes shall come out of Egypt and Ethiopia shall soon stretch forth her hands unto God," was a widely diffused way of thinking that supported various attempts to identify Africa (signified by "Ethiopia") to be the true home of diaspora blacks and the repository of a noble and accomplished culture.

The early Rastafari also drew upon two important texts that were circulating in Jamaica in the 1920s. *The Holy Piby* was published by the prophet Robert Athyli Rogers in New Jersey in 1924 and soon found its way to Jamaica along with the Rev. Fitz Balintine Pettersburgh's *The Parchment Scroll of Black Supremacy*. Both texts emphasized the dignity of black people and their need for self-determination. Additionally, each stressed the need for a new Bible that would speak directly to the descendants of slaves. The influential Rastafarian teacher, Leonard Howell, copied passages from both of them into his *The Promised Key*.

The catalyst for the first Rastafari preachers, however, was the crowning of Ras Tafari Makkonen as Emperor Haile Selassie I of Ethiopia on November 2, 1930. Rastas continue to see his coronation as a momentous occasion, even though they differ on his significance. The Ethiopian monarchy traced itself back to the biblical king Solomon, and when Ras Tafari Makonnen ascended to the throne he received the titles King of Kings, Lord of Lords, and Conquering Lion of the Tribe of Judah. Some Jamaicans were quick to see the resonance of those titles with biblical prophecies (e.g., in Rev. 19:16) and identified the new king as Christ returned to earth to liberate the scattered children of Ethiopia and serve as their new monarch.

Leonard Howell, often identified as the first Rasta, advanced the concept of Haile Selassie's divinity, starting in 1933. Howell began preaching in Kingston but found little success; he then moved to Jamaica's eastern parish of St. Thomas. Possibly drawing on Hindu sources, Howell gave himself the prophetic name Gangunguru Maragh, which translates as "teacher of great wisdom, king of kings." He published *The Promised Key* under that name around 1935. In 1940, he established a communal settlement called the Pinnacle, which lasted until 1954.

Archibald Dunkley, Joseph Hibbert, and Robert Hinds were also among the first teachers who proclaimed the divinity of the Ethiopian king. Dunkley convinced himself through his own study of the Bible that Haile Selassie was indeed the Messiah and he taught against the spirit possession common in Revival groups. Hibbert claimed to possess secret wisdom that could be found in the apocryphal book of Maccabees and was known for his occult powers. Hinds was initially a supporter of Howell, but then established himself as the prophet of his own group, the King of Kings Mission. Hinds's followers observed the Passover ritual because they saw themselves as exiles in Jamaica, waiting to return to Africa.

The early Rastafari experienced substantial hostility in Jamaica; they were, after all, avowed enemies of the status quo. In 1960, some of the brethren in Kingston sought the help of the University College of the West Indies in dispelling misconceptions about Rastafari. The result was a report that recounted the history of the group, including various founding figures, previous encounters with law enforcement and the continuing deterioration of relations between Rastas and civil authorities, beliefs about Hailie Selassie, and the desire for repatriation, among other things. The report warned against stereotyping Rastas as criminal renegades and offered recommendations that the Jamaican government should send a mission to Africa to set the stage for immigration, improve housing opportunities for impoverished Rastas, and offer job training and radio and press facilities for them, among other things.

BELIEFS AND PRACTICES

From its beginnings, Rastafari has been a loosely unified movement with authority diffused among many individuals. Although "mansions" and "houses" have coalesced around different figures, Rastafari today features significant diversity and efforts at centralization have met with little success. For example, not all Rastas wear dreadlocks; nor do all smoke *ganja* or marijuana; not all take the Nazirite vow from Numbers 6; and not all assert the divinity of Haile Selassie. Some hope for repatriation to Africa in the near future whether through divine intervention or individual effort, while others focus on political reform in Jamaica and elsewhere. It is difficult to generalize about Rastafari, since there are always exceptions.

Rastafari focuses on individuals discovering the truth for themselves, through introspection and through reasoning sessions with other Rastas, often with the aid of the "holy herb," ganja (see Gen. 3:18 and Rev. 22:2). Haile Selassie remains a central figure even if his status is understood in different ways. Africa is revered as both the homeland and the Promised Land.

Rastafari is also suffused with a biblical consciousness, which helps Rastas understand, among other things, the nature of God (Jah), the significance of Selassie, their identity as the true Israelites, their need for exodus from the oppressive structures that deny them dignity and self-determination, and their situation of exile in Babylon even as they yearn for Zion.

Many Rastafari adopt the "dreadlocks" hairstyle and they provide multiple reasons for what dreads symbolize, including a lion's mane in imitation of the conquering lion of Judah. Many also adopt an "ital" (from "vital" without the initial "v") way of life, which emphasizes a "natural" diet that eschews any additives and focuses on fruits and vegetables. Many Rastas have also adopted an idiosyncratic way of speaking in which "I" words predominate, where "I and I" refers to the unity between the individual and the deity or to two individuals, "I man" refers to a Rasta who is conscious of inner divinity, "the I" as a form of address recognizes another person's inherent value; "ital" refers to vital, natural foods, and "irator" and "iration" refer to the creator and creation. In addition "oppression" is redescribed as "downpression," and "understand" as "overstand," for example. Rastafari speech both reinforces group solidarity and supports the oppositional project of "chanting down Babylon" by using language to create an alternative reality.

IMPACT

Early on, Rastafari spread beyond Jamaica, and emigrants from Jamaica took it to the United Kingdom, Canada, and the United States, among other places. But it achieved its greatest international popularity through reggae music, with Bob Marley (1945–1981) being its most prominent ambassador. The association of Rastafari with a popular form of music, however, also exposed it to commodification and misunderstanding. Also as Rastafari has spread, it has faced issues such as the continuing negative impact of Jamaican patriarchal attitudes toward women and the question of whether people who are not of African descent can become Rastas. But Rastafari remains a dynamic and attractive religious tradition throughout the world.

See also: Candomblé; Charisma and Leadership in New Religious Movements; *Holy Piby, The*; Race and New Religious Movements; Santería; Umbanda; Vodou.

Further Reading

Barnett, Michael. 2018. *The Rastafari Movement: A North American and Caribbean Perspective.* New York: Routledge.

Chevannes, Barry. 1994. *Rastafari: Roots and Ideology.* Syracuse, NY: Syracuse University Press.

Hill, Robert A. 2001. *Dread History: Leonard P. Howell and Millenarian Visions in the Early Rastafarian Religion,* reprint. Chicago: Research Associates School Times Publications and Frontline Distribution International, Inc.

Maragh, G. G. (Leonard Percival Howell). 1993, reprint. *The Promised Key*. Brooklyn, NY: Publishers Group.

Van Dijk, Frank Jan. 1993. *JAHmaica: Rastafari and Jamaican Society, 1930–1990*. The Hague: Koninklijke Bibliotheek.

PRIMARY SOURCE DOCUMENT

From G. G. Maragh, *The Promised Key* (c. 1935)

Leonard Howell was a prominent Rastafari preacher who wrote the movement's primary tract, The Promised Key, *in 1935. Howell published the tract using his Hindu pen name, G. G. Maragh. An excerpt follows below.*

The glory that was Solomon greater still reigns in Ethiopia. We can see all the Kings of the earth surrendering their crowns to His Majesty Ras Tafari the King of Kings and Lord of Lords Earth's Rightful Ruler to reign forever and ever.

Upon His Majesty Ras Tafari's head are many diadems and on His garments a name written King of Kings and Lord of Lords oh come let us adore him for he is King of Kings and Lord of Lords, The Conquering Lion of Judah, The Elect of God and the Light of the world.

His Majesty Ras Tafari is the head over all man for he is the Supreme God. His body is the fullness of him that fillet all in all. Now my dear people let this be our goal, forward to the King of Kings must be the cry of our social hope. Forward to the King of Kings to purify our social standards and our way of living, and rebuild and inspire our character. Forward to the King of Kings to learn the worth of manhood and womanhood. Forward to the King of Kings to learn His code of Laws from the mount demanding absolute Love, Purity, Honesty, and Truthfulness. Forward to the King of Kings to learn His Laws and social order, so that virtue will eventually gain the victory over body and soul and that truth will drive away falsehood and fraud. Members of the King of Kings arise for God's sake and put your armor on.

Dear inhabitants of the Western Hemisphere, the King of Kings warriors can never be defeated, the Pope of Rome and his agents shall not prevail against the King of Kings host warriors you all must stand up, stand up, for the King of Kings.

All ye warriors of the King of Kings lift high King Alpha's Royal Banner, from victory to victory King Alpha shall lead his army till every enemy is vanquished.

ETHIOPIA'S KINGDOM

Dear inhabitants of this world King Ras Tafari and Queen Omega are the foundation stones of the Resurrection of the Kingdom of Ethiopia.

Their prayer and labour for our Resurrection is past finding out; no library in this world is able to contain the work of their hands for us, for they work both day and night for our deliverance.

As for this generation of the 20th century you and I have no knowledge how worlds are build and upon what triggers Kingdoms are set.

In King Alpha's Encyclopedia he will explain to us all, how worlds are being built and upon what trigger Kingdoms are set on. He will also explain to us the capacities of generations.

Speaking for the Universe and the womanhood of man Queen Omega the Ethiopian woman is the crown woman of this world. She hands us Her Rule-Book from the poles of supreme authority she is the Cannon Mistress of creation.

King Alpha and Queen Omega are the paymasters of the world, Bible owner and money mint. Do not forget they are Black People if you please.

Owing to the universal rend of our ancient and modern we are at this juncture of our history scattered over the Globe into little sectional groups.

All our local bands throughout the globe are bent towards King Alpha's Royal Repository, the Royal Authority is to admit all Bands, Mission Camps, Denominations into the supreme Royal Repository.

Queen Omega being the balming mistress of many worlds she charges the powerhouse right now.

Have we any authority from King Alpha? Yes we are vessels of the divine honor. Have we any authority from the world? Assuredly yes indeed, King Alpha signs for our destiny and gave us His Supreme Affidavit a trillion centuries after the end of eternal life.

Source: Maragh, G. G. *The Promised Key*. Kingston, Jamaica: Harding Commercial Printery, 1935.

Rosicrucianism

The origins of Rosicrucianism are nebulous. The religion is often attributed to a fourteenth-century pilgrim named Christian Rosenkreuz, a potentially allegorical figure who wrote about the power of the "Rose Cross" in several sources that were ultimately published in the seventeenth century, namely, *Fama Fraternatis* (1614) and *Confessio Fraternatis Rosae Crucis* (1615). These texts have a social reformatory bent, identifying the need to abolish hunger and disease as primary aims of religious practice, and are tinged with millennialism, predicting an imminent end to the current world order. More likely these texts were composed by Johann Valentin Andreae (1586–1654), a Lutheran theologian, whose various writings were tinged with references to Gnosticism, Hermeticism, and occult religiosity and who wrote of the Order of the Rose Cross in other documents. Though the Rose Cross clearly references the Christian origins of Rosicrucianism, not all subsequent iterations of the movement are specifically Christian in nature, even while adopting

Christian Rosenkreutz, by some accounts, is the founder of Rosicrucianism, a mystical Christian movement and secret order. His writings, including the engraving above, posited that humankind was born with a "divine spark," which should be cultivated through ascetic and magical practices and could span multiple lifetimes. By other accounts, Rosenkreutz is fictional, a nom de plume, for a Gnostic and Lutheran theologian, Johann Valentin Andreae. (Wellcome Library)

the symbol. In fact, certain elements of Rosicrucian thought (such as the notion of reincarnation) directly defy orthodox Christian theology, thus its original ties to Christianity, even of a mystical variety, have not spared its proponents from accusations of heresy.

At base, Rosicrucianism posits that there exists a divine order and a human order, the latter inhabiting a tainted, physical world. Every human being, however, has a divine "spark," found in the heart, which can actually transform the person from the inside out if cultivated through ascetic or sometimes religio-magical practices. Often this transformation from essentially human to essentially divine may take several lifetimes. Since the ultimate aim is the complete reformation of humanity, the sudden emergence of these texts and the response to them spawned notions that a global, secret society was poised to spark a scientific, cultural, religious, and political reformation of Europe and the world.

There have been numerous, often secret, Rosicrucian orders that have emerged over the centuries, bearing similarities to esoteric movements such as Freemasonry whose initiates fiercely guard their rites and rituals. However, Rosicrucianism experienced a renaissance in the nineteenth and early twentieth centuries, spawning numerous societies, including Fraternatis Rosae Crucis, Societas

Rosicruciana, the Ancient and Mystical Order of the Rosy Cross, and the Rosicrucian Order, Crotona Fellowship (ROCF).

The ROCF was founded in England in 1920 by George A. Sullivan (1890–1942). Members participated in secret rituals, which enabled them to progress through "degrees" of initiation (similar to Freemasonic societies) and combined magical practices with worship and study. Sullivan maintained that these practices were ancient and ROCF was simply a revival of an ancient tradition. The group dissolved following Sullivan's death. The immediate impact of the ROCF was less pronounced than its long-term legacy. Though the group never achieved significant membership, two major religious figures were involved: Gerald Gardner (1884–1964) and Peter Caddy (1917–1994). Gardner is viewed by many as the founder of modern witchcraft and a primary figure in the development of Wicca. Thus, the practices and ideas of the ROCF influenced a major new religious movement. Gardner also maintained, like Sullivan, that he was simply reviving an age-old religious movement and was not creating something new. Caddy, who along with wife Eileen (1917–2006) founded the Findhorn Foundation, a New Age community in England, belonged to the ROCF and adapted the ethos of the society, particularly its focus on developing individual power through positive thinking and community ritual.

Not all new religious movements linked to Rosicrucianism identify as strictly Rosicrucian societies. The Hermetic Order of the Golden Dawn was another occult religious society that emerged in England in the late nineteenth century. Its founders were Freemasons who were also steeped in Rosicrucian texts, practices, and lore, which they combined with Theosophy's belief in Great Masters or individuals who had been guiding humanity toward spiritual enlightenment for millennia. The focus on transformation from human to divine reflected Rosicrucian beliefs in human transfiguration, though members of the Golden Dawn often believed it could happen in their lifetimes.

Operating at around the same time, across the Atlantic Ocean, was Noble Drew Ali's (1886–1929) Moorish Science Temple, which was influenced by both Rosicrucian and Freemasonic beliefs and rituals. Born Timothy Drew, Ali claimed that black people were descended from the Moors, thus defying their racialized characterization of "negroes" and designating them the true, biblical people—a nation unto themselves. Ali was particularly drawn to esoteric religious traditions for their symbolism, exclusivity, and the fact that they often claimed ancient lineages despite their modern time stamp. In fact, despite his claims that it arose from original revelation, Ali's *The Holy Koran of the Moorish Science Temple of America* was heavily influenced by other texts, one of which was *Unto Thee I Grant*, written by Rosicrucian author Sri Ramatherio (translated in 1925 by Rosicrucian, Harvey Spencer Lewis (1883–1939)). The text focuses on the foibles and characteristics of humanity and how, among other things, each person has an obligation to transform the self to act for the greater good and the transformation of humanity as a whole.

The list of Rosicrucian societies and Rosicrucian-inspired groups is long. Rosicrucianism, though unknown to many, has influenced countless new traditions and societies, particularly those considered esoteric in character.

Though most are defunct, Rosicrucianism as a broad esoteric religious tradition appeals to people's desire to partake in something unknown but to a rarified few, which promises not only a total transformation of oneself, but ultimately, of the world.

See also: Ali, Noble Drew (1886–1929); Caddy, Eileen (1917–2006); Findhorn Foundation, The; Freemasonry; Gardner, Gerald (1884–1964); Gnostic Groups; Hermetic Order of the Golden Dawn, The; Hermeticism; Millennialism; Moorish Science Temple of America, The; New Age, The; Occultism and Esotericism; Wicca.

Further Reading

Fleming, John V. 2013. *The Dark Side of the Enlightenment: Wizards, Alchemists, and Spiritual Seekers in the Age of Reason.* New York: W.W. Norton & Company.

McIntosh, Christopher. 2011. *The Rose Cross and the Age of Reason: Eighteenth-century Rosicrucianism in Central Europe and its Relationship to the Enlightenment.* Albany: SUNY Press.

Melton, J. Gordon. 1990. *Rosicrucianism in America.* New York: Garland.

Ross, Rick Alan (1952–)

Although he was not among the very first deprogrammers of the 1970s, in the 1980s, Rick Ross quickly earned a reputation as an implacable opponent of groups he identified as destructive cults. Ross acknowledges participating in some "involuntary" deprogrammings but asserts that his preferred form of "cult intervention" involves a voluntary exchange of information between himself and the cult member. Ross holds no degrees in psychology, religious studies, or related fields and bases his knowledge of cults on personal experience and reading of popular accounts.

Ross gained some notoriety when he was consulted by the Federal Bureau of Investigation in 1993 during the fifty-one-day siege of the Mount Carmel Center near Waco, Texas. Ross's advice reinforced the image of the Branch Davidians as helpless pawns who were being manipulated by an unscrupulous and possibly mentally deranged leader.

Ross's advice, as well as the testimony he offered in court for a time, and his public appearances have relied on an explanation for cult membership that by the 1980s was a standard position within the anticult movement. Relying on figures like Robert Jay Lifton (1926–) and Margaret Thaler Singer (1921–2003), Ross has argued that members of groups he identifies as "destructive cults" are the victims of a process of coercive persuasion or thought reform. Virtually anyone could be taken in by such practices. Manipulative leaders exploit the members of destructive cults, financially, spiritually, and sometimes sexually, for their own gratification.

During the time that it was the most prominent anticult organization in the United States, Ross worked closely with the Cult Awareness Network (CAN) and frequently received referrals for deprogrammings from staff members at CAN's headquarters. That relationship, while initially profitable, eventually led to the downfall of CAN and a serious setback for Ross.

Though his contacts at CAN, Ross became involved in the deprogramming of a young man, Jason Scott, whose mother wanted to extricate him from an evangelical Pentecostal church to which she and her children had belonged. Scott wanted to stay and resisted his deprogramming. He eventually escaped from Ross and his hired enforcers and sued them, and CAN, for kidnapping him against his will. Although no convictions were delivered on criminal charges, a civil suit resulted in a $5 million verdict against the defendants. CAN was bankrupted and Ross, though he eventually settled with Scott, suffered a financial setback.

Nonetheless, Ross continues to battle against what he sees as destructive cults. He maintains an extensive website, originally for the Rick Ross Institute, which was renamed in 2013 the Cult Education Institute for the Study of Destructive Cults, Controversial Groups and Movements (www.culteducation.com).

See also: Anticult Movement, The; Brainwashing; Branch Davidians; Cult Awareness Network, The; Deprogramming; Exit Counseling; Singer, Margaret Thaler (1921–2003).

Further Reading
Ross, Rick Alan. 2014. *Cults Inside Out: How People Get In and Can Get Out.* North Charleston, SC: CreateSpace.

Shupe, Anson, & Susan E. Darnell. 2006. *Agents of Discord: Deprogramming, Pseudo-Science, and the American Anticult Movement.* New Brunswick, NJ: Transaction Publishers.

Russell, Charles Taze (1852–1916)

From an early age, Charles Taze Russell was serious about his religion. Born in Pennsylvania in 1852, Russell reportedly mixed an early business acumen with a penchant for proselytization. As a child he would chalk Bible verses on any surface available in the hope of converting the unfaithful. By the age of twenty, he had moved from Presbyterianism to Congregationalism, but soon rejected the Calvinist theology of both, finding it impossible to reconcile the concept of hell with a merciful God. In 1870, he chanced upon the teachings of former Millerite and Seventh-day Adventist preacher, Jonas Wendell (1815–1873), whose arguments against eternal hell and the reality of the immortal soul and about the imminence of Christ's Return appealed to Russell. Soon thereafter, Russell founded his own Bible study group.

RELIGIOUS FOUNDER

Though Russell shared the Biblicism and millennialism of the Seventh-day Adventists, he soon diverged from them in his belief that when Christ returned, he would create Eden on earth, rather than destroy it. He also argued that Christ's Return would be invisible and that it had already occurred—in 1874. Christ would only reveal himself to the world during the final Battle of Armageddon. Russell never claimed revelation as the source of his conclusions; he arrived at them by diligent study of the Bible, for which he even employed the help of Hebrew and Greek tutors to help him read the text in its original languages.

A desire to spread his discoveries regarding the Christian millennium, as well as his theological denials of eternal hell and the immortal soul, led Russell to publish prolifically—something that would become a defining feature of the new religious movement he would found, the Watch Tower Bible and Tract Society (better known as the Jehovah's Witnesses).

Before it was known by this name, however, Russell's group was simply called the "Bible Student Movement," reflecting the original model by which Russell arrived at his discoveries. The group was formally incorporated in 1884. From 1886 to 1904, Russell wrote and published his greatest work, which was originally called *Millennial Dawn*, but later renamed *Studies in the Scriptures*. Over seven volumes, Russell expanded upon his millennial vision, weaving together biblical texts with his own interpretation and commentary. For example, the second volume, *The Time is at Hand* (1889), lays out how he came to the scripturally grounded conclusion that Christ had already returned. Similarly, the fifth volume, *The At-One-Ment between God and Man*, painstakingly shows how Russell's reading of the Bible led him to determine that Christ's atonement was for all, negating the necessity of hell.

Along with his book series, Russell founded the journal, *The Watch Tower*, which was circulated among Jehovah's Witnesses and distributed by missionaries to any who would take one. It was the editing and publication of the journal that reportedly led to tension and the eventual dissolution of his marriage to Maria Francis Ackley (1850–1938). The pair had met in 1879, but her desire to assume a more prominent editorial role chafed Russell, though she cited "immoral conduct" with another woman as a primary cause (something that her husband would flatly deny). Russell would eventually call the marriage a "mistake." They divorced in 1897, after which he threw himself more fully into the missionary and ministerial work of the society.

LIFE AND LEGACY

Russell maintained a packed travel schedule throughout his life, believing it his mission to spread the urgent millennialist message. As a result, his status would only rise in the movement, leading many Jehovah's Witnesses to believe that he was somehow chosen or inspired by God and even that Russell's coming may have been predicted in the Bible. Russell continued to deny such speculations throughout his life, arguing throughout his missions that others would come to his understanding of the Bible, just as he had.

However, his travels ultimately took a physical toll. Weakened from his time away from home, he died from cystitis in October 1916, remaining President of the Society until his last breath. He was succeeded as president by Joseph Franklin Rutherford (1869–1942). Arguably, his greatest contributions were his numerous publications, which have reached circulation in the tens of millions and are published in over thirty-five languages.

See also: Millennialism; Millerites, The; Prophecy in New Religious Movements; Watch Tower Bible and Tract Society, The (Jehovah's Witnesses).

Further Reading

Russell, Charles Taze. 1896–1904. *Studies in the Scripture.* Volumes I–VII. Available at: https://archive.org/details/StudiesInTheScripturesVolumes1-7.

Zydek, Fredrick. 2010. *Charles Taze Russell: His Life and Times, the Man, the Millennium, and the Message.* Winthrop, CT: Winthrop Press.

S

Salafism

The term Salafism derives from the Arabic word *salaf,* meaning "righteous predecessors," and is generally thought to refer to the first three generations of Muslims. Salafism, as a reform movement within Sunni Islam, arose in the late nineteenth century among those who wished to rid Islam of modern innovations or *bid'ah,* and emulated those early Muslims who followed closely the *Sunnah,* or the tradition of the Prophet Muhammad. Iranian Muslim, Jamal al-Din al-Afghani (1838–1897), is cited as an originator of Salafist thought. Though Shiite, his efforts against British colonial rule, which he saw as a problematic influence, were adopted by those most responsible for Sunni Salafism. Al-Afghani encouraged all efforts to rid Muslims of British and, more broadly, Western, rule.

There are two primary branches within Salafism: modernist and purist. Modernist Salafists argue that rigid adherence to tradition has led to calcification in Muslim belief and believe that a return to this earlier moment of theological and institutional creativity would help break the movement out of archaic patterns. Purist Salafists, on the other hand, argue against modern adaptation and seek a full return to the practices of the seventh and eighth centuries as well as a particular reading of the Qur'an. It is the Purist position that has inspired terrorist organizations such as al-Qaeda and millennialist movements such as the Islamic State (ISIS). Nonetheless, most Salafists are not affiliated with extremism or violence and seek to practice pure Islam in their daily lives.

EVOLUTION AND BELIEFS

Salafism of both modernist and purist varieties first took hold in Egypt. Al-Afghani's disciple, Muhammad Abduh (1849–1905), adapted his predecessor's beliefs to the Egyptian context and disseminated Salafist ideas through an early network of like-minded individuals called the Islamic League. Later, Abduh's writings would influence Hassan al-Banna (1906–1949), founder of the Muslim Brotherhood. The Muslim Brotherhood is one of the earliest and possibly the most influential Islamic revival movement. Originally conceived as a means of eradicating poverty and encouraging charity among Egyptian Muslims, the movement turned increasingly to political activism as Western influences appeared to infiltrate the government. This pattern holds for other Salafist-influenced movements in Middle Eastern countries such as Lebanon, where Salafists criticized the government for westernizing and neglecting the needs of Muslims who felt disenfranchised. Muslim Brotherhood member Sayyid Qutb (1906–1966) whose writings would influence both Islamic revivalists and Islamic radicals, was reflective of this activist turn and was ultimately executed for his part in the unsuccessful plot to execute Egyptian president, Gamal Abdel Nasser (1918–1970).

Central to Salafism is a notably literalist approach to the reading and interpretation of the Qur'an. The effects of this reading are myriad. For example, Salafists, especially purists, shun all trappings of Western culture, including attire. They believe that the West, in general, represents *al-Jahiliyya*, or "ignorance." Salafists also differentiate between *salaf* and *khalaf*: those who are authentic believers and those who are pretenders, respectively. In this way, the greatest targets of Salafist revivalism are fellow Muslims whom they feel have strayed from the true faith due to Western influence and globalization.

Contrary to popular conceptions of Salafist or other fundamentalist movements, that members are asked to blindly follow the rules unthinkingly, Salafists eschew the notion of *taqlid*, which compels Muslims to obey the pronouncements of Muslim legal scholars without examining doctrinal questions themselves. Rather, Salafism is built on the idea that Muslims must personally learn and absorb Muslim theology and law and must study the Qur'an for themselves (a practice known as *ijitihad*). This attitude of returning to the sources reflects the original concern of al-Afghani and others that Qur'anic and theological interpretation had been the purview of a rarified few, rather than the property of all Muslims willing to do the work. The effect of this emphasis on personal interpretation was that certain classical doctrines came under question, including that of *jihad*. Jihad, "striving," typically referred to the inner struggle all Muslims undergo to obey Allah and follow the teachings of Muhammad. However, jihad's "lesser" form emerged during this time, which enabled Muslims to wage defensive war against those associated with al-Jahiliyya. Since the West had struck first (dating back to the Crusades by the reckoning of some), then all Muslims were effectively playing defense. This concept was expanded by some (prompted by Qutb's book *Milestones* [1964]) to mean that it was the duty of all Muslims to spread Islam and to impose Islamic law or *Sharia* throughout the world.

AFTER 9/11

The attacks on the World Trade Center in New York and the Pentagon on September 11, 2001, have increased the tendency to conflate all Salafist forms of Islam with terrorism (or more troublingly, all of Islam with terrorism). Certainly, al-Qaeda drew upon Salafist principles, among other intellectual sources, to ground its platform that Western interference and acts of violence justified a defensive jihadist position—and any violence that might issue from it. More recently, ISIS has employed Salafist principles, specifically those that seek to emulate the early caliphate of those first generations of Muslims. ISIS takes this position to an extreme by seeking to recreate, literally, the early caliphate both geographically and institutionally in the Arabian peninsula.

However, Salafism is not synonymous with these groups, and many Salafists, particularly those who consider themselves modernists, wish to distance themselves from them. This has not prevented both Sunni and Shia Muslims from critiquing Salafism as backward-looking and narrow in its use and interpretation of the Qur'an. The fear of Muslims in countries where Islam is not a majority is that the actions of Salafists will affect them adversely; the fear of Salafists is that such attitudes will lead to Western, not Islamic, victory.

See also: Al-Qaeda; Globalization and New Religious Movements; ISIS; Millennialism.

Further Reading
Egerton, Frazer. 2011. *Jihad in the West: The Rise of Militant Salafism*. Cambridge: Cambridge University Press.
Lauzière, Henri. 2016. *The Making of Salafism: Islamic Reform in the Twentieth Century*. New York: Columbia University.
Meijer, Roel, ed. 2014. *Global Salafism: Islam's New Religious Movement*. New York: Oxford University Press.
Qutb, Sayyid. 1964. *Milestones*. Cairo, Egypt: Kazi Publications.

Santería

One of the many new religions that took shape among Africans who were forcibly taken to the New World by slave traders, Santería developed in Cuba during the nineteenth and early twentieth centuries. Also known as *la regla de ocha* (the rule of the orishas) and *la regla Lucumí* (the rule of the Lucumí), Santería creatively adapted practices and beliefs about the African *orishas* who personified *ashé* or divine power and incorporated elements of Christianity. Like other new religions

In Santería, individuals dance to invite the spirits, who are identified with both Roman Catholic saints and African orishas, to join them in the ritual. When the spirits arrive, they dispense advice for both individuals and the community and healing. (Sandra Foyt/Dreamstime.com)

534 Santería

among Africans and their descendants, Santería responded to the cultural and social dislocation experienced by people who lost their ties to homeland, tribal group, and family and had the religion of their masters, Christianity, imposed upon them.

ORIGINS

More than five hundred thousand slaves came to Cuba, with the bulk arriving in the three decades before slavery was formally banned in 1868. Many of those individuals were Yoruba, though that designation itself was a recent invention. Yoruba-speaking people in Cuba were known as Lucumí, a term of uncertain origin. In urban areas of Cuba, both free blacks and slaves of the same ethnic background were grouped into *naciones* (nations). Many participated in societies for mutual aid, religious practice, and social activities, following a practice developed earlier in Spain.

Although the Roman Catholic Church attempted to use those societies, *cabildos*, for religious instruction, they also became incubators for remembering and creatively transforming African religions. Since Santería identifies Roman Catholic saints with African orishas, it constitutes both an accommodation and resistance to colonial power. After Cuba fully achieved independence from Spain in 1902, the cabildos became the bases for the *ilés* or houses of Santería, which were led by "godfathers" or "godmothers" who presided over a network of spiritual kin.

BELIEFS AND PRACTICES

The creator God in traditional Yoruba cosmogonies, Olodumare, has ordained a destiny for everyone. Since he is portrayed as having withdrawn from active engagement with the world, the orishas act as God's agents in the world and manifest his ashé or power. Of the many African orishas, only some play a prominent role in Santería. Ellegua, for example, is a trickster. He opens paths and is the master of the crossroads; he is a powerful magician. Santería ceremonies begin and end with an acknowledgment of Ellegua. In the complex set of connections that characterizes each of the orishas, Ellegua is associated with St. Anthony of Padua, the number 3, the colors red and black, and white chickens, roosters, opossums, and rum. When he dances, he acts like a clown and he carries a hooked staff. Yemaya, on her part, is associated with the Virgin Mary of Regla, Spain, maternity, the number 7, the colors blue and white, the duck, turtle, and goat. In her dancing, she can evoke either placid or raging seas, and her emblem is the fan shell. Orishas may also have associations that cross gender lines. The powerful male orisha Shango, for example, is associated with St. Barbara.

Practitioners of Santería (*santeros* or *santeras*) work with the orishas to discern God's will for them and act in accordance with it. Accordingly, ritual practices are central to Santería. Although noninitiates may attend ceremonies, one becomes a full member of an *ilé* through a process of initiation, the ritual of *asiento* or *kariocha*. That process involves identifying the specific orisha with whom the initiate will enter into a lifelong relationship.

There are multiple ways to enter into contact with the orishas. Sacrifice, including animal sacrifice, nourishes the orishas with the ashé of the sacrificial victim and nourishes the members of the community with the animal's flesh. Divination, in various forms, can be used to seek help from the orishas to address pressing problems, particularly ones related to health, finances, or love. Divination relies on the conviction that the world is orderly and that the orishas can help individuals discern the meaning of apparently random events.

The most dramatic and intimate interaction between humans and the orishas comes through trance. Rhythmic drumming and dancing can produce altered states of consciousness in which an orisha descends on or "mounts" an individual. The temporarily incarnated orisha, who displaces the consciousness of the individual, can then provide counsel of various sorts to individuals and the community as a whole. Sacrifice, divination, and the experience or witnessing of altered states of consciousness strengthen the bonds between individuals and the worshipping community, on one hand, and between the members of the *ilé* and the unseen but powerful world of the orishas, on the other.

THE SECOND DIASPORA

The development of Santería in Cuba was paralleled by the development of Candomblé in Bahia, Brazil, Vodou in Haiti, Shango and Orisha worship in Trinidad, and other similar new religions throughout the Caribbean. In that sense, worship of the orishas was already an international religious complex in the nineteenth century. Santería in the United States, however, grew most rapidly among recent immigrants in the years after Fidel Castro's successful communist revolution in 1959 and since then has attracted members with no ethnic ties to either Africa or Cuba.

Santería has also figured prominently in court cases about religious freedom in the United States. In 1993, for example, the U.S. Supreme Court ruled in favor of the Church of the Lukumi-Babaluaye, Inc. in its suit against the city of Hialeah, Florida. The court ruled that the attempt to prevent animal sacrifice within the city's limits constituted an unnecessary burden on the plaintiff's constitutional rights. A 2009 case in Euless, Texas, reached the same conclusions.

See also: Candomblé; Race and New Religious Movements; Rastafari; Umbanda; Vodou.

Further Reading

Brandon, George. 1993. *Santeria from Africa to the New World: The Dead Sell Memories.* Bloomington: Indiana University Press.

Brown, David H. 2003. *Santería Enthroned: Art, Ritual, and Innovation in an Afro-Cuban Religion.* Chicago: University of Chicago Press.

Carr, C. Lynn. 2015. *A Year in White: Cultural Newcomers to Lukumi and Santería in the United States.* New Brunswick, NJ: Rutgers University Press.

Murphy, Joseph M. 1988. *Santería: An African Religion in America.* Boston: Beacon Press.

Satanic Panic

From 1980 through the early 1990s, fear of dangerous actions inspired by Satan swept through North America and spread to Europe and beyond. Although that burgeoning concern had much in common with the fear of treacherous "cults" that had developed in the late 1960s, it was more narrowly focused. Triggered by memoirs such as *Michelle Remembers*, which purported to recount incidents of "Satanic ritual abuse" during the childhood of its titular subject, and other reports from parents who feared that their children were being subjected to similar abuse in daycare centers, rumors about an extensive organized Satanic underground that was preying on innocent children quickly found credulous audiences in the news and entertainment media and among some psychologists and law enforcement officials.

Coauthored by Michelle Smith and her therapist, Dr. Lawrence Pazder, *Michelle Remembers* recounts the emotionally wrenching sessions during which Michelle began to remember fragments of what had apparently happened to her as a young child. Two things stand out in Michelle's story. First, the identification of the abuse that Michelle apparently suffered as a child depended on what came to be known as "recovered memories." Such recollections were widely held by many members of the therapeutic community and by the general public to be accurate representations of things that had actually happened. Second, Michelle's therapist, who later became her husband, played a substantial role in developing a context in which the bits and pieces that Michelle brought up in conversation could be made parts of a coherent, meaningful whole.

In 1983, the fears stoked by *Michelle Remembers* and many other books in the same genre erupted in a series of accusations made against teachers at the McMartin Preschool in Manhattan Beach, California. After one parent reported to the police that she suspected that her estranged husband and one of the teachers at the school had sexually abused her young son, a flood of accusations, eventually numbering some 350, ensued. The accusations, including references to Satanic practices, were endorsed by therapists and ultimately taken to a trial that lasted six years and cost taxpayers more than sixteen million dollars. No convictions were secured and all charges were eventually dismissed.

The failure of the McMartin case initiated the end of the Satanic panic of the 1980s and 1990s. Once the prosecution failed to provide evidence of Satanic practices, at least some therapists and law enforcement officials began to look much more skeptically at the grandiose claims about an organized Satanic underground. In 1993, when the Branch Davidian affair monopolized public discussion of alternative religions, the fear of Satanic groups began to fade into the background.

See also: Branch Davidians; Church of Satan, The; Satanism.

Further Reading

Hicks, Robert D. 1991. *In Pursuit of Satan: The Police and the Occult.* Buffalo, NY: Prometheus Books.

Nathan, Debbie, & Michael Snedeker. 1995. *Satan's Silence: Ritual Abuse and the Making of a Modern American Witch Hunt.* New York: Basic Books.

Victor, Jeffrey. 1993. *Satanic Panic: The Creation of a Modern Legend.* Chicago: Open Court.

Satanism

Satanism has proven to be a very elastic term, and therefore a fuzzy category, particularly in popular usage. During the "Satanic Panic" of the 1980s and early 1990s, many observers feared the presence of Satanists virtually everywhere. Further, a variety of memoirs from purported victims and testimonies elicited by therapists fed a journalistic effort to identify a vast Satanist underground that was preying on children throughout the world. A report from Federal Bureau of Investigation agent Kenneth Lanning, composed in 1992, showed the dizzying array of groups that could be included under the general heading of Satanism and thus were suspected of being involved in "Satanic Ritual Abuse." The groups ranged from the expected, such as the Church of Satan or its offshoot the Temple of Set, to the astonishing, including, Buddhism, Hinduism, Islam, Mormonism, and even Roman Catholicism.

It is clear from Lanning's list that "Satanism" has been broadly used as a pejorative term for things that scared (at least some) people. The generalizing depiction of "Satanism" performed the same kind of boundary-setting work that the term "cult" did, even as the two of them overlapped. It distinguished legitimate from illegitimate forms of religion and focused attention and energy on exposing and eradicating illegitimate groups. Although existing Satanic groups have been able to prove conclusively that they are not guilty of the acts conjured up by the Satanic Panic, attempts to regulate alternative religious groups continue to be made throughout the world.

Efforts made during the height of the Satanic Panic to classify various forms of Satanism, distinguishing, for example, experimental from occult from self-styled from traditionalist Satanists, quickly foundered on their own logical weaknesses. The fear of Satanism and the motivations behind that fear were too amorphous to inspire effective categories. But even though the Satanic Panic collapsed, only to be replaced by alarms about other alternative forms of religion, the general public has been left with a vague unease about the prevalence of an ill-defined Satanism.

THE (PRE)HISTORY OF SATANISM

Scholars have shown in detail both that contemporary Satanism has a substantial past and that it stands as a distinctively modern phenomenon. The figure of Satan himself, of course, has a long history. His depiction as "the adversary" in biblical texts has attracted the attention of many who have wanted to set themselves in opposition to the prevailing culture and social norms of their day. Satan has long been a symbol of resistance to the status quo, but the often Romantic appeal to Satan to ground criticisms of church and society never really achieved the status of a fully developed religious belief system with concomitant ritual activity. That would not take place until the 1960s in California.

With very few exceptions, contemporary Satanism, as an organized religious system with specific ritual practices, traces its origins to Anton Szandor LaVey (1930–1997) who founded the Church of Satan on April 30, 1966, in San

Francisco. There have been multiple offshoots from LaVey's church, but his influence has reached well beyond the confines of his particular organization. Through his interviews in the media, dramatic public actions, and especially his writings, such as *The Satanic Bible*, LaVey has extended his impact throughout the world. Surveys have shown that *The Satanic Bible* remains the primary gateway through which individuals come into contact with the Satanic milieu, which overlaps with the broader cultic milieu.

TYPES OF SATANISM

Despite LaVey's widespread influence, there is considerable variety within the contemporary Satanic milieu. LaVey's particular form of Satanism is rationalist. He does not see Satan as an actual being, but rather as a metaphor. The language that LaVey uses in his creedal formulation, "The Nine Satanic Statements," which appears in *The Satanic Bible*, is telling. The first eight statements begin with the phrase "Satan represents." In LaVey's system, Satan represents a particular attitude or orientation to this world, which is, after all, the only world there is. LaVey encourages his readers to exercise relentless doubt and to question all established truths. He positions himself as the first to proclaim the truths contained in *The Satanic Bible* and to call for the establishment of a new religion much better suited to the true nature of human beings. But he also asserts that those who have similar courage and insight can come to the same conclusions.

Esoteric Satanism, on the other hand, relies on the reception of special gnosis by particular prophetic figures. It sees Satan as a real supernatural being and can draw on multiple esoteric religious traditions to form a religious system. The Temple of Set, which split off from LaVey's Church of Satan provides a good example. Its founder, Michael Aquino, claims to have received many revelations from the ancient Egyptian deity, Set. Those revelations are set out in a series of scriptural texts that form the backbone of the Temple's religious system.

Whether rationalist or esoteric, contemporary forms of Satanism can also be understood as forms of "self-religion." Thus, they have things in common with many "New Age" religious systems. Self-religion is this-worldly and focuses on the development of the individual. LaVey, for example, located his Church of Satan on the border between psychiatry and religion. He wanted his audience to throw off the fetters imposed on them by established religions, especially Christianity, and to embrace their true selves. He conceived of his religion as a form of controlled selfishness, in which individuals would embrace, for example, indulgence instead of abstinence, so long as it did not hurt anyone else.

See also: Church of Satan, The; Cult; New Age, The; Satanic Panic.

Further Reading

Dyrendal, Asbjørn, James R. Lewis, & Jesper AA. Petersen. 2016. *The Invention of Satanism*. Oxford: Oxford University Press.

Introvigne, Massimo. 2016. *Satanism: A Social History*. Leiden: E. J. Brill.

Petersen, Jesper Aargard. 2009. *Contemporary Religious Satanism*. Burlington, VT: Ashgate.

Richardson, James T., Joel Best, & David G. Bromley. 1991. *The Satanism Scare*. East Brunswick, NJ: Transaction Publishers.

Van Luijk, Ruben. 2016. *Children of Lucifer: The Origins of Modern Religious Satanism*. Oxford: Oxford University Press.

Sathya Sai Baba Movement, The

Sathya Sai Baba (1926–2011), born Sathyanarayana Rajuin, was allegedly born by miraculous conception—a fact touted by his mother and employed by his followers to highlight Sai Baba's inherent divinity. From an early age, he exhibited magical ability, which he first tested to perpetrate childhood pranks around his village, Puttaparthi in India. At thirteen, however, he temporarily lost consciousness and began exhibiting changes in his demeanor. Then on October 20, 1940, he declared himself to be both the incarnation of Shirdi Sai Baba (1838–1918), a saint claimed by both Hindus and Muslims, whose accolades included serving as an avatar for the Hindu deity, Shiva, and of Shiva as well. This was seemingly confirmed when, to accompany this announcement, he proceeded to materialize various objects out of thin air.

Sathya Sai Baba gained fame for his magical ability, which he attributed to his innate divinity, having been reincarnated as a saint who was also an avatar for Shiva. Though grounded in Hindu principles, the Sathya Sai Baba movement ultimately claimed to be nondenominational, achieving a global presence in the late twentieth century. The movement has its own university (depicted above) located in Puttaparthi, Andhra Pradesh, India, which was the birthplace of Sathya Sai Baba. (Gerold Grotelueschen/Dreamstime.com)

For the next decade, Sai Baba grew in fame for his magical abilities, specifically his materializations. He was able to make precious items appear, such as rings, but also could conjure *vibhuti*, an ash-like substance that he employed in healing many who flocked to him. His movement grew in India and, though he never personally visited, it took root in the United States because of lecture series given by his disciples. His message was disseminated through transcribed discourses, which were ultimately compiled into a compendium known as *Sathya Sai Speaks*, with entries ranging from 1953 to 2009. Though his roots are Hindu, both his religious message and his religious institution, Sathya Sai International Organization (SSIO), founded in the 1960s, were intentionally nondenominational.

Sai Baba died in 2011, though he told his followers that he would exist in human form until 2022, at which point he would incarnate as Sri Prema Sai Baba, who will be an avatar of Shakti, a powerful, all-encompassing force central to Kundalini Yoga. His practitioners give Sai Baba *darshan*, meaning worship, which denotes his status as a deity (and one who supposedly would end an era of history known as the dark age or kali yuga). In India, he has been recognized at various points by the government for his service, even appearing on a postage stamp issued in 1999 and then again in 2013. However, he was also plagued with allegations of fraud, money laundering, and sexual abuse—accusations that his family and followers deny.

BELIEFS AND PRACTICES

Sai Baba's central teaching is that each human being is inherently divine and that the entirety of life's purpose is to realize this divinity through *sadhana* (spiritual discipline), which combines individual meditation and prayer, group singing and devotion, and community service. This leads organically to a religious movement that is universalist in principle and helps to explain the institution's commitment to nondenominationalism. Sai Baba urged practitioners to avoid discrimination of all kinds—religious, racial, class/caste—since ultimately all are part of the same divine "One" and the "One" resides in all of them. Practitioners are enjoined to love all and to live their lives focused on creating harmony and peace through proper conduct and nonviolence.

Though practices vary from center to center and practitioner to practitioner, the SSIO states in its charter that all members are expected to attend to spiritual discipline daily and to abide by a specific code of conduct. The code of conduct ranges from reminders to partake in daily meditation and weekly spiritual singing, to encouragement to study the discourses of Sai Baba and to engage in community outreach, to admonitions against giving into personal desires and speaking poorly of others. Overall, the code of conduct reminds individual practitioners to stay vigilant in their practices and to become vital, contributing members of both religious and global community. Sai Baba was adamant that practitioners not retreat from the world and critiqued ascetic practices as world-renouncing. Today modern practitioners (particularly those from Western nations) are drawn to the movement for its focus on individual spiritual growth, personal wellness (including the practice of vegetarianism), and global community projects.

INSTITUTION AND LEGACY

According to the website of SSIO, there are approximately two thousand Sathya Sai Baba Centers located in 126 countries, with members in nearly 180 countries. Estimates place membership anywhere between ten to one hundred million. This significant discrepancy results from the fact that the definition of "member" may range from casual dabbler to devotee. Membership is advertised as "free and open to all," but particularly "sincere seekers," enabling those from diverse faith backgrounds to visit the Centers, learn from Sai Baba, and not necessarily leave their home tradition. Demographically, members both inside and outside of India hail from upper-middle-class backgrounds and are well educated. All are invited to weekly services, which revolve around singing and various devotional and meditative activities. There is also great emphasis on volunteerism, specifically in charitable endeavors, ranging from food distribution, to medical aid, to disaster relief.

Beyond religious centers, a radio network, and a publishing house devoted to the writings of Sai Baba, SSIO oversees medical and educational institutions. Sai Baba desired community outreach and spiritual advancement to be linked, prompting him to found multiple hospitals, schools, and drinking water supply stations, where services are offered free of charge. In fact, the SSIO is alternatively called the Sri Sathya Sai Seva Organization, where *seva* means "service." Thus, the cultural impact of Sathya Sai Baba's message certainly equals his spiritual legacy, which follows his belief that the spiritual discipline inherently produces care for the world and those around you.

See also: Charisma and Leadership New Religious Movements; Healing, Health, and New Religious Movements; Hindu New Religious Movements; Magic and New Religious Movements; Yoga.

Further Reading

Baba, Sathya Sai. 1953–2009. *Sathya Sai Speaks*. Volumes 1–42. Available at: http://www.sathyasai.org/discour/content.htm.

Kim, Hanna H. 2014. "Sathya Sai Baba and the Repertoire of Yoga." In Mark Singleton and Ellen Goldberg, eds., *Gurus of Modern Yoga*. New York: Oxford University Press.

Srinivas, Smriti. 2008. *In the Presence of Sai Baba: Body, City, and Memory in a Global Religious Movement*. Leiden; Boston: Brill.

Srinivas, Tulasi. 2010. *Winged Faith: Rethinking Globalization and Religious Pluralism through the Sathya Sai Baba Movement*. New York: Columbia University.

Science and Health with Key to the Scriptures

HISTORY

Science and Health with Key to the Scriptures is a new scripture written by Mary Baker Eddy (1821–1910), the founder of Christian Science. Christian Science emerged as a parallel tradition to New Thought in the late nineteenth century. The religion's distinguishing features are beliefs that all matter is illusory and the only reality is spirit or God, evil is unreal, sin results from the wrongful belief that evil is real, and through prayer and right thinking, illness can be banished and salvation achieved. All of these concepts, as well as explanations for how to connect with the "Mind" of Christ to heal ailments, are unpacked in *Science and Health*.

Eddy began writing *Science and Health* in 1872. It was first published in 1875 by W.F. Brown & Co—the same year that Church of Christ, Scientist was founded. Eddy considered it her most important achievement, even though she intended for the text to be read alongside the Bible, not to replace or supplant the traditional Christian canon. Passages in the "Key to the Scriptures" were specifically designed to correspond to various passages in the Bible and to illuminate the spiritual message of the biblical text. Reflecting her belief that these two texts were all one needed to advance spiritually and achieve salvation, Eddy named *Science and Health* as the official pastor of the Church. Each Sunday, in congregations around the world, "Readers" stand and read a passage from the Bible and one from *Science and Health*. The program is standardized and thus the same for every congregation, ensuring that all Christian Scientists hear the same message.

Eddy continued to make changes to *Science and Health* or to commission new editions due to typographical errors made by her first two publishers. All later editions were published by the University Press of Cambridge. By her death in 1910, there had been 418 editions of *Science and Health*; there have been further editions, but the Church ceased numbering them. The Church now includes the full text of *Science and Health* on its website, though during the 1990s, it was reported that over ten million copies had sold.

CONTENT AND FEATURES

Science and Health is organized topically, with various chapters dealing with specific theological, practical, cosmological, and philosophical issues. For example, the first chapter, "Prayer," unpacks the purpose, preparation, and efficacy of prayer for the Christian Scientist; the chapter on "Marriage" describes the spiritual purpose and theological challenges of marital relationships; and the "Science, Theology, Medicine" chapter seeks to show how "Divine Science," Eddy's great discovery, relates to both Western medicine and Christian theology. Clearly, not every traditional aspect of Christian theology is addressed, reflecting the nature of *Science and Health* as supplemental, not standalone. Those topics to which Eddy devotes a chapter begin with passages from the Bible that speak to the theme of the chapter. In both the printed and online versions, marginal descriptions are included to help the reader find a specific point or passage in the text (e.g., in the "Creation" chapter, there is the marginal descriptor, "No material creation").

The "Key to the Scriptures" follows the topical chapters and is intended to provide a "spiritual interpretation" of particular passages of the Bible. Much like the thematic chapters, not every chapter in the Bible is given specific treatment—in fact, only Genesis and the Book of Revelation are addressed specifically. Once again, Eddy's aim is to shed light upon certain elements of the Bible that are the most crucial for Christian Science thought and practice. Additionally, she created a "Glossary" of biblical terms (such as "Adversary" or "Holy Spirit"), for which she provides interpretations with a Christian Science twist ("Adversary" becomes "one who opposes or denies" and "Holy Ghost" becomes Divine Science).

Science and Health closes with a chapter called "Fruitage," which comprises a series of testimonials by those who read the text and experienced spiritual advancement and physical healing.

See also: Christian Science; Eddy, Mary Baker (1821–1910); Healing, Health, and New Religious Movements; New Scriptures and New Religious Movements; New Thought.

Further Reading

Eddy, Mary Baker. 1934. *Science and Health with Key to the Scriptures*. Boston: Published by the First Church of Christ, Scientist.

Gill, Gillian. 1998. *Mary Baker Eddy*. Reading, MA: Perseus Books.

Weddle, David L. 1991. "The Christian Science Textbook: An Analysis of the Religious Authority of *Science and Health* by Mary Baker Eddy." *Harvard Theological Review* 84, no. 3 (July): 273–297.

Science Fiction and New Religious Movements

At first glance, religion and science fiction may seem to have little in common. However, both traffic in the examination of imagined worlds, accept that contact with supernatural or heavenly beings is possible, believe that global change by supernatural means can happen, and accept that fantastic or miraculous events are real. From certain vantage points, religion *is* a form of science fiction, since its claims to truth are speculative, requiring faith, not fact, to confirm them. Thus, it is not surprising that science fiction may begin to exhibit elements of religion or that new religious movements in particular may exhibit qualities of science fiction.

FROM FICTION TO RELIGION

Perhaps the clearest example of the synthesis of science fiction and religion is the Church of Scientology. Around the same time that he was developing the concepts that would form the basis of Scientologist belief and practice, L. Ron Hubbard (1911–1986) wrote science fiction. His sci-fi works spanned publications in "pulp" magazines, such as *Astounding Science Fiction*, short stories, such as his short story collection, *Kingslayer* (1949), and novels, such as *Battlefield Earth* (1982), which would eventually be made into a film by notable Scientologist, John Travolta (1954–).

Unsurprisingly, Hubbard's science fiction reflected his growing religious interests, and vice versa. For example, *Dianetics* (1950) posited that human beings were capable of greater, potentially superhuman, feats if they trained their minds and released past trauma, a notion reflective of the themes of his sci-fi corpus. Additionally, Hubbard frequently wrote about space travel, alternate planets and galaxies, and extraterrestrial life forms, versions of which would appear in the theology of Scientology, particularly in versions of human evolution and the creation of the universe.

544   **Science Fiction and New Religious Movements**

Some religions that take inspiration from science fiction are less earnest and more satirical. The Church of the Flying Spaghetti Monster, or Pastafarianism, arose as an internet hoax. Its founder, Bobby Henderson (1980–), created the religion as a means of critiquing the Kansas State Board of Education's insistence on teaching both intelligent design and the theory of evolution. The description of the religion reads like a science fiction novel, albeit a farcical one where the creator of the world resembled a bowl of spaghetti and meatballs, heaven involved a beer volcano, and hell boasted strippers with sexually transmitted diseases. Despite its origins, the spoof religion has attracted acolytes who, though not protected by the First Amendment, are permitted to wear religious "attire" (colanders as hats) in ID photos.

STRANGER THAN FICTION

Other religions were not quite so literally born of science fiction, but came to resemble the genre nonetheless. UFO religions, for example, seem to spring from the screen of a 1950s flying saucer film, but their origins are unequivocally religious. Former racecar driver Claude Vorilhon (1946–), was contacted by the Elohim (a plural term for God in the Hebrew Bible/Old Testament), a race of advanced, extraterrestrial beings. From them, Vorilhon, who took the prophetic name Raël, learned that all life on earth had been created by the Elohim in laboratories. His initial contact produced new translations of the Bible, as well as efforts to promote cloning instead of reproduction, in order to advance humanity according to the example of their extraterrestrial creators. In other new religious movements, UFOs simply make an appearance, rather than acting as foundational to their religious system. In 1985, Louis Farrakhan (1933–) the current leader of the Nation of Islam claimed that he had ascended to the heavens (much like the Prophet Muhammad as recorded in the Qur'an) where he boarded the Mother Ship and was greeted by the Prophet Elijah Muhammad (1897–1985), who was not actually dead.

The advance of technology, particularly the invention of the internet, has made possible the existence of new religions, including those with sci-fi ties, that may not have existed otherwise. For self-proclaimed Vampires, even their most established institutions such as the Temple of the Vampire exist predominantly online. The same goes for practitioners of Jediism, a religion that began as the result of a census campaign. Jedi are the intergalactic knights connected to the mysterious "force" in the *Star Wars* films, who many have noted resemble certain mystical strains of world religions. Jediism has even exited the virtual world into the real, establishing Jedi temples in the United States.

For the most part, the public finds the parallels between science fiction and religion strange, but innocuous. However, in certain cases, the resemblance to science fiction has been used to ridicule or belittle a new religion. Heaven's Gate, a new religious movement that made media waves following the ritual suicide of thirty-nine of its members in March 1997, was called a "science fiction cult" by various news outlets. The assumption behind this characterization is that the members of Heaven's Gate had confused fiction with reality rather than being active religious agents with a complex belief system based on Christian millennialism, new age religion, and belief in UFOs. This terminology was also used to highlight the danger of cults, since in cases like Heaven's Gate, it seemed clear that its members had lost touch with reality and took their lives to perpetuate a fantasy.

The marriage between science fiction and religion will continue to produce movements, so long as there are those who find the sacred in the strange.

See also: Cult; Heaven's Gate; Hubbard, L. Ron (1911–1986); Jediism; New Religions on/ and the Internet; Pastafarianism (Church of the Flying Spaghetti Monster); Raëlians, The; Science, Technology, and New Religious Movements; Scientology; UFO Religions; Vampirism; Vorilhon, Claude (Raël) (1946–).

Further Reading

Cowan, Douglas E. 2010. *Sacred Space: The Quest for Transcendence in Science Fiction, Film, and Television.* Waco, TX: Baylor University Press.

Jones, Douglas FitzHenry. 2012. "Reading 'New' Religious Movements Historically: Sci-Fi Possibilities and Shared Assumptions in Heaven's Gate." *Nova Religio* 16, no. 2: 29–46.

Kripal, Jeffrey J. 2011. *Mutants and Mystics: Science Fiction, Superhero Comics, and the Paranormal.* Chicago: University of Chicago Press.

Zeller, Benjamin E. 2012. "Heaven's Gate, Science Fiction Religions, and Popular American Culture." In *Handbook of Hyper-Real Religions.* pp. 59–84. Leiden: Brill.

Science, Technology, and New Religious Movements

Accounts of Galileo Galilei's (1564–1642) investigation at the hands of the Roman Inquisition, Christian fundamentalists banning the theory of evolution from science classes, and religious denial of climate change seem to confirm this familiar trope that science and religion don't mix. In reality, the history of the interactions between religion and science is far more complex, and religious people are not so simply categorized as anti- or ascientific.

Many major religions have embraced scientific discovery—sometimes begrudgingly, sometimes eagerly. There have also been a host of new religious movements that have embraced science and technology. And they have not been passive recipients of scientific innovation. New religions have adapted science to work for them, bending the standard definition of scientific "truth" to align with theological and spiritual ends—a fact that has led critics to deny the designation of science to these traditions. Nonetheless, science and religion have mixed and will continue to mix in the world of new religions.

SEEING IS BELIEVING

When it comes to the promises made by religions, one can distinguish between those that offer more general rewards and those that offer more immediate results. General rewards are found in many major religions, often including offers of eternal life in exchange for adhering to a particular belief system; such rewards usually require little or no evidence to support them. Religions that offer more immediate results provide an instant test of the validity of their practices or beliefs, such as miraculous healings. Many new religions that premise their origins and belief systems on a scientific basis dabble in such immediacy. Proclaiming that you have scientific "proof" of belief or ritual can be an attractive draw for potential members in a religious marketplace suffused with those promising future rewards—particularly when this proof comes in the form of better health, longer life, and even advanced abilities.

The appeal to quantifiable evidence in modern religious practice is often associated with the progenitors of the movement known as New Thought. Though diffuse in its practices and iterations, its origins are often tied to the work of Phineas Quimby (1802–1866). While experimenting with Mesmerism—a belief system that incorporated the use of magnets placed at strategic points on the body to heal various ailments—Quimby discovered that it was the patients' belief in the efficacy of the practice, rather than the practice itself, that healed. One of Quimby's clients was Mary Baker Eddy (1821–1910). Eddy had suffered from illness throughout her life and had little success with Western medicine. She sought Quimby's help and eventually came to her own discovery, known as Divine Science, following a near-death experience. Eddy determined that matter was illusory (including disease, which was the result of wrong thinking or "sin") that God was mind. As a means of guiding people toward patterns of right thinking, Eddy wrote *Science and Health with Key to the Scriptures* (1875), intending for it to be read alongside the Bible to unlock the latter's true or "scientific" meaning. She would eventually found an institution for Divine Science, known as the Church of Christ, Scientist.

New Thought, or the notion that right thinking (or believing) can lead to salvation and produce tangible results, spawned or influenced many movements. The Unity School of Christianity, founded by Charles (1854–1948) and Myrtle Fillmore (1845–1931), was born from a combination of New Thought and Christianity. Unity employs the language of science to advocate for the proof of various Christian doctrines, such as the reality of the afterlife, and for the practical impact of prayer and certain bodily practices, such as vegetarianism, on one's earthly and eternal life.

TECHNOLOGY AND MYTHOLOGY IN THE TWENTIETH CENTURY

Not all new religions employed science as a means of "proof" in their religious systems. The International Society for Krishna Consciousness (ISKCON), for example, often maintained that it was a science, even more than a religion, even while disparaging the soullessness of science and the focus on quantitative results. ISKCON members, or Hare Krishnas, positioned Krishna Consciousness as the antidote to Western science, which was overly materialistic. They claimed that "true" science, based in Vaishnavic Hindu practices, challenged the true nature of all material reality. By engaging the language of science, but without the method, ISKCON legitimized its claims. It sought to enjoy the imprimatur of science, not through a reliance on evidence-based results, but through the cultivation of mythologies that appealed to science and technology.

The appeal to science in mythologies is found in several new religions that combined Islam with racial uplift at the beginning of the twentieth century. Noble (Timothy) Drew Ali (1886–1929), founder of the Moorish Science Temple, claimed that black people were descendants of Moors, for whom the true religion was Islam. By reworking their historical and mythic origins, members of the temple could shed the racial distinction of "negro" and instead claim to be "Moors." An outgrowth of this new mythos was the Moorish Manufacturing Corporation, which created products intended to keep Moors pure and racially distinct, thus employing modern industrial technology for religious ends. Ali's contemporary and founder of the Nation of Islam, Elijah Muhammad (1897–1975) invoked science to highlight both the technological advancement of black people, who were chosen by God to reign over earth, and the sinister origins of the white race. Among God's chosen was evil scientist, Yacub, who created white people in his laboratory to subvert God's providence. This experiment set in motion a prophetic narrative that would require black people to be subjugated by whites until a specific moment in the future (which Muhammad assured was their present one) when God's chosen people would ultimately ascend to their true position once again.

UFO religions have spanned not only science but the mythological world invoked in science fiction. UFO sightings have existed for centuries, but in the latter half of the twentieth century, they became an object of cultural fascination, mostly of the popular variety. However, a number of new religions arose from this milieu on the following premise: if there are other forms of life in the universe, there was a distinct possibility that they could aid humanity technologically and spiritually, and that they were in fact divine or supernatural in nature.

Founded by Ernest (1904–1971) and Ruth Norman (1900–1993), the Unarius Academy of Science opposes the label of religion, arguing that it is a science, that simply provides the greater meaning behind scientific principles, such as gravity and atomic energy. Unarius stands for Universal Articulate Interdimensional Understanding of Science; the interdimensional aspect refers to the fact that both Normans served as channels for extraterrestrial beings who provided advanced sacred knowledge of the physical universe. Equally drawn to the idea that there were beings desirous of communicating with earthlings was George King (1919–1997) who, drawing on Theosophy, argued that among extraterrestrials were a set of "Cosmic Masters" who had helped humanity advance throughout history. Upon these beliefs, King founded the Aetherius Society, so named for the primary extraterrestrial intelligence that contacted King. Its practices reflect a combination of Theosophical and New Age beliefs. Other UFO groups, like the Raëlians, place greater emphasis on science and advocate for advanced technology. After being visited by extraterrestrials called the Elohim (a name for God in the Hebrew Bible), founder Claude Vorilhon, Raël (1946–), revealed that human beings were created in a lab. This has led the group to advocate for modern, albeit controversial, scientific practices such as cloning.

548   Science, Technology, and New Religious Movements

Perhaps the best-known UFO religion of the twentieth century is Heaven's Gate. Founded by Marshall Herff Applewhite or "Do" (1931–1997) and Bonnie Lu Nettles or "Ti" (1927–1985), Heaven's Gate mixed Christian millennialism, New Age spirituality, and an interest in various branches of science, including astronomy and aeronautics. Ti and Do revealed that they were actually extraterrestrials who had taken human form to help humanity advance to The Evolutionary Level Above Human. The precise nature of this transition would change over time, precipitated in part by Nettles's untimely death. Eventually, the appearance of the Hale-Bopp Comet was perceived as a sign that the moment had come to shed their earthly vessels; the remaining members of Heaven's Gate committed ritual suicide in March 1997.

RELIGIONS OF THE FUTURE

In an era when technology advances swiftly, it is not surprising that religions have arisen that employ technology deliberately in their theology and systems of practice. Scientology, primarily through the use of the E-Meter, has engaged with technology since its founding in the mid-twentieth century. It even refers to its practices and teachings as "tech." Founder L. Ron Hubbard (1911–1986) published *Dianetics* in 1950, his antidote to modern psychology, which posited the existence of the "reactive" and "conscious" mind. The reactive mind stored memories of past trauma as "engrams," which stunted people in myriad ways. To rid people of engrams, they would undergo "auditing," which involved use of the E-Meter to measure electromagnetic response as their auditor asked them a series of questions. Over time, the individual could become "clear" of all past trauma. The Church of Scientology grew out of Dianetics when those who underwent auditing began to report memories of past lives. Hubbard revealed that each person was actually a Thetan, an eternal, immortal being; through multiple reincarnations, the Thetan had forgotten who he or she was, a feature of the trauma stored in the reactive mind. By combining the modern technology, quantifiable results, with a religious mythology, Scientology offered a religion for a technological age.

There are also many religions that have grown as a result of the internet—or, perhaps, would not have existed if not for the internet, such as Jediism or Vampirism. Kopimism, a combination of the words "copy" and "me," is a religion *of* the internet. Kopimists are those who consider free access to information on the internet a sacred right. Though the movement is quite diffuse, a feature of the emphasis on secrecy for its members, there are Kopimist priests and administrators known as "ops," who arrange interaction points among members. The lack of belief in any higher power or any discernible institutional body has led critics to characterize Kopimism as a parody religion, at best, and as the dangerous result of a problematic merging of technology and religion.

Despite those who fear that science, technology, and religion have been too greatly conflated, there are those who feel drawn to these religions for their perceived modernity. Arguably, adaptation is a natural process for religions and those that are able to cast themselves as aligned with science and technology may have an advantage in a modernizing age.

See also: Aetherius Society, The; Ali, Noble Drew (1886–1929); Applewhite, Marshall (1932–1997), and Bonnie Lu Nettles (1927–1985); Christian Science; Dianetics; Eddy, Mary Baker (1821–1910); Healing, Health, and New Religious Movements; Hubbard, L. Ron (1911–1986); International Society for Krishna Consciousness (ISKCON); Jediism; Kopimism; Mesmerism; Millennialism; Moorish Science Temple of America, The; Muhammad, Elijah (1897–1975); Nation of Islam, The; New Age, The; New Religions on/ and the Internet; New Thought; Quimby, Phineas (1802–1866); Raëlians, The; *Science and Health with Key to the Scriptures*; Science Fiction and New Religious Movements; Scientology; Theosophy; UFO Religions; Unarius Academy of Science, The; Unity School of Christianity; Vampirism; Vorilhon, Claude (Raël) (1946–).

Further Reading

Bigliardi, Stefano. 2016. "New Religious Movements, Technology, and Science: The Conceptualization of the E-Meter in Scientology Teachings." *Zygon* 51, no. 3: 661–683.

Rapport, Jeremy. 2011. "Corresponding to the Rational World: Scientific Rationales and Language in Christian Science and the Unity School of Christianity." *Nova Religio* 14, no. 4: 11–29.

Rapport, Jeremy. 2016. "New Religions and Science." In James R. Lewis & Inga Tøllefsen, eds., *The Oxford Handbook of New Religious Movements*. New York: Oxford University Press.

Zeller, Benjamin E. 2011 [2010]. *Prophets and Protons: New Religious Movements and Science in Late Twentieth-century America*. New York: New York University Press.

Zeller, Benjamin E. 2014. "Science." In George D. Chyrssides & Benjamin E. Zeller, eds., *The Bloomsbury Companion to New Religious Movements*. London: Bloomsbury Academic.

Scientology

Since its beginnings in the early 1950s, the Church of Scientology has remained one of the most controversial new religions of the twentieth and twenty-first centuries. Grounded in L. Ron Hubbard's (1911–1986) exploration of the human mind, Scientology has developed into a very complex organization devoted to the preservation and promulgation of what it sees as Hubbard's unprecedented insight into how to cure humanity of its multiple ailments and unleash the power inherent in every individual.

ORIGINS AND HISTORY

Scientology attributes to Hubbard an extraordinary biography, including his initiation into the Blackfoot tribe as a child, travels to the Far East and other expeditions, expertise as a pilot, and meritorious service in the U.S. Navy, among other things. After spending two years at George Washington University, Hubbard embarked on a career as a writer of genre pulp fiction, primarily

550   Scientology

Western and science fiction. But Hubbard's greatest achievement began while he was convalescing from injuries suffered in World War II. With the time to devote himself fully to formulating his ideas, Hubbard came to the conclusions that were eventually published in 1950 as *Dianetics: The Modern Science of Mental Health*.

Hubbard touted Dianetics (from the Greek *dia*, "through" and *nous* "mind") as a system of thought and attendant practices that could dramatically improve the lives of individuals and ameliorate an array of social problems. As the subtitle of his book suggests, Hubbard initially conceived Dianetics as a scientific approach to improving mental health. At the core of his system was the concept that humans have both a conscious, "analytical" mind and a "reactive" mind. The reactive mind stores memories of past traumatic events as "engrams," which can be reactivated when any element associated with the initial incident is encountered. When that happens, individuals will suffer from various psychological and even physical illnesses that compromise their ability to function at peak capacity.

Hubbard believed that he had developed a process, or a "technology," through which individuals could diminish and ultimately dissipate the negative effects of their stored engrams. The process of "auditing," a form of counseling that follows a careful script developed by Hubbard, was designed both to bring engrams to the surface and progressively reduce their inhibiting effects.

Hubbard had high hopes for his new form of therapy and he was initially buoyed by the enthusiastic reception that *Dianetics* received, including its spending six months on the *New York Times* best-seller list. Many individuals adopted Hubbard's therapeutic ideas and even developed independent practices of Dianetics.

Two primary factors, however, led Hubbard to reconceive his system in the early 1950s. First, the medical and psychological establishment expressed no interest in, and even opposition to, Hubbard's insights, which marked the beginning of an antipathy toward psychiatry that Hubbard and now Scientology continues to express. Second, some of those undergoing auditing were reporting memories that reached beyond their current lifespans to past lives. Hubbard's move toward incorporating Dianetics into the broader system of Scientology (from the Latin *scio* to know and the Greek *logos* knowledge; "knowing how to know") was gradual. By late 1954, however, he was describing Scientology as a religion that focused on the human spirit or "thetan." The thetan constitutes the fundamental identity of each individual; it is eternal and consequently experiences multiple incarnations, thus explaining individuals' memories of past lives. In 1955, Hubbard incorporated the Founding Church of Scientology in Washington, D.C.

Hubbard's efforts to establish Scientology as a religion continued to prompt controversy both in the United States and Europe. Although the Church was granted tax-exempt status by the U.S. Internal Revenue Service (IRS) in 1956, that status was revoked in 1967 because the revenues of the Church were found to benefit primarily individuals. A prolonged legal and publicity battle ensued. It was only resolved on October 1, 1993, when Scientology regained its status as a religion in the eyes of the IRS. Scientology's status as a religion continues to be a point of contention in some European countries, particularly Germany.

PRACTICES AND BELIEFS

Although auditing and training are the fundamental activities for practitioners of Scientology, Hubbard did attempt to distill the basic beliefs of the Church in an official creed, composed in 1954. In what may reflect the opposition Hubbard encountered from the outset, the first section of the creed insists on the rights of all humans to choose their own ideas, organizations, and religious practices. The second section asserts that humans are basically good and are seeking, above all, to survive. In fact the imperative or urge to survive is what animates Scientology's presentation of the eight dynamics of human life, which are symbolized in Scientology's eight-pointed cross. In order, they refer to the survival of the self, the family, the group, the species, all life forms, the physical universe, the life source or the spirit, and infinity or God. The third section of the creed emphasizes that no one has the right to destroy the sanity or reduce the survival of anyone else. Finally, the fourth section asserts that the spirit alone can save or heal the body. The Creed of Scientology captures only a small portion of the Church's teaching, but it does introduce some of Scientology's distinctive ideas. In general, though, practice, rather than abstract belief, is central to Scientology.

At one level, Scientology constitutes what Rodney Stark and William Sims Bainbridge have called a "client cult," in which individuals contract with the organization for specific services, such as courses based on Scientology's principles or auditing sessions. Accordingly, those individuals may have only intermittent interactions with the organization. Some Scientologists, however, join the Sea Organization (or Sea Org), so named because from 1968 to 1975 Hubbard had the leadership of the Church live on board a fleet of ships. The Sea Org constitutes a religious order within the Church of Scientology and provides leadership for the many different organizations sponsored by the Church. Members sign a billion-year contract with the Church and in turn receive food, lodging, and auditing services without charge. Breaking the Sea Org's rules or leaving altogether are treated as serious infractions and merit sanctions ranging from being assigned to the Rehabilitation Project Force or being declared a "suppressive person" with whom Scientologists should not associate.

Scientology offers to its practitioners an elaborate, ongoing process, called the "Bridge to Total Freedom," by which they can continue to develop their human capacities. The fundamental goal for Scientologists is to achieve through auditing the state of "Clear." Clears are freed from the debilitating effects of stored engrams and can enjoy multiple psychological and even physical benefits. One statement of Scientology's goal is to clear the entire planet.

The state of clear, however, is only one step along the Bridge. Beyond it lie successive stages related to the spiritual status of Operating Thetan or OT. As the Church puts it on its primary website (www.scientology.org), at the level of OT one becomes wholly oneself as an immortal spiritual being. Although Scientology holds that Hubbard designed fifteen OT levels, only eight have so far been released.

Movement across the Bridge is time consuming and costly. Graduation from one level to the next, even as it promises extraordinary expansion of one's capabilities, demands extraordinary dedication. In addition to deepening practice of auditing, the successive OT levels lead the practitioner deeper into the worldview and mythology of Scientology. Although the Church treats the information associated with the OT levels as esoteric religious knowledge that should be revealed only to initiates at the appropriate time, information about that knowledge has been produced in several court cases and is now readily accessible online, despite the efforts of the Church to retain control of its teachings.

One of the most widely known, and frequently ridiculed as on the television show *South Park*, elements of Scientology's teaching is the creation story associated with OT level III. The account begins some seventy-five million years ago and focuses on the actions of the galactic ruler Xenu. In response to overpopulation in his area of the galaxy, Xenu brought billions of people to earth and destroyed them, using hydrogen bombs. Their thetans, however, survived and now cling to modern individuals, causing them even more suffering than their engrams. Those thetans need to be released from individuals through auditing.

CONTROVERSIES

Scientology has been embroiled in controversy from its origins. Rejection by medical and psychiatric gatekeepers helped turn Hubbard's new science of mental health into a religion. The early diversity of the practice of Dianetics led Hubbard to exert greater control over his discoveries, but individuals continue to put Hubbard's insight into practice independently, particularly since the rise of David Miscavige (1960–) to a position of leadership after Hubbard's death.

Like other new or alternative religions, Scientology has been the focus of exposés by disgruntled former members, which have appeared as books and have also served as sources for journalists who have written critical accounts of the Church. The celebrity status of some former members—Scientology has long courted celebrities for the increased visibility they bring to the religion—guarantees a large audience for the negative views of opponents. Actress Leah Remini (1970–), for example, has both written an autobiography critical of her time in the Church and beginning in 2016 hosted a documentary series, *Leah Remini: Scientology and Its Aftermath*, that provides a forum for other ex-members to express their grievances. The entanglement of Scientology with Hollywood, most notable in actor Tom Cruise's fervent public endorsements of Scientology, was at the heart of Lawrence Wright's (1947–) *Going Clear* (2013), which was also made into an HBO special.

The current leader of Scientology, David Miscavige, has received particularly sharp criticism from former members, including some like Mark "Marty" Rathbun (1957–), who once held leadership positions. Rathbun led the Religious Technology Center, the organization responsible for protecting all of the copyrights held by Dianetics and Scientology. He left the Church in 2004 but continued to practice Scientology and has written several books about the Church, including *The Scientology Reformation* and *What Is Wrong with Scientology*, and continues to produce a blog that is critical of both the current hierarchy of the Church and some of the Church's critics.

In the United States, Scientology has been publicly portrayed as the epitome of a dangerous cult, with a special focus on both the costs involved in moving along the Bridge and the purportedly totalitarian control the Church exerts over its most dedicated members in the Sea Org. The Church's protracted battle with the IRS, which revolved around its claim to status as a religion, has been echoed by clashes with government agencies and the general public in other countries. In Germany, for example, the status of Scientology as a religion remains in dispute and Scientologists suffer from widespread discrimination and restrictions on their activities.

Many of Scientology's critics claim that it is losing members, but the Church insists that it continues to make palpable progress toward its goal of clearing the planet. Because of the occasional nature of many individuals' relationship with the Church, it is difficult to determine trustworthy membership numbers. But despite the virtually constant opposition it has faced, it seems unlikely that the Church of Scientology will disappear at any time in the near future. The benefits that it offers continue to attract a devoted audience.

See also: Dianetics; Freezone Scientology; Hubbard, L. Ron (1911–1986); Occultism and Esotericism.

Further Reading

Hubbard, L. Ron. 2007 [1950]. *Dianetics: The Modern Science of Mental Health.* Commerce, CA: Bridge Publications.

Lewis, James R., ed. 2009. *Scientology.* New York: Oxford University Press.

Lewis, James R., & Kjersti Hellesøy, eds. 2017. *Handbook of Scientology.* Leiden: E. J. Brill.

Urban, Hugh B. 2011. *The Church of Scientology: A History of a New Religion.* Princeton, NJ: Princeton University Press.

Westbrook, Donald A. 2019. *Among the Scientologists: History, Theology, Praxis.* New York: Oxford University Press.

Wright, Lawrence. 2013. *Going Clear: Scientology, Hollywood, and the Prison of Belief.* New York: Knopf.

Sect

Like "cult," the term "sect" has had a long history in the academic study of religion. But it also has been given a different, negative meaning in popular discourse, particularly in Europe. In French ("secte"), Italian ("sette"), and German ("sekte"), the term carries the same pejorative force that "cult" has in English. It is therefore crucially important to examine carefully every use of "sect" for its intended meaning.

RELIGIOUS SECTS

The discussion of sects in the sociology of religion initially focused on Christianity. Max Weber, for example, proposed a simple distinction: people are born into churches but they join sects. Weber's student Ernst Troeltsch offered a more complex account. Acknowledging that sects were typically viewed negatively by churches, Troeltsch argued that even though Christian sects had their roots in the Christian message, they were detached from the world and generally attracted members from the lower classes. Joining Weber and Troeltsch as influential contributors to the developing "church-sect typology," H. Richard Niebuhr reinforced Weber's notion that a sect was a voluntary organization with an exclusive membership and reemphasized Troeltsch's contention that sects appealed primarily to the lower social classes. Niebuhr also stressed the dynamic nature of sects, arguing that they could rarely sustain themselves for more than a generation and that, if they persisted, they moved inevitably toward becoming churches.

As the church-sect typology became part of the working vocabulary of scholars of religion, it provided clear gains in the understanding of some specific groups. But those gains were offset by the loss of conceptual clarity that came with the proliferation of additional types and subtypes of sects and also the diverse proposals for categorizing the relationship of individual sects to their broader religious contexts. J. Milton Yinger and Bryan Wilson were among the scholars who developed elaborate typologies of sects and their relations to other religious bodies. Eventually, Benton Johnson proposed returning to the clarity and simplicity of something like Weber's original distinction. Using the single criterion of tension with society, Johnson proposed that a church is a religious group that accepts its social environment, while a sect is a group that rejects its social environment.

The concept of a sect has been used in different ways in the study of new religions. Sociologist of religion Roy Wallis, for example, draws a sharp distinction between sects and cults. For Wallis, the identifying characteristic of a sect is its claim to unique status and authority. Sects are founded on what he calls "epistemological authoritarianism." They admit only one way of doing things and frequently vest extensive power and centralized authority in an individual or very small group. Wallis argues that a sect is very different from a cult, which is seen by its members as only one of a variety of ways in which they might pursue salvation.

Sociologist Rodney Stark, with various collaborators, has outlined a different approach. Stark focuses on what he calls the "religious economy" or the total amount of religious activity in a given society. He views the process of secularization as self-limiting and emphasizes that secularization provokes religious responses, which keep the religious economy in a state of flux. Stark observes that as churches progressively accommodate themselves to their social environments, they run the risk of alienating their members who have endorsed a higher tension with society. Some of those disgruntled members have the potential to undertake reform efforts that would undo the effects of accommodation and increase the tension between the church and its social environment. In some instances, when they explicitly split off from their parent bodies through schism, those reformers could become the founders of sects.

On the other hand, for Stark cults are groups that are new to a specific social environment, either through invention by religious entrepreneurs or through importation from other societies. In other words, sects form by schism; cults form by innovation. Both of them respond to the increasing secularization of churches. To the extent that sects and cults persist, they also risk responding to the powerful lure of accommodation; once they do, they also can experience their own schisms and challenges from innovative alternative groups. In Stark's view, the complex interplay of the secularization of dominant religious groups, sectarian revivals, and innovative cult formations constitutes the perpetually dynamic system of a religious economy.

DANGEROUS SECTES

The use of the term "secte" and its analogues in Europe echoes the pejorative use of the term by Christian churches against their sectarian competitors. Although Germany has been particularly concerned with the Church of Scientology and other countries, such as Belgium and certain parts of Switzerland, have developed legislation against "sectes," France has been the most aggressive in passing legislation and providing general support to its own anti-secte movement. French anti-secte activists have often drawn directly on the ideas of members of the American anti-cult movement, including Cynthia Kisser (1949–), the former Executive Director of the Cult Awareness Network and psychologist Margaret Singer (1921–2003).

During the 1990s, the French government issued several reports about the perceived dangers of sectes, and in 1998 it established the Interministerial Mission to Battle against Sectes. Then, in 2001 France passed the About-Picard law, named for the two members of parliament who drafted it. The law was aimed at secte movements (some 173 of which had been identified in a 1996 government report) that purportedly undermined individuals' human rights and fundamental freedoms. In Europe, France continues to take the strongest stance against stigmatized new religions.

See also: Anticult Movement, The; Cult; Cult Awareness Movement, The; Singer, Margaret Thaler (1921–2003).

Further Reading

Introvigne, Massimo. 2004. "Something Peculiar about France: Anti-Cult Campaigns in Western Europe and French Religious Exceptionalism." In James R. Lewis, ed., *The Oxford Handbook of New Religious Movements*, pp. 206–220. Oxford: Oxford University Press.

Stark, Rodney, & William Sims Bainbridge. 1985. *The Future of Religion: Secularization, Revival, and Cult Formation.* Berkeley: University of California Press.

Wilson, Bryan. 1990. *The Social Sources of Denominationalism: Sects and New Religious Movements in Contemporary Society.* Oxford: Oxford University Press.

Seekers

Especially in their earliest phases, new religions find members among those who have weakened or nonexistent ties to other religious groups. Those who are firmly embedded in religious communities and generally satisfied with their experience are less likely to abandon certainty and security for a precarious new group. On the other hand, those who are experiencing ongoing dissatisfaction and/or have loosened their ties to a particular group are correspondingly more likely to entertain alternative religious affiliations. That is particularly true for those who have defined themselves as seekers.

Religious seeking has always been an option for some people. In 1841, for example, the Transcendentalist Ralph Waldo Emerson (1803–1882) identified himself as an "endless seeker." Many of those in the metaphysical subculture of the late nineteenth to mid-twentieth century—the audience for Theosophy, Spiritualism, UFO beliefs, and other alternative forms of wisdom—also saw themselves as seekers. But the continuing social and cultural pluralism that has come to define many contemporary societies and the widespread weakening of the hold that many traditional religious groups have exercised on their members have fostered structural conditions that promote individuals' self-definitions as seekers.

Even those who remain within largely traditional religious groups may define themselves as religious or spiritual seekers. In fact, several observers have noticed a shift in patterns of religious and spiritual life away from individuals being content to dwell in a carefully bounded and well-regulated religious community governed by external authority toward an individually focused ongoing religious or spiritual quest that recognizes the primacy of the individual rather than the community. Seekers are not lost souls, but rather individuals who eagerly search for religious and spiritual wisdom. Through interactions with various subcultures, they can gain guidance about both what to search for and how to do it.

Seekers tend to reject external authorities and contend that individual experience is self-authenticating. Even the wisdom purveyed by influential teachers, such as New Age leaders, is subjected to personal verification. Seekers gravitate toward "self-religions," which both aim at the cultivation of the self and invest all authority in the seeking individual. Self-religions have been particularly evident in the general New Age milieu, often motivated by the conviction that each individual has a "higher" or even "Christ" self that needs to be rediscovered and developed. But other new religious groups, such as Anton LaVey's Church of Satan, have focused on individual self-gratification without positing that there is any kind of "higher" self.

Although there is movement between more traditional religious groups and new religions, many who understand themselves as seekers are part of the diffuse cultic milieu, which British sociologist Colin Campbell (1940–) identified as the diverse and constantly mutating elements of the cultural underground of society. Similarly, Christopher Partridge (1961–) describes an "occulture" as a repertoire of oppositional, hidden, stigmatized, and rejected beliefs and practices. Individual seekers feel free to take from those broad currents of religious and spiritual thought and practice the elements that make the most sense to them and nourish their personal development. Many see their seeking as a lifelong pursuit that may take them through acquaintance or even temporary affiliation with various groups and traditions. The traffic of individuals like David Spangler (1945–) into and out of the New Age community at Findhorn in Scotland and the passage of individuals into and out of the Heaven's Gate group provide good examples of the often restless movement of seekers through the cultic milieu.

While those who see themselves as lifelong seekers may be available for conversion to new religions, their affiliation is liable to be temporary, just as their allegiances are likely to be multiple at any given time. Such seekers are more likely to have ongoing "conversion careers" marked by the temporary alignment of their interests with those of successive groups over time. In that way, seekers contribute to both the perpetuation and the dynamism of the cultic milieu or occulture. By moving from acquaintance or affiliation with one group to another, they help spread new religious and spiritual ideas beyond their points of origination. But their penchant for searching over dwelling in a stable community does not contribute to the stability of the groups with which they come into contact.

In terms of the typology of cults articulated by Rodney Stark and William Sims Bainbridge, seekers definitely form an audience for new and alternative religious and spiritual ideas and practices. They may also act as clients by purchasing specific goods or services, such as ritual implements like crystals or participation in New Age workshops, from various providers. But they rarely make sustained contributions to the well-organized and carefully demarcated and governed communities that constitute cult movements. Such movements may be populated by seekers who have convinced themselves that they have found something worth abandoning their commitment to searching for a community in which they can dwell for the foreseeable future.

The circulation of seekers through the cultic milieu or occulture constitutes of a substratum of individuals that nourishes the formation and reformation of new religions. As long as they remain in motion, however, they also contribute to the instability of the very groups with which they affiliate.

See also: Conversion; Cultic Milieu; Disaffiliation and Ex-Membership in New Religious Movements; Findhorn Foundation, The; Heaven's Gate; New Age, The.

Further Reading
Roof, Wade Clark. 1993. *A Generation of Seekers: The Spiritual Journeys of the Baby Book Generation.* San Francisco: HarperSanFrancisco.

Roof, Wade Clark. 1999. *Spiritual Marketplace: Baby Boomers and the Remaking of American Religion.* Princeton, NJ: Princeton University Press.

Stark, Rodney, & William Sims Bainbridge. 1985. *The Future of Religion: Secularization, Revival, and Cult Formation.* Berkeley: University of California Press.

Sutcliffe, Steven. 2003. *Children of the New Age: A History of Spiritual Practices.* New York: Routledge.

Sutcliffe, Steven. 2017. "Seekership Revisited: Explaining Traffic in and out of New Religions." In Eugene V. Gallagher, ed., *Visioning New and Alternative Religions: Projecting the Future,* pp. 33–46. New York: Routledge.

Wuthnow, Robert. 1998. *After Heaven: Spirituality in America since the 1950s.* Berkeley: University of California Press.

Self-Realization Fellowship (Yogananda)

ORIGINS AND FOUNDER

Fueled by a wave of interest in the mystical "East," Swami Vivekananda (1863–1902) served as a point of contact for Western audiences regarding Hindu beliefs and practices and opened the door for future "gurus" to build upon the religious groundwork he had laid. The same year that Vivekananda was making a splash at the World's Parliament of Religion in Chicago, Mukunda Lal Ghosh (1893–1952)—later Paramahansa Yogananda—was born in Gorakhpur, India.

Yogananda's parents were disciples of Lahiri Mahasaya (1828–1895), a master of Kriya yoga. When Yogananda was only an infant, Mahasaya blessed him and told his mother that her son would be a "yogi" who would convert many to the path of Kriya yoga. Seemingly proving this pronouncement true, Yogananda began seeking a spiritual teacher in his youth. In 1910, he was apprenticed to Swami Sri Yukteswar Giri (1855–1936), with whom he spent the next decade learning Kriya yoga, with the explicit purpose of spreading it in the West. During that time, he took formal vows as a monk in the Swami Order and assumed the name Yogananda, meaning "bliss through divine union" in Sanskrit.

In 1920, Yogananda traveled to Boston, Massachusetts, for the International Conference of Religious Liberals. Much like his predecessor, Vivekananda, both he and his message (which he summarized in a speech titled "The Science of Religion") were enthusiastically received. Soon thereafter he founded the Self-Realization Fellowship (SRF). Yogananda opened its first meditation center in Boston, with the aid of lifelong disciples, Minott W. (1892–1960) and Mildred Lewis (1897–1988) and Alice Hasey, better known as Sister Yogamata (1885–1963). A speaking tour throughout the United States soon followed, and in 1925, Yogananda founded the international headquarters for SRF in Los Angeles. The movement was legally incorporated as a nonprofit religious organization in 1935.

From 1935 to 1936, Yogananda returned to India, primarily to visit his dying mentor, Sri Yukteswar Giri, though he would also find time to initiate Mahatma Gandhi (1869–1948) and other prominent Indian figures into Kriya yoga. Outside of this brief return, Yogananda would spend over thirty years of his life living and lecturing in the West, primarily the United States. During that time, he attracted some one hundred thousand converts to the Fellowship and lectured to exponentially more. Crucial to the success of the movement were those (almost exclusively white and primarily upper-middle class) disciples of Yogananda who would go on to spread his message of Kriya yoga and his writings, which he began producing in earnest beginning in 1936. He began with a series called the "Self-Realization Fellowship Lessons" intended for study at home. However, it was his *Autobiography of a Yogi* (1946) that would bear the most sustained and significant cultural impact. Until his death, Yogananda was working on a series of commentaries on the Bhagavad Gita as well as the Christian Gospels (titled *The Second Coming of Christ: The Resurrection of Christ within You*). He died in

March of 1952, and reportedly, his body showed no signs of decay even weeks after his death.

Even after his death, Yogananda and his teachings maintained spiritual authority within SRF. Institutional authority was another story. The first president of SRF was Rajarsi Janakananda (born Jesse James Lynn; 1892–1955), who served until his death in 1955. Reflecting the ethos of equality within SRF, the next two presidents were women: Daya Mata (born Rachel Faye Wright; 1914–2010), who served from 1955 to 2010, followed by Mrinalini Mata (born Merna Brown; 1931–2017), who served from 2010 to 2017. The current president is Brother Chidananda (born Christopher Bagley in 1953). Since Yogananda's death, all presidents have been white converts to the religion, a fact that highlights both SRF's popularity in the West as well as its amalgamation of Hinduism with modern cultural and Western religious ideals.

BELIEFS AND PRACTICES

Born from Hinduism, SRF's primary aims are conceived along those lines. The goal of all spiritual practice is to realize that the "self" (hence the name "self-realization") is actually a part of God or God-consciousness (in Hinduism, the term would be Brahman or Atman rather than God). The realization of this fact is achieved through meditation on God, which, besides fundamentally altering one's spiritual outlook, will conquer all physical and mental diseases or "inharmonies." However, the language used to describe the achievement of divine consciousness also takes on Christian or modern spiritual overtones. For example, SRF maintains that the teachings of Jesus and those of Kriya yoga are effectively synonymous, particularly in the belief that all reality is one with God. Confirming Yogananda's belief in the interchangeability of not just Hindu and Christian but "Eastern" and "Western" religious and cultural systems is the fact that he listed these as part of the fundamental ideals of SRF. In this way, SRF poses itself not as a Hindu sect but as the realization of universal religion.

The primary means of achieving divine consciousness is Kriya yoga (also called "the sacred science"), which translates to the "path of practice." According to Yogananda, it was practiced not only by the earliest of Hindus but by Jesus Christ and his disciples. Kriya yoga is mentioned in the Bhagavad Gita, but it was reportedly lost as a practice until the nineteenth century, when it was picked up by Lahiri Mahasaya and others. The practice is passed on through a guru-disciple relationship, a lineage that is still emphasized in the SRF even despite the availability of Yogananda's teachings designed for home study. The discipline of Kriya yoga begins with a series of preparatory techniques. First are "energization exercises," which prepare the body for meditation, generally through the regulation of breath. These exercises are followed by the Hong-Sau technique of concentration, which is designed to focus one's thought and to clear the mind of distractions. With the mind now clear, the practitioner will next employ the aum technique, which involves meditation on and aural repetition of the word "aum," which represents the divine presence. Having completed these steps, Kriya yoga can be attempted, whereby one uses the energy generated by focusing on the aum to control and enhance the energies in one's body, particularly the spine and brain. By controlling these energies in the body, one moves slowly toward inner peace and oneness with God.

The practice of Kriya yoga forms the center of SRF religious life. All other activities, both sacred and secular, are intended to prepare one for practicing Kriya yoga or to further enhance the divine consciousness realized in its practice. Thus, one could study the eclectic scriptures of SRF, which, besides the teaching of Yogananda, include the Gospels, the Bhagavad Gita, and the *Rubaiyat*, a poem written by Persian poet Omar Khayyam. Prayer is also a fundamental element of SRF practice, which Yogananda taught should be used for the betterment of others rather than ourselves. Though much of this practice, including prayer and Kriya yoga, is undertaken on one's own, there are also opportunities for communal prayer and worship, particularly when a significant amount of energy is required to bring a desired end to pass (as would be accomplished in the "World Prayer Circle").

CULTURE AND CONTROVERSY

Over the years, Yogananda and SRF attracted a number of famous individuals to the fold. George Harrison of the Beatles counted Yogananda as a major spiritual influence and donated proceeds from album sales to SRF at one time. Both Harrison and Elvis Presley made visits to SRF in Los Angeles.

Despite its success among religious seekers in general, not simply the famous ones, SRF has experienced both internal and external strife. Kriyananda (born James Donald Walters; 1926–2013), a disciple of Yogananda, was summarily dismissed in 1962 after serving two years as vice president of the Board of SRF. The reasons for his dismissal are murky; however what followed was not. In 1990, SRF filed suit against Kriyananda for the use of Yogananda's teachings in his own religious venture, the Church of Self-Realization. The court ultimately sided with SRF, believing their claims that Yogananda had intended to leave the rights to his life's work to the Fellowship. From the outside, SRF has faced criticism from both Hindus and Christians who view the mixing of their views as problematic and a self-serving marketing ploy to gain more members.

Despite these trials, SRF currently operates five hundred temples, centers, and ashrams in 175 countries. It maintains a quarterly magazine titled *Self-Realization* and offers weekly services at its various locations and a variety of workshops, retreats, and humanitarian activities throughout the year. Though the vast majority of members participate in SRF virtually or through participation at local sites of worship, there are those who continue to follow in the footsteps of Yogananda and become monks and nuns. In this way, SRF fits seamlessly into the modern, Western religious landscape that offers something for everyone.

See also: Hindu New Religious Movements; Occultism and Esotericism; Vedanta Society, The; Vivekananda, Swami (1863–1902); Yoga.

Further Reading

Foxen, Anya P. 2017. *Biography of a Yogi: Paramahansa Yogananda and the Origins of Modern Yoga.* New York: Oxford University Press.

Self-Realization Fellowship. "Self-Realization Fellowship." Available at: http://www.yogananda-srf.org/Default.aspx.

Yogananda, Paramahansa. 1998 [1946]. *Autobiography of a Yogi.* Los Angeles: Self-Realization Fellowship.

Seventh-day Adventism

Seventh-day Adventism is one of those religions about which many people have heard, but few know anything about, other than the fact that it qualifies for the label of "cult." Despite this gap in knowledge, Seventh-day Adventism is among the most successful new religious movements of recent centuries, counting nearly twenty million people as members across the globe (as of 2015), and spawning other new religious movements along the way.

ORIGINS AND EARLY HISTORY

On an October night in 1844, thousands of expectant millennialist Christians known as Millerites awaited the imminent return of Christ: an event they knew would precipitate the end of the world. The group was named for its founder William Miller (1782–1849), who, through a complicated series of biblical calculations, predicted that Christ's Second Advent would occur sometime between March 21, 1843, and March 21, 1844. When those dates passed without incident, Miller (consulting the Bible and realizing he had made a calculation error) named October 22, 1844, as the anticipated moment. That date would later become known as "The Great Disappointment," when Christ, again, failed to appear.

Though some would reject the Millerite movement altogether following this nonevent, some simply reinterpreted the significance of that date. One interpretation argued that on October 22, 1844, a "spiritual," rather than a physical "rapture" had taken place (rapture being the moment when Christ returns and raises all believing Christians into the sky; see I Thess. 4:13–17). This spiritual rapture marked the end of the period of probation and the beginning of a period of judgment, an event that meant that the end of the world was imminent. Included among those who chose to "spiritualize" the event in such a way were Hiram Edson (1806–1882) and James White (1821–1881), but most importantly, James's wife, Ellen (1827–1915). Ellen White's visions were the source of this new interpretation and the forthcoming belief system that became Seventh-day Adventism.

The first few decades of the Seventh-day Adventist movement were characterized by a loosely connected set of people, many of whom still belonged to other churches. Seeing the need for a more formal institution, its early leaders formally established the Seventh-day Adventist Church in May 1863 in Battle Creek, Michigan, where it would maintain its headquarters until 1989 (after which it moved to Maryland). At the time of its establishment, the church had thirty-five thousand

Seventh-day Adventism

members. However, both its message through vigorous missionary work and its institutions, particularly Adventist hospitals, spurred the growth of the Church. By the mid-twentieth century, the Adventists counted around two hundred thousand members in the United States and nearly twice that abroad.

BELIEFS AND PRACTICES

Like many Protestant churches who maintain that the Bible is their primary authority, Seventh-day Adventists were initially reluctant to formalize any other text or doctrine as canonical. Nonetheless, both the writings of Ellen G. White, namely, her prophetic book *The Great Controversy* (1858) and certain other documents created by the Church have taken on official status among Seventh-day Adventists. For example, the 1980 document, *Seventh-day Adventists Believe: A Biblical Exposition of 27 Fundamental Doctrines* (to which one more was added in 2005, making the tally twenty-eight fundamental beliefs) is cited as the clearest delineation of Adventist belief.

Given its birth from a millennialist Christian movement—the Millerites—central to Seventh-day Adventist belief is the reality of Christ's imminent return. Many of their beliefs and practices concern preparing both body and soul for Christ's return to ensure salvation in this period of God's judgment. Given that traditional Christianity is also concerned with salvation and preparing for Christ's return, Seventh-day Adventists hold many conventional beliefs: that humans are fallen and therefore inherently sinful; that Christ's death atoned for the sin of humanity, but only those who believe in his sacrifice can partake of that atonement; and that God is all-powerful, all-knowing, and merciful even as he judges their deeds. However, their particular brand of Christianity also diverges from the "mainstream." For example, Adventists believe in continuing revelation, as evidenced first through the visions of Ellen White, though they believe that further prophets may arise to prophesy things to come, and in their reintroduction of certain biblical practices eschewed in many Christian churches.

Foremost among Seventh-day Adventists' beliefs is the importance of a "seventh-day" Sabbath (hence, their name). Thus, instead of holding the Sabbath on the first day, Sunday, as is the custom in traditional Christianity, they hold it on the seventh day, Saturday, which was the custom of the biblical Hebrews and modern Jews. It is their belief that their practice is the more biblical and true to the original guidelines of the earliest Church. Prayer, worship on the Sabbath, and study of the Bible are the primary means through which Seventh-day Adventists practice their faith, though they also partake of missionary and humanitarian work.

Though no longer strictly prescribed as they were during the earliest decades of the movement, White and the first Seventh-day Adventists instituted a series of dietary and health measures to help purify the body. Similar to their adherence to the Jewish Sabbath, Seventh-day Adventists took seriously the Old Testament proscriptions (see Lev. 11) against unclean foods, such as pork and shellfish, better known as the rules of "kashrut" or keeping kosher. In line with other dietary and health trends in nineteenth-century religions, Seventh-day Adventists also advocated for a vegetarian diet and for abstaining from alcohol and tobacco. These practices inspired Adventist John Harvey Kellogg to develop foods that would work for this biblical diet, particularly in the realm of hearty, grain-based breakfast cereals, for which the modern company Kellogg is still known.

The Church is governed by a "Presbyterian" structure, meaning that, at the highest level of organization, there is a group of appointed individuals, known as the General Conference, who govern the Church (though there is an office of the president). Decisions about polity and practice trickle down from the top through local conferences and then local churches. Clergy and missionary officials are appointed by local conferences to each local church.

CULTURE AND CONTROVERSY

Seventh-day Adventism has also given birth to various offshoots. The Adventist doctrine of "present truth" keeps alive the expectation that prophetic guidance can be experienced in any generation. Most (in)famous among the splinter groups are the Branch Davidians, formerly the Davidian Adventists, who were involved in a fifty-day siege with the Bureau of Alcohol, Tobacco, and Firearms and the Federal Bureau of Investigation that ended in a tragic fire on April 19, 1993. Their leader, David Koresh (1959–1993), adopted the mantle of prophecy once held by Ellen White and interpreted the events around him as indicators of Christ's imminent return and the central role of the Branch Davidians in the events that would follow.

The Church has also had a somewhat ambivalent relationship to women in roles of spiritual authority. Despite the prominence of Ellen White as a founder of the religion and a promise to "defend" and "elevate" the status of women (as stated on its website), the Church has voted against female ordination (as recently as 2015). Though women are certainly encouraged to seek fulfillment in all areas of life, in both a professional and familial sense, their role in the Church is supplementary and supportive. In general, the Church is socially conservative, eschewing extramarital sex, abortion, birth control, and same-sex partnerships or marriage—views that align them with many Christian churches in the United States and globally.

In contemporary culture, Seventh-day Adventists are most commonly associated with strict religiosity and social conservatism (as seen by the character of Mrs. Kim on *Gilmore Girls* [2000–2007]). More recently, however, the story of Desmond Doss (1919–2006), a Seventh-day Adventist and conscientious objector, was depicted in the film *Hacksaw Ridge* (2016). Doss (portrayed by Andrew Garfield) would go on to win the Congressional Medal of Honor for his actions at Okinawa during World War II. Though the film may not universally reverse the stereotyping of Seventh-day Adventism as a cult, like all positive portrayals of religious individuals, it may help to lessen the stigma and bring greater understanding to a form of Christianity that is more similar to traditional Christianity than it is different.

See also: Branch Davidians; Food and New Religious Movements; Gender and New Religious Movements; Healing, Health, and New Religious Movements; Koresh, David (1959–1993); Millennialism; Miller, William (1782–1849); Millerites, The; Prophecy in

New Religious Movements; Watch Tower Bible and Tract Society, The (Jehovah's Witnesses); White, Ellen G. (1827–1915).

Further Reading

Bull, Malcolm, & Keith Lockhart. 2006. *Seeking a Sanctuary: Seventh-day Adventism and the American Dream*. Second Edition. Bloomington: Indiana University Press.

Pearson, Michael. 1990. *Millennial Dreams and Moral Dilemmas: Seventh-day Adventism and Contemporary Ethics*. Cambridge: Cambridge University Press.

Seventh-day Adventist Church. 2005 [1980]. *The Seventh-day Adventists Believe: A Biblical Exposition of 28 Fundamental Doctrines*. Available at: https://szu.adventist.org/wp-content/uploads/2016/04/28_Beliefs.pdf.

Vance, Laura L. 1999. *Seventh-day Adventism in Crisis: Gender and Sectarian Change in an Emerging Religion*. Urbana; Chicago: University of Illinois Press.

White, Ellen G. 1858. *The Great Controversy between God and Satan*. Battle Creek, MI: James White.

Sex, Sexuality, and New Religious Movements

Religious institutions are invested in sex. More specifically, religions are often in the business of linking sex and sexuality to theological doctrines regarding sin and salvation; practical and societal understandings of morality; systems of membership; and interpretations of proper marital relationships. Look no further than the familiar religious proscriptions against premarital or adulterous sex or, more recently, the religious arguments proffered for and against same-sex relationships or marriages. Sex, and sexuality as the biological manifestation of sexual preference, are, simultaneously, the realization of physical intimacy, the product of human instinct, and the ways families are made, communities are built, and institutions sustained. Sex is also a way that power is built and exploitation of vulnerable communities is enabled in religious institutions.

New religious movements are no different and are very often sites of transgressive sexual practices or sexual exploration. They are also sites where the regulation of sex becomes a means of regulating people to good or ill effect. And as institutions that are typically in a higher state of tension with society, new religious movements are often subjected to a higher state of scrutiny than more established religions when it comes to sexual practices, whether fair or not.

SEXUAL EXPERIMENTATION

Various new religious movements have challenged norms regarding conventional sexual relationships and encounters. Very often the form of this challenge operates in two primary ways: regulation or liberation.

Among the groups that seek to regulate sex, perhaps none is better known than the Shakers. Led by (Mother) Ann Lee (1736–1784), the Shakers practiced (and continue to practice) celibacy. Lee, who had experienced the death of all four of her children in infancy, received a revelation that confirmed for her that

Sex, Sexuality, and New Religious Movements 565

pregnancy, as the product of sex, and sex itself were the root of sin. As vessels preparing for the imminent arrival of Christ, individuals' bodies should remain pure and their human instincts subjugated into work and devotion to God. The movement reached its height during the nineteenth century, but has suffered for its lack of progeny: as of 2019, the Shakers counted only two remaining members. Several centuries later, another millennialist movement, this time a Christian UFO group called Heaven's Gate, also dissolved all marital and sexual relationships in preparation for advancement to The Evolutionary Level Above Human. Believing that they would transported to a UFO and transformed into a new form, they emulated on earth what they believed would be an existence totally devoid of human urges.

Not all groups that regulate sex go the route of celibacy. While studying at Yale Theological Seminary, John Humphrey Noyes (1811–1886) made an important discovery: Christ had already returned in AD 70. This meant that human beings needed to and could live "perfectly," while on earth. Part of this perfection involved the renunciation of all proprietary sexual and romantic relationships in favor of a system of "complex marriage," which he implemented at his communal religious society, the Oneida Community. Members were not celibate, but all sexual encounters were undertaken with the aim of showing love and devotion to God. Noyes himself was in charge of ordering these sexual encounters to ensure that attachments did not form; he also implemented the practice of male continence (where a man would not ejaculate during sex), which focused the act on God, not on personal pleasure, and avoided unwanted pregnancies. Children or "stirpicults" did occur, but who could have a child and by whom were also strictly regulated so as to ensure a more "perfect" next generation. This experiment in sexual relationships has been critiqued as the product of Noyes's desire for control; though this picture is one-sided, given the number of people who did join with knowledge of the community's practices, the practice of complex marriage dissolved as Noyes aged.

Sex is also tied to the creation of perfect, "sinless" children among Unificationists. The Unification Church, founded on the teachings of Rev. Sun Myung Moon (1920–2012), is renowned for its mass weddings of thousands of adherents, very often with partners they have just met. In *Divine Principle* (1952), Moon laid out an alternative biblical history where Eve not only ate the fruit but committed a sexual sin with the serpent and then with Adam, thereby tarnishing the sinless family that she and Adam were set to create. Jesus, who in most Christian tellings is the antidote to the first couple's sin, did not fulfill his duty of marrying and forming a sinless family based on total love and devotion to God. Thus, it was Reverend Moon who, along with his wife Hak Ja Han (1943–), who are the True Parents of a perfect humanity. All those married in a Unificationist "Blessing Ceremony" are enjoined to treat sex as an act whose sole purpose is to create sinless children, which is the ultimate manifestation of divine love.

On the opposite side of the spectrum are those groups that seek to liberate sexuality from societal, and often religious, constraints. Pierre Bernard (1875–1955) founded the Tantrik Order based on his own interpretation of Tantric Buddhism.

Rather than restrict pleasure from sex to channel sacred power, as Indian Tantrics do, Bernard advocated for spiritual fulfillment through sexual release and arousal.

It was during the sexual revolution of the 1960s, however, that many new religions seemed to propose open and free love as a component of spiritual practice. Neopagans of various orientations argued that spiritual exploration through sex was divine. In his Osho Movement, Bhagwan Shree Rajneesh (1931–1990) compelled the members of his compound, Rajneeshpuram, to feel free to express themselves sexually with one another, while simultaneously claiming that true spiritual advancement meant moving past the need and act of sex (as he had done). The Family (Children of God) brought a Christian bent to free love by arguing that Jesus Christ joined couples during sex (an act known as "loving Jesus") and masturbation; members were also famous for their recruitment technique of "flirty fishing," which involved sending young members to flirt with potential converts to bring them into the fold. Also born during this era, the Church of Satan, which is premised on the idea that one should act on, not repress, one's instincts, advocates for acting on one's sexual desires (while also adamantly advocating for consent).

SEXUAL EXPLOITATION

Besides the tropes of brainwashing and the megalomaniacal leader, accusations of sexual impropriety or exploitation top the list of assumptions about dangerous "cults." Though there is more falsehood than truth to this generalization, there are certainly examples of sexual deviance among new religions—examples that have been touted by anticult activists as proof of the link between new religions and sexual abuse.

Though by no means exclusively so, two groups are perceived as particularly vulnerable to sexual abuse: women and children. Claims of sexual exploitation of female disciples have been leveled at many leaders of new religious movements who have reportedly leveraged spiritual advancement for sex (such as Satchitananda (1914–2002) of Integral Yoga). In 2018, the new religious movement NXIVM came under fire for allegedly enslaving female disciples who were forced to perform sexual acts for those who paid to attend its seminars; both the founder Keith Raniere (1960–) and his associate, Allison Mack (1982–), were convicted for various crimes. Raniere was sentenced to 120 years in prison.

Occasionally the two vulnerable groups overlap. Fundamentalist Mormons are those who continued to practice plural marriage after it was outlawed by the Church of Jesus Christ of Latter-day Saints in 1890. The vast majority of Fundamentalist Mormons maintain marriages between consenting adults, but certain groups, such as the Fundamentalist Latter-day Saints (FLDS) have witnessed its leaders go to jail for statutory rape. Prophet Warren Jeffs (1955–), currently serving a life sentence for two counts of rape (though more are alleged), still leads the FLDS from jail. While incarcerated, Jeffs has reportedly called for a cessation of all sexual activity between married couples and mandated procreation to occur at the hands of only fifteen handpicked men. David Koresh (1959–1993), former leader of the Branch Davidians, also dissolved marriages among those living at the Mount Carmel Center in Waco, Texas. Through an inspired reading of the Bible, Koresh believed that all children born of him would rule in heaven when Christ returned. While mandating celibacy among the Branch Davidians, Koresh took multiple wives, several of whom were underage, and by whom he had children. These allegations of statutory rape were among those leveled at Koresh during the fifty-one-day siege between the Branch Davidians, the Federal Bureau of Investigation, and the Bureau of Alcohol, Tobacco, and Firearms, which ended in a deadly fire on April 19, 1993.

The stereotype of cultic sexual abuse has also led to erroneous accusations of sexual impropriety, such as those that occurred during the Satanic Panic. Rumors of Satanic ritual abuse emerged in the 1980s and 1990s, touched off by books like *Michelle Remembers* (1980), where a young woman recovered repressed memories of her reported sexual abuse at the hands of Satanists. Though the credibility of these claims was later undermined, this led to a swath of accusations, most famously toward a set of California daycare workers, for supposedly subjecting children to Satanic sexual rituals.

SEXUAL ORIENTATION

Though movements for LGBTQ+ rights are expanding in the twenty-first century, certain new religious movements have been well advanced in this regard. Raëlism, a UFO religion positing that aliens known as the Elohim created all life on earth, including humans, in their labs, has consistently defended the rights of LGBTQ+ individuals to love and marry. Though eschewing procreation (they advocate cloning and scientific processes for human advancement), they believe that human beings were designed exactly as they were meant to be by their creators. Similarly supportive of the LGBTQ+ community and notions of fluid gender and sexual identity are many Neopagan groups. The notion of free love and sex as a means of celebrating the fecundity of nature were common among Neopagan practices—which included the celebration of gay and lesbian relationships.

On the other hand, certain new religious movements have emerged as vocal opponents of same-sex marriage and of homosexuality in general. Seventh-day Adventists describe all same-sex behavior as antithetical to God's plan and to biblical prescriptions. The Latter-day Saints, whose system of salvation is centered upon the creation of an eternal family argues similarly that same-sex relationships disrupt Heavenly Father's plan for humanity: to create large families who will live together for eternity in the Celestial Kingdom. Nonetheless, the Latter-day Saints have made strides toward greater acceptance of LGBTQ individuals; in 2019, they allowed children of LGBTQ+ couples to become baptized and lifted the label of "apostasy" for those in same-sex marriages. However, the Church still employs the language of "same-sex attraction" versus homosexuality to denote a belief that sexuality is an action that can be redirected rather than an aspect of one's identity.

See also: Anticult Movement, The; Branch Davidians; Children and New Religious Movements; Children of God (The Family International); Church of Jesus Christ of

Latter-day Saints, The; Church of Satan, The; Fundamentalist Mormons; Heaven's Gate; Integral Yoga; Koresh, David (1959–1993); Lee, (Mother) Ann (1736–1784); Marriage and Relationships in New Religious Movements; Millennialism; Moon, Rev. Sun Myung (1920–2012); Neopaganism; Noyes, John Humphrey (1811–1886); NXIVM; Oneida Community, The; Rajneesh, Shree Bhagwan/Osho (1931–1990); Rajneesh/Osho Movement, The; Raëlians, The; Satanic Panic; Satanism; Seventh-day Adventism; Shakers, The; Tantrik Order, The; Unification Church, The; Women in New Religious Movements.

Further Reading

Foster, Lawrence. 1984. *Religion and Sexuality: The Shakers, the Mormons, and the Oneida Community*. Urbana: University of Illinois Press.

Goodwin, Megan. 2014. "Sexuality Studies." In *The Bloomsbury Companion to New Religious Movements*. London: Bloomsbury Academic.

Goodwin, Megan. 2016. "Sex and New Religions." In *The Oxford Handbook of New Religious Movements*, 2nd ed. Oxford: Oxford University Press.

Vance, Laura L. 2008. "Converging on the Heterosexual Dyad: Changing Mormon and Adventist Sexual Norms and Implications for Gay and Lesbian Adherents." *Nova Religio* 11: 56–76.

Wright, Stuart, & James Richardson, eds. 2011. *Saints Under Siege: The Texas State Raid on the Fundamentalist Latter Day Saints*. New York: New York University Press.

Seymour, William (1870–1922)

EARLY YEARS AND RELIGIOUS BEGINNINGS

In the early twenty-first century, Pentecostalism is a global religion counting nearly three hundred million adherents. The explosion of this variety of Christianity owes its start to a half-blind, African American preacher named William Seymour (1870–1922). Born the child of former slaves in Reconstruction-era Louisiana, Seymour's youth was characterized by experiences of extraordinary prejudice and abject poverty, compounded by the sudden death of his father. Seymour would leave his childhood home in the 1890s for the Midwest, but ultimately return to the South—Houston—by 1903. Along the way, he discovered his religious calling.

Born a Roman Catholic, Seymour converted to Methodism when in Indianapolis, but would shortly thereafter join a "Holiness" Church. The Holiness movement was a movement within American Protestantism that emphasized baptism by the Holy Spirit (which often manifested in ecstatic worship), belief in the imminent return of Christ, and faith healing (among other spiritual abilities enabled by the Holy Spirit). Following his move to Cincinnati, Seymour contracted smallpox, which would ultimately leave him blind in one eye. He attributed this affliction to his reticence to accept God's call to ministry—which he remedied by determining to become a minister and studying at a local Bible college.

Moving to Houston in 1903, Seymour bounced around, between jobs and churches, dabbling in different holiness varieties, until he met Charles Parham (1873–1929). Parham was the founder of the "Apostolic Faith" movement, a precursor to Pentecostalism (Pentecost refers to the story in Acts 2 when the Apostles received the gift of tongues). Pentecostalism's signifying belief is that speaking in tongues is the true mark of baptism by the Holy Spirit. Seymour was attracted to this message and took classes at Parham's new Bible school, though because he was black in the Jim Crow-era South, he was compelled to sit outside of the classroom and listen through the window. Gathering a reputation as a gifted preacher (though he had not yet received the gift of tongues), Seymour began preaching alongside Parham in 1906 (though Parham was reportedly reticent to preach to mixed-race audiences); soon thereafter, he accepted a call to serve as pastor in Los Angeles.

ASUZA STREET

Recounted famously by Frank Bartleman (1871–1936), what happened at Asuza Street in Los Angeles shortly after the arrival of Seymour in 1906 serves as the creation story for modern Pentecostalism. His first pastoral job in Los Angeles having fallen through, Seymour started a Bible and prayer meeting at a friend's home, where he finally received the gift of the Holy Spirit. The meeting attracted so many in its few months that it soon moved to a building on Asuza Street. Remarkable for its time, the movement was racially diverse from its outset, a fact that drew people to it and created the environment for a vast religious phenomenon that would spread swiftly.

Though Bartleman cited the San Francisco earthquake, which occurred on April 18, 1906, as a precipitating event for the "Asuza Street Revival," the outpouring of the Holy Spirit, the explosion of spiritual gifts including speaking in tongues, and the seemingly daily growth in membership of Seymour's church were already evident in the weeks that preceded the apocalyptic natural disaster. By September of that year, Seymour began publishing *The Apostolic Faith*, a nod to Parham, though Seymour would soon surpass him in influence and prestige as the founder of Pentecostalism.

LATER YEARS AND LEGACY

The immediate success of Seymour's revival was also marred by controversy and opposition. In the remaining decade of his life, while he toured the United States spreading the good news of Holy Spirit baptism, Seymour endured opposition from other Holiness Groups and perhaps, most painfully, from Charles Parham who preached against the excesses and racial diversity of the growing movement. By 1914, the Asuza Street mission had become a small congregation; he would serve as its pastor for his remaining days. Yet, the movement he began endured and thrived all over the world long after he was gone.

See also: Charisma and Leadership in New Religious Movements; Healing, Health, and New Religious Movements; Millennialism; Pentecostalism; Race and New Religious Movements.

Further Reading

Bartleman, Frank. 1973 [1925]. *Asuza Street: An Eyewitness Account to the Birth of the Pentecostal Revival*. New Kensington, PA: Whitaker House.

Espinosa, Gastón. 2014. *William J. Seymour and the Origins of Global Pentecostalism: A Biography and Documentary History.* Durham, NC: Duke University Press.

Liardon, Roberts. 2014. *The Great Asuza Street Revival: The Life and Sermons of William Seymour.* Sarasota, FL: Embassy Publishing.

Shakers, The

ORIGINS AND HISTORY

The United Society of Believers in Christ's Second Appearing, more famously (and more pejoratively) known as the Shakers or "Shaking Quakers," is perhaps best known for its unconventional beliefs and practices regarding relationships, the equality of the sexes, and communal living. Yet, in many ways, the Shakers were representative of the many millennial Christianities endemic to the eighteenth and nineteenth centuries: they expected the imminent arrival of God's Kingdom and the new world order it would bring.

The religious movement from which the Shakers arose was founded by James and Jane Wardley, whose ecstatic form of worship earned them their reputation for "shaking." Preaching on the impending Kingdom, the Wardleys attracted a young, gifted woman by the name of Ann Lee in the late 1750s. Lee's prophetic abilities and visionary theology propelled her to leadership in the group; in 1770, she would be revealed

Hancock Shaker Village, found in Hancock and Pittsfield, Massachusetts, was home to the religious community known as "the Shakers," or the United Society of Believers in Christ's Second Appearing, from 1790 to 1960. Originally from England, the Shakers settled in America, becoming renowned for their radical gender equality, their practice of celibacy, and, later, their skilled craftsmanship and carpentry. (Lee Snider /Dreamstime.com)

as the Second Coming of Christ. Lee was the spiritual and theological center of the movement, a fact that remains true today for those few Shakers remaining. Through a series of revivals, the fledgling movement grew slowly, while simultaneously inviting public scrutiny, even persecution, for some of their more heretical practices.

In 1774, Lee and a handful of followers sailed to the new world following a revelation, which showed that the religion would flower in the comparably more tolerant, American soil. Settling in Watervliet, New York, the Shakers began a preaching tour of New England, gaining converts along the way. It was after Ann Lee's death, however, that the religion experienced a period of sustained growth under Joseph Meacham (1742–1796). From 1787 to 1796, multiple communities across New England were established and incorporated. It was Meacham who created the communal style of living practiced by the Shakers. Communities were divided into "families" governed by both men and women. Though men and women were often separated in living quarters and in day-to-day living, all lived together as "Brothers" and "Sisters," which, appropriately, were the titles by which members went.

The period of 1830–1860 was known as the "era of manifestations," during which the Shakers experienced their peak in members as well as manifestations of the spirit—spurred by the general culture of revivalism then present in the United States. The Civil War stymied the progress of the Shakers and the group would never again achieve the relative popularity of its heyday.

BELIEFS AND PRACTICES

Much of Shaker theology and practice engaged progressive ideas about gender and sexuality. For example, Mother Ann revealed that God was both male and female. This idea debunked traditional notions of male superiority by showing that both men and women were made in God's direct image. This gender dualism extended to the notion of Christ's first and second advents. Jesus was the first, male incarnation of Christ, thus the second advent would feature the female aspect of God, taking the form of a woman. There is some dispute among modern Shakers as to whether Mother Ann was the female incarnation of Christ or whether she was "Second Eve," who would help bring humanity toward God and serve as "helpmeet" to Christ. Neither view affects the millennialist Christian outlook of the Shakers, who believe that Christ has returned and the Kingdom arrived.

Perhaps Shakers are most famous for their practice of celibacy, which stems from their belief that sex was the root of all sin and procreation a sign of humanity's fallen state. By remaining celibate and through the consistent confession (and renunciation) of their sins, Shakers are living as they should under the Kingdom of God. Though there were Shaker children (when families converted to Shakers, for example), the general lack of children led to innovations in gender roles. Men and women shared responsibilities and authority in the church and in the community. Though work was separated by gender, with men undertaking more hard labor and women more household tasks, the emphasis is on the importance and necessity of both genders in serving the community. Following the model for communal societies, Shakers share all goods and living spaces; avoiding personal possessions and attachments enables each Shaker to focus on obeying God.

572 Shakers, The

Given their total focus on God and remaining free of sin, Shakers have also earned a reputation as conscientious objectors. They are openly pacifistic in their views, a fact that may have inadvertently impacted their ability to gain converts (particularly at that crucial moment following the Civil War).

Similar to their parent group, the Quakers, Shakers worshipped in "meeting houses," designed to reflect the equalitarian beliefs of its members. Lacking an elevated pulpit or any trappings of church ceremony, meeting houses contain rows of benches facing each other across the room, enabling a communal form of worship. Though worship is encouraged to proceed according to the spirit, meaning those who feel moved can speak, today Shaker worship services proceed in a more orderly fashion (though dance and song are still central components). Nonmembers are always welcome to services.

LEGACY AND FUTURE?

Due in great part to their stringent lifestyle and relational standards, turnover among the Shakers was high. At their peak in the mid-nineteenth century, the Shakers counted six thousand members. Numbers continued to dwindle over the next century and beyond. As of 2017, there were only two remaining Shakers in the only active Shaker community in Sabbathday Lake located in New Gloucester, Maine. Despite their status as cultural curio, the Shakers have retained a lasting reputation in the area of furniture making. An Amazon.com search reveals countless books on Shaker furniture making and the history of Shaker aesthetics.

See also: Lee, (Mother) Ann (1736–1784); Marriage and Relationships in New Religious Movements; Millennialism; Sex, and Sexuality, and New Religious Movements.

Further Reading

Bial, Raymond. 2008. *The Shaker Village.* Lexington: University of Kentucky Press.

Stein, Stephen J. 1994. *The Shaker Experience in America: A History of the United Society of Believers.* New Haven, CT: Yale University Press.

Whitson, Robley E. 1983. *The Shakers: Two Centuries of Spiritual Reflection (Classics of Western Spirituality).* Mahwah, NJ: Paulist Press; Ex-Seminary Library Edition.

PRIMARY SOURCE DOCUMENT

Excerpt from F. W. Evans, *Compendium of the Origin, History, Principles, Rules and Regulations, Government, and Doctrines of the United Society of Believers in Christ's Second Appearing . . . (1859)*

An excerpt from the guiding Shaker text, Compendium of the Origin, History, Principles, Rules and Regulations, Government, and Doctrines of the United Society of Believers in Christ's Second Appearing, *is as follows*.

6. As she [Ann Lee] advanced in years she was strongly impressed with a sense of the deep depravity of human nature, and of the odiousness of sin, especially the impure and indecent nature of sexual coition for mere gratification. To her mother she often expressed her feelings respecting these things, and earnestly desired to be kept and preserved from sin, and from those abominations her soul so much abhorred. . . .

9. In the year 1758, and 23d year of her age, she united herself to a society called *Shakers* which was under the ministration of Jane and James Wardley, formerly of the Quaker order. The people of that society were of blameless deportment, and were distinguished for the clearness and swiftness of their testimony against sin, the strictness of their moral discipline, and for the purity of their lives.

10. The light of this people led them to an open confession of every sin they had committed, and to take up a full and final cross against everything they knew to be evil. This endowed them with great power over sin; and here Ann found that protection she had so long desired, and which corresponded with her faith at that time. She was baptized into the same Spirit, and by degrees traveled to the full knowledge and experience of all the spiritual truths of the Society.

11. To her followers she said; "I love the day that I first received the Gospel. I call it my birthday. I cried to God, without intermission, for three days and three nights, that he would give me *true desires*. And when I received a gift of God, I did not go away and forget it, and travel no further; but I stood faithful, day and night, warring against all sin, and praying to God for deliverance from the *very nature of sin*. And other persons need not expect to find power over sin without the same labor and travel of soul.

12. I felt such a sense of my sins that I was willing to confess them before the whole world. I confessed my sins to my elders, one by one, and repented of them in the same manner. When my elders reproved me, I felt determined not to be reproved twice for the same thing, but to labor to overcome the evil for myself.

13. Soon after I set out to travel in the way of God, I labored a-nights in the work of God. Sometimes I labored all night, continually crying to God for my own redemption. Sometimes I went to bed and slept; but in the morning, if I could not feel that sense of the work of God that I did before I slept, I would labor all night. This I did many nights, and in the daytime I put my hands to work, and my heart to God; and when I felt weary and in need of rest, I labored for the power of God, and the refreshing operations thereof would release me, so that I felt able to go to my work again.

14. Many times, when I was about my work, I have felt my soul overwhelmed with sorrow. I used to work as long as I could keep it concealed,

and then would go out of sight, lest anyone should pity me with that pity which was not of God. In my travel and tribulation my sufferings were so great, that my flesh consumed upon my bones, bloody sweat pressed through the pores of my skin, and I became as helpless as an infant. And when I was brought through, and born into the spiritual kingdom, I was like an infant just born into the natural world. They see colors and objects, but they know not what they see. It was so with me; but before I was 24 hours old, I saw, and I knew what I saw."

15. Ann was wrought upon after this manner for the space of nine years. Yet she often had intervals of releasement, in which her bodily strength and vigor was sometimes miraculously renewed; and, at times, her soul was filled with heavenly visions and Divine revelations. By these means the way of God and the nature of his work gradually opened upon her mind with increasing light and understanding.

16. The Divine manifestations she received from time to time were communicated to the Society, and tended greatly to enlighten the minds and strengthen the faith of the members, and to increase and confirm the testimony. Her mind, ever intent upon the great work of salvation, was greatly affected concerning the lost state of mankind. But the real foundation of that loss was still concealed from her view; nor could she see any prospect of recovery under the existing circumstances; for she had long been convinced that there was nothing in all the professions and practices of professors that could save them from sin here, or furnish to them any reasonable hope of salvation hereafter.

17. She spent much time in earnest and incessant cries to God, to show her the foundation of man's loss, what it was, and wherein it consisted; and how the way of salvation could be discovered and effectually opened to mankind in the state they were then in, and how the great work of redemption was to be accomplished.

18. The ultimate fruit of the labor and suffering of soul that Ann passed through was to purify and fitly prepare her for becoming a temple in whom the same Christ Spirit that had made a *first* appearance to Jesus, at his baptism by John in the Jordan (the river of Judgment), at which time he received the anointing which constituted him Jesus Christ, could make a *second* appearing; and through whom the God of heaven could set up a Church, or "kingdom, which should never be destroyed"; for all previous Churches had been destroyed by and through the operation of the fleshly lusts of their own members. They all commenced in the Spirit, and with a cross; but, through self-indulgence, "ended in the flesh."

Source: Evans, F. W. *Compendium of the Origin, History, Principles, Rules and Regulations, Government, and Doctrines of the United Society of Believers in Christ's Second Appearing.* New York: D. Appleton and Company, 1859.

Shamanism

Virtually everything about shamanism and its contemporary offshoot neo-shamanism is disputed. The word "shaman" purportedly derives from a Tungus language root and may mean "one who knows." Some argue that the term "shamanism" should only be used for the religious practices of a handful of groups in Siberia. Others have posited that the term should refer to the practices of indigenous societies throughout the world who contact the spirit world for healing and other benefits. In that perspective, shamanism becomes a generalized and generalizing category that gathers together material from very different cultural contexts. That position is best exemplified by the influential Romanian historian of religions Mircea Eliade (1907–1986), whose *Shamanism: Archaic Techniques of Ecstasy* (first published in French in 1951) gave impetus to the understanding of shamanism as a global phenomenon. Since Eliade believed that his form of comparative religion could give birth to a new humanism, he would not have been surprised about the uses to which his general picture of shamanism would later be put.

Shamanism next made a public appearance in the widely read works of the anthropologist Carlos Castenada (1925–1988). During his work for his doctorate, Castaneda claimed to have met a Yaqui Indian "man of knowledge" don Juan Matus from northern Mexico. Castaneda's books about don Juan reached a broad popular audience, particularly in the counterculture, eager to replicate Castaneda's shamanic learning. But academic anthropologists persistently raised questions about Castaneda's veracity.

In 1980, Michael J. Harner (1929–2018) published *The Way of the Shaman*. Harner had trained as an academic anthropologist and done field work in the Ecuadorian and Peruvian areas of the Amazon. During his field work in the early 1960s, Harner participated in the ceremonial consumption of ayahuasca, a plant-based psychoactive substance brewed into a tea. His experience convinced him of the reality of the shamans' vision of a world divided into the Upper, Lower, and Middle realms and their ability to travel between them. Harner remained in academia until 1987, dividing his time between academic writing and the pursuit of shamanic practice. He established the Foundation for Shamanic Studies in 1979 (see www.shamanism.org), which continues to offer workshops in shamanic practice to all who are interested. The foundation also offers support to individuals and groups who are attempting to protect or revive indigenous forms of shamanism.

Although both Harner and Castaneda (who used peyote) consumed psychoactive substances as part of their shamanic training, in fact most traditional shamans rely on other ways, such as drumming, of fostering ecstatic states. But the connection between shamanism and drugs, nevertheless, attracted certain religious seekers.

Harner's transition from scholar to scholar-practitioner to full-time shaman and teacher of shamanism captures how shamanism moved out of the realm of scholarship and into the realm of religious practice in the last quarter of the twentieth century. In the process, several things have happened. First, shamanism has been shorn of its cultural specificity. In traditional shamanic societies, shamans either

576 Shamanism

inherited their positions or were chosen by the community after having visionary experiences. They worked on behalf of their communities, bringing physical and psychological healing and various kinds of wisdom from other worlds into this world. Being a shaman was open only to a very few. In contrast, the type of "core shamanism" that Harner and others promote constitutes a homogenized blend of shamanic elements from multiple cultures, whether they come from Siberia, the Amazon, or the American plains. Core shamanism is something that individuals can choose to pursue as a spiritual practice; there is no limit to the number of people who can adopt shamanic practices. In addition to the democratization of the practice of shamanism, the focus has shifted to what shamanic ritualizing can do for the individual, not the community. Neo-shamanism thus fits within the array of "self-religions" that are sometimes grouped under the umbrella category of "New Age."

Despite efforts of Harner's Foundation, however, neo-shamanism has not escaped charges that it is engaging in illegitimate cultural appropriation that is actually harming indigenous peoples rather than helping them. For example Lynn V. Andrews (1940–), who has written the *New York Times* best-sellers *Jaguar Woman* (1985) and *Medicine Woman* (1981), claims to have worked with shamans on four continents for more than three decades (see https://lynnandrews.com /pages/about-lynn). But the First Nations Community of Manitoba, Canada could find no traces of the shamans that she named as being active there. Aboriginal people have also doubted her claims to have encountered shamans in Australia. Such invented or distorted accounts of indigenous practices, many claim, can do real damage to native peoples. Several Native American authors have also critiqued what they call "white shamanism" as a contemporary form of cultural imperialism and draw parallels between cultural and territorial annexation. Some of the negative effects of neo-shamanism can be seen in the global movement of spiritual tourists who can move from Siberia to Amazonia in search of authentic religious "highs" without much concern about what their presence does to the peoples whose worlds they are entering.

Neo-shamanism, then, has to be seen as part of the general global flow of religious practices and ideas that characterizes contemporary life. Certain individuals claim, within that flow, the privilege of forming eclectic personal religious systems out of whatever practices and ideas with which they come into contact. The commodification of indigenous cultures, however, can have serious, and often negative, consequences for native peoples themselves.

See also: Ayahuasca; Globalization and New Religious Movements; Healing, Health, and New Religious Movements; New Age, The.

Further Reading

Castaneda, Carlos. 1968. *The Teachings of Don Juan: A Yaqui Way of Knowledge*. Berkeley: University of California Press.

De Mille, Richard, ed. 1980. *The Don Juan Papers: Further Castaneda Controversies*. Santa Barbara, CA: Ross-Erikson.

Eliade, Mircea. 1972. *Shamanism: Archaic Techniques of Ecstasy*, rev. ed. Princeton, NJ: Princeton University Press.

Harner, Michael J. 1980. *The Way of the Shaman.* New York: Harper & Row.

Wernitznig, Dagmar. 2003. *Going Native or Going Naïve? White Shamanism and the Neo-Noble Savage.* Lanham, MD: University Press of America.

Shembe, Isaiah (c. 1870–1935)

Isaiah Mdliwamafa Shembe was the founder of the Ibandla lama-Nazaretha or Nazareth Baptist Church, an African-Initiated Church that took shape in the KwaZulu-Natal area of colonial South Africa at the beginning of the twentieth century. The members of the Church remember Shembe as being marked for great things, even from his conception. Multiple stories about Shembe draw parallels between his life and that of Jesus. Shembe frequently experienced dreams, visions, and other forms of communication that established and then reinforced his status as a prophet. Members of the Church insist that God's revelation to human beings did not stop with the death of Jesus, but that it has continued in modern-day Africa with Shembe.

Even before he began his own church in 1910, Shembe had come to equate the Jehovah of the Christian Bible with the Zulu Creator God Nkulunkulu, anticipating the mix of African and Christian elements that would characterize his church. Shembe spent some time with a Methodist mission church and was baptized by full immersion into the African Native Baptist Church (ANBC) led by the Rev. W. M. Leshege in 1906. Soon after, Shembe separated from his family and the ANBC to function as an itinerant preacher in the years leading up to 1910. The founding of his own church was initiated when a group of recent converts that he brought to a station of the American Board of Foreign Missions for further instruction was rejected because they were dressed in Zulu clothing.

Although Shembe was not literate, he was deeply familiar with the Christian Bible and he developed his own distinctive understanding of it. He insisted on the observation of the Sabbath on Saturday, the seventh-day, in keeping with both his personal exegesis of the Bible and confirming prophetic inspiration. Shembe asserted that Christian churches that observed the Sabbath on Sunday were denying their followers a chance at salvation.

Shembe's church observes four sacraments: baptism, the Lord's Supper, dancing as worship, and the wearing of special uniforms. Baptism must be by full immersion in accordance with Shembe's understanding of the biblical requirements. The Lord's Supper is celebrated only on special occasions, rather than weekly or daily. Participants must undergo a period of fasting and self-examination to prepare themselves for the ritual. The ritual dancing that the Nazarites perform is traced to Psalm 150 as a justification for the use of drums, horns, and stylized movements in giving praise to God. Finally, the members of the church wear white robes on ritual occasions, with the understanding that their robes are the same as those worn by the heavenly host, something that Shembe himself saw in multiple visions.

Members of the Nazareth Baptist Church think of themselves as God's Chosen People. They lead sober, conservative lives and understand themselves to be keeping the Nazarite vows mentioned in Numbers 6. They identify one of the two sacred places that Shembe established soon after founding the Church as the "New Jerusalem." That holy city of Ekuphakameni ("the exalted place"), located on the outskirts of Durban, South Africa, was founded to serve both as the headquarters and a ritual center for the Church. As the new Zion, it serves as a place of pilgrimage for the most important gathering of members of the Church each July.

The second holy site for the Church is the mountain Nhlangakazi ("the place of the great/big reed"). It, too, is identified as a site where Shembe had multiple prophetic experiences, including a temptation by the devil that echoes Jesus's temptation in Matthew 4. It was on the mountain that Shembe received the commission to spread the message of his church to everyone. Members of the Church conduct an annual pilgrimage to Nhlangakazi, which is roughly thirty kilometers from Ekuphakameni, every January.

Unlike some new religious movements, Shembe's church was able to survive his death in 1935 and to continue to attract converts both from other Christian groups and from traditional African religions across tribal lines. On Shembe's death, leadership passed to his son, Johannes Galilee Shembe (1904–1977). The Nazareth Baptist Church, however, has experienced a series of schisms, with various members of the Shembe family contending for control over both his memory and the headquarters at Ekuphakameni. Though the Nazareth Baptist Church has fragmented, the movement as a whole remains a vital presence in southern Africa.

See also: African New Religious Movements; Church of the Lord (Aladura); Kimbangu, Simon.

Further Reading
Cabrita, Joel. 2014. *Text and Authority in the South African Nazaretha Church*. New York: Cambridge University Press.
Tishken, Joel. 2013. *Isaiah Shembe's Prophetic Uhlanga: The Worldview of the Nazareth Baptist Church in Colonial South Africa*. New York: Peter Lang.

Singer, Margaret Thaler (1921–2003)

On the basis of her public speaking, testimony in court, and popular writings, Margaret Singer was one of the most influential participants in the contemporary anticult movement. Trained as a clinical psychologist, she was best known within that field for her work on family therapy. But that limited notoriety was thoroughly eclipsed by the role that she played in the public "cult wars" of the late twentieth century through her espousal of ideas about brainwashing, thought reform, and coercive persuasion.

An early presentation of Singer's position appeared in an article in the popular magazine, *Psychology Today* in 1979. She suggested that as many as two to three million individuals had suffered negative psychological effects of membership in "cults." Singer's analysis was based on interviews she conducted with more than three hundred members and ex-members. She found their experiences to be sufficiently similar as to constitute a single pattern and urged therapists to learn about the various cults to help potential patients.

By the appearance in 1995 of *Cults in Our Midst*, Singer claimed to have worked with more than three thousand current and former members, although all references to them had been made anonymous. She concluded that cults constituted an urgent threat to public health and the very fabric of democracy. Disregarding evidence about how many people actually joined and stayed in cults, Singer amplified the perceived threat by stressing that everyone is vulnerable to predatory cults.

Although Singer offered a rudimentary typology of cults, in the end, she minimized differences among them. She also denied any interest in the specific ideologies of individual groups and preferred to focus on what she saw as the similarities in the processes by which they attracted and retained members. Building on the work of Robert Jay Lifton (1926–) on Chinese and Korean attempts at indoctrination in the 1950s and her mentor Edgar Schein's work on thought reform, Singer built the case that cults practiced coercive persuasion.

Singer's warnings about the dangers of cults found a responsive audience in the loose coalitions of worried parents, mental health professionals, attorneys, and other activists who, since the early 1970s, had animated a movement in opposition to the perceived growing "cult problem." Singer offered a simple, but powerful, explanation for why children of the middle and upper classes had abandoned college and the promises of careers for new and strange religions.

As parents attempted to remove their children from stigmatized groups through legal means, Singer became a sought-after provider of expert testimony in the 1970s, providing more than thirty depositions and testimonies. In her statements, Singer expressed a strong form of brainwashing theory by which cults overcame the free will of individuals and achieved virtually complete control over them. By the early 1980s, however, scholars had raised critical questions about the brainwashing hypothesis as it applied to new religious movements.

In 1983, the American Psychological Association (APA) appointed a task force to examine the theory of coercive persuasion. Although Singer was appointed to chair the study of Deceptive and Indirect Methods of Persuasion and Control and the task force included prominent figures in the anticult movement, in 1987, the APA declined to accept the report of the task force, citing its lack of academic rigor and biased approach. The American Sociological Association also formally weighed in against the brainwashing hypothesis. With that, the tide began to turn against the use of Singer's ideas in court. Singer and others who held similar views were no longer accepted as expert witnesses.

Singer attempted to preserve her reputation and livelihood, however, by suing the APA for defamation in both 1993 and 1994. Both suits were quickly dismissed. The failure to sustain the brainwashing theory as a legal tool contributed to the dwindling practice of coercive deprogramming through the 1990s as various forms of "exit counseling" became the most prominent ways of working with cult members. It is clear, however, that the continuing public endorsement of the brainwashing hypothesis, which can be traced in part to Singer's work, has not kept pace with its legal and academic rejection.

See also: Anticult Movement, The; Brainwashing; Cult; Deprogramming; Exit Counseling.

Further Reading

Shupe, Anson, & Susan E. Darnell. 2006. *Agents of Discord: Deprogramming, Pseudo-Science, and the American Anticult Movement*. New Brunswick, NJ: Transaction Publishers.

Singer, Margaret Thaler. 1979. "Coming Out of the Cults." *Psychology Today* January: 72–82.

Singer, Margaret Thaler, with Janja Lalich. 1995. *Cults in Our Midst: The Hidden Menace in Our Everyday Lives*. San Francisco: Jossey-Bass Publishers.

Smith, Joseph (1805–1844)

EARLY LIFE AND FIRST VISIONS

Joseph Smith Jr. was born on December 23, 1805, in Vermont. Smith's parents, Joseph Sr. and Lucy, were both of solid New England stock, but were unsettled in religious affiliation and livelihood. While Lucy was devout, if not orthodox, Joseph Sr. was definitely a seeker, dabbling in various religions including Universalism. His lack of settled identity set the stage for Joseph Jr.'s own spiritual grappling in his adolescence. Especially when, after moving to Palmyra, New York, the Smith family was caught up in the religious revivals then burning through the town. Finding no definitive answers from the variety of Christian denominations available, in 1820 Smith retreated to the woods where he prayed to God for answers and immediately received a vision of God and Jesus. The two heavenly personages instructed him that all other churches were apostate and that he would create a new church on the foundation of the restored gospel. Three years later, he received a subsequent vision in his bedchamber, this time from a figure outside of the Christian canon known as the angel Moroni. Moroni instructed Joseph that, when deemed worthy, he would translate a set of golden plates buried in a hill nearby. As he awaited that moment, Joseph married Emma Hale and began to gather a group of devoted believers. In 1827, he was commissioned to dig up the plates, after which he began the process of dictating to Martin Harris, and then to Oliver Cowdery, what he translated. *The Book of Mormon* was completed and published in March 1830; in April 1830, Joseph along with those early believers founded the Church of Jesus Christ of Latter-day Saints (LDS Church).

The story of Joseph's visions has since been elevated to the status of scripture because these miraculous encounters, and the knowledge of the restored gospel they revealed, mark Smith and his LDS Church as distinct from competing Christianities. However, Smith also benefited from the familiarity of his claims; many like him were also claiming direct experiences of the divine, thus his story was not so far-fetched as to be dismissed outright. On the other hand, he differentiated himself, and his nascent church, by claiming to have found and translated a new and wholly extra-biblical scripture.

BUILDING THE CHURCH

Whether it was the appeal of the precocious youth or a religious context replete with those seeking a new and better church, the Church began to spread and with it the reputation of Joseph Smith. Young, handsome, resourceful, and a charismatic speaker, Smith cut a dashing figure in a competitive religious market. Reports multiplied of those spellbound by Smith's oratorical ability, particular the way he could weave together biblical and present history in seamless fashion. Even more remarkable was the fact that he was virtually uneducated—a fact most "Saints" argue highlights the truth of his calling and his message.

However, it was his lack of education that critics would often cite as one of the reasons to doubt Smith's abilities as a leader and as a true man of God. At best, his critics found him to be a deluded, albeit earnest lunatic, and at worst, a conman or megalomaniacal tyrant. The last label arose as a result of rumors concerning Smith's most controversial revelation, that of plural marriage. Uncharitable interpretations of this revelation read Smith as a lascivious and sex-crazed figure, drunk on his own power. Though the LDS Church has discontinued the practice, they do not attribute the practice to Smith's own human urges, but to his belief, as interpreted from God's revelation, that marriage and the production of many children were essential to achieving what Saints call "exaltation," or ascension to the highest level of heaven.

Joseph Smith, founder of The Church of Jesus Christ of Latter-day Saints (the Mormon Church). Smith claimed to have been visited by the angel Moroni, who told him of the location of ancient gold plates, from which he transcribed and published *The Book of Mormon*. Smith founded the Mormon Church in 1830. (Library of Congress)

For the Latter-day Saints, the most important label by which Smith is known is prophet. Besides being the originator of the Church (at least in modern history), he was arguably the most productive LDS prophet. Thus, the leap to paint the early LDS Church as a cult of personality misunderstands the scope of his influence and his accomplishments. The fact that the church sustained itself after his martyrdom reveals that Smith was accomplished at church-building. In his capacity as prophet, he recorded a series of direct revelations over a period of fifteen years that would form the basis of the Church's religious thought, practice, and community. Among these innovations were a new and growing set of scriptures, a unique

582 Soka Gakkai

cosmological vision that placed human beings on a path to deification, a set of unique rituals and distinctive site of worship in the Temple, and an intricate and expansive church infrastructure and hierarchy.

DEATH AND LEGACY

Smith's continuing contributions to the Church, however, met an untimely end. As he and the Saints had made their progress west, beginning in 1830 and stopping at various locations until arriving in Nauvoo, Illinois, during the early 1840s, they had tallied a growing list of enemies from within and without. Both types of foe would converge on Smith in late spring of 1844, when he signed off on the destruction of a printing press owned by a former Saint, whose first and only paper had been devoted to smearing his name. Smith, his brother Hyrum, and two members of the Quorum of Twelve Apostles, John Taylor and Willard Richards, were arrested by the Illinois militia and escorted to a jail cell in Carthage to await trial for the charge of treason. On June 27, 1844, a mob descended on the jail and murdered both Joseph and Hyrum Smith. Falling from a window after being pierced by bullets, Smith reportedly yelled, "Oh Lord my God," dying shortly thereafter. Though these words have become legendary in a more popular sense, it is the pages of scripture and the language of revelation for which Smith will be remembered among the Saints.

See also: Charisma and Leadership in New Religious Movements; Church of Jesus Christ of Latter-day Saints, The; Fundamentalist Mormons; Prophecy in New Religious Movements; Sex, Sexuality, and New Religious Movements.

Further Reading
Brodie, Fawn. 1995. *No Man Knows My History: The Life of Joseph Smith.* New York: Vintage Books.

Bushman, Richard. 2007. *Joseph Smith: Rough Stone Rolling.* New York: Random House.

Jessee, Dean C., Ronald K. Esplin, and Richard Lyman Bushman, eds. *The Joseph Smith Papers.* Multiple Volumes. Salt Lake City, UT: Church Historian's Press.

Soka Gakkai

Part of the wave of religious innovation that occurred in Japan during the nineteenth and twentieth centuries, Soka Gakkai is a lay Buddhist new religion in the Nichiren Shōshū tradition. It now has as many as ten million members throughout the world and has expanded its religious mission by actively advocating for disarmament, human rights, sustainable development, and other issues, often in cooperation with the United Nations.

Although it traces its teachings to the Japanese Buddhist priest Nichiren Daishonin (1222–1282), the contemporary history of Soka Gakkai begins in the 1920s when Japanese educator Tsunesaburo Makiguchi and his protégé Josei Toda converted to Nichiren Buddhism. In 1930, they founded the Soka Kyoiku Gakkai, or Educational Society for the Creation of Value, which was critical of Japanese educational practices. That group opposed both the established Japanese state religion and Japan's participation in World War II. Both the founders were sentenced to prison for refusing to require their adherents to enshrine in their homes talismans from the Grand Shrine at Ise, which contradicted Nichiren Buddhist principles. Makiguchi died there in 1944. The organization took a decisive religious turn when Toda experienced enlightenment in prison while reading the Lotus Sutra.

After his release, Toda renamed the group Soka Gakkai, "Value-Creating Society," in 1946. He became the second president of Soka Gakkai in 1951. He urged members to make 750,000 converts, and by the end of the 1950s, Soka Gakkai claimed over one million adherents. That focus on aggressive proselytizing (*shakubuku*), derived in part from the conviction that the Nichiren tradition is the only true form of Buddhism, earned the rancor of rival religious groups in Japan.

Soka Gakkai was imported to North America by Japanese women who had married members of the United States military after World War II. In the United States, Soka Gakkai has spread primarily through established social networks of religious seekers. In part to attract potential members, the current website (www.sgi.org) of Soka Gakkai International, provides a history of the group, a selection of writings of the third and current honorary president Daisaku Ikeda (1928–), stories from Soka Gakkai members about how the religion has transformed and guided their lives, and instructional texts and videos. Those materials, along with the writings of Nichiren, serve as the basis for members' study of Buddhism.

PRACTICES

The Lotus Sutra is the focal point of Soka Gakkai and chanting of praise for the sutra is the central ritual action. Practitioners are instructed to perform their chanting in front of a *gohonzon*, a scroll with *nam-myoho-renge-kyo* written down the center. The scrolls are held to be replicas of the original calligraphic mandala made by Nichiren in 1279. Such scrolls can be simple or ornate and may be located within a more complex home shrine. In whatever form it takes, the *gohonzon* provides a focus for individuals as they chant their praise for the Lotus Sutra and recite portions of it. Such chanting is most frequently undertaken by individuals in their homes, but it can also be a group practice. The purpose of chanting is to bring individuals to the fundamental realization of their own inner Buddha nature and to cultivate the qualities of courage, wisdom, and compassion that come with that understanding. Although Soka Gakkai practice focuses on the individual, members may also gather for monthly discussions and mutual support in areas where there are sufficient numbers.

Members are still encouraged to convert others, especially since Soka Gakkai believes that the world is in the latter days of the Buddha's dharma. According to Nichiren, that period began in 1052 and the only opportunity for salvation or achieving Buddhahood is to focus on the Lotus Sutra and reject all other teachings.

584 Spiritual but Not Religious

Although it does not promulgate any specific rules of conduct, in Soka Gakkai, the realization of one's inner nature is also supposed to prompt social action. In the broadest sense, practitioners are supposed to draw on the power of the Lotus Sutra to create an ideal world of peace and happiness for all creatures. Soka Gakkai desires a "human revolution," in which the transformation of individuals ultimately leads to change on a global scale.

CONTROVERSIES

From its origins, Soka Gakkai depended on the Nichiren priesthood; for example, priests were responsible for providing copies of the *gohonzon* for all new members. But in 1991, after more than a decade of tension, the members of Soka Gakkai, numbering some 95 percent of the Nichiren organization, were excommunicated by the priests. Each group claimed to be the true successors of Nichiren. Soka Gakkai was able to weather that challenge by forming relationships with priests who themselves had left the formal Nichiren organization.

In Japan, Soka Gakkai's desire for social change has led it to get involved in politics. Members of Soka Gakkai founded the political party Komeito in 1964. At that time, some people in Japan worried that the new party violated the separation of religion and politics established in the Japanese constitution. By 1970, all formal ties between Komeito and Soka Gakkai had been severed, but only in the early twenty-first century did Komeito begin to shed the general perception that it was a religious party.

In the United States, Soka Gakkai has generally avoided the sharp criticisms and social opposition leveled against some other new religions and maintained a relatively low level of tension with its immediate social environment. It has not been known for aggressive proselytizing, intense relationships between followers and a single guru, or unconventional sexual or other practices associated in the public discourse with "cults."

See also: Japanese New Religious Movements.

Further Reading

Dobbelaere, Karel. 2001. *Soka Gakkai: From Lay Movement to Religion.* Salt Lake City, UT: Signature Books.

Hammond, Phillip, & David Machacek. 1999. *Soka Gakkai in America: Accommodation and Conversion.* Oxford: Oxford University Press.

Hochswender, Woody, Greg Martin & Ted Morino. 2001. *The Buddha in Your Mirror: Practical Buddhism and the Search for Self.* Santa Monica, CA: Middleway Press.

Ikeda, Daisaku, et al. 2000. *The Wisdom of the Lotus Sutra: A Discussion,* Vol. I. Santa Monica, CA: World Tribune Press.

Spiritual but Not Religious

What does it mean to be "Spiritual but not Religious" (SBNR)? For some, this religious designation is a thoroughly modern and American one, born from a variety of forces: the increasing number of those unaffiliated with a formal religious institution or "nones," globalization and the ever-expanding access to alternative traditions, the advent of seeker culture in the 1960s, and the rise of New Age religions and the influx of Asian religious traditions, among others. What these forces produced was a sea of individuals who either rejected formal institutional religious labels or who associated "religiousness" with institutional control and "spirituality" with individual advancement or evolution. Along these lines, some would argue that the religion of SBNR is the religion of the individual, and therefore not a formal new religious movement at all.

Increasingly, however, scholars have sought to locate those who identify as SBNR in a longer historical narrative, one that spans continents and centuries and coheres a supposedly inchoate group into a broader movement. Arguably, the roots of SBNR lie firmly in the rise of modern Europe. The Reformation, which deemphasized the role of the Church in mediating salvation and emphasized reading and interpreting the Bible for oneself, and the Enlightenment, which placed an imprimatur on the rational mind to know truth, were (perhaps unwitting) intellectual and cultural contributors to the notion that the individual should be involved in shaping her religious life.

In the American context, following the Revolutionary War and the formal disestablishment of state religion, religions of many varieties proliferated. Individuals could choose a religious home that worked for them; correspondingly, religions adapted to the exploding variety by learning to market themselves to be competitive. In the nineteenth century, a profusion of philosophical and religious movements, such as Transcendentalism and New Thought, emphasized the divine capability of human beings to understand ultimate reality or truth and even to change their physical circumstances through the power of their mind. In the twentieth century, such notions of human capacity were bolstered in the years post–World War II, when immigration laws were changed and the counterculture was born—both events that introduced the youth of America to the notion that truth existed outside the political and religious institutions of their youth. Religious and cultural borrowing marked many so-called New Age religions, which merged multiple religious strains into movements that promised the individual practitioner anything from better health to advancement to a higher plane of existence. And with the advent of the internet, suddenly easy consumption of religious texts and artifacts made it possible for those identifying as SBNR to create their own religious world with a key stroke.

BELIEFS AND VARIETIES

Identifying them as different than mere agnosticism, scholar Linda Mercadente divides SBNRs into five categories. First, are the "Dissenters," those who actively distance themselves from organized religion for a variety of reasons, including personal history. "Casuals" are those who partake of religious or spiritual practices on an as-needed basis; this could include attending a religious service, practicing meditation, or seeking out the services of a spiritual practitioner. Often "Casuals" engage in spiritual activities for the sake of their emotional or physical betterment. Those who are "Explorers" are constantly on a spiritual quest and are unlikely or uninterested in finding a permanent religious home. They often dabble in multiple spiritual practices at once or move from one spiritual practice to the next. "Seekers" are those looking to recover an identity lost (often they are disillusioned with their former institution) and do hope to commit to new religious identity ultimately. Finally, "Immigrants" are those who have found a new spirituality and are actively acclimating to its requirements (or lack thereof). These categories are not discrete, in that SBNRs may exhibit traits of several of these types or switch between them according to where they are on their spiritual path.

Practices are eclectic and vary from practitioner to practitioner. Often those who identify as SBNR employ Hindu and Buddhist practices, such as yoga and meditation, or Chinese homeopathic techniques, such as acupuncture, as a means of seeking mystical union or "centering" themselves. There are also those who engage in astrology, mediumship, or crystals, hallmarks of New Age spirituality, to channel sacred power and beget a desired outcome. For a great many SBNRs, much of their religious practice involves reading and study.

A MODERN SPIRITUALITY

Though there is not a definitive demographic profile for those who identity as SBNR, more often than not, the designation is employed by those who are young, male, and English-speaking.

In some ways, the religion of SBNR seems to reflect the contemporary landscape of religion, which is market and consumer-driven, geared toward marketing religions tailor-made to the modern seeker. It is this image that leads critics of SBNRs to characterize them as lacking religion or even being spiritually lazy, simply choosing what is most interesting on a given day. Critics accuse SBNRs of creating "me-focused" religions that accelerate cultural isolation and secularization. Postcolonial scholars are also particularly skeptical of the cultural borrowing that occurs by SBNRs, perceiving such appropriation as occurring without knowledge of the theological, cultural, and communal reasons for a given practice or belief, thus voiding it of meaning.

Despite these critiques, being SBNR does not appear to be a dying trend. Though the unaffiliated are not synonymous with those who are SBNR, the numbers continue to grow among those who choose to find religious fulfillment outside of traditional institutional forums.

See also: Globalization and New Religious Movements; New Age, The; New Thought; Seekers; Transcendentalism.

Further Reading

Albanese, Catherine. 2008. *A Republic of Mind and Spirit: A Cultural History of Metaphysical Religion.* New Haven, CT: Yale University Press.

Fuller, Robert C. 2001. *Spiritual but Not Religious: Understanding Unchurched America.* New York: Oxford University Press.

Mercadante, Linda A. 2014. *Belief without Borders: Inside the Minds of the Spiritual but not Religious.* New York: Oxford University Press.

Schmidt, Leigh. 2012. *Restless Souls: The Making of American Spirituality*, 2nd ed. Berkeley: University of California Press.

Spiritualism

In the twenty-first century, the term "Spiritualism" often conjures images of the search for spirituality or individual professions of being "spiritual but not religious." Though there are certainly aspects of Spiritualist practice that speak to modern trends in religiosity—namely, the ability to progress through an often individualized spiritual discipline—Spiritualism is a distinctive religion that holds, at its base, the belief that there is a spiritual realm and that humans can communicate with it. In its simplest terms, Spiritualism is about talking to the dead.

HISTORY AND BACKGROUND

Though the origins of Spiritualism as a religious movement are murky (and disputed), most historians argue that it involved the Fox Sisters and a series of phenomena known as the Hydesville Rappings. In 1848, Hydesville, New York, was situated at the heart of the "Burned-over District," which was so named because of the many religious revivals and new religions that had occurred there over a short time. At that time, two of its inhabitants, Margaret "Maggie" (1833–1893) and Kate (1837–1892) Fox, began to hear noises, which they described as "rappings" in their house, which had a reputation for being haunted. The girls (who were twelve and fifteen, respectively) sought to reproduce the noises by invoking the spirit (or spirits) they believed was responsible for them. Kate and Margaret soon amassed a devoted group of followers, including many radical Quakers who privileged not only the internal but external reality of spiritual experiences. The earliest group to consider themselves "Spiritualists" believed not only in the truth of the phenomena but also that the girls were mediums—those who could channel spiritual entities. Kate and Margaret began to exhibit their abilities, including the ability to fall into hypnotic trances or to perform "automatic writing" (writing the words of a spirit while possessed by it) in front of paying audiences and to conduct public séances.

From the platform built by the Fox sisters, the popularity and prestige of mediums, séances, and Spiritualism grew. Mediums, particularly those that gave public exhibitions (often known as "trance lecturers or performers"), often ascended to the rank of celebrity; Cora Scott (1840–1923) is a prime example. Thus, many who dabbled in Spiritualism were attracted by the mystique and charisma of certain key Spiritualists, attending lectures or séances (a group ceremony aimed at contacting the dead) to mingle among them. Others wished to speak to their dead loved ones. However, there were many who wanted more than the opportunity to speak to those they had lost: they wanted to learn from these spirits, who now inhabited a realm no living person could. Some like Andrew Jackson Davis (1826–1910) and Helena Petrovna Blavatsky (1831–1891) (the cofounder of

Theosophy, an offshoot of Spiritualism) became Spiritualists to seek alternative sources of divine knowledge. It was the possibility of such sacred knowledge that set apart religiously minded Spiritualists from those Spiritualists who came primarily as spectators.

Over its first few decades, the religious movement proceeded as a diffuse network of mediums and Spiritualist circles, sometimes formed into alliances or organizations, in the United States and, increasingly, Europe. A number of Spiritualist periodicals circulated to keep Spiritualists apprised of developments or informed of major events. Additionally, some Spiritualists began forming themselves into "churches," including the National Spiritualist Association of America, which convened a National Convention and declared March 31, 1870, the official birth of modern Spiritualism. In the United Kingdom, the next largest hub of Spiritualist practice, the Spiritualists' National Union, was founded in 1890. These organizations still exist but do not constitute all varieties of Spiritualism. Many Spiritualists choose to practice individually or in smaller circles, seeking séances outside of more established institutional networks; these Spiritualists may casually identify with the Spiritualist Church or with another religion entirely.

BELIEFS AND PRACTICES

According to the National Spiritualist Association of Churches (www.nsac .org), Spiritualism is a science (since the basis of its belief system are empirically verifiable phenomena), a philosophy (since it examines the laws of nature), and a religion (since it seeks to comply with the spiritual laws of nature, which are also those of God). The primacy of science emphasizes for a twenty-first century audience the continuity of the nineteenth-century beliefs in psychic and spiritual phenomena as central to Spiritualism's beliefs and practices. However, Spiritualists do maintain a set of principles, which emphasize the belief in an Infinite Intelligence (or God), that this entity manifests itself in the physical and spiritual world, and the belief in the immortality and eternal progression of the soul toward total knowledge and consciousness that continues after death (proven, of course, by continued contact with the deceased). Many of these ideas stem, at least in part, from the ideas of Emanuel Swedenborg (1688–1772), who claimed to have spoken to spirits and who argued that spirits represent intermediaries between God and human beings. Contrary to popular portrayals of spirits, then, all contact with the deceased is not ghoulish, but divine.

Similar to its offshoot Theosophy, belonging to Spiritualist circles did not preclude one from belonging to another religion. For some, Spiritualist practice simply enhanced one's religious practices by providing an alternative path to religious truth. James Freeman Clarke (1810–1888), a Unitarian who practiced Spiritualism, argued along these lines. In fact, the National Spiritualist Association of America states as one of its "Objects" that Spiritualists promise to "protest" any attempts to compel religious belief in any one particular way.

Other "Objects" of Spiritualism including "teaching" its principles, "advocating" for spiritual healing, and "encouraging" each person, Spiritualist or not, to continually seek truth. Beyond these general mandates, Spiritualists are enjoined to follow "natural or universal laws" (which are also God's laws), which are impersonal and eternal, and seek balance among all living things (e.g., the "Golden Rule" is foremost among these laws). And while physical mediumship in its previous form—filled with rappings, trances, and supernatural phenomena—is rare, mediums and séances are still the primary form of worship and gathering for Spiritualists, though the focus is much more focused on seeking direct sacred knowledge than on talking with loved ones.

Spiritualism also maintains a close relationship with alternative healing practices and ideologies, differentiating between mediums and spiritualist healers. The latter are those who employ their connection with the spiritual realm to cure ailments and illnesses, which aligns them with many nineteenth-century and modern movements that argued for a mental or spiritual alternative to Western medicine.

CULTURAL LEGACY

Similar to other new religions born in the nineteenth century (e.g., Theosophy and Christian Science), Spiritualism provided a context for women to inhabit positions of authority. Most mediums were women. This fact illuminates two essential conclusions: first, the historical belief that women were more susceptible to spiritual contact (both good and bad) lent them authority in their role as mediums, and second, Spiritualism represented a means of rejecting traditional authority as much as it meant rejecting the finality of death. In general, and particularly in the nineteenth century, Spiritualism and social reform seemed to go hand in hand. Many key Spiritualists, such as Paschal Beverly Randolph (1825–1875), who was an abolitionist, bucked traditional political and social institutions, much as they bucked traditional religious institutions.

Given the nature of Spiritualist phenomena, there are have been multiple allegations of fraud leveled at mediums and other Spiritualists through history. Beginning with the Fox sisters, critics accused those involved with séances of fabricating phenomena and cheating people of their money. Though many Spiritualists maintained the veracity of their spiritual experiences, the religion was not helped by those who were caught perpetrating fraud or, in the case of Maggie Fox, those who confessed to such activities. In the 1880s, the Society for Psychical Research was founded by British Spiritualists primarily to investigate fraudulent phenomena among their rank. However, what occurred as a result of their public revealing of huckster mediums was the decline of physical mediums overall and with them, much of Spiritualism's broad market appeal. In the mid-to-late nineteenth century, there were apparently millions of Spiritualists solely in the United States. In the early twenty-first century, the global population of Spiritualists numbers around a quarter of a million. Spiritualism, in its many forms, is still a significant new religious movement today; however, it has never again achieved the level of prestige or number of participants it had in its first decades.

See also: Blavatsky, Helena Petrovna (1831–1891); Christian Science; Fox, Kate (1837–1892), and Margaret (1833–1893); Fraud and Deception in New Religions; Ghosts, the Paranormal, and New Religious Movements; Occultism and Esotericism; Swedenborg, Emanuel; Theosophical Society, The; Theosophy; Women in New Religious Movements.

Further Reading

Braude, Ann. 2001. *Radical Spirits: Spiritualism and Women's Rights in the Nineteenth Century.* Second Edition. Bloomington: Indiana University Press.

Carroll, Bret E. 1997. *Spiritualism in Antebellum America (Religion in North America).* Bloomington: Indiana University Press.

Leonard, Todd Jay. 2005. *Talking to the Other Side: A History of Modern Spiritualism and Mediumship, A Study of the Religion, Science, Philosophy and Mediums that Encompass this American-Made Religion.* Lincoln, NE: iUniverse.

Starhawk (1951–)

One of the most influential contemporary American Pagan teachers, Starhawk (née Miriam Simos) took her religious name in her early twenties after experiencing a series of dreams in which she met the Goddess. Starhawk traces her interest in Paganism and Goddess worship to events in her teens, but, like many who have become contemporary Pagans, at that time, she did not have the language and categories to name her experience. That changed when, during her time at UCLA, she met several witches and eventually spent time with Z. Budapest (1940–), who founded the women-only Susan B. Anthony Coven #1 in 1971 in Los Angeles.

By 1975, Starhawk was devoting herself to teaching and writing about Paganism in the San Francisco area, which had a thriving community of Pagans of various orientations. While there, she studied with Victor Anderson (1917–2001) who claimed to be a hereditary witch in the Faery tradition. Starhawk's teaching, which has always had a pronounced feminist emphasis, inspired the formation of several covens of practicing witches who observed Pagan holidays based on the solar calendar.

In 1979, Starhawk and collaborators sponsored the first annual public ritual of the Spiral Dance, which was also the title of her first and most widely read book, published in 1979. Starhawk identifies herself as part of the Reclaiming tradition, which, among other things, reclaims the power of the ancient Goddess and women's religious and political agency and addresses social, political, and, increasingly, ecological injustices. Like much of contemporary Paganism, the Reclaiming tradition is loosely organized, but Starhawk, along with others, was an important figure in the Reclaiming collective that lasted from 1978 to 1997.

Although Starhawk has held many classes and workshops on contemporary Witchcraft and Paganism, she has reached a much broader audience through her writing. For many contemporary Pagans, *The Spiral Dance*, which combines general observations about Paganism with specific ritual scripts, has been a point of entry into Paganism and a valued guide for many practicing Pagans. The text has even been part of the curriculum of Cherry Hill Seminary, which has been offering online courses to support the development of Pagan ministers since 2000. It has also been translated into multiple languages.

Starhawk's career as a teacher highlights the diversity of sources on which contemporary Paganism draws; substantial differences within the movement, such as the question of mixed gender versus all women covens; the attraction that Paganism exerts on some who feel that their religious experiences are not validated by established religious groups; and the power of the printed word to draw others into the movement.

See also: Neopaganism; New Scriptures and New Religious Movements.

Further Reading

Salomonson, Jone. 2002. *Enchanted Feminism: The Reclaiming Witches of San Francisco.* New York: Routledge.

Starhawk. 1999. *The Spiral Dance: A Rebirth of the Ancient Religion of the Great Goddess.* Special 20th anniversary ed. San Francisco: HarperSanFrancisco.

Vakem, V., & Joh Sulak, eds. 2001. "Starhawk." In *Modern Pagans: An Investigation of Contemporary Pagan Practices*, pp. 6–16. San Francisco: RE/search Publications.

Steiner, Rudolf (1861–1925)

Rudolf Steiner, founder of Anthroposophy, is perhaps better known for the various programs he founded or inspired, including the Waldorf educational system, organic and biodynamic farming, and a socially conscious financial system. All of these programs arose from the esoteric religious movement he created.

Born in Austria, Steiner trained to become a natural scientist. However, having experienced supernatural phenomena since childhood, he found himself increasingly drawn to philosophical and spiritual subjects. Eventually, these pursuits led him to Theosophy, an occult religious system claiming that human beings could access other sacred realms and could converse with supernatural beings, known as the Great Masters, who aided people in their path to spiritual enlightenment. Steiner served as secretary for the German chapter of the Theosophical Society from 1902 to 1912.

Over time, however, Steiner grew disillusioned with Theosophy, specifically its emphasis on Asian religious sources. Steiner founded Anthroposophy on the notion that occult knowledge was just as prominent in Christianity. He also believed that Jesus needed to be elevated from the traditional Theosophical view that he was another avatar of a Great Master, rather than the culmination of spiritual history to that point. A prolific writer even prior to his split from Theosophy, Steiner's work increasingly reflected the Christian esoteric bent of his thought.

Steiner quickly branched out into other industries and fields of knowledge believing that individual spiritual advancement necessitated societal advancement as well. He advocated for a new form of medicine, which employed a variety of homeopathic techniques, as well as emphasized a therapeutic technique known as "eurythmy," which sought to heal the soul and the mind along with the body. Steiner's educational, social, and economic theories operated on the assumption of unity, equality, and a division of labor, emphasizing the importance of human rights in all social systems.

Steiner's accomplishments were marred by his racial theory of evolution. Adopted from Helena Petrovna Blavatsky (1831–1891), Steiner posited that the highest level of spiritual evolution was represented by the "Aryan" race, as seen in white, European (specifically Germanic) culture. Though Steiner would ultimately deny that categories such as race and ethnicity had any importance, due to the essential unity of all humanity, these views had a long afterlife and influenced racial-political systems such as National Socialism. (This is also a point of irony, as Steiner had been accused by Adolf Hitler [1889–1945] as being a defender of the Jews and a Jew himself.)

Steiner continued to lecture even as his health failed. He died on March 30, 1925, survived by his religious movement, and his achievements in the field of education, agriculture, and economics, among others.

See also: Anthroposophy; Blavatsky, Helena Petrovna (1831–1891); Occultism and Esotericism; Race and New Religious Movements; Science, Technology, and New Religious Movements; Theosophical Society, The; Theosophy.

Further Reading
Lachman, Gary. 2007. *Rudolf Steiner: An Introduction to His Life and Work*. London: TarcherPerigree.

Steiner, Rudolf. 1908. *How to Know Higher Worlds: A Modern Path of Initiation*. London: Theosophical Publishing Society.

Steiner, Rudolf. 1914 [1902]. *Christianity as Mystical Fact*. London: G.P. Putnam & Sons.

Subud

Often, described as a "spiritual movement," rather than a religion, "Subud" is actually an acronym that derives from three Sanskritic words: "*Susila Budhi Dharma*," which means that someone lives a life that is "truly human" (susila), exhibits awareness of an intrinsic force in all living creatures that pulls them along the proper spiritual path (budhi), and lives with a sense of surrender toward God's will and the overall order of the universe (dharma). Though the movement was founded by and among Muslims, its founder and practitioners maintain that the practice of Subud is accessible to everyone, regardless of their gender, race, nationality, and religious affiliation.

The Indonesian and Javanese Muslim Muhammad Subuh Sumohadiwidjojo (1901–1987), also called Pak Subuh or "Bapak," founded Subud in the 1930s, following a series of mystical experiences (reportedly over one thousand days in a row) where he was completely overpowered by a powerful light that propelled him through a series of movements quite similar to a traditional Muslim prayer sequence. He realized that he was being guided by God and, once he surrendered to the experience, he was able to discern a set of "inner teachings" revealed to him in the process. Bapak's experience came to be called *latihan kejiwaan*, which means "spiritual training," and is the central practice of Subud. In the coming years, Bapak would gather a group of followers, though he categorically rejected the title of "prophet" or "leader," believing that *latihan* should act as an accompaniment to established religious traditions.

Subud spread to the West by way of journalist Husein Rofé (1922–), who arrived in Jakarta in the 1950s. His writings on Subud captured the attention of Westerners interested in Asian mystical and esoteric traditions. Among those invested in such knowledge was John G. Bennett (1897–1974), whose work on psychology and spirituality would heavily influence the founder of The Fourth Way, G. I. Gurdjieff (1878–1949), and his most prominent disciple, P. D. Ouspensky (1878–1947). Disciples of The Fourth Way and Subud, though sharing an intellectual lineage, would eventually part ways over questions of the will: the former believed spiritual practice led to an autonomous, objective will or "observing self," whereas the latter believed the will needed to be surrendered to God. Despite such schisms, interest in Subud would build throughout the twentieth and into the twenty-first centuries; today, there are around two thousand practitioners of Subud in Indonesia and ten thousand practitioners worldwide, predominantly in Europe and the United States.

Practitioners are not subjected to any particular set of rules nor required to hold any set of specific beliefs in common. It is expected that they will interpret their own experience of the divine and, accordingly, allow others to have the same degree of interpretive leeway. Proselytization is strictly prohibited and all members are expected to arrive open to their own experiences and by their own free will. Bapak was heavily influenced by Sufism, the mystical branch of Islam, which is particularly clear in the focus on the development of individual, internal knowledge, prolonged training of "the self," and the ability to understand the hidden meaning of sacred texts. This is replicated most clearly in the practice of *latihan*, which focuses on intuitive knowledge and immediate experience of the divine; unlike Bapak's original experience or those often described by mystics of other traditions, most mystical experiences engaged by Subud practitioners occur internally and after sustained focus, rather than spontaneously.

Subud practice takes place at "centers," and generally adherents participate twice a week. Men and women are separated and *latihan* is guided by those known as "helpers." Though one is told to listen for an inner voice revealing truth, this does not mean practice is staid or quiet. Practitioners will often sing, dance, move around, cry, chant, or anything else that the divine guides them to do in that moment. Latihan can occur individually as well.

The primary organization of Subud is the World Subud Association (WSA), which has fifty-four national associations serving its thousands of members. These associations each have committees that serve the institutional side of Subud and helpers who serve the spiritual side. Since the 1970s, WSA has focused on serving various social welfare projects as well.

See also: Fourth Way, The; Gurdjieff, G. I. (1866–1949); Mysticism; Ouspensky, P. D. (1878–1947); Sufi New Religious Movements.

Further Reading

Geels, Antoon. 1997. *Subud and the Javanese Mystical Tradition*. Richmond, Surrey: Curzon Press.

Roof, Wade Clark. 2000. *Contemporary American Religion.* New York: Macmillan Reference.

Webb, Gisela. 1995. "Subud." In Timothy Miller, ed., *America's Alternative Religions.* Albany: SUNY Press.

Sufi New Religious Movements

Sufism is the mystical branch of Islam. Like its counterparts in Judaism (Kabbalah) and Christianity (Gnosticism), it emphasizes the individual's inward experience of the divine rather than adherence to a particular set of traditions. Though Sufism is essentially coterminous with Islam (many Sufis claim that the Prophet Muhammad was the first Sufi), a number of Sufi new religious movements have arisen since the seventh century, highlighting the fact that Sufism continues to spark religious innovation. Additionally, Sufism, as a broad tradition, shares with new religious movements the fact that it has faced staunch opposition from certain factions, specifically among conservative Muslims, who feel those who practice it stray too far from Islamic practice and law.

SUFI BELIEF AND PRACTICE

Though some argue that Sufism acts as a separate "denomination" of Islam alongside Sunni and Shi'a, most Muslims engage in Sufi practice as a component of their Sunni or Shi'i beliefs. Neither can Sufism be considered a singular tradition in a practical sense, since it did not emerge as a unified movement and practices vary geographically, historically, and often from practitioner to practitioner. Numerous Sufi "orders" exist, each with their own lineage and preferred set of practices.

Nonetheless, most share in common the belief that union with God is the goal. Similar to other mystical strains in major world religions, traditional Sufism posits that only a few Muslims can achieve knowledge characterized as *batin* or "hidden." Thus, while Sufi practice occurs everywhere, only a few are actually privy to special divine knowledge and can achieve its central goal. The greatest obstacle for most is their individual soul, or *nafs*; only those able to relinquish their ego completely achieve divine oneness. A Sufi mystic proceeds through various stages of progression or *maqamat*, each of which poses its own challenges and marks a practitioner as more or less advanced in spiritual practice. Sufis are expected to exhibit *tawakkul*, or absolute faith in God.

Sufis engage in a number of practices, known as *tariqa*, targeted at opening an inward connection to God. Practices are usually passed from teacher to student, reflecting the transfer of "divine light." Chief among them is *dhikr* (translated as "remembrance" in Arabic), which is the consistent repetition of the names of God. The intention of this repetition is to enter into a state of deep focus, which allows one to achieve oneness with God. Meditation, or *muraqaba*, is also a central Sufi practice, which can be achieved through dhikr or through the practice of concentrating the senses, heart, and mind on God, seeking to shut out external stimuli.

Often Sufis will engage in a certain asceticism to shut out the needs of the body to focus on the needs of the soul; though this is by no means ubiquitous among Sufis. Sufis may also express or exhibit their knowledge in myriad forms; poetry is one such method made famous by Rumi (1207–1273), whose works have been popularized throughout the world.

MODERN SUFISM

A number of Sufi traditions have emerged over the centuries, some of which could be categorized as Sufi sects or orders, occurring within the parameters of Sufi Islam, and some of which are Sufi inspired, emerging outside of this lineage and leading to their qualification as new religious movements.

Subud is an Indonesian new religious movement founded by Muhammad Subuh Sumohadiwidjojo (1901–1987), better known as Bapak. Following a series of mystical experiences in the 1930s, where he felt God revealed to him secret, inner teachings, Bapak gathered a group of followers focused on living a proper, spiritual life focused on knowing God through one's own mind and soul. Heavily inspired by Sufism, he developed much of the practice of Subud (known as *latihan kejiwaan*, or "spiritual training") from Sufi sources and ideas. In particular, the emphasis on individual experience of God, the ability to understand the deeper meaning of Islamic texts, and the development of divinely implanted inner knowledge were Sufi in origin.

Universal Sufism, on the other hand, emerged as a tradition inspired by but external to Islam and emphasizes the universality of all religions, borrowing elements of major world traditions like Christianity and Buddhism in its practice and belief. Deriving much of its Sufi elements from Idries Shah (1924–1996), considered the greatest exponent of Sufism in the Western world, and Hazrat Iniyat Khan (1882–1927), founder of the Sufi Movement (later the Sufi Order International), Universal Sufism employs a number of traditional Sufi techniques. Chief among them are *dhikr*, to achieve unity with God, and sama, a Sufi ceremony that includes music and dance to incite "active" meditation, as made famous by the Whirling Dervishes of the Mevlevi Order. The movement has achieved its greatest popularity in Western nations where traditional Sufism is less established.

Other syncretic Sufi traditions, such as the Chilean new religious movement, Arica; the American organization, Bawa Muhaiyaddeen Fellowship; or the British group, Beshara, abound, highlighting the perceived adaptability of Sufism to modern Western models of spirituality. On occasion, Western converts, such as Ahmed Murad Chisti (born Samuel L. Lewis; 1896–1971), founded their own Sufi Orders; Chisti's "Dances of Universal Peace" emerged from his initiation into Universal Sufism. Others, like Hakim Bey (born Peter Lamborn Wilson; 1945–), are attracted to certain elements of Sufism, such as its poetry, rather than to the religious tradition as a whole. Nonetheless, there are those who criticize the appropriation of Sufism or the selection of only certain elements of Sufi practice untethered from Islamic belief.

See also: Bey, Hakim (1945–); Gnostic Groups; Kabbalah; Mysticism; Subud.

Further Reading

Gatling, Benjamin. 2013. "The Guide after Rumi: Tradition and its Foil in Tajik Sufism." *Nova Religio* 17, no. 1: 5–23.

Khan, Adel Hussain. 2015. *From Sufism to Ahmadiyya: A Muslim Minority Movement in South Asia.* Bloomington: Indiana University Press.

Rausch, Margaret J. 2003. *Pilgrims of Love: The Anthropology of a Global Sufi Cult.* Bloomington: Indiana University Press.

Sedgwick, Mark. 2016. *Western Sufism: From the Abbasids to the New Age.* New York: Oxford University Press.

Swedenborg, Emanuel (1688–1772)

Like the many people who read and cited his work and the movements that would claim descent from him, Emanuel Swedenborg is difficult to categorize. He was a scientist, a mystic, a theologian, and a prophet; he was steeped in Enlightenment thought and new scientific methods, while maintaining a strict devotion to the Christian Bible and, on occasion, communicating with, and even visiting, the divine realm.

In early the 1740s, Swedish inventor Swedenborg began experiencing spiritual dreams and visions at night, many of which revolved around a feeling of impurity and sinfulness. By 1745, he was recording frequent contacts with spiritual beings, who eased his mind as to his spiritual worth and provided him insights into divine truth, including the hidden meaning in the Bible. It was not long after that he began publishing theological writings, though he was compelled to publish in England due to Sweden's stringent antiheresy laws. His first and most influential book, *Secrets of Heaven* (1749), introduced his most famous theory of "correspondence." Rather than take the Bible as the literal word of God, people must learn to read it for its inner, spiritual message—for every natural or human fact, he argued, there was a corresponding spiritual or sacred reality.

More treatises followed, which expanded on his early theory, recounted his extraordinary experiences, and revealed special knowledge of the impending Christian millennium. In *The Heavenly Doctrine* (1758), he revealed that the Last Judgment had occurred the previous year (1757) and that Christ had returned, not physically, but via an internal revelation given to Swedenborg, who related it to the world. His book, *Heaven and Hell* (1758), recorded his ascent to heaven and his descent to hell, where he learned, among other things, that hell is entirely human-made: God does not condemn, but rather, human beings choose to live without God by living lives of deceit and selfishness.

Beginning in the late 1750s, Swedenborg began to experience visions that mark him as a prophet and occasionally as a medium. In 1759, he grew agitated while attending a dinner party, claiming that there was fire that would soon destroy his home. Sure enough, he rushed home to find that a fire had been successfully extinguished three houses down from his own. He also was called upon by various people, including the Queen of Sweden, Louisa Ulrika (1720–1782), to locate certain objects or to relay messages to those previously deceased.

Though he had been successful at spreading his ideas without raising the ire of Sweden's Lutheran Church, eventually his luck ran out. Never subjected to the accusation of heresy, though several of his followers would be, his works were deemed to contain numerous errors and were banned in Sweden. In response, Swedenborg composed his last book, *True Christianity* (1771), in which he laid out his thoughts regarding Christian, specifically Lutheran theology, and essentially established the basis for a "new church." This "new church" or "new Jerusalem" would be representative of the "fifth" age of spiritual history, where humanity would move past reliance on texts (which were easily corrupted) and enter the fullness of sacred knowledge. Shortly after completing this book, which would prove foundational for followers of his ideas, Swedenborg suffered a stroke. He died in 1772.

Swedenborg never set out to create his own church. Nonetheless, numerous movements have emerged that either claim to be

Emanuel Swedenborg was an eighteenth-century Swedish scientist and mystic whose visions of heaven ultimately led him to theorize about the nature of all reality and the hidden meaning of the Christian Bible. His works were banned, though they experienced a renaissance in the nineteenth and twentieth centuries by those who believed his theological assertions, particularly that of correspondence, were convincing. (*History of all the Religious Denominations in the United States.* Harrisburg, PA: John Winebrunner, 1848)

influenced by his works or claim to be the true interpreters of his works. Of the former are those like the Transcendentalists, particularly Ralph Waldo Emerson (1803–1882), who was particularly influenced by Swedenborg's notion of correspondence and incorporated it into many of his major works. Among the latter is the New Church, also known as the Swedenborgian Church, which was founded in England, but has found its greatest success in the United States. Yet, there were many who would not adapt Swedenborg's work into a formal philosophical or ecclesiastical system, but still found his works on their library shelves, including religious leaders like John Wesley (1703–1791), Henry James Sr. (1811–1882), and D. T. Suzuki (1894–1966), who translated some of Swedenborg's works into Japanese.

598   **Swedenborg, Emanuel**

See also: Millennialism; Mysticism; New Church, The; Prophecy in New Religious Movements; Transcendentalism.

Further Reading

McNeilly, Stephen, ed. 2003. *On the True Philosopher and the True Philosophy: Essays on Swedenborg.* West Chester, PA: Swedenborg Foundation.

Swedenborg, Emanuel. 2001 [1758]. *Heaven and Its Wonders and Hell. From Things Heard and Seen.* West Chester, PA: Swedenborg Foundation.

Swedenborg, Emanuel. 2015 [1758]. *The New Jerusalem and Its Heavenly Doctrine.* South Orange, NJ: A&D Books.

T

Tantrik Order, The

HISTORY

In the Western imagination, "tantra" is a practice that seems to bear few trappings of religion, but conjures images of celebrities discussing marathon sessions of sex and exotic, salacious texts such as the *Kama Sutra*. Practitioners of Tantric yoga, a discipline within Tibetan Buddhism, have argued that such a perspective is impossibly narrow and ignores the greater goal of all tantric practice, which is liberation from the cycle of reincarnation and annihilation of the self. The process of translating an ancient religious practice into a Western spiritual-sexual discipline reflects a common pattern beginning in the nineteenth century. Westerners, fascinated with Asia in general and Asian religions in particular, began to adopt Buddhist and Hindu (among other) beliefs and practices and to mold them into new religions, palatable to a Western market clamoring for access to "esoteric" religions. Such was the case for Pierre Bernard (1875–1955), founder of the Tantrik Order.

Pierre Bernard (born Perry Baker) was born in 1875 in Iowa, though his early life is shrouded in mystery. What is known is that, as a teenager, he traveled to India to study Sanskrit, for which he claimed to have earned the title of "shastri" (one with facility in Sanskrit) and been initiated into secret, Tantric circles. Returning to the United States, specifically California, by the early twentieth century, he had gained a reputation, primarily through the creation of his "clinics," as an adept at self-hypnosis and yoga as a means of healing. In 1906, Bernard formally founded the Tantrik Order of America and its accompanying mouthpiece, the *International Journal: Tantrik Order*. Marketing for the Tantrik Order emphasized the exclusive or esoteric knowledge made available through Bernard and the possibility of harnessing divine power through ancient practices, including many that bore a sexual component.

By 1910, Bernard had relocated to New York, opening his "Oriental Sanctum," a clinic that boasted both yoga instruction open to all and a members-only Tantric circle upstairs. By this time, the press had taken note of Bernard who called himself "the Omnipotent Oom," and began to shine a spotlight on his exploits, resulting in his arrest on the charge of kidnapping and a brief stint in jail. In the years following his release, Bernard and his most devoted followers relocated to a large estate in New York, which they named the "Clarkstown Country Club" and which served as the site of a utopian Tantrik community. A stream of wealthy patrons began to attend his clinics, heightening his profile and enabling him to purchase a series of spaces for Tantric Clinics in many major cities in the country. However,

600 Tantrik Order, The

complaints by the community to the local police compounded by persistent media attention led Bernard to relinquish his role as the head of the Tantrik Order. He retreated into secular life as a successful businessman, dying at the age eighty in 1955. With him, the Tantrik Order lost its initiative, but the practice of Tantra, as he conceived of it, remained for years to come.

BELIEFS AND PRACTICES

The term "tantra" (from the Sanskrit) means to expand, to extend, to stretch. Tantra is also the name for the ritual manual detailing methods for this particular type of yogic practice. The fifth tantra or "maithuna" deals with sex, though the descriptions are quite dry—not the erotic novella of Western imagination. In Tantric Buddhism, the aim of all practices, including sex, is to obtain and retain creative power or "Shakti." Intercourse stimulates Shakti through simulation of the union with the creator God, Shiva, but the aim is not release (or orgasm) but retention.

American Tantrism as taught in the Tantrik Order maintains the opposite position, which is that it is release during intercourse that empowers the individual practitioner. Arising during the twilight of the Victorian Era, the Tantrik Order offered a view of sex that challenged the predominant cultural imperative in the West to suppress sexual instincts. For practitioners of Tantra then and today, sex is treated as a sacrament, or as a means of bringing the body in contact with divine power. Rather than deny the body, American "Tantrikas" practice the idea that the body, particularly those aspects involved in sex and reproduction, is crucial to all spiritual exercises and to personal spiritual empowerment. All rituals involve the senses somehow, with many specifically targeted at sexual arousal as a means invoking divinity and then employing that divinity to perform "supernatural acts," which can produce effects spanning from physical healing to killing an enemy. Though extraordinary, these "magical" effects are a smaller component of the greater aim to gain control over the divine power created through sexual activity.

CULTURE AND CONTROVERSIES

Beginning with its founder, Bernard, the Tantrik Order was embroiled in scandal. Besides his arrest for kidnapping, Bernard, unsurprisingly, came under scrutiny for engaging in a series of sexual relationships with his female students. It was these accusations that eventually led him to close his first clinic in California and to relocate to New York. However, rumors of his sexual exploits continued to plague him, a fact not helped by the "orgies" occurring at the Country Club in upstate New York.

Nowadays, with the Tantrik Order defunct, its offspring, American Tantrism, is viewed as one among many practices for those seeking alternative spiritual paths or, more particularly, for couples looking to "spice up" their love lives. Scholars and practitioners of Tantric Buddhism remain critical of the cultural borrowing and re- (or mis-) interpretation of an ancient tradition inherent in American

Tantrism. Nonetheless, Tantra is still a part of the American religious lexicon, one that ties sex to spiritual evolution.

See also: Sex, Sexuality, and New Religious Movements.

Further Reading

Douglas, Nik. 1997. *Spiritual Sex: Secrets of Tantra from the Ice Age to the New Millennium.* New York: Pocket Books.

Urban, Hugh. n.d. "The Omnipotent Oom: Tantra and its Impact on Modern Western Esotericism." Available at: http://www.esoteric.msu.edu/VolumeIII/HTML/Oom .html.

Urban, Hugh. 2007. *Tantra: Sex, Secrecy, Politics, and Power in the Study of Religion.* Delhi, India: Motilal Banarsidass Publishers.

Temple of Set, The

Founded in 1975 by Michael Aquino after his split with Anton LaVey and the Church of Satan, the Temple of Set is a contemporary theistic and esoteric Satanic group. Aquino had been a central member of LaVey's Church and served as editor of the newsletter *The Cloven Hoof.* But when LaVey decided that he would sell initiation into the Church's priesthood, Aquino opposed him.

In his formal letter of resignation Aquino stated his distinctive position. Where LaVey viewed Satan as a symbol of rebellion, Aquino sees Satan as a supernatural entity identified with the ancient Egyptian deity Set. Where LaVey claimed rational insight into the human condition as the basis of his thinking, Aquino claims divine revelation.

Aquino has attested that he had begun to receive revelations from a Satanic source even while he was still a member of the Church of Satan, starting in 1970. The first communication that Aquino received, by a process of inspiration, was the *Diabolicon.* The text speaks directly in the voice of Satan. Then, nearly a year before his departure from the Church of Satan, Aquino received another Satanic communication, *The Ninth Solstice Message.* Those texts attributed to Aquino a very different kind of authority from LaVey's and formed the foundation of a different kind of church. Only twelve days after he formally severed his relationship with LaVey, Aquino received another communication in the same fashion as the others. *The Book of Coming Forth by Night*, portrayed as a recovery of ancient wisdom, became the foundational document for the Temple of Set (www.xeper.org).

The religious system of the Temple of Set differs substantially from that of the Church of Satan. For the Setians, Satan is a real being, the original pre-Judeo-Christian deity Set. Aquino is Set's chosen messenger for this era. The complex religious system can be summarized in the term *Xeper*, pronounced *khefer*; it means to "become." Becoming, or achieving self-awareness, self-knowledge, and self-creation, is a central and arduous task in the Temple of Set.

Aquino has developed an elaborate initiatory process for aspiring Setians. Moving through the ranks takes substantial intellectual effort. The Temple of Set does not court casual members; it seeks those who will read widely and study carefully. In an appendix to one of his works, Aquino lists 125 pages of recommended reading and the rest of his writings are studded with recommended readings, films, and other materials, much of it devoted to ancient Egypt. The sober intellectualism of the Temple of Set stands in marked contrast to the playful hedonism of the Church of Satan.

Like the Church of Satan, the Temple of Set has not been immune to schisms. In the early 1980s, Ronald Keith Barrett (1944–1998), who had become High Priest in 1979, declared that he, like Aquino, had an inspired "Word" to communicate. The new word was *Xem*, pronounced *khem* and meaning "to give direction to the changes initiated by Xeper." Barrett's insistence that his new revelation, contained in his own *The Book of Opening the Way*, was a necessary addition to the *xeper* revelation struck Aquino as a challenge to his own authority.

Barrett resolved the conflict by resigning from the Temple of Set in May of 1982. The Order of Anubis (www.orderofanubis.org) has striven to maintain the orthodoxy of Barrett's original teachings and claims to be the most authentic vehicle for the "infernal mandate" that Aquino took over from LaVey and Barrett took over from Aquino. From the 1980s through the early 2000s, Aquino has moved into and out of his original position of high priest in response to various challenges. He remains the central intellectual figure in the Temple.

The Temple of Set is governed by a Council of Nine, which appoints both a high priest(ess), currently Peggy A. Hardy, and an executive director. The Temple recognizes six degrees of initiation. The first degree constitutes a probationary period during which the Temple and the initiate can assess the appropriateness of membership for the individual. Although the Temple focuses on the individual pursuit of *xeper*, members may concentrate on specific fields of study by joining a particular Order and may pursue fellowship with other Setians in Pylons.

See also: Charisma and Leadership in New Religions; Church of Satan, The; Satanism.

Further Reading

Aquino, Michael. 2010. *The Temple of Set*, 11th ed. (draft). San Francisco: Self-published.

Dyrendal, Asbjørn, James R. Lewis, & Jesper AA. Petersen. 2016. *The Invention of Satanism*. Oxford: Oxford University Press.

Introvigne, Massimo. 2016. *Satanism: A Social History*. Leiden: E. J. Brill.

Thelema

Thelema is the esoteric religious tradition founded by British occultist Aleister Crowley (1875–1947). Crowley began his occult religious career as a member of the Hermetic Order of the Golden Dawn. However, his affiliation shifted when he was visited by a being named Aiwass, a messenger of the Egyptian god Horus, who imparted sacred knowledge to Crowley, which he would write down in *The Book of the Law* (1904).

Chief among the ideas revealed in the text was the notion that to "do what thou wilt shall be the whole of the law! Love is the law, love under will." This notion that the human will was the greatest force in the universe was the basis of Thelema, which is a Koine Greek term for "will." Crowley believed that a new era

Thelema   603

known as the Age of Horus was emerging, which would be governed by the Law of Thelema. The origins of Thelemic thought are eclectic, drawing from both Western and Eastern esoteric traditions, ancient Hermeticism, and ceremonial magic. The majority of its divine pantheon is drawn from Egyptian religion, however, there is no requirement in Thelema that belief in a higher power is necessary.

Beyond adherence to the Law of Thelema, Thelemic ritual and belief are eclectic, with little required as far as orthodoxy (right belief) or orthopraxy (right practice). Thelemic magic, or magical practice aimed at actualizing the "True Will" in oneself and the universe, is the broad term for most rituals undertaken by Thelemites. Some have critiqued Thelema for the potential selfishness of its creed to "do what thou wilt." Though the *Book of the Law* does specify that one should defend oneself (even to the death) if this right is occluded, it also indicates that one should not prevent others from realizing their own will.

Crowley founded the Abbey of Thelema in 1920, though there is little formal organizational structure for those who consider themselves Thelemites; many subscribe to traditions that claim Thelema as a precursor. In this way, Thelema has influenced numerous new religious movements, such as the Ordo Templi Orientis, an occult religious group that emerged in England in the twentieth century, and certain sects of Neopaganism. Among scholars, more controversial is the assertion that Thelemic elements appear in Scientology.

The shadow of Thelema is long and its impact has largely been felt outside of the movement. John Whiteside Parsons (1914–1952), for example, was a rocket scientist and Thelemite, who believed that science and magic represented opposite sides of the same coin.

See also: Crowley, Aleister (1875–1947); Hermetic Order of the Golden Dawn, The; Hermeticism; Magic and New Religious Movements; Neopaganism; Occultism and Esotericism; Ordo Templi Orientis; Parsons, John Whiteside (1914–1952).

Further Reading

Crowley, Aleister. 2004 [1904]. *The Book of the Law*. Newburyport, MA: Weiser Books.

Melton, J. Gordon. 1983. "Thelemic Magick in America." In Joseph H. Fichter, ed., *Alternatives to American Mainline Churches*. Barrytown, NY: Unification Theological Seminary.

Urban, Hugh B. 2004. "The Beast with Two Backs: Aleister Crowley, Sex Magic and the Exhaustion of Modernity." *Nova Religio* 7, no. 3: 7–25.

PRIMARY SOURCE DOCUMENT

Excerpt from Aleister Crowley's *The Book of the Law* (1904)

The Book of the Law, *written in Cairo, Egypt between April 8 and 10 in 1904, is the text seen as central to the spiritual philosophy of Thelema. The text is composed by Aleister Crowley, who claimed that the book was dictated to him by an extraordinary being called Aiwass. The book's three chapters are written in the first person by three of Thelema's main deities: Nuit, Hadit, and Ra-Hoor-Khuit. What follows is an excerpt from the sacred text.*

Chapter I
The Book of the Law

1. Had! The manifestation of Nuit.
2. The unveiling of the company of heaven.
3. Every man and every woman is a star.
4. Every number is infinite; there is no difference.
5. Help me, o warrior lord of Thebes, in my unveiling before the Children of men!
6. Be thou Hadit, my secret centre, my heart & my tongue!
7. Behold! it is revealed by Aiwass the minister of Hoor-paar-kraat.
8. The Khabs is in the Khu, not the Khu in the Khabs.
9. Worship then the Khabs, and behold my light shed over you!
10. Let my servants be few & secret: they shall rule the many & the known.
11. These are fools that men adore; both their Gods & their men are fools.
12. Come forth, o children, under the stars, & take your fill of love!
13. I am above you and in you. My ecstasy is in yours. My joy is to see your joy.
14. Above, the gemmèd azure is
15. The naked splendour of Nuit;
16. She bends in ecstasy to kiss
17. The secret ardours of Hadit.
18. The wingèd globe, the starry blue,
19. Are mine, O Ankh-af-na-khonsu!
20. Now ye shall know that the chosen priest & apostle of infinite space is the prince-priest the Beast; and in his woman called the Scarlet Woman is all power given. They shall gather my children into their fold: they shall bring the glory of the stars into the hearts of men.
21. For he is ever a sun, and she a moon. But to him is the winged secret flame, and to her the stooping starlight.
22. But ye are not so chosen.
23. Burn upon their brows, o splendrous serpent!
24. O azure-lidded woman, bend upon them!
25. The key of the rituals is in the secret word which I have given unto him.
26. With the God & the Adorer I am nothing: they do not see me. They are as upon the earth; I am Heaven, and there is no other God than me, and my lord Hadit.

27. Now, therefore, I am known to ye by my name Nuit, and to him by a secret name which I will give him when at last he knoweth me. Since I am Infinite Space, and the Infinite Stars thereof, do ye also thus. Bind nothing! Let there be no difference made among you between any one thing & any other thing; for thereby there cometh hurt.

28. But whoso availeth in this, let him be the chief of all!

29. I am Nuit, and my word is six and fifty.

30. Divide, add, multiply, and understand.

31. Then saith the prophet and slave of the beauteous one: Who am I, and what shall be the sign? So she answered him, bending down, a lambent flame of blue, all-touching, all penetrant, her lovely hands upon the black earth, & her lithe body arched for love, and her soft feet not hurting the little flowers: Thou knowest! And the sign shall be my ecstasy, the consciousness of the continuity of existence, the omnipresence of my body.

32. Then the priest answered & said unto the Queen of Space, kissing her lovely brows, and the dew of her light bathing his whole body in a sweet-smelling perfume of sweat: O Nuit, continuous one of Heaven, let it be ever thus; that men speak not of Thee as One but as None; and let them speak not of thee at all, since thou art continuous!

33. None, breathed the light, faint & færy, of the stars, and two.

34. For I am divided for love's sake, for the chance of union.

35. This is the creation of the world, that the pain of division is as nothing, and the joy of dissolution all.

36. For these fools of men and their woes care not thou at all! They feel little; what is, is balanced by weak joys; but ye are my chosen ones.

37. Obey my prophet! follow out the ordeals of my knowledge! seek me only! Then the joys of my love will redeem ye from all pain. This is so: I swear it by the vault of my body; by my sacred heart and tongue; by all I can give, by all I desire of ye all.

38. Then the priest fell into a deep trance or swoon, & said unto the Queen of Heaven; Write unto us the ordeals; write unto us the rituals; write unto us the law!

39. But she said: the ordeals I write not: the rituals shall be half known and half concealed: the Law is for all.

40. This that thou writest is the threefold book of Law.

41. My scribe Ankh-af-na-khonsu, the priest of the princes, shall not in one letter change this book; but lest there be folly, he shall comment thereupon by the wisdom of Ra-Hoor-Khu-it.

42. Also the mantras and spells; the obeah and the wanga; the work of the wand and the work of the sword; these he shall learn and teach.

43. He must teach; but he may make severe the ordeals.

44. The word of the Law is *Θελημα*.

45. Who calls us Thelemites will do no wrong, if he look but close into the word. For there are therein Three Grades, the Hermit, and the Lover, and the man of Earth. Do what thou wilt shall be the whole of the Law.

46. The word of Sin is Restriction. O man! refuse not thy wife, if she will! O lover, if thou wilt, depart! There is no bond that can unite the divided but love: all else is a curse. Accursèd! Accursèd be it to the æons! Hell. . . .

Source: Crowley, Aleister Crowley. *The Book of the Law: Liber Al vel Legis.* April, 1904. Available at: https://hermetic.com/legis/ccxx/chapter-i.

Theosophical Society, The

ORIGINS

The Theosophical Society, founded in New York 1875, served as the institutional vehicle for Theosophy, the religious system founded by Helena Petrovna Blavatsky (1831–1891) and Henry Steel Olcott (1832–1907), with the latter serving as its first president (until his death in 1907). The Society formed around the religious genius of Blavatsky, whose claims to and publications about the secret, sacred or "occult" knowledge she received from a collection of spiritually enlightened beings (some living, many deceased), known as Mahatmas or "Great Masters," began to gain a following. It was Olcott, however, who would lend the movement its traditionally "Eastern," religious bent, having studied and traveled extensively in south Asia.

At its outset, the Theosophical Society established itself as nonsectarian, meaning any could join, regardless of religious affiliation, and open to all regardless of sex, race, or other demographic distinctions. The only stipulations of membership were to seek universal truth through the work of comparative religion and to investigate tirelessly the power inherent in humanity and creation. Blavatsky argued that the Theosophical Society represented one of an infinite number of attempts by a hidden "spiritual hierarchy," known as the "Masters of Ancient Wisdom," to help guide their earthly counterparts to a higher plane of evolutionary existence.

Though Olcott and Blavatsky were undoubtedly the intellectual and theological inspiration for the Theosophical Society, it was cofounder William Quan Judge (1851–1896) who took on the bulk of administrative duties, formalizing Theosophical thought in his writing and seeing after the institutional health of the movement. Judge helmed the North American branch of the movement and established the independent Theosophical periodical, *The Path*, which, besides Blavatsky's writings, served as the Society's primary vehicle for disseminating the message of Theosophy through the nineteenth century. By 1895, Judge counted 102 American branches with approximately six thousand members.

ORGANIZATION AND INSTITUTION

The Society was (and continues to be) organized into "lodges," which equated to local parishes where nearby Theosophists could gather as well as the physical structures in which Theosophists met. Besides the Society's gradual expansion in North America, its greatest success occurred in India, where Blavatsky and Olcott landed in 1878, establishing a center in Adyar. However, Blavatsky's death in 1891 shook the movement, causing a schism between the American and Adyar factions. Olcott and rising star Annie Besant (1847–1933) accused Judge of forging letters from Mahatmas, to which Judge responded by severing the American branch from the Theosophical Society entirely. Ironically, it was Judge's group that would retain the title of Theosophical Society, with Olcott and Besant titling their organization, Theosophical Society—Adyar. Further schisms would ensue within both the American and Adyar branches, each claiming to represent the true realization of Blavatsky and Olcott's spiritual aims.

The Theosophical Society suffered its fair share of controversies, beginning with Blavatsky. Blavatsky was accused of both plagiarism and falsification of supernatural phenomena. Critics accused Blavatsky of plagiarizing much of her writing from ancient, Eastern texts, particularly those composed while she claimed to be guided by a Great Master. Even more salacious were the accusations against Charles Leadbeater (1854–1934), a second-generation leader in the Society. Leadbeater resigned from the Theosophical Society in 1906 following revelations that he had advised prepubescent boys to masturbate as a means to relieve sexual thoughts. Echoing a more contemporary understanding of adolescent sexuality, Leadbeater argued that young people were too often forced to repress their sexuality, which could have damaging effects on their psyche. He was reinstated in 1908 when Annie Besant assumed leadership of the Society following Olcott's death.

Though these accusations hurt the movement for a time, the Theosophical Society still maintains a presence today, boasting members in almost seventy countries around the globe. Other esoteric movements would follow, such as the Rosicrucian Fellowship and the I AM Activity, undoubtedly influenced by groundbreaking religious work of Blavatsky, Olcott, Judge, and the Theosophical Society. The advent of the internet brought with it a pronounced digital presence for the Society as well as a realization of Blavatsky's hope that Theosophy would be a practice used by many to enhance their individual, spiritual journeys.

See also: Blavatsky, Helena Petrovna (1831–1891); I AM Activity, The; Olcott, Henry Steel (1832–1907); Theosophy.

Further Reading

Besant, Annie. 2015. *Theosophy and the Theosophical Society*. London: Forgotten Books.

Blavatsky, Helena Petrovna. *The Key to Theosophy*. Available at: http://www.theosociety.org/pasadena/key/key-hp.htm.

Crow, John L. 2012. "Taming the Astral Body: The Theosophical Society's Ongoing Problem of Emotion and Control." *Journal of the American Academy of Religion* 80, no. 3: 691–717.

Lavoie, Jeffrey D. 2012. *The Theosophical Society: The History of a Spiritualist Movement*. Boca Raton, FL: BrownWalker Press.

Theosophy

HISTORY AND BACKGROUND

Theosophy was born at a crucial moment in the history of religious innovation. Spiritualism, a nineteenth-century religious movement grounded in the belief that contact with the dead was possible, attracted a robust following, primarily in the Eastern United States. Spiritualists gathered for séances, usually led by a medium—someone with a particular capacity to speak with or even channel the supernatural—seeking contact with lost loved ones or secret knowledge of a spiritual plane beyond earthly existence. Theosophy's founding also coincided with the "West's" nineteenth-century romance with the mysterious, exotic "East." As European colonial powers extended their reach into southern and eastern Asia throughout the century, Asian religious texts, people, ideas, and systems became objects of study and fascination throughout the Western Hemisphere.

What both Spiritualism and Eastern religions offered seeking Westerners, such as Theosophy's founders, Helena Petrovna Blavatsky (1831–1891) and Henry Steel Olcott (1832–1907), was the promise of "esoteric" (meaning "restricted to insiders") and "occult" (meaning "hidden") knowledge. Blavatsky was a Spiritualist and medium whose contact with the spirit realm led her to the belief that there were supernatural beings who had crucial, sacred knowledge to reveal to those willing. Such spiritual beings were among the "Great Masters," or Mahatmas—namely, beings, living or dead, who were spiritually evolved—and it was from them that she gleaned the sacred knowledge at the root of Theosophy. It was through her contact with Olcott in Spiritualist circles, however, that the movement gained its particular, Asian religious bent. Though Blavatsky had traveled to south Asia, Olcott had spent a sustained amount of time studying and living in India. Beyond the fact that many of the Great Masters with whom Blavatsky claimed contact hailed from south Asian countries, Theosophical theology bore the marks of Asian religious contact, particularly in terms of its doctrine of reincarnation—one, like other "borrowed" ideas, that bore the mark of Theosophy's own, innovative interpretation.

Reflecting the fact that Theosophy was not simply a sect of Spiritualism or, more loosely, of Hinduism or Buddhism, Blavatsky, Olcott, and William Judge (1851–1896) (the most institutionally minded of the three) founded the Theosophical Society in New York in 1875. From there, the movement expanded to Europe, particularly England, throughout the United States, and, following Blavatsky's and Olcott's move in 1878, in India. This period between the 1870s and the 1880s saw the heyday of Theosophical thought, as Blavatsky published prolifically, beginning with *Isis Unveiled* (1877), followed by *The Secret Doctrine* (1888), and *The Key to Theosophy* (1889), among others. For his part, Olcott served as president of the Society, traveled extensively to disseminate its message (particularly in India), and gained a reputation as a spiritual healer.

Blavatsky's death in 1891 brought with it a period of strife for the Society, which witnessed a schism between its American branch (led by Judge) and its Indian or Adyar branch (led by Olcott and, following his death in 1907, Annie Besant). Though Judge would take on Blavatsky's mantle as the most productive writer of Theosophical thought, both branches are in existence today, though neither claims the levels of membership during its turn-of-the-twentieth-century peak.

BELIEFS AND PRACTICES

The term Theosophy derives from two Latin words: "Theos," meaning God, and "Sophia," meaning "wisdom." Thus, literally defined, Theosophy translates to "wisdom of God." Blavatsky was not the first to employ the term, a fact she acknowledged by citing early Christian fathers and Hindu yogis in their use of the term. However, her intention in highlighting these earlier usages in two seemingly disparate religions, was to show that Theosophy, as a religious belief system and discipline, could be found in all religions; in other words, Theosophy was a "universal religion." This meant, most basically, that all religions were similarly invested in pursuit of knowing and understanding God, which was simply "Truth," and for this reason, all religions were simply branches of the universal religion, Theosophy. The symbol of Theosophy, besides joining together symbols from major world religions—such as the aum of Buddhism, the Egyptian Cross of Christianity, and the Star of David of Judaism—reiterates Theosophy's primary motto that "there is no religion higher than truth." Blavatsky maintained that one could be both a member of another religion and a Theosophist—Theosophy simply opened any religious practitioner's eyes to a greater field of sacred knowledge, thus enhancing their lived religious practice.

Complicating the notion that someone could be a "Theosophist" was a highly developed religious cosmology and theology that effectively supplanted those of other religions. Central to this system of religious thought was the idea that there was a secret, sacred hierarchy of beings whose goal was to advance humanity as a whole toward spiritual enlightenment, even perfection—also referred to as the "intelligent evolution of all existence." Members of this hierarchy, or the "Great Masters," had intervened in the course of human history in two ways: by speaking through mediums like Blavatsky or by returning to earth in human form to guide humanity through their actions and knowledge. The Masters themselves were at different stages of spiritual evolution. Some, like the Buddha or Jesus Christ, were "Higher Avatars," or those who were highly spiritually advanced and now lived on a different, higher, supernatural plane of existence. Others, like George Washington or other admirable, historical figures of a given day were "lesser Avatars," those who were advanced beyond most of humanity, but who had not evolved enough to warrant reincarnation onto another plane.

It was through the Masters that Blavatsky, and later Judge, explained the Theosophical theory of reincarnation. Whereas in Buddhism and Hinduism, reincarnation occurred as a result of karma accrued through one's earthly actions. The aim of both practices was to cease the cycle of reincarnation, by nullifying the effects of one's karma through right action and through the realization of God-consciousness (Hinduism) or self-annihilation (Buddhism). However, in Theosophy, reincarnation is desired and perpetual. Through each reincarnation, a spiritual being learns more and advances, ultimately leading to reincarnation on other planes. Not only spiritual but physical reincarnation was possible. Theosophy maintained that all matter was alive, vital and thus, perpetually reincarnated into other forms. This focus on the intersection of both the physical and material realms led to those like Judge to call Theosophy a "religious science."

From Theosophy's doctrine of reincarnation grew Blavatsky's theory of "root races." Blavatsky argued that humanity had progressed (and continued to progress) through a series of stages known as "root races," arguing that, as a whole, humanity was in the era of the fifth (out of seven) or "Aryan" root race. Though she maintained that "race" was simply a convenient way of categorizing humans according to stages of evolution, she did ascribe racial and ethnic characteristics to the earlier or "lower" stages, thus setting up a potential racial hierarchy (with the Aryans, who were white, at the pinnacle). Adolph Hitler (1889–1945) certainly interpreted the term "Aryan" through the lens of racial stratification, thus adopting this supposedly spiritual term for his own purposes (which we now know included the destruction of entire groups of people, particularly Jews).

It is unfair and problematic, however, to tie the impact and uses of Theosophy to the world's most infamous racist. For most, Theosophy represented a means of realizing a personal path to spiritual enlightenment without the fear of eternal damnation for choosing the "wrong" path. Thus, Theosophists are most often engaged with individual practices such as meditation and personal study. When they do gather, they do so most often in Theosophical "lodges," where they can seek guidance from other Theosophists, or perhaps from one of the Mahatmas who walk among us—or even from those long dead, through ritual communion with the spirit realm. If one were to visit the Theosophical Society of America's current website, one could see a number of classes offered; from the individual to those more group focused, all are geared toward imparting "ageless wisdom," particularly of the Asian religious variety, for members and nonmembers alike.

See also: Anthroposophy; Blavatsky, Helena Petrovna (1831–1891); I AM Activity, The; Olcott, Henry Steel (1832–1907); Theosophical Society, The.

Further Reading

Blavatsky, H. P., & Michael Gomes. 1997. *Isis Unveiled: Secrets of the Ancient Wisdom Tradition, Madame Blavatsky's First Work; A New Abridgement by Michael Gomes.* Wheaton, IL: The Theosophical Publishing House.

Cranston, Sylvia. 1993. *H.P.B: The Extraordinary Life & Influence of Helena Blavatsky Founder of the Theosophical Movement.* Los Angeles: TarcherPerigee.

Olcott, Henry Steel. 1954. *Old Diary Leaves: The Only Authentic History of the Theosophical Society, Second Series, 1878–1883.* Wheaton, IL: The Theosophical Publishing House.

Steiner, Rudolf, & Catherine Creeger. 1994. *Theosophy: An Introduction to the Spiritual Processes in Human Life and in the Cosmos.* London; Chicago: Anthroposophic Press.

The Theosophical Society of America. Available at: www.theosophical.org.

Thoreau, Henry David (1817–1862)

EARLY LIFE AND TRANSCENDENTALISM

Best remembered as the reclusive writer who retreated to the woods "to live deliberately," Henry David Thoreau personified the nature-focused, self-reliant ethos of the Transcendentalist movement (Thoreau 2008, 83). Born in the

Thoreau, Henry David

geographical epicenter of Transcendentalism—Concord, Massachusetts—in 1817 and to parents whose religious proclivities ranged from iconoclastic to liberal, Thoreau was primed at a young age to seek spiritual fulfillment outside of the four walls of a church.

His youthful anticlericalism has led many scholars of Thoreau to paint him as irreligious (or even antireligious). Arguably, Thoreau simply had not found a religious system that worked for him, until he came under the wing of the father of the Transcendentalist movement, Ralph Waldo Emerson. Thoreau was attracted to the premise of Transcendentalism, namely, that every person is inherently divine, a fact that can be realized by continually seeking new and higher truths in oneself and in nature. For Thoreau, the primary means of seeking truth occurred in two complementary ways: in writing and in communion with the wilderness. It was Emerson who encouraged Thoreau to pursue a writing career—beginning with a journal and then extending to poetry and prose—but it was Thoreau who determined that his subject was the natural world, which he perceived as the entryway to all sacred knowledge.

"WRITING" NATURE

It was this desire to "write nature" that led Thoreau to construct a house near Walden Pond, which he would inhabit from 1845 to 1847. While there, Thoreau spent his days walking, subsisting on the land, and writing. There, he wrote his first book, *A Week on the Concord and Merrimack Rivers* (published in 1849), which was an elegy to his elder brother, John. Some speculate that the tragic death of John from tetanus in 1842 may have spurred Henry on his spiritual quest, a fact reflected in the increasingly religious language of his journal and his subsequent writings.

It was *Walden* (published in 1854), however, the novelized account of his two-year experiment, that both upped his literary capital and expressed his primary contribution to the Transcendentalist movement. The book captures the day-to-day life of living close to nature and the personal, spiritual insights that such proximity revealed. Thoreau also published several essays describing his excursions to Maine under the guidance of Penobscot Indian guides (eventually gathered together as *The Maine Woods*, published posthumously in 1864). Thoreau had been fascinated with American Indians from a young age, perceiving them as the greatest source of original knowledge of the wilderness. Additionally, in many of his writings, the influence of Asian, particularly Hindu, religious texts such as *The Laws of Manu* and the *Bhagavad Gita*, was clear. Thoreau and many other Transcendentalists found in such texts what they perceived to be Transcendental ideas, such as the practice of internal contemplation and the connection between the human and natural worlds. Critics have chided Thoreau for his adoption of both American Indian and Indian belief systems for his own spiritual purposes, a critique that was common during the nineteenth century and particularly among Transcendentalists.

Following his stay in Walden, he became a surveyor for part of the year as a means of funding his writing agenda. Since surveying involved walking the grounds of Concord and observing nature, it also provided him with material for his works and a means of continuous communication with nature. His final unpublished manuscript, tentatively titled *Wild Fruits*, was intended to serve as a Transcendentalist "new testament," filled as it was with simple observations of the nature he saw around him and the religious effects they wrought on him as observer.

Described as odd-looking and a bit irascible in temperament, Thoreau often burned relational bridges by the sheer fact of his passionate beliefs. However, his deathbed was attended by admirers and friends, even those rebuffed at one time or another by his critique. After becoming ill in 1860, his health continued to decline until his death on May 6, 1862, at the age of forty-four. His mythic and mysterious last words were reportedly "moose" and "Indian."

See also: Transcendentalism.

Further Reading

Richardson, Robert D. 1988. *Henry Thoreau: A Life of the Mind*. Berkeley: University of California Press.

Thoreau, Henry David. 2008. *Walden*. Oxford: Oxford University Press.

Thoreau, Henry David, Bradford Torrey, & Francis H. Allen. 1984. *The Journal of Henry David Thoreau*. Volumes I–XIV. Salt Lake City, UT: Gibbs M. Smith, Inc.; Peregrine Smith Books.

Walls, Laura Dassow. 2017. *Henry David Thoreau: A Life*. Chicago: University of Chicago Press.

3HO

Along with many other groups, 3HO, which stands for "Healthy, Happy, Holy Organization," emerged out of the tidal wave of immigration to the United States following the lifting of restrictive immigration bans in 1965. Arriving during a time when interest in Asian religious ideas and practices, particularly yoga, was at a peak, 3HO built on this interest to create a quintessential new religious movement for an age characterized by the eclectic religious desires of spiritual seekers who desire an "holistic" movement that merges spiritual, mental, and bodily practice.

BEGINNINGS AND TRAVELS TO AMERICA

Harbhajan Singh Puri (later Khalsa, which means "pure") (1929–2004), better known as "Yogi Bhajan" by the members of 3HO, was raised in a Sikh family in Punjab (a province of India now divided between India and Pakistan). However, religious eclecticism surrounded him from the start: his mother was Hindu and he was educated by Catholic nuns. Throughout his life and as a result of his career as a civil servant in India, Bhajan traveled a great deal, which facilitated his desire to learn from a variety of spiritual masters. While a practicing Sikh, Bhajan also studied deeply in yogic traditions, particularly Kundalini (often known as "tantric") yoga. After a time, he became an instructor at an ashram in New Delhi, a role that would precipitate his move to Canada in 1968 where he would begin to teach classes at the local YMCA and begin, somewhat informally, to spread his burgeoning religious message. When a faculty position in yogi studies at the University of Toronto fell through, Bhajan shifted his missionary focus, turning instead to Los Angeles, California. Around the time of this move in 1969 at the height of the American counterculture, he formally founded the Healthy, Happy, Holy Organization and adopted the name Yogi Bhajan.

The initial followers of the movement were white and middle class, and generally qualified under the category of "hippie." More specifically, they were seeking alternatives to Western religion, culture, and specific practices, such as diet and medicine. Though members were initially called "yogis," in the 1970s. Bhajan brought 3HO into greater alignment with Sikhism and thereafter, 3HO members were referred to as Sikhs.

During his tenure as leader of 3HO, Bhajan expanded the religion into the areas of business and politics. He founded Khalsa International Industries, which produces a variety of health foods, and Akal Security, a major private security company. Upon his death in 2004, several political figures spoke glowingly on his behalf, noting that he was an exemplary citizen; Bill Richardson, the Governor of New Mexico, ordered that flags be lowered to half-mast out of respect. Until his death, Bhajan was the spiritual heart of the movement. His death led to a vacuum in authority, which led to chaos for a time—including a suit brought against Bhajan's widow, Inderjit Kaur Puri, by Bhajan's former assistant, charging misuse of funds.

BELIEFS AND PRACTICES

3HO developed out of Sikhism, which employs certain major practices of Hinduism. It also absorbed various aspects of New Age religious and countercultural movements more broadly. Adapted out of Sikhism is their code of conduct called "rahit," which includes adherence to the five Ks: kesh (uncut hair, often held in a turban, which is typically white for 3HO members); kangha (a comb worn at all times as a reminder and symbol of cleanliness); kara (an iron bracelet to be worn as a reminder to adhere to Sikh laws of conduct and belief); kachera (an undergarment worn to remind Sikhs to be ready to defend their religion at any time); and kirpan (a ceremonial dagger, sewn into clothing, as a reminder to defend those who are oppressed). Ritual adherence to these specific practices begets formal initiation into the Sikh khalsa (something not attempted by all Sikhs). Members of 3HO must also adopt Sikh surnames—Singh, for men, and Kaur, for women—as well as Khalsa as an additional surname. Besides the teachings of Yogi Bhajan, the central sacred text for 3HO is the Guru Granth Sahib, the "living guru" for all Sikhs. From there, however, differences emerge.

The central revelation of 3HO was the truth and practice of Hinduism's Kundalini yoga. The primary purpose of Kundalini yoga is to harness the body's energies as a source of power, which one then uses to move along the path to total consciousness (or awareness of one's essential oneness with the entire, divine universe). Through a variety of practices, including bodily control (of breath primarily, but of other bodily functions as well), physical practice (often called "kriya," which mixes yogic postures, breath, and sound), repeating specific mantras, among other things, the body, mind, and soul are brought into balance, and therefore greater spiritual awareness and bodily health. Members of 3HO believe that Yogi Bhajan's teachings helped to usher in the Aquarian Age (which formally began in November 2011), a time during which the truth of kundalini yoga will become a necessary piece of everyday life as the capacity of the human mind for knowledge continues to grow. This belief gives 3HO a decidedly millennialist cast.

Given its name, the pursuit of health is central to 3HO practice. 3HO promotes vegetarianism. On the 3HO website, the saying "You are What you Eat" accompanies a detailed list of what you should eat as well as the spiritual benefits of such a diet. Foods are divided between sattvic (the most important foods, which bring clarity and lightness to the practitioner) and rajasic (for occasional use, which bring will power and forcefulness). To be avoided are tamasic foods, those connected to instinct or desire which are often associated with mindless eating disconnected from spiritual practice. Additionally, mind-altering substances such as alcohol and drugs are to be avoided as they disrupt the meditative practice of kundalini.

Though much of the practice of 3HO could be characterized as self-focused, it also emphasizes the importance of "seva," or selfless service. Once one has harnessed the energy evoked by kundalini practice, one is not only to employ this energy to open the mind to higher levels of consciousness, but to channel this energy into helping others. Reflecting the holistic character of the religion's practice, 3HO members are also to direct this energy at maintaining mutually fulfilling familial and personal relationships. The Kundalini Research Institute offers a course on "Conscious Communication," which emphasizes the importance of saying only what you can "put your totality behind" (www.3ho.org).

3HO TODAY

The movement has faced backlash for certain practices. For example, Yogi Bhajan purportedly recommended separating children from their parents to better connect them to the broader khalsa and to instill in them the importance of self-imposed spiritual discipline. This pronouncement received pushback from 3HO members, particularly women (and later, some of the children who underwent separation).

As with many new religious groups that hail from a specific tradition, while offering something distinctive and new, 3HO has also experienced pushback from the Sikh community, or the very "khalsa" of which it claims to be an integral part. Sikhs generally refer to members of 3HO as "Gora" (meaning white) Sikhs, a fact that reflects the origins of the movement in the white, hippie counterculture but also the phenomenon of cultural and religious appropriation that has become common among white Westerners. Given the syncretic nature of 3HO's belief system, Sikhs are concerned with the promotion of this new religion as a sect of Sikhism. Additionally, Bhajan's occasional references to his own status as a messianic figure go against modern Sikh beliefs that the Guru Granth Sahib was the only religious authority necessary. Despite this critique, however, relations between 3HO and Sikhs have been relatively cordial, and 3HO members enjoy qualified acceptance in the community of North American Sikhs. For this reason, scholars of new religious movements have often ignored the group, a welcome fact for 3HO members who see themselves as a continuation of something very old, not partakers of something new.

Since the group flies under the radar somewhat, it is hard to get an estimate of how large the movement is today. The 3HO website projects a robust movement, offering classes, information for anyone interested in the Healthy, Happy, Holy lifestyle, and connections to a broader institution known as the "International Kundalini Yoga Teachers Association." Given a contemporary culture that is enamored of yoga, individual spiritual growth, bodily health, and non-Western religious truth, it is no surprise the movement survives—and thrives.

See also: Healing, Health, and New Religious Movements; Millennialism; Seekers; Tantrik Order, The; Yoga.

Further Reading

Bhajan, Yogi, & Hargopal Kaur Khalsa. 2013. *Laws of Life: The Teachings of Yogi Bhajan.* Santa Cruz, NM: Kundalini Research Institute.

Jakobsh, Doris. 2008. "3HO/Sikh Dharma of the Western Hemisphere: The 'Forgotten' New Religious Movement?" *Religion Compass* 2, no. 3: 385–408.

O'Connell, Joseph T., Milton Israel, Willard G. Oxtoby, W. H. McLeod, & J. S. Grewal. 1988. *Sikh History and Religion in the Twentieth Century.* Toronto: The Centre for South Asian Studies, the University of Toronto.

3HO Organization. "Healthy, Happy, Holy Organization." Available at: https://www.3ho .org/.

Transcendental Meditation

Like other New Age religions that brought ancient Hindu knowledge to a Western spiritual marketplace, such as Yogananda's Self-Realization Fellowship, Transcendental Meditation or TM found a home among a burgeoning group of religious seekers who were dissatisfied with their traditional religious homes. TM offered a path not only to spiritual but to physical, wellness and advancement, thus fed a religious Zeitgeist characterized by those clamoring for religions that treated "the whole person."

The movement began in India under the guidance of Maharishi Mahesh Yogi (born Mahesh Prasad Varma; 1918–2008). Beginning in 1941, the Maharishi (which means "seer") served as the secretary to Guru Dev (or Swami Brahmananda Saraswati; 1868–1953) who instructed his young disciple in ancient Vedic knowledge, including deep meditation techniques or dhyana yoga. Since Guru Dev was a Brahmin and the Maharishi was not, the latter could not be named as the master's successor. However, prior to his death, Guru Dev asked the Maharishi to teach deep meditation, soon known as Transcendental Meditation, to the world.

The Maharishi obliged. During the 1950s and 1960s, he toured the United States and Europe and quickly attracted a group of devoted followers, which included celebrities such as the Beatles. The Maharishi became a celebrity in his own right, which provided a new platform from which to spread the message of TM. This he accomplished in two primary ways: through publication and through the establishment of TM "centers" where TM teachers could train; this included the purchase of Parsons College in Iowa, which would serve as the site of the movement's university. The Maharishi is author of around thirty books, most significantly *Science of Being and Art of Living* (1963), which details the practice of TM, and his own translation of the first six chapters of the Bhagavad Gita (originally published in 1967). The Maharishi established thousands of TM centers and, until he became too ill to do so, trained instructors of TM at his home base in the Netherlands.

After the Maharishi died in 2008, leadership passed to Maharaja Adhiraj Rajaraam (originally Tony Nader; 1955–), who is the current leader of the TM movement.

BELIEFS AND PRACTICES

TM revolves around the practice of silent meditation, usually involving the internal repetition of a particular mantra. Practitioners are recommended to sit in a comfortable (not yogic) meditation stance for twenty minutes a day with eyes closed. Each practitioner selects a mantra, which they keep secret and are discouraged from speaking aloud at any time so that the mantra is only associated with internal focusing techniques. Generally, the only other person who knows the practitioner's mantra is the TM teacher who assigned it. TM teachers are trained not only in meditation but in discerning the proper mantra for each student. The wrong mantra, according to the Maharishi, could have deleterious effects for the practitioner and even reverse the beneficial effects of TM. Most mantras derive from the Vedas.

New practitioners of TM participate in a course given by a TM teacher, which usually occurs over seven days. Besides an initial worship ritual where they pay homage to the Holy Teachers of TM and receive their individualized mantra, practitioners participate in intensive meditation sessions where the TM teacher monitors their meditation technique. After this initial course, practitioners may take additional classes, but they generally hone their meditation techniques individually. In general, TM is a practice undertaken alone, though instances occur where communal meditation is possible. In some cases, these individuals may seek to become TM teachers themselves, for which they must embark on a four-month training course.

Like many New Age religions, TM is millennialist in outlook. During his life, the Maharishi announced the coming of the "Age of Enlightenment." This new era would usher in a time of peace, joy, and wellness, prompted by the spread of TM. As more people practiced TM, the more advanced humanity became and the better the world would be for it.

INSTITUTION AND CULTURAL LEGACY

TM has been touted for its health benefits and critiqued by the medical community for overstating these beneficial effects. The current leader of TM, Rajaraam, is a medical doctor and neuroscientist whose work on the effects of TM on human cognition and, in some cases, curative effects on neural disorders, seems to align TM's spiritual practice with the medical community. Many practitioners of TM report feeling less stressed and anxious as well as seeing discernible changes in their blood pressure. However, members of the medical community have cited the bias of most research studies of TM as they are often conducted and published by its practitioners. Other studies that have been conducted seem to disprove the effects of TM or equate its impact with other stress management techniques.

Medical critiques aside, today, TM counts nearly ten million practitioners across the globe who find benefit in the practice, both spiritual and otherwise. Celebrities such as Jerry Seinfeld, Kristen Bell, Martin Scorsese, and Oprah Winfrey, among others, practice and promote TM in both official (Winfrey has devoted an episode of her show "Oprah the Next Chapter" to TM and its benefits) and unofficial (such as posts of celebrities in deep meditative stances on their social media pages) ways. Those interested in practicing TM can attend courses (for which they pay a fee) through a TM Center or through the "Find a Teacher" tab on the TM website (www.tm.org/). TM has been employed in corporate settings and in schools as a means of managing stress and providing constructive outlets for energy, respectively.

See also: Health, Healing, and New Religious Movements; Hindu New Religious Movements; Millennialism; New Age, The; Seekers; Self-Realization Fellowship (Yogananda); Yoga; Yogi, Maharishi Mahesh (1918–2008).

Further Reading

Forem, Jack. 2012. *Transcendental Meditation: The Essential Teachings of Maharishi Mahesh Yogi.* Carlsbad, CA: Hay House, Inc.

Mason, Paul. 2015. *Roots of TM: The Transcendental Meditation of Guru Dev & Maharishi Mahesh Yogi.* Penzance, UK: Premanand.

Yogi, Maharishi Mahesh. 2001 [1963]. *Science of Being and Art of Living: Transcendental Meditation.* New York: Meridian.

Yogi, Maharishi Mahesh. 2016 [1967]. *Maharishi Mahesh Yogi on the Bhagavad Gita: A New Translation and Commentary.* London, UK: Arkana.

Transcendentalism

HISTORY

Transcendentalism has suffered from the problem of categorization: is it a literary movement? A philosophy? A religion? All of the above? This lack of definition, however, can be understood as a function of Transcendentalism's founding premise: that all definitions are useless if they stop a person from seeking ultimate and divine truth.

Though its cultural imprint has born long-lasting effects, Transcendentalism existed as a movement in New England during the mid-to-late nineteenth century, born out of the liberal Christian denomination, Unitarianism. At that time, Unitarians broke from their parent denomination, Congregationalism, rejecting the Calvinist theology of the latter, specifically its emphasis on total human depravity. Unitarians argued, instead, that God had granted human beings the ability to discover truth and achieve salvation through the work of their own, divine reasoning faculties. "Free inquiry"—the belief that truth should be pursued unhindered by religious institutions or doctrines—and "self-culture"—the practice of continually improving the mind through focused study and religious contemplation—became the denomination's most distinctive features.

Some began to feel that the Unitarians had not taken the practice of free inquiry far enough. In 1832, Ralph Waldo Emerson (1803–1882), a Unitarian minister, left his pulpit on the grounds that he could no longer administer the Lord's Supper, for he felt it was an empty ritual. He represented a number of "radical" Unitarians who felt that their denomination was far too beholden to archaic Christian practices and beliefs. These individuals would only begin to coalesce into a movement in 1836. In this year, the Transcendental Club (or "Hedge's Club"—so named for Frederic Henry Hedge (1805–1890), whose visits from Maine prompted the meetings) was founded and Emerson published *Nature*, which was viewed as the definitive statement of Transcendental thought. These events were soon followed, in 1838, by Emerson's delivery of the "Harvard Divinity School Address," where he declared that humans were inherently divine and could perform miracles akin to Jesus. This address began the "Transcendentalist Controversy," in which the Unitarian Church began to fracture between those who wished to retain a definitively Christian identity and those who did not, but wished to privilege free inquiry over all else (the Transcendentalists). Theodore Parker added fuel to the fire in 1841, with his sermon "The Transient and Permanent in Christianity," in which he declared all of historical Christianity "fleeting," calling instead for a return to "Absolute Religion." This controversy would continue to embroil Unitarianism until the 1860s, by which point the majority of Transcendentalists had left the church for other endeavors, or moved along the spectrum toward a more conservative version of Transcendentalist principles.

BELIEFS AND PRACTICES

There are many sources of Transcendentalist thought, not least of which was the liberal Christian theology of Unitarianism. However, Emerson, Parker, George Ripley, Bronson Alcott, and other of the most prominent Unitarians, were heavily influenced by both British Romanticism and German Idealism. From the Romantics, especially Samuel Taylor Coleridge (1772–1841) and Thomas Carlyle, they gleaned the notion of a "religious principle," or intuitive connection to the divine mind or "Oversoul." Those whose minds were trained to channel the Oversoul could claim direct access to the ultimate, never-ending truth—a feature of their thought that they also adopted from their interpretations of Hindu and Buddhist religious thought. Equally influential was the related idea, gleaned from the work of Immanuel Kant in particular, that humans were in possession of both Reason (an intuitive source of spiritual knowledge) and Understanding (the capacity to absorb information from the world outside), but that it was Reason that shaped people's understanding of reality. Transcendentalism got its name from Kant, whose "transcendental idealism," posited that human perception of the world (rather than information gathered from the world itself) was the true source of all knowledge.

For Transcendentalists, these philosophical influences put the human being—specifically the human mind—at the center of all spiritual practice and as the source of all sacred knowledge. "Self-reliance" became the mantra of Transcendentalists, who came to believe that no outside authority was needed to learn ultimate truth. Retreat to nature, then, became a necessary element of Transcendentalist practice—both to blot out the distractions of civilization and Christian institutions and to tap into the divinity inherent in the natural world. In *Nature*, Emerson famously described becoming the "transparent eyeball," where he felt fully connected and absorbed into nature and thus felt his own divinity at its fullest.

CULTURE AND LEGACY

Transcendentalists never formed themselves into a church, functioning mainly as a group of thinkers and reformers who shared a general commitment to total free inquiry and self-reliance. However, there were several projects or institutions that sought to realize Transcendental thought in a practical sense. Most famous—and arguably most successful of them all—was *The Dial*, a periodical devoted to publishing works by Transcendentalist authors or pieces sympathetic to Transcendental thought, which was helmed by Margaret Fuller (1810–1850) from 1841 to 1843. Less successful was Bronson Alcott's Temple School, which posited a Transcendentalist model of education, whereby he would awaken students to their own, internal store of knowledge through persistent, Socratic-style questioning. The school ultimately foundered for lack of investment. Equally ambitious and ill-fated was Brook Farm, the utopian community founded by George and Sophia Ripley in 1841. Extending the motto of self-reliance to its fullest extent, the Ripleys sought to build a completely self-sustaining commune built on the theories of Charles Fourier. The community would suffer a devastating fire in 1846, which, along with pending bankruptcy, forced the dissolution of the experiment.

Not an institutional success in any lasting sense, the work of Transcendentalists is preserved primarily as literature, often relegated solely to English classes. However, the roots and focus of Transcendentalism were fundamentally religious, aimed as they were on the eternal progression of the human mind and soul to their most divine form.

See also: Thoreau, Henry David (1817–1862).

Further Reading

Buell, Lawrence, ed. 2006. *The American Transcendentalists: Essential Writings (Modern Library Classics)*. New York: Modern Library Paperback Edition; Random House Publishing Group.

Geldard, Richard. 2005. *The Essential Transcendentalists*. New York: Penguin Group.
Gura, Philip. 2008. *American Transcendentalism: A History*. New York: Hill and Wang.
Packer, Barbara. 2007. *The Transcendentalists*. Athens: University of Georgia Press.

Twelve Tribes, The

The division of ancient Israel into twelve tribes, each named for one of the sons of the patriarch Jacob (Israel), has inspired the formation of several very different new religious movements, each claiming to represent the true Israel. Different groups, including representatives of British Israelism and its more racist and anti-semitic offshoot Christian Identity, have claimed to be the ancestors of the ten lost tribes that were deported when Assyria conquered the Northern Kingdom of Israel in 722 BCE. One of the "mansions" of Rastafari has identified itself as the Twelve Tribes of Israel since its foundation by Vernon Carrington (1936–2005, known as the prophet Gad) in 1968. Such groups have in common the desire to reestablish ancient Jewish practices from different time periods.

So it is with the group that began in 1973 as the Vine Street Christian Community in Chattanooga, Tennessee, became the Northeast Kingdom Community Church after relocating to Island Pond, Vermont, in 1979, adopted the name of Messianic Communities in the early 1990s, and finally became known as the Twelve Tribes in 1995. The group grew out of Elbert Eugene Spriggs's (1937–) experience with the Jesus Movement of the 1970s. In 1973, Spriggs and his wife began a Bible study group for young people. They also began to buy and renovate Victorian homes in Chattanooga and eventually opened several Yellow Deli restaurants, all of which attracted a young clientele.

By 1975, the Vine Church had separated from the First Presbyterian Church after the latter cancelled morning services on Super Bowl Sunday. Spriggs began holding outdoor services called "Critical Mass" and also began performing baptisms even though he was not ordained. His actions attracted opposition both from Christian pastors and from the anticult group FREECOG, which had been formed to combat another offshoot of the Jesus Movement, the Children of God. Tensions in Chattanooga led the Church to establish an outpost in Island Pond, Vermont, in 1978 and then to move there wholesale in 1979. External agitation against the group culminated in a trumped-up 1984 raid that briefly remanded 112 children into state custody. But tensions diminished after that event.

Like the Children of God, the Vine Church preached a Christian millennialist message. The world was entering its last days and soon the faithful would be saved by the return of Jesus. As its theology developed, Spriggs's group put special emphasis on what it saw as the practices of the earliest Jewish followers of Jesus. Relying particularly on Acts 2 and 4, the Church endorsed Christian communalism and self-sufficiency. In addition to the restaurants it sponsored, the group promoted other small-scale craft businesses, such as making candles, soaps, and lotions, so that the various homes could be self-sufficient.

The group endorses a conservative sexual ethic promoting chastity before marriage, modest dress, and a general removal from the temptations of the world.

Substantial effort is devoted to proselytization through the publication and distribution of the self-published *Freepaper*, the outfitting of a special bus and sailing ship, and the commissioning of "walkers" who would spread the word beyond the group's established communities. Children are homeschooled.

The Twelve Tribes see the restoration of Israel, of which they are the spiritual descendants, as the first step in a millennial scenario that will culminate with the return of Jesus (who they call by his Hebrew name "Yashua") and the rewards of the Holy and the Righteous (virtuous nonmembers) and the damnation of the unjust.

Ritual life in the Twelve Tribes includes daily gatherings at dawn and dusk that focus on reinforcing the community through reconciliation and forgiveness. The communities observe the Jewish Sabbath but also the First Day from sundown Saturday to sundown Sunday. Although Spriggs (who later took the Hebrew name Yoneq and encouraged others to adopt Hebrew names) is the founder of the group, leadership of the group is shared by elder members.

Missionary efforts throughout the world have been successful enough that the group in the early twenty-first century numbered in the low thousands. Four tribes are located in the United States, another four in Europe, two in Latin America, and one each in Australia and Canada.

See also: Children of God (The Family International); Christian Identity; FREECOG (Free the Children of God); Millennialism; Rastafari.

Further Reading

Palmer, Susan J. 2010. "The Twelve Tribes: Preparing the Bride for Yashua's Return." *Nova Religio* 13: 59–80.

Swantko, Jean 2004. "The Twelve Tribes Messianic Communities, the Anti-Cult Movement, and Governmental Response." In James T. Richardson, ed., *Regulating Religion: Case Studies around the Globe*. New York: Kluwen Academic/Plenum Publishers.

UFO Religions

In their construction of comprehensive views of the cosmos, many religions posit that there is another world, or worlds, in addition to this earthly one. Moreover, under certain circumstances there can be movement or at least communication between this world and what lies beyond. Special individuals, for example, can ascend from this world to one above, as Muhammad (c. 570–632 CE) did when he took his famous night journey from Jerusalem into the heavens (see Qur'an 17:1) or David Koresh (1959–1993) did when he took a similar journey while in Jerusalem in 1985. Alternatively, beings from other worlds can visit or communicate with this one, often to commission individuals with a special task, as occurred with Joseph Smith (1805–1844) and with Jesus in the beginning of Mark's gospel (see Mark 1:9–11). Such traffic between worlds can inspire religious individuals and even provoke the development of new religions.

Set against that background, beliefs that humans have contacted alien beings and that aliens, traveling in "flying saucers," have come to earth conform to a familiar religious pattern. Some UFO enthusiasts, often inspired by Erich von Däniken's *Chariots of the Gods* (1968, fiftieth anniversary edition 2018), believe that aliens have been in contact with humans throughout history and they sometimes offer innovative understandings of ancient texts, such as Ezekiel's vision of the heavenly chariot (Ezekiel 1) or the star that guided the biblical wise men to Bethlehem (see Matt. 2). Scholars, however, date the modern religious history of contacts with aliens to the eighteenth century, specifically, the claim of Emmanuel Swedenborg (1688–1772) to have visited planets in this solar system and beyond. But religious systems based on actual contacts with unidentified flying objects and their passengers would not develop until the mid-twentieth century.

FROM SIGHTINGS TO CONTACTS

The history of actual UFO religions begins after World War II. The turning point occurred on June 24, 1947, when Kenneth Arnold (1915–1984) observed a group of nine shining disks in the air over the Cascade mountains while flying his private plane near Washington's Mount Rainier. By the end of that year some 850 sightings had been reported in the United States alone. Five years later, George Adamski (1891–1965), who had been actively involved in occult and theosophical circles since the 1930s, claimed to have contacted aliens in flying saucers on November 20, 1952.

The humanoid "Space Brother" that Adamski first encountered used the name Orthon and claimed to have lived on earth a long time ago but, having become spiritually advanced, now lived on Venus. The two communicated largely through telepathy, with Orthon warning Adamski about the dangers of nuclear war, a theme that would appear in many other accounts of contacts with aliens. Adamski documented his encounter with Orthon in the best-selling *Flying Saucers Have Landed* (1953), written with British author Desmond Leslie (1921–2001). Adamski's next book *Inside the Space Ships* (1955) recounted his travels to Venus and elsewhere and his meeting with "the Master," an extraterrestrial sage. Adamski's revelations paved the way for other contactees to tell their stories. Some of his work is preserved by the Adamski Foundation (www.adamskifoundation.com).

Among the others who came forward with stories of contacts with aliens was George Van Tessel (1910–1978), who founded the Ministry of Universal Wisdom in 1953 in Giant Rock, California. Van Tessel claimed that in 1952 he began to receive telepathic communications from a being called Ashtar, who is the chief of the intergalactic forces. The following year Van Tessel actually was contacted by aliens from Venus at Giant Rock. From 1953 to 1977, Van Tassel held annual Giant Rock Spacecraft Conventions, which attracted a wide range of UFO enthusiasts.

Like Orthon, Ashtar was very concerned about the massive destructive potential of the hydrogen bomb, which could not only destroy life on earth but could have reverberations for that section of the galaxy. When the detonation of hydrogen bombs did not produce widespread destruction, Ashtar's message switched to emphasizing how his forces had helped to protect the planet.

As would happen with many other UFO religions, including Heaven's Gate, the Raëlians, and the Aetherius Society, Ashtar took a particular interest in straightening out the contemporary interpretation of the Bible. Ashtar identified both Jesus and his mother as beings from space who had volunteered to help humankind.

Van Tessel held weekly sessions at Giant Rock to promote the message from Ashtar. Soon, however, others claimed to be receiving similar messages and it became impossible to contain them within a single organizational framework. Messages from Ashtar waned in the 1960s but reappeared in the 1980s in books like *Ashtar: A Tribute* (1985) published by a channeler under the name of Tuella. Ashtar and Ashtar Command still maintain a presence on the internet (see, e.g., http://ashtar.galactic.to/ and http://sanandaseagles.com/pages/ashtar_command .html).

More successful in maintaining organizational control of messages from extraterrestrial beings has been the Aetherius Society, founded in 1956 by George King (1919–1997). Like Adamski, King had been active in theosophical and occult groups before his first encounter with alien beings. King's first encounter happened on May 8, 1954, when he learned from the Cosmic Master Aetherius that he was to be the earthly voice for the "Interplanetary Parliament." Over his life, King received more than six hundred "transmissions" from extraplanetary beings. The Society is distinctive in its ability to retain control over King's teachings (see www.aetherius.org) even after his death. Within the Aetherius Society, King's writings have the status of scripture. *The Twelve Blessings* (1958) is portrayed as a

UFO Religions **625**

continuation of Jesus's Sermon on the Mount (see Matt. 5–7) and was delivered to King by Jesus himself again identified as one of the Cosmic Masters.

Other scriptures have been communicated to humans by extraplanetary beings or intelligences also. Perhaps most noteworthy is *The Urantia Book* (UB, 1955), which was received by an individual known only as the "sleeping subject" in increments from 1906 to 1955. As with the Ashtar communications, the UB is depicted as coming from a vast cosmic bureaucracy, members of which have become interested in helping those on earth. The Raëlian movement has also produced scriptures, especially *Intelligent Design: The Message from our Designers* (2005). Just as inspiration from God, gods, the Holy Spirit, or angels, for example, guaranteed the legitimacy of earlier scriptures, so does the contact with aliens guarantee the legitimacy of many contemporary scriptures.

Even in new religions that are not strictly considered UFO religions, contact with extraplanetary beings or forces can play an important role. Elijah Muhammad (1897–1975), founder of the Nation of Islam, described a UFO known as the Mother Plane or Wheel, which was in a small planet measuring one-half mile by one-half mile. Elijah Muhammad believed it was described in Ezekiel 1. The Mother Wheel played an important part in legitimizing Louis Farrakhan's (1933–) authority when he reinvigorated the Nation of Islam. Farrakhan claimed that in 1985 he ascended to the Mother Wheel. When he entered it, he met Elijah Muhammad, who had not died but remained alive. Like others before him, Farrakhan received a prophetic commission and full knowledge of God's message while he was with the original Messenger of the Nation of Islam.

Flying Saucers also feature in the central text of a short-lived millennialist movement that achieved notoriety in the 1990s. In 1992, Hon-Ming Chen (1955–), who had been teaching social science at the Chai-Nan Junior College of Pharmacy in Taiwan, experienced a revelation in which God told him to devote his attention to the religious life. Prior to his experience of revelation, Teacher Chen, as he was known within Chen Tao (God's Salvation Church), had been a member of a UFO group in Taiwan. Convinced that the United States was the Pure Land of God, Chen moved his group there, eventually settling in 1997 in Garland, Texas. Chen taught that God would appear in human form on March 31, 1998, after appearing on cable television three days earlier. Chen laid out his millennialist scheme in *God's Descending on Clouds (Flying Saucers) to Save People* (1997). Other new religions, such as the United Nuwaubian Nation of Moors, which has gone through multiple incarnations, have also featured various UFO beliefs.

Carl Jung's (1875–1961) characterization of UFOs as "technological angels" suggests that descriptions of UFOs transpose into a contemporary idiom a more ancient perception that there are worlds other than this earth, whose inhabitants can, on occasion, communicate with us. From that vantage point, it seems likely that UFOs will continue to play a role in new religions.

See also: Aetherius Society, The; Chen Tao; Farrakhan, Louis (1933–); Heaven's Gate; Millennialism; Nation of Islam, The; New Scriptures and New Religious Movements; Raëlians, The; Swedenborg, Emanuel (1688–1772); Unarius Academy of Science, The; United Nuwaubian Nation of Moors, The; *Urantia Book, The.*

Further Reading

Lewis, James R., ed. 1995. *The Gods Have Landed: New Religions from Other Worlds*. Albany: State University of New York Press.

Partridge, Christopher, ed. 2003. *UFO Religions*. New York: Routledge.

Tumminia, Diane G., ed. 2007. *Alien Worlds: Social and Religious Dimensions of Extraterrestrial Contact*. Syracuse, NY: Syracuse University Press.

Umbanda

Among the many creole new religions that have developed in Brazil, Umbanda is a relative newcomer, having taken shape in the 1920s and 1930s in Rio de Janeiro. Umbanda is distinctive in drawing on American Indian and European traditions as well as African ones. In fact, the "de-Africanization" of Umbanda, in the form of *Umbanda Pura* (Pure Umbanda), increased its attractiveness to white, urban, middle-class participants and perhaps helped them avoid the persecution to which Afro-Brazilian religions were subjected, most recently by various Pentecostal Protestant groups. But the "whitening" of Umbanda has also provoked backlash from those arguing for "re-Africanization." Nonetheless, the practices and imagined cosmos of Umbanda bear multiple resemblances to those of Candomblé and other Afro-Brazilian religions.

A syncretic religious tradition born in Brazil, Umbanda draws upon African traditional religions, Kardecism (a branch of European Spiritualism, or "Spiritism"), and indigenous American practices. An Umbanda altar, such as that depicted above, includes icons representative of the various spirits or deities invoked and worshipped by Umbanda practitioners, such as the preto-velhos, "old-blacks," which are spirits of enslaved Africans and Afro-Brazilians. (Carlos Pinheiro/Dreamstime.com)

ORIGINS

From the start, Umbanda incorporated a diverse set of influences. Principal among them was the spiritualism of the French writer Léon Rivail, who adopted the religious name Allan Kardec. Kardec compiled his communications with the spirit world into what functioned as a philosophy and even a form of science in France, called *Spiritisme*. But after his works reached Brazil, beginning in 1857, his system took on more religious characteristics and became known there as *Espiritismo* or *Kardecismo*. *Kardecismo*'s association with philosophy and its claim to scientific evidence of the existence of spirits made it attractive to middle- and upper-class urban Brazilians who wanted no part of what they saw as lower class and even barbaric Afro-Brazilian religions. Rio was the center of interest in *Kardecismo*, though it attracted adherents throughout the country.

Some Brazilian spiritualists, however, were dissatisfied with Kardecist orthodoxy and attracted by the power they knew was attributed to African and other spirits. They began to incorporate elements of various Afro-Brazilian religions into their practice. Scholars have identified those influences as having come from a religious substratum called Macumba that focused on African spirits or deities known as *orixás* in Brazil. But others also caution that the term "Macumba" was a pejorative used to associate certain practices with "African" lower classes.

Whatever the status of Macumba as a distinct religious tradition, Umbanda clearly incorporated elements from Kardec's spiritualism and from African religions that had been brought to Brazil through the slave trade and transformed there. In some of its forms, Umbanda also borrows ideas from other religious traditions, underlining its eclecticism and universalism.

In addition to *Umbanda Pura*, variants of Umbanda include *Umbanda Kardecista*, which retains many Kardecist ritual practices, and *Umbanda Oriental*, which emphasizes esoteric sources from indigenous religions, Hinduism, Rosicrucianism, and Theosophy, among others. *Umbanda Africana* emphasizes continuity with African and Afro-Brazilian practices and more closely aligns with Candomblé. *Umbanda traçada* or *misturada* forthrightly acknowledges drawing from multiple sources. It is more accurate to view Umbanda as a family of related religious groups arranged along a continuum rather than as a single, hierarchically organized religion.

Although specific founders are difficult to isolate, the first center of the new religion Umbanda was founded by Zélio de Moraes in the mid-1920s in Niterói in the state of Rio de Janerio. By 1938, it had moved across the bay to Rio. Umbanda has thrived since its founding and now counts adherents in the tens of millions. It has also traveled with Brazilian immigrants to other Latin American countries and the United States.

PRACTICES AND BELIEFS

Unlike both mainline Kardecism and Candomblé, Umbanda identifies four distinct groups of spirits with whom practitioners may interact. The first, *caboclos*, are the spirits of indigenous Native Americans; the second, *preto-velhos* ("old-blacks"), are the spirits of slaves. The third category, *exus*, encompasses the only spirits associated with Africa, including the orixá Exu himself, who under Catholic influence in Brazil became identified with the devil and acquired female counterparts known as *pombagiras*. The fourth group of spirits is *crianças* or children. Umbanda's spirits are organized into a complex system of seven lineages, in which spirits are also associated with Catholic saints. The main lineages are also subdivided.

All forms of Umbanda share two fundamental tenets: a belief that spirits can actively intervene in human affairs and the practice of spirit possession through which the spirits communicate with humans. Participants identify their central practice as *caridade*, charity. The spirits demonstrate their charity toward humans through consultations that occur when the spirits manifest themselves through various forms of possession. When temporarily incarnated during a ceremony, the spirits can provide spiritual guidance, healing, and practical advice that may include referral to secular specialists, such as lawyers or doctors. They can also provide protection against actions instigated by other, malevolent, spirits. Many Umbanda centers also provide direct financial assistance to members experiencing difficulties. The work of providing charity binds the members of a center to each other and also to the spirits who graciously provide their help.

The focus on charity in Umbanda contrasts starkly to the negative mirror image of Umbanda, called *Quimbanda*. The earliest collective effort to systematize Umbanda, undertaken in Rio in 1941 at a congress of Umbanda leaders, strove to heighten the contrast between the good works done by Umbanda and the negative impacts of the black magic the group identified with Quimbanda. The leaders identified Umbanda as pure, clean, white, charitable, and beneficent. Quimbanda, on the other hand, was identified with the black arts and exploitation. The distinctions drawn were clearly not solely religious. Many practitioners of Umbanda have sought to distance it from both Afro-Brazilians and the lower classes. For them, the existence of Quimbanda reinforces their understanding of Umbanda's, particularly Umbanda Pura's, superiority.

See also: Candomblé; Kardecism (Spiritism); Race and New Religious Movements; Santería; Spiritualism; Vodou.

Further Reading

Brown, Diana DeG. 1994. *Umbanda: Religion and Politics in Urban Brazil*. New York: Columbia University Press.

Capone, Stefania. 2010. *Searching for Africa in Brazil: Power and Tradition in Candomblé*, Lucy Lyall Grant, trans. Durham, NC: Duke University Press.

Murrell, Nathaniel Samuel. 2010. *Afro-Caribbean Religions: An Introduction to their Historical, Cultural, and Sacred Traditions*. Philadelphia: Temple University Press.

Schmidt, Bettina E., & Steven Engler, eds. 2016. *Handbook of Contemporary Religions in Brazil*. Leiden: E. J. Brill.

Unarius Academy of Science, The

The groups that developed in the second half of the twentieth century based on contact with alien beings or "flying saucers" understood themselves in various ways. Some, like the Aetherius Society, connected themselves with earlier religions, such as Christianity, or figures, such as Jesus. Others insisted that they were not religious at all but rather scientific and philosophical systems based on an accurate and expansive understanding of the universe. The Unarius Academy of Science sees itself as part of the latter group, even though outsiders have classified it as a "contactee" or UFO religion.

Founded in 1954 in southern California as the Unarius Science of Life, Unarius was built on the experiences of Ernest Norman (1904–1971) and his wife Ruth Norman (1900–1993). Ernest was active in post–World War II metaphysical circles, including Spiritualist churches; Ruth was part of the same cultic milieu. Ernest also received messages transmitted from both Venus and Mars. He published both his first books of channeled messages, *The Truth About Mars* and *The Voice of Venus*, in 1956; many more volumes would follow.

The generative moment for Unarius occurred in 1954 at a psychic convention when Ernest gave Ruth a "past-life reading," which disclosed that she had formerly been the Egyptian pharaoh's daughter who found the infant Moses. The idea that humans had all lived past lives would become a central tenet of Unarius. Around the same time a visit to a medium yielded the information that Ernest has once lived as Pharaoh Akhenaton.

Soon the floodgates to memories of more past lives opened. Ruth had a dramatic experience of illness after which she informed Ernest that she had learned that he was Jesus returned to earth to reestablish his mission. Ruth learned that she, too, had a role in the story of Jesus, having in a past life been Mary of Bethany, who was supposed to be the wife of Jesus. Over time, more and more past lives of the founders of Unarius came to light, including memories of lives lived in Atlantis. Those stories grafted them not only into the biblical narrative but also into the fabric of human history. From that perspective, the Unarius message was both new and very old. Its roots in antiquity gave it legitimacy, but it was an unprecedented insight for the present and near future.

Unarius remains dedicated to the study and application of "the *self-healing science* of reincarnation" (see https://unarius.org/index.php?page=discover-your -past-lives). Through classes and workshops held onsite at the Unarius headquarters in El Cajon, California, east of San Diego, and through courses of study that can be undertaken at home, Unarius continues to hold out the possibility of individuals living "more constructive, creative, and peace-filled lives." To support the goals of Unarius, its website offers an array of books, audiotapes, CDs, and even the opportunity to livestream the shows that it produces for public-access TV.

The focus on past lives is one of the two major emphases of Unarius. The other ties it to the world of contacts with alien beings and UFOs. Ernest continued to channel messages from various "spiritual planets" until his death in 1971. The teachers on those planets were portrayed as advanced, benevolent beings who wanted to educate and heal those on earth. Unarius developed a complex view of the universe as composed of energy, which vibrates in various waves and frequencies. Scientific understanding of that energy enables individuals to be in contact with both extraplanetary intelligences and past lives.

630   Unification Church, The

The Normans gradually assembled a small circle of students through the 1950s and 1960s. Two who joined in the 1960s, known within the group as Antares (Charles Spiegel, 1921–1999) and Cosmon (Thomas Miller, 1946–), also began to channel messages from the "Space Brothers" and to discover the past lives they had led. Ruth herself had begun to receive transmissions in 1969 before her husband's death. After Ernest's death, the pace of Ruth's reception of messages increased. In 1973, she learned that because of her progress she had been recognized as a "healing archangel," Queen Uriel. Uriel would become the dominant persona for Ruth until her death and she often appeared in costume and with regalia fitting her exalted status.

Soon after her recognition as Uriel, Ruth began to express the conviction that the Space Brothers would actually come to earth in spaceships from thirty-two planets to share their higher knowledge superior technology with those on earth. The newly arrived scientists would set up a hospital and a university and would recover the lost libraries of Atlantis and Lemuria, among other wondrous things. The return was initially set for 1975 but was deferred until 2001, in part to coincide with Uriel's one hundredth birthday. In preparation for the arrival of the Space Brothers, Uriel purchased sixty-seven acres in Jamul, California, east of San Diego, to serve as a landing site for the ships.

Ruth Norman did not live to see 2001 and that year passed without the arrival of any extraterrestrial visitors. From that perspective, prophecy was again disconfirmed. Although the failure of the ships to show up led some Unarians to doubt their commitment, others remained unshaken. Neither the delay in the arrival of the Space Brothers, ridicule from outsiders, nor, after the 1997 suicides, the need to distinguish Unarius from the UFO religion of Heaven's Gate has destroyed Unarius. A small band of the faithful, and a much larger mailing list, continues to receive and study the messages of the Normans.

See also: Aetherius Society, The; Channeling; Cultic Milieu; Heaven's Gate; Mediums; Millennialism; Prophecy in New Religious Movements; UFO Religions.

Further Reading

Lewis, James R., ed. 1995. *The Gods Have Landed: New Religions from Other Worlds.* Albany: State University of New York Press.

Partridge, Christopher, ed. 2003. *UFO Religions.* New York: Routledge.

Tumminia, Diane G. 2005. *When Prophecy Never Fails: Myth and Reality in a Flying-Saucer Group.* New York: Oxford University Press.

Tumminia, Diane G., ed. 2007. *Alien Worlds: Social and Religious Dimensions of Extraterrestrial Contact.* Syracuse, NY: Syracuse University Press.

Unification Church, The

According to many popular observers, in the 1960s through the 1970s, the United States experienced an explosion in the number of new religious movements. Called "cults" by their frightened detractors, those groups seemed particularly adept at drawing adherents from members of the experimental youth culture of the 1960s.

For a time, none of the groups was as notorious as the Unification Church, founded by a Korean preacher, the Rev. Sun Myung Moon (1920–2012).

Popularly known as the "Moonies," the church quickly became infamous for its members' intense dedication to recruiting, often in public spaces. In response, distraught parents attempted to "rescue" their adult children from the group by using strategies such as temporary legal conservatorships and sometimes violent deprogramming. The Unification Church became a grudging participant in the "cult wars" that pitted concerned families and their allies against members of new religions, new religious groups, and their own allies.

ORIGINS

The foundation of the Unification Church goes back to Moon's extraordinary experience on Easter morning in 1936, when he was sixteen years old. As Moon recalls in his autobiography, he was desperately seeking answers through prayer to questions such as why the world was filled with so much sorrow and pain. His prayers were answered dramatically when Jesus himself appeared to Moon. He learned that he was commissioned to do the work of God on earth to save humanity and bring joy to God. Moon also reports that his initial experience opened the way for other revelations from Jesus.

Despite his early experiences, Moon did not begin a public ministry until 1946. In the meantime, he studied electrical engineering in both Seoul and Tokyo. But after the end of World War II, he returned to Pyongyang. There, he joined many other Korean religious leaders who claimed prophetic status and preached amalgams of Confucianism, Christianity, and indigenous traditions. Moon finally established the Holy Spirit Association for the Unification of World Christianity on May 1, 1954. Two years earlier, Moon had already completed the first written account of his teachings, the *Divine Principle*, which became the focus of study, teaching, and missionary appeals for his church.

Divine Principle offers an interpretive retelling of biblical history. It advances Moon's central, and controversial, contentions that both Adam and Eve and later Jesus failed to accomplish for human beings what God had originally intended. In Moon's view, Adam and Eve were supposed to perfect themselves and establish a sinless family in the Garden of Eden, but Eve committed a sexual sin with the serpent and also joined with Adam prematurely. As a result, they were expelled from Eden and humanity thereafter stood in need of restoration. Jesus, too, was supposed to have married, formed a perfect, sinless family, and returned humanity to the state that God had originally envisaged. Since Jesus, too, failed in that mission, humanity remained in need of restoration.

Divine Principle claims to contain new truths that are appropriate for the time of the Second Advent, when the new, perfect world originally intended by God will finally be established. Moon's teachings, therefore, have always had a millennialist character. That emphasis became more pronounced in the 1990s and 2000s when Moon declared that he and his wife, Hak Ja Han (1943–), were actually the True Parents of humankind. He proclaimed that they would inaugurate the

632 Unification Church, The

new world through their teachings and specifically by uniting couples through the central ritual of the Blessing Ceremony—often in dramatic mass weddings. Family life became essential to the process of restoration, with the goal of bringing sinless children into the world.

FROM KOREA TO THE UNITED STATES

Moon's presentation of salvation history, with him and his wife at its hinge point, became the basis for a vigorous missionary religion. The Unification Church prospered in Korea, despite strong opposition, and soon spread to Japan. The first Unificationist missionary, Young Oon Kim, reached the West coast of the United States in 1959. She slowly attracted a few converts and quickly set up church headquarters in the San Francisco Bay area. Other missionaries soon followed, but conversion efforts through the 1960s were disorganized and yielded meager results. In the early 1970s, however, earlier scattershot efforts gave way to a single organization and membership increased into the low thousands. Rev. Moon himself began to devote more attention to proselytization in the West and the organization sponsored public spectacles, such as the "God Bless America" rallies at Yankee Stadium and the Washington Monument in 1976. Increased public presence, however, also earned the movement more opposition, which only increased when the deaths in Jonestown in 1978 inflamed public opposition to "cults."

From the 1970s into the 1980s, Unificationists increased their institutional presence in the United States. In 1975, for example, the Unification Theological Seminary was established in Barrytown, New York. From 1972 on, the Church sponsored annual International Conferences on the Unity of the Sciences. The Church also developed a number of subgroups, such as the Professors World Peace Academy, the New Ecumenical Research Academy, and the International Religious Foundation. Paragon House was founded to publish materials from various church projects, and in 1982 the *Washington Times* newspaper was established to spread Unificationism's particular brand of anti-communism. In addition, the Church invested its funds in numerous businesses throughout the world. The proliferation of groups associated with the Church and its involvement in profit-making also earned it strong criticism. Critics portrayed the various groups as deceptive "fronts" and the involvement in business raised doubts about the religious purpose of the Church.

Through all of those developments Rev. Moon remained the unquestioned leader of the Church. Even when he served nearly a year in prison from 1983 to 1984 for a tax evasion conviction that many mainline religious leaders questioned, Moon remained firmly in charge.

In the 1990s, Moon became more direct in proclaiming his own role in the history of salvation. In speeches, Moon emphatically described his own unique position with his wife as the True Parents of humankind and even acknowledged that he was the hoped-for Messiah. The Church recognized the importance of Moon's speeches by including them with the *Divine Principle* in the canon of the Completed Testament Age. When Rev. Moon died in 2012, however, the restoration of humanity had not yet been accomplished.

THE UNIFICATIONIST MOVEMENT AFTER REV. MOON

Rev. Moon led the Unification Church in its various forms for nearly sixty years. During the later stages of his life, he moved toward establishing a plan for succession. But because Rev. Moon had fourteen children with his second wife Hak Ja Han (seven sons and seven daughters) and also identified his wife as one of the True Parents, there were multiple individuals who could claim to be his successor. Despite Rev. Moon's efforts conflict ensued and schism became a real possibility.

The Moon's eldest son, Hyo Jin (1962–2008), proved unsuitable for leadership, and the next oldest, Heung Jin (1966–1984), died in a car wreck. Rev. Moon then focused on his third oldest son, Hyun Jin (1969–). After his education at Columbia University, Harvard University, and the Unification Seminary, Hyun Jin began to assume various leadership roles within the movement. In 1998, for example, Hyun Jin was appointed the vice president of the Family Federation for World Peace and Unification. Significantly, in 2000, Rev. Moon decided that Hyun Jin would inherit the ability to perform the Blessing Ceremony.

By 2008, however, Hyun Jin's status as his father's designated successor came under attack by several of his siblings, including his younger brother Hyung Jin (1979–), his other brother Kook Jin (1970–), and his sister In Jin (1965–). Each of the siblings developed bases of power within the movement from which they leveled criticisms of their brother. In addition, Rev. Moon's wife aimed to establish herself as the leader of the Unification Church, particularly in Korea. Although they agreed on many fundamentals, each of the would-be successors espoused a different vision for the future of the movement. Their contesting visions of the future continue to play out and threaten to divide Unificationism into multiple factions.

See also: Brainwashing; Conversion; Cult; Deprogramming; *Divine Principle*; Millennialism; Moon, Rev. Sun Myung (1920–2012).

Further Reading

Barker, Eileen. 1984. *The Making of a Moonie: Brainwashing or Choice?* Oxford: Blackwell Publishers.

Bromley, David G., & Anson D. Shupe, Jr. 1979. *"Moonies" in America: Cult, Church, and Crusade.* Beverly Hills, CA, Sage.

Chryssides, George D. 1991. *The Advent of Sun Myung Moon: The Origins, Beliefs and Practices of the Unification Church.* London: Macmillan.

Introvigne, Massimo. 2017. "Unification Movement Schismatic Groups (2012-Present)." Available at: https://wrldrels.org/2017/04/23/unification-movement-schisms-2/.

Mickler, Michael L. 2006. "The Unification Church/Movement in the United States." In Eugene V. Gallagher & W. Michael Ashcraft, eds., *Introduction to New and Alternative Religions in the United States*, 5 Vols., pp. 158–183. Westport, CT: Greenwood.

Mickler, Michael L. 2013. "The Post-Sun Myung Unification Church." In Eileen Barker, ed., *Revisionism and Diversification in New Religious Movements*, pp. 47–65. Burlington, VT: Ashgate.

Moon, Sun Myung, 2009. *As a Peace-Loving Global Citizen.* Washington, DC: The Washington Times Foundation.

Unitarian Universalism

HISTORY

As its name suggests, Unitarian Universalism is a Protestant denomination born of two liberal (meaning "open") Christian denominations, Unitarianism and Universalism. Both denominations were nurtured in the years following the American Revolution in Massachusetts. Both reflected a burgeoning liberal theological trend that privileged a rational reading of the Bible and led them to dispute certain tenets of Calvinist doctrine.

Universalism is so named for its central liberal doctrine: the universal salvation of humanity or the idea that when Christ died, he died for all. Throughout Christian history, theologians had toyed with the doctrine of universal salvation, but it was John Murray (1741–1815), an English immigrant and former Anglican, who named his church for it. Murray established the first Universalist congregation in Gloucester, Massachusetts, in 1774. Murray and Hosea Ballou (1771–1852) are referred to as the fathers of Universalism. Affected by the revivals of the eighteenth and nineteenth centuries, Universalist congregations were often places of emotive worship and a democratic ethos among the parishioners, reflected in the fact that those among the lower or working-class were particularly drawn to the movement. The first general meeting of the Universalist Church of America (UCA) occurred in 1785.

Unitarianism, on the other hand, became the religion of the Boston elite in the early nineteenth century. So named for their rejection of the doctrine of the Trinity as irrational, Unitarianism had appeared in Poland and England beginning in the seventeenth century, though its nineteenth-century Boston iteration arose out of Congregationalism. Congregationalism, the system of church governance founded by the Puritans, gave power to individual congregations and denied the use of creeds as "tests" of one's faithfulness. For this reason, individual congregations began to move away from orthodox Calvinist views, electing ministers who reflected this liberal point of view, such as Jonathan Mayhew and Charles Chauncy, who were progenitors of Unitarianism. The "father" of Unitarianism is William Ellery Channing (1780–1842), whose 1819 sermon, "Unitarian Christianity," outlined the denomination's belief system. Channing also coined the term "self-culture," which referred to the central Unitarian principle that human beings could come closer to God by constantly bettering the mind through study based on total "free inquiry." The American Unitarian Association (AUA) was officially formed in 1825 as a loose association of Unitarian ministers.

Beginning as early as the mid-nineteenth century, efforts had been made to build bridges between the two liberal denominations. Having recently experienced a schism between the more conservative and more radical (traditionally known as the Transcendentalist) branches, Unitarians spent the latter half of the nineteenth century trying to find theological consensus. During this time, Unitarian membership seemed to stagnate, even fall—a crisis similar to the Universalists. After peaking in the 1830s, Universalism's numbers seemed to dwindle. However, historical and demographic differences prevented the two liberal denominations from merging until far into the twentieth century. Then, in 1961, under the leadership of Dana McLean Greeley (1908–1986) (then president of the AUA), the

Unitarian and Universalist denominations officially merged becoming Unitarian Universalism, with the Unitarian Universalist Association (UUA) serving as the denomination's primary governing body (with Greeley as its first president).

BELIEFS

At their respective starts and throughout the nineteenth century, both Unitarianism and Universalism were staunchly Christian denominations. Belief in the existence of God, the exemplary life and sacrifice of Jesus of Nazareth, and the authority of the Bible were crucial elements of faith. However, the influx of humanist principles in the twentieth century eroded the devotion of Unitarians and Universalists to specifically Christian elements of the faith, privileging instead the spiritual fulfillment of each individual person from whatever source works for them.

Today, Unitarian Universalism belief grounds itself in the "Seven Principles," which emphasize each person's worth and the necessity of restorative social justice around the globe. Reflecting their liberal Christian origins, several of the principles highlight the importance of the individual conscience to determine what is true and to pursue that truth unfettered by religious doctrine. Further, while Unitarian Universalism has not dispensed with the Bible as a primary source of truth, they have also added other "sources," both textual and otherwise, to their list of religious authorities, including intuitive or direct experience of the divine, scriptures from non-Christian religions, and the natural world (the latter showing the lingering influence of Transcendentalism on Unitarian Universalism).

INSTITUTION AND CULTURE

Reflecting the Congregationalist roots of Unitarianism, Unitarian Universalism is noncreedal. For this reason, individual congregations are generally ecumenical in nature, paying homage to the truth of all belief systems, while reflecting the individual character of their location and the makeup of their membership. Unitarian Universalist churches exist in fellowship with one another, meaning that they recognize a common commitment to the principles of the UUA and often participate in "pulpit exchanges," where ministers will preach at sister congregations. Though the denomination is most prominent in the United States, particularly in the northeast, it maintains congregations on each continent, with Europe having the highest concentration of Unitarian Universalists outside of the United States.

Unitarian Universalism maintains a steady position as a denomination welcoming of all people—even those with different belief systems (a fact reflected in the many religious symbols usually found on church altars). The UUA was one of the first denominations to ordain openly gay clergy and maintains a steady number of female clergy (including the current president of the UUA). Overall, Unitarian Universalism has earned a reputation as a welcoming, if not always theologically precise, home for religious individuals seeking a devotional environment where personal experience is paramount, all religious views are welcome, and a commitment to social justice is central.

See also: Transcendentalism; Thoreau, Henry David (1817–1862).

Further Reading

Buehrens, John, & Forrest Church. 1998. *A Chosen Faith: An Introduction to Unitarian Universalism.* Boston: Beacon Press.

McKanan, Dan, ed. 2017. *A Documentary History of Unitarian Universalism.* Volumes 1–2. Boston: Skinner House Books.

Robinson, David. 1985. *The Unitarians and the Universalists.* Westport, CT; London, UK: Greenwood Press.

United Nuwaubian Nation of Moors, The

During the twentieth century, several new religions arose to address the erasure of identity and deprivation of fundamental human rights that represented the continuing effects of slavery and colonialism for African Americans. Those movements, including the Moorish Science Temple of America and the Nation of Islam, drew upon diverse materials from Islam, Black Nationalism, black Freemasonry, and other esoteric currents of thought. The United Nuwaubian Nation of Moors, initiated by Dwight D. "Malachi" York (1945–) in 1967, is perhaps the most creative group to develop in that black cultic milieu.

ORIGINS

It is difficult to distinguish legend from fact in the biography of York, just as it is with Noble Drew Ali (1886–1929) and W. D. Fard (1877–?). York claims to have been born in the Sudan on June 26, 1945, but the Federal Bureau of Investigation (FBI) places his birth in Maryland. York admits to having a criminal past, and he served time in prison between 1965 and 1967. Although he may have encountered Islam in prison, like many other inmates, his career as a religious leader began after his release when he became a student of Sheik Daoud Faisal (1891–1990) at the State Street Mosque in Harlem.

York had a voracious appetite for wisdom of all sorts and was soon composing his own pamphlets. He attracted a small group of friends to a group he called Ansaar Pure Sufi. In the first of many transformations, he renamed the group the Nubian Islamic Hebrews in 1968 and styled himself Imam Isa (Jesus); his followers donned African robes and fezzes. Like many of his predecessors, York was focused on discovering the true identity and history of African Americans. He argued that they were originally from a specific area of the Sudan and hence were Nubians or Nuwaubians. Over time, he extended that history back to ancient Egypt and Sumer. Beyond that, he concluded that the Sumerian and Egyptian civilizations had actually been founded by extraterrestrials from the planet Rizq.

BELIEFS AND PRACTICES

York's account of human origins shows the diverse elements of his ideology. York has recorded his teachings in an extensive library of "scrolls," of which *The Holy*

Tablets serves as the central text. In his writings, York situates himself in a lineage of prophets that includes Marcus Garvey (1887–1940), W. D. Fard, Noble Drew Ali, Elijah Muhammad (1897–1975), and Clarence 13X Smith (1928–1969), among others. As divinely inspired writings, *The Holy Tablets* are both the source of the Hebrew Bible, New Testament, and Qur'an and the correction of the errors in those texts.

York teaches that the Hebrew Bible, Christian Scriptures, and Qur'an both describe false gods and prescribe illegitimate worship of them. He is especially critical of the practice of blood sacrifice and its transformation in the Eucharist; he views such rituals as reflection of earlier ones when extraterrestrials would eat human bodies or feed off their energies. The gods to which such rituals are directed are simply posing as deities to control humans. The true God is Anu and York came to identify himself as an incarnation of Anu named Yaanuwn, whose task was to save the 144,000 faithful (see Rev. 7:1; 14:1) before the destruction of this world.

As early as 1973, the movement, now called the Ansaaru Allah Community, had set up communal living arrangements in the neighborhood around Brooklyn's Bushwick Avenue. At that time, their religious life focused on the mosque and members were urged to live modest, sober lives, similar to the members of the Nation of Islam. Much of the group's teaching focused on the recovery of true identity and the unmasking of false gods.

CONFLICTS

Like other communal groups, the Ansaaru Allah Community came into conflict with both neighbors and law enforcement. A series of fires near its Brooklyn mosque from 1976 to 1991 drew the attention of the FBI, which York's group shared with other black movements.

Ultimately, in 1993, York decided to move his followers to 475 acres in rural Edenton, Georgia. There York set about constructing the "Mecca of the West," Tama-Re. The move coincided with the addition of another layer to his already complex mythology. In Georgia, York and his followers claimed to be members of a Native American Tribe, the "Yamassee of the Creek Nation." That new identity reflects York's 1992 claim that the original humans were actually brown, not black as he had been preaching since the beginning. The architecture of York's new settlement reflected his sources of inspiration. Tama-Re features a forty-foot-high black pyramid and a smaller gold one; it has statues of Egyptian deities, and even a figure of a black Jesus crucified on an Egyptian Ankh and wearing an Indian headdress.

The apparent strangeness of the group attracted neighbors' wary attention. Local law enforcement was eager to believe claims orchestrated by disgruntled former members that York was molesting children. On May 8, 2002, the FBI and local police raided Tama-Re. York was initially charged with 116 counts of child molestation. On January 23, 2003, York pleaded guilty to a litany of charges. Despite the recantation of a key witness, York was found guilty and remanded to prison, where he still remains.

See also: Freemasonry; Moorish Science Temple of America, The; Nation of Gods and Earths, The (The Five Percent Nation), Nation of Islam, The; Noble Drew Ali (1886–1929); Race and New Religious Movements.

Further Reading

Bailey, Julius. 2015. "Sacred Not Secret: Esoteric Knowledge in the United Nuwaubian Nation of Moors." In Stephen C. Finley, Margarita Simon Guillory, & Hugh R. Page, Jr., eds., *Esotericism in African American Religion: "There is a Mystery,"* pp. 210–224. Leiden: Brill.

Easterling, Paul. 2015. "The 'Nu' Nation: An Analysis of Malichi Z. York's Nuwaubians." In Stephen C. Finley, Margarita Simon Guillory, & Hugh R. Page, Jr., eds., *Esotericism in African American Religion: "There Is a Mystery,"* pp. 198–209. Leiden: Brill.

Palmer, Susan. 2010. *The Nuwaubian Nation: Black Spirituality and State Control.* Burlington, VT: Ashgate.

York, Malachi Z. n.d. *The Holy Tablets.* Available at: http://holytablets.nuwaubianfacts.com/.

Unity School of Christianity

Like some branches of New Thought, Unity School of Christianity, also known as Unity Church or Unity, merged Christian language and theology with an emphasis on the power of the mind to achieve heavenly salvation and earthly fulfillment. Boasting members like Maya Angelou (1928–2014) and Erykah Badu (1971–), Unity appeals to those desirous of a modernized Christianity that believes anything is possible through Christ and the awesome power of the self.

ORIGINS AND FOUNDER

Throughout their lives, Charles (1854–1948) and Myrtle Fillmore (1845–1931) both suffered from chronic disabilities or maladies. Neither found relief in Western medicine. Then in the 1880s while living in Kansas City, Missouri, the Fillmores found New Thought, a diffuse movement that emphasized the possibility of curing maladies and improving one's circumstances through the work of one's mind ("mind cure"). Soon after beginning their New Thought classes, the Fillmores felt their health improve, a result they attributed to the methods learned in their courses and the power of prayer. In the process, Myrtle discovered the motto that would ground the theology of Unity Church: "I am a child of God, and therefore I do not inherit sickness."

Accompanying their interest in alternative forms of healing, the Fillmores—Charles, in particular—dabbled in the many religious movements and philosophies then arriving and arising in the United States. For them, there was a natural marriage between spiritual and physical health, since most physical maladies had a spiritual source. Feeling that their experiences and knowledge about the power of prayer and right thinking deserved a more public airing, the two began publishing their message in the periodical *Modern Thought* beginning in 1889 (it became *Unity Magazine* in 1891, which is still the movement's periodical today). This led to the creation of a prayer group in 1890 called "Silent Unity."

Though the Fillmores had no intention of founding a formal religious institution, by the early twentieth century, they had enough of a following through their prayer group and mailings that Charles and Myrtle were ordained as Unity ministers and a site of operations was established in Kansas City. Later, Unity Village was established outside of Kansas City, which became the formal headquarters of Unity Church. Charles continued to publish prolifically, even after Myrtle's death in 1931. His books, including *The Twelve Powers of Man* (1930), *The Metaphysical Bible Dictionary* (1931), and *Atom-Smashing Power of the Mind* (1949), rose to the level of scripture among Unity members.

BELIEFS AND PRACTICES

Unity Church aligns with New Thought in many of its principles, simply giving them a nondenominational Christian bent. The five "universal spiritual principles" of Unity, as listed on their website, are: the absolute goodness and omnipresence of God, the divinity and inherent goodness of human beings, the power of thought to "create" life experiences, the power of prayer to "change" and "transform" one's life, and the notion that these principles must be lived to be effective (www.unity.org). Rather than a personified and historical God, like the God presented in the Bible, Unity Church maintains that God is a powerful spiritual energy or infinite mind from which all creation, including humans, emanate and draw strength. Also, Jesus is divine, though not in some special sense, given that all human beings are children of God and divine themselves. Unity members believe that Jesus was the greatest model of human divinity and divine potential. Thus, they do not believe that Christ's sacrifice absolved some inherent sinfulness, but rather that Jesus helped them to realize the divinity they possessed all along. Additionally, Unity Church members read and use the Bible as a source of spiritual knowledge. However, they understand the book as a compilation of multiple authors over time; rather, Unity Church members should look for the metaphysical significance of the various authors' stories, which act as examples of souls at various stages of spiritual evolution.

Prayer is the central practice of Unity, specifically affirmative prayer. Unity differentiates its style of prayer from petitionary prayer, which focuses on asking God for something. Rather, affirmative prayer is an act of creation, whereby the individual meditates on a desired outcome, focuses on tapping into the divine within, and affirms what will come. In other words, rather than asking God to heal an ailment, an individual would say, "I am guided to perfect health." Not only can one perform affirmative prayer for oneself, but one can "request a prayer" from others, which builds on the belief that the more thought is directed at a given issue, the greater likelihood that the desired end will come to pass.

640 *Urantia Book, The*

Affirmative prayer may also be used by Unity members when there is a major tragedy or catastrophe. For example, in October 2018, Hurricane Michael devastated the panhandle of Florida; in response, Unity Worldwide ministries responded by issuing a call for donations, aid, and prayer. Besides prayer, which is most often undertaken on an individual basis, Unity conducts services, maintains an ordained clergy and missionary arm, and offers classes on various aspects of Unity philosophy—often taking the work of Charles Fillmore as the chosen content.

UNITY IN CONTEMPORARY SOCIETY

As a branch of New Thought, Unity has come under fire for being a pseudoscience that replaces scientific methods with positive thinking. Despite such critiques, Unity boasts around 170,000 members worldwide, with ministries on nearly every continent. The Church is still headquartered at Unity Village in Kansas City, where members come for retreats and annual conferences, and where the most visible vehicle of the church, *Unity Magazine*, is published.

See also: Christian Science; Healing, Health, and New Religious Movements; New Thought.

Further Reading

Anderson, Alan, & Deb Whitehouse. 2003. *New Thought: A Practical American Spirituality.* Bloomington, IN: AuthorHouse.

Fillmore, Charles. 2010 [1930]. *The Twelve Powers of Man.* Whitefish, MT: Kessinger Publishing, LLC.

Fillmore, Charles. 2017 [1949]. *Atom-Smashing Power of the Mind.* Scotts Valley, CA: CreateSpace Independent Publishing Platform.

Vahle, Neal. 2002. *The Unity Movement: Its Evolution and Spiritual Teachings.* West Conshohocken, PA: Templeton Foundation Press.

Urantia Book, The

First published in 1955, *The Urantia Book* (UB) presents itself as a collection of revelations to humans by extraplanetary intelligences. The revelations were received by an individual known only as "the sleeping subject." Convinced readers of the UB insist that the conduit through whom the revelations flowed did absolutely nothing to change or edit them. The true authors of the UB are claimed to be a specially formed "revelatory corps" or commission assembled specifically to communicate the UB's cosmic wisdom.

The UB was revealed in segments from 1906 to 1955. The "contact personality" was a patient of Chicago psychologist Dr. William S. Sadler (1875–1969). Sadler gradually became persuaded of the truth of what his patient told him and became instrumental in bringing the UB to the world. Sadler initially shared the developing set of revelations with a small group of interested people, but their publication marked both the end of the reception of revelations and a new, more public, phase in the reception of the UB. Sadler functioned as the head of the earthly

The Urantia Book comprised a series of revelations by an extraterrestrial entity through a person known as "the sleeping subject." Spanning thousands of pages, its contents reflected communications occurring from 1906 to 1955 that addressed everything from the creation of the universe to the true nature of God and Jesus. It was published by Psychologist Dr. William S. Sadler, whose patient had experienced these revelations. (Jeannievda/Dreamstime.com)

"Contact Commission" but he steadfastly refused to claim any sort of prophetic status for himself. The message of the new scripture, he asserted, should stand on its own.

CONTENTS

The UB is a substantial volume. It contains 196 separate "papers" and totals nearly 2,100 pages. The text relays a complex story about the origins and nature of the universe; the creation of our earth, known in the text as Urantia; the nature of human beings; and the identity of God. It presents the cosmos as a vast collection of universes overseen by a complex bureaucratic organization. Permission to reveal the UB, for example, had to be granted by the appropriate universe administrators, including those at the highest levels. The UB thus represents the distilled wisdom of the entire cosmos.

The UB also positions itself as the fifth in a sequence of "bestowals" that have been given to the inhabitants of Urantia to hasten their spiritual evolution. Those bestowals set the history of Urantia in a cosmic scale. The first bestowal occurred some five hundred thousand years ago with the teachings of an entity known as

642   *Urantia Book, The*

the "Planetary Prince." He was followed, thirty-eight thousand years ago by Adam and Eve, then by "Machiventa Melchizedek," and, two thousand years ago by Jesus. As the progression of bestowals suggests, the UB inserts familiar biblical figures into its cosmic context.

In fact, Jesus figures very prominently in the UB. Nearly eight hundred pages of the text are devoted to the "Jesus Papers." Like other texts produced by new religions, the UB asserts that the canonical accounts of Jesus are either untrustworthy or incomplete. From its perspective, the subsequent history of Christianity has been based on a shaky foundation. One aim of the UB, then, is to set the record straight.

In the UB, the mission of Jesus is set within the expansive cosmology articulated in the first part of the text. Jesus is identified as Michael of Nebadon, the "Creator Son" of our local universe and sometimes referred to as "Christ Michael." In keeping with the scope of the UB, Jesus is presented as having been part of six previous bestowals in other parts of the universe. Jesus's time on Urantia helped him develop an understanding of what creatures experience and helped to prepare him to exercise his cosmic sovereignty. The UB presents Jesus as a friend, companion, and counselor for human beings.

According to the UB, Jesus's mission on earth was not to set up a new religion but rather to reveal the nature of the Father to all on Urantia and throughout the local universe of Nebadon and also to lead people to a greater understanding of themselves, their Creator Father, and their place in the cosmos. For example, in one of its versions of the Lord's Prayer, the UB instructs the petitioner to ask "Give us this day the vivifying forces of light, / And let us not stray into the evil bypaths of our imagination, / For yours is the glorious indwelling, the everlasting power, / And to us the eternal gift of the infinite love of your Son" (UB 144.5.2, p. 1622). Accordingly, the UB devalues certain aspects of the biblical account of Jesus, such as his suffering, death, and resurrection. In the UB, for example, Jesus's physical body slept during his three days in the tomb and immediately disintegrated when he arose in his new "morantia" form, somewhere between the material and spiritual, with his personality intact.

CHALLENGES

Despite strong efforts to ensure that the UB was received as the final revelation of our extraplanetary guides, some devoted readers of the UB claimed that those same extraordinary intelligences were continuing to provide guidance beyond the UB. The mainstream of the UB's readership, however, rejected such attempts to supplement its teachings.

The UB and its readers have not been immune to the widespread critiques of cults in the later twentieth and early twenty-first centuries. Martin Gardner (1914–2010), a popular science and mathematics writer, published an entire book debunking the UB. Linking the UB with *The Book of Mormon*, the writings of Ellen White, Unificationism's *Divine Principle*, and even the Qur'an, Gardner exclaimed in exasperation that "one Bible is enough!" Despite such fulminations, however, the UB retains a devoted readership and other new scriptures continue to be produced.

See also: Anticult Movement, The; New Scriptures and New Religious Movements.

Further Reading

Bradley, David. 1998. *An Introduction to the Urantia Revelation.* Arcata, CA: White Egret Publications.

Gallagher, Eugene V. 2014. *Reading and Writing Scripture in New Religious Movements: New Bibles and New Revelations.* New York: Palgrave/Macmillan.

Gardner, Martin. 1995. *Urantia: The Great Cult Mystery.* Amherst, NY: Prometheus Books.

Hammer, Olav, & Mikael Rothstein. 2012. "Canonical and Extracanonical Texts in New Religions." In Olav Hammer & Mikael Rothstein, eds., *The Cambridge Companion to New Religious Movements*, pp. 113–129. Cambridge: Cambridge University Press.

Mullins, Larry, with Meredith Justin Sprunger. 2000. *A History of the Urantia Papers.* Boulder, CO: Penumbra Press.

PRIMARY SOURCE DOCUMENT

Excerpts from *The Urantia Book*—"The Meaning of Jesus"

The Urantia Foundation was established in 1950 with the primary purpose of safeguarding their venerated religious text, The Urantia Book. *As custodians of the text, the member of the foundation also sought to spread its teachings. Excerpts from* The Urantia Book *is as follows.*

Although Jesus did not die this death on the cross to atone for the racial guilt of mortal man nor to provide some sort of effective approach to an otherwise offended and unforgiving God; even though the Son of Man did not offer himself as a sacrifice to appease the wrath of God and to open the way for sinful man to obtain salvation; notwithstanding that these ideas of atonement and propitiation are erroneous, nonetheless, there are significances attached to this death of Jesus on the cross which should not be overlooked. It is a fact that Urantia has become known among other neighboring inhabited planets as the "World of the Cross."

Jesus desired to live a full mortal life in the flesh on Urantia. Death is, ordinarily, a part of life. Death is the last act in the mortal drama. In your well-meant efforts to escape the superstitious errors of the false interpretation of the meaning of the death on the cross, you should be careful not to make the great mistake of failing to perceive the true significance and the genuine import of the Master's death.

Mortal man was never the property of the archdeceivers. Jesus did not die to ransom man from the clutch of the apostate rulers and fallen princes of the spheres. The Father in heaven never conceived of such crass injustice as damning a mortal soul because of the evil-doing of his ancestors. Neither was the Master's death on the cross a sacrifice which consisted in an effort to pay God a debt which the race of mankind had come to owe him.

Before Jesus lived on earth, you might possibly have been justified in believing in such a God, but not since the Master lived and died among your fellow mortals. Moses taught the dignity and justice of a Creator God; but Jesus portrayed the love and mercy of a heavenly Father.

The animal nature—the tendency toward evil-doing—may be hereditary, but sin is not transmitted from parent to child. Sin is the act of conscious and deliberate rebellion against the Father's will and the Sons' laws by an individual will creature.

Jesus lived and died for a whole universe, not just for the races of this one world. While the mortals of the realms had salvation even before Jesus lived and died on Urantia, it is nevertheless a fact that his bestowal on this world greatly illuminated the way of salvation; his death did much to make forever plain the certainty of mortal survival after death in the flesh.

Though it is hardly proper to speak of Jesus as a sacrificer, a ransomer, or a redeemer, it is wholly correct to refer to him as a *savior*. He forever made the way of salvation (survival) more clear and certain; he did better and more surely show the way of salvation for all the mortals of all the worlds of the universe of Nebadon.

When once you grasp the idea of God as a true and loving Father, the only concept which Jesus ever taught, you must forthwith, in all consistency, utterly abandon all those primitive notions about God as an offended monarch, a stern and all-powerful ruler whose chief delight is to detect his subjects in wrongdoing and to see that they are adequately punished, unless some being almost equal to himself should volunteer to suffer for them, to die as a substitute and in their stead. The whole idea of ransom and atonement is incompatible with the concept of God as it was taught and exemplified by Jesus of Nazareth. The infinite love of God is not secondary to anything in the divine nature.

All this concept of atonement and sacrificial salvation is rooted and grounded in selfishness. Jesus taught that *service* to one's fellows is the highest concept of the brotherhood of spirit believers. Salvation should be taken for granted by those who believe in the fatherhood of God. The believer's chief concern should not be the selfish desire for personal salvation but rather the unselfish urge to love and, therefore, serve one's fellows even as Jesus loved and served mortal men.

Neither do genuine believers trouble themselves so much about the future punishment of sin. The real believer is only concerned about present separation from God. True, wise fathers may chasten their sons, but they do all this in love and for corrective purposes. They do not punish in anger, neither do they chastise in retribution.

Even if God were the stern and legal monarch of a universe in which justice ruled supreme, he certainly would not be satisfied with the childish scheme of substituting an innocent sufferer for a guilty offender.

The great thing about the death of Jesus, as it is related to the enrichment of human experience and the enlargement of the way of salvation, is not the *fact* of his death but rather the superb manner and the matchless spirit in which he met death.

This entire idea of the ransom of the atonement places salvation upon a plane of unreality; such a concept is purely philosophic. Human salvation is *real*; it is based on two realities which may be grasped by the creature's faith and thereby become incorporated into individual human experience: the fact of the fatherhood of God and its correlated truth, the brotherhood of man. It is true, after all, that you are to be "forgiven your debts, even as you forgive your debtors."

The cross of Jesus portrays the full measure of the supreme devotion of the true shepherd for even the unworthy members of his flock. It forever places all relations between God and man upon the family basis. God is the Father; man is his son. Love, the love of a father for his son, becomes the central truth in the universe relations of Creator and creature—not the justice of a king which seeks satisfaction in the sufferings and punishment of the evil-doing subject.

> **Source:** *The Urantia Book*, Paper 188. "The Time of the Tomb." Available at: https://www.urantia.org/urantia-book-standardized/paper-188-time-tomb. This work uses quotations from the English-language translation of *The Urantia Book* published by Urantia Foundation, © 1955, 2008 Urantia Foundation, 533 Diversey Parkway, Chicago, Illinois 60614, USA; +1 (773) 525–3319; https://www.urantia.org; all rights reserved. The views expressed in this work are those of the author and do not necessarily represent the views of Urantia Foundation or its affiliates.

Utopianism in New Religious Movements

Utopias are a natural outgrowth of civilization; so long as there are people, there will be those who believe that the perfect society can, does, or should exist. Many religions may have utopian strains, often tied to millennialist impulses or the belief that change, whether gradual or immediate, will produce a new world order, often on the heels of some major world event such as the Second Coming of Christ.

But not every religion channels these impulses into the creation of a utopian society: one that seeks to prepare for, replicate, or even realize a perfect world here on earth. New religions are often inclined to create utopian movements—a feature of their engineering as groups that either branch from old traditions or emerge autonomously, pitching themselves as the best or newest pathway to salvation in this life and the next. And while most utopian experiments fail, some have stood the test of time, mostly in historical memory, but for a rare few, in actuality.

GENERAL CHARACTERISTICS

No single religious utopia is like another, but certain patterns can be discerned. Perhaps most notable is the fact that new religious utopias are generally communitarian; practicing some form of communal living, the sharing of property and wealth, an ethos of self-sufficiency, and an equal distribution of labor. For new religious utopias, these characteristics are often steeped in theological meaning, as they are in certain Christian utopias that seek to approximate the Kingdom of God where distinctions of wealth and status will cease to matter. The creation of self-sufficient "communes" coupled with the conviction of religious doctrine can often lead to some division between the utopia and the outside world in varying degrees.

Numerous new religious movements also experiment with traditional gender roles as well as marital and sexual relationships. In many cases, gender roles are completely dissolved and "work" ceases to be described in gendered terms. Marriage and sex are also regulated—sometimes both are done away with completely or regulated due to some overriding theological principle. Relationships, as a primary means of attachment to the world, are supposed to be subsumed in the pursuit of communal and individual spiritual advancement or perfection. Increasingly, new religious utopias have exhibited an environmentalist bent, invoking sustainable agricultural and energy policies as a part of their religious programs.

Finally, many new religious utopias, though rarely achieving great numerical strength and often the target of significant external (and sometimes internal) critique, hope that their brand of religiosity will attract others. Though time and experience may lead to a particular utopian community to increase its exclusivity and close ranks, most at the outset believe they have something to share with the world worth emulating.

HISTORIC EXAMPLES

Beginning in the late eighteenth century, several religious utopias emerged in the United States. The Shakers, though born in England prior to the American Revolution, took root in the new republic under the leadership of Mother Ann Lee (1736–1784). Mother Ann revealed that the root and result of sin were sex and procreation, respectively. As a result, Shakers, though living communally, live celibately (aided by the fact that their sleeping arrangements are segregated by gender). In the community, men and women share the workload, though they often perform tasks typically affiliated with each gender, and authority in the church. The community survives, but is currently reduced to two surviving members.

Similar to the Shakers, the Oneida Community was renowned for its marital, procreative, and sexual practices—though for the opposite reason. Following his realization that Christ had already returned in AD 70, John Humphrey Noyes (1811–1886) declared that people could begin living perfectly as they would in the Kingdom of God. As part of this perfection, monogamous marital relationships were to be dissolved; in their place, Noyes implemented a system of complex marriage at Oneida, which he founded in 1848. In this system, all members were married to one another and sexual relationships occurred between multiple partners to avoid attachment (and as ordered by Noyes). Procreation was strictly regulated and only those couples matched by Noyes himself could produce "stirpiculits," children born at Oneida. Total gender equality was also encouraged—labor was not divided according to gender and women wore distinctive uniforms that included pants to facilitate more heavy labor. Eventually, the defection of second-generation members and an aging Noyes led to a dissolution of the community as a religious utopia. It still lives on as a successful manufacturer of silver goods.

The Amana Society is another such entity that began as a religious utopia and evolved into a for-profit business. Born from German Pietism, the Amana Colonies were founded in Iowa in the mid-nineteenth century. All colony members worked and each received a base salary intended for use at the various self-sustaining industries and stores in the community. Traditional social rank was dissolved in view of the German Pietist belief that all could have an individual connection to God; traditional gender roles remained intact. Eventually, financial strain forced a split between the Amana Church and the Amana Society, effectively dissolving the religious connection to the work of the community. Both survive today.

Various nineteenth-century Transcendentalists were associated with two short-lived utopian experiments in Massachusetts: Brook Farm and Fruitlands. Though both societies were influenced by the socially conscious works of Charles Fourier (1772–1837), whose work was not religiously based, Transcendentalists like Bronson Alcott (1799–1888) were drawn to such utopias given their tendency to buck the constraints of established institutions and the belief that one must be constantly engaging in self-betterment, which furthered spiritual advancement. Both movements dissolved due to financial woes and the flagging engagement of their members.

MODERN UTOPIAN MOVEMENTS

Not all utopias dissolved so gradually. Peoples Temple founded the Agricultural Mission at Jonestown, Guyana as a realization of its Christian Socialist principles, including total equality of races and genders, the eradication of poverty, and self-sufficiency in a world on a course for global disaster. Its founder, Jim Jones (1931–1978) envisioned Jonestown as a haven for those unable to find purchase in a, racist, ageist, and classist United States. Unfortunately, the utopia ended in tragedy when over the course of November 17–18, 1978, over nine hundred members of the community committed revolutionary suicide, the result of mounting pressure from outside, Jones's increasing paranoia, and the belief that their martyrdom would help them move into another, better place. Without the same loss of life, the Osho Movement, which existed as its own incorporated city (Rajneeshpuram) in Oregon during the 1980s, would dissolve amidst accusations of criminality. The community was founded by Shree Bhagwan Rajneesh (1931–1990), who believed that by total love and commitment to one another, which included advocacy of free love, gender equality, and limited procreation, its followers would advance to a higher spiritual plane.

Synonymous in the public consciousness with the "danger" of religious utopias (or new religions in general) is the Family International (The Children of God) of the 1970s and 1980s. Christian and millennialist in orientation, members of the Family lived communally, pooled resources, and practiced sexual emancipation (a fact which some argued reflected the counterculture of its time). The movement still survives today, though communalism is no longer practiced.

Several new religious utopias merged ecological and spiritual pursuits. Damanhur, founded in 1975 in the Piedmont region of Italy, after a failed attempt to build an underground temple, evolved into several centers around the globe that focus on meditation and peaceful cohabitation of people and the natural world. In Tennessee, the Farm is an intentional community founded at the height of counterculture in the 1970s; it combines communal living, vegetarianism, holistic medicine (particularly midwifery), and a focus on individual spiritual catharsis. Though diminished in size, the community still exists today and has founded numerous nonprofit companies, focused on humanitarian and environmental aims. Finally, the Findhorn Foundation arose as the result of its founders' communication with advanced beings, whose messages served as a gathering point for New Age religionists. The movement would eventually diversify, running a local hotel and becoming renowned for their sustainable gardening practices; it still exists as a mecca for those interested in alternative channels of ultimate truth.

See also: Amana Society; Children of God (The Family International); Damanhur; Environmentalism and New Religious Movements; Farm, The; Findhorn Foundation, The; Gender and New Religious Movements; Jones, Rev. Jim (1931–1978); Lee, (Mother) Ann (1736–1784); Marriage and Relationships in New Religious Movements; Millennialism; New Age, The; Noyes, John Humphrey (1811–1886); Oneida Community, The; Rajneesh, Shree Bhagwan/Osho (1931–1990); Rajneesh/Osho Movement, The; Peoples Temple; Sex, Sexuality, and New Religious Movements; Shakers, The; Transcendentalism.

Further Reading

Gómez, Javier León. 2019. "Religiousness and Spirituality in the New Utopian Movements." *Religions* 10, no. 166: doi:10.3390/rel100030166.

Jennings, Chris. 2016. *Paradise Now: The Story of American Utopianism.* New York: Random House.

Mandelker, Ira L. 1984. *Religion, Society, and Utopia in Nineteenth-Century America.* Amherst: University of Massachusetts Press.

Peterson, Anna L. 2005. *The Seeds of the Kingdom: Utopian Communities in the Americas.* Oxford: Oxford University Press.

Pitzer, Donald E., ed. 1997. *America's Communal Utopias.* Chapel Hill: The University of North Carolina Press.

Valley of the Dawn, The

Brazil has been the site for the development of many new religions, from Candomblé and Kardecist Spiritualism in the nineteenth century, to Umbanda and various forms of Pentecostalism and New Age spirituality in the twentieth. The largest Brazilian new religious movement, the Valley of the Dawn (Vale do Amanhecer in Portuguese), officially named the Social Works of the Spiritualist Christian Order, was founded in 1969 and since has spread to other countries in South America and Europe as well as to the United States. It now claims as many as eight hundred thousand adherents.

The Valley of the Dawn originated in the religious experiences of Neiva Chaves Zelaya (1925–1985). A widowed truck driver who sought work in the construction of the new Brazilian capital Brasilia in 1955, Neiva began to experience visions in 1958. After an initial resistance to accept them, she became a full-time medium in 1959. For a while she cooperated with a more established medium in the formation of a small religious group, but by 1969, she felt called to establish her own group, drawing on Spiritist practices, UFO lore, and elements of Christianity, among other things. She met Mario Stassi in 1965 and he became a coleader of the new group, helping to structure the eclectic worldview that was developing through Tia ("Aunt") Neiva's interactions with the spirit world.

Crucial to Tia Neiva's status within the group was her ability to channel Pai Seta Branca ("Father White Arrow"), an Amerindian chieftain who in a previous life had been incarnated as St. Francis of Assisi. In the group's cosmology, however, Pai Seta Branca was actually a "Planetary Master," a highly evolved being who had first come to earth more than thirty thousand years ago to aid the evolutionary development of humankind. Unfortunately, humans have forgotten their own history. Pai Seta Branca is communicating that knowledge to Tia Neiva because humanity is on the verge of a new millennium.

Pai Seta Branca, however, is only one of some thirty thousand spirits who can communicate with humans. Members of the Valley of the Dawn, which is the name used both for the organization and for its settlement outside of one of the satellite cities of Brasilia, believe that anyone has the capacity to serve as a medium. There are thousands of mediums in residence at the group's Brazilian headquarters.

The Valley of the Dawn settlement focuses on two prominent ritual spaces. The Temple is where outsiders come for healing rituals and the Burning Star, an artificial lake in the shape of a six-pointed star is where members conduct their own rituals. Both spaces feature eclectic and very colorful architecture, including statues, images of spirits, and more abstract elements, and members adopt elaborate, colorful costumes.

Several different rituals focus on the "disintegration" of negative energies and bad karma to pave the way for the new millennium. Outsiders frequently come to the Temple for healing, which is provided at no cost. The mediums believe that physical and other problems are caused by negative spirits. The spirits are divided into four categories and suggest the complex religious heritage of the group. There are the spirits of former slaves, native Brazilian and Indian spirits, spiritual doctors, and also extraterrestrials from the planet Capela, to which highly evolved individuals will return at the dawn of the millennium.

In the healing process, the afflicting spirits are identified, extracted from the patient, and taught the correct doctrine by the medium. The patients are then freed and the mediums put them into contact with benign spirits. Those suffering from physical ailments are also referred to medical doctors. Ideally, the patients will come back and join the Valley of the Dawn where they, too, can develop their capacities to contact the spirits.

See also: Candomblé; Globalization and New Religious Movements; Kardecism (Spiritism); Mediums; UFO Religions; Umbanda.

Further Reading

Hayes, Kelly E. 2013. "Intergalactic Space-Time Travelers: Envisioning Globalization in Brazil's Valley of the Dawn." *Nova Religio* 16: 63–92.

Introvigne, Massimo. 2013. "The Vale do Amanhecer: Healing and Spiritualism in a Globalized Brazilian New Religious Movement." *Sociologia: Revista da Faculdade de Letras da Universidade do Porto* 26: 189–200.

Pierini, Emily. 2018. "Healing and Therapeutic Trajectories among the Spirit Mediums of the Brazilian Vale do Amanhecer." *International Journal of Latin American Religions* 2: 272–289.

Váquez, Manuel A., & José Cláudio Souza Alves. "The Valley of the Dawn in Atlanta, Georgia: Negotiating Incorporation and Gender Identity in the Diaspora." In Cristina Rocha & Manuel A. Vásquez, eds., *The Disapora of Brazilian Religions*, pp. 313–337. Leiden: E. J. Brill.

Vampirism

In the first decades of the twenty-first century, it seemed that vampires were everywhere. The image of vampires, influenced by books and films like the *Twilight* series and television shows like *The Vampire Diaries*, evoked a broader cultural fascination with these undead creatures of the night and presented an image of vampires as dangerous predators and as objects of desire. This fascination is by no means new—vampire lore and legends extend for centuries. However, the advent of Vampire Religion, or Vampirism, is a relatively contemporary phenomenon.

ORIGINS AND HISTORY

The concept of a vampire arose in medieval Europe, the result of confusion about how bodies decompose. During decomposition, the deceased body's skin shrinks and recedes, making nails and teeth appear longer. The body also produces a black liquid from the mouth and nose, that some believed to be blood. From there the vampire legend spooled into stories of blood-thirsty, lustful beings spawned by the Devil. In popular novels, like Bram Stoker's *Dracula* (1897), vampires subverted traditionally Catholic symbols and ideology: they were repelled by the cross and, instead of giving blood as Christ did through the transubstantiated host, they took it. Thus, vampires represented the forces of darkness against Christian forces of goodness. As with many things religious, there is a fine line between fear and awe. Thus, it was not a far stretch for fear to become rapt interest to become worship.

The first group of self-identified vampires emerged in the 1970s. They maintained they must consume animal or human blood for its nutritional (claiming their bodies cannot absorb nutrients from other foods) and spiritual properties. These individuals came together after contacting Dr. Jeanne Keyes Youngson who founded The Count Dracula Fan Club (today, The Vampire Empire) in 1970. They began convening at gatherings called "Dark Shadows" conventions, which prompted the publication of materials about vampire life. From this group arose The Temple of the Vampire (TOV), which was founded by George C. Smith and granted tax-exempt status in the United States in 1989. *The Vampire Bible* was published later that year.

Though it began as a mail-order religious community, the group maintains a mostly virtual presence on the internet. It asserts itself as the only "authentic international organization in the world that represents the true Vampire Religion" (http://templeofthevampire.com/history). Further, the TOV maintains that its roots reach back into history, claiming that it is an ancient order that has been called other names throughout history, such as The Temple of the Dragon.

BELIEFS AND PRACTICES

Vampire Religion is not monolithic. Since much of Vampire Religion is practiced individually, with the exception of annual gatherings or conventions, variations in belief and practice are common. Some may include blood-drinking as a sacramental rite of communion, others may worship or pray to Vampires as greater beings of immense power. Most imagine (or hope) that they themselves will become a vampire at some point—in this life or the next.

However, the TOV sets out a very clear set of doctrines, beginning with the idea that the Vampire represents the next level in human evolution. Similar to The Church of Satan, the TOV emphasizes the importance of individual freedom and fulfillment, ideas that are reflected in "The Vampire Creed," which appears in *The Vampire Bible*. Ironically, the TOV prohibits the drinking of blood or all ritual activities that could potentially harm another person. For them, the power of the Vampire does not come through literal consumption, but through realization of untapped power, which allows a person to achieve peak health, wealth, and even immortality. The vast majority of TOV rites are targeted at absorbing this power through contact with or invocation of Vampire Gods. *The Vampire Bible* lays out a seven-step ceremony for achieving such contact and can be performed in community or individually.

TOV members believe that Vampires are the original founders of the world's religions, which they created to control human beings. Vampires, then, are the actual rulers of the world and humans are merely a lower species from which to absorb energy and power. For the lucky few who have realized the truth about vampires, they need not be controlled by those rulers. Each member of the TOV is said to bear a "dayside" and a "nightside" in his or her personality. The dayside exhibits qualities of skeptical materialism and cynicism over the stupefying power of traditional religion. The nightside is characterized by magical abilities, many associated with vampires such as shapeshifting, flight, glamour, and immortality. Achieving the abilities of the nightside is a difficult process and one granted only to those who have learned the teachings of the TOV and participated in the various religious rituals intentionally.

COMMUNITY AND CULTURE

The TOV is incredibly secretive and exclusive. Becoming a member of the TOV begins by giving a donation, monetary or otherwise. Only then will a member receive *The Vampire Bible*, along with other religious accouterments like the Vampire Temple Ring, and become initiated into its teachings. From there, the member proceeds along various levels or "circles" of membership, which mark his or her progress in achieving vampiric traits. At the Third Circle, an individual becomes a Vampire Priest or Priestess (members of "The Priesthood of Ur"), but the highest level marks one as a Vampire Sorcerer or Sorceress.

The number of those who practice Vampire Religion is small; many dabble with the faith, but do not remain for the long term. This does not necessarily mean that they leave occult religion, or even vampirism, behind. Vampire Religion is simply one expression of modern Vampire culture.

See also: Church of Satan, The; Ghosts, the Paranormal, and New Religious Movements; New Religions on/and the Internet; Sex, Sexuality, and New Religious Movements.

Further Reading

Browning, John Edgar. "The Temple of the Vampire." *World Religions and Spirituality.* Available at: https://wrldrels.org/2016/10/08/temple-of-the-vampire/.

Laycock, Joseph. 2009. *Vampires Today: The Truth about Modern Vampirism.* Westport, CT: Praeger Publishers.

Temple of the Vampire, The. 1989. *The Vampire Bible.* Lacey, WA: Temple of the Vampire.

Vedanta Society, The

ORIGINS AND HISTORY

The Vedanta Society was founded during a period of peak Western fascination with Asian religions. Other new religious movements such as Theosophy and its institutional structure, the Theosophical Society, reflected both a dissatisfaction with traditional, Western religious forms and a belief that the "East" held valuable and hidden secrets about divine truth.

In 1893, Swami Vivekananda (1863–1902), a Hindu monk and disciple of Ramakrishna (1836–1886) (for whom the Ramakrishna Mission, which Vivekananda represented, was named), traveled to Chicago for the World's Parliament of Religion. Vivekananda's time at the Parliament was a resounding success. There he presented many of the views that would serve as the basis for the Vedanta Society, including the essential wisdom of all religions, while presenting Hinduism as the religious system furthest along the path to divine enlightenment. He became an instant celebrity, with people clamoring for his views and guidance. As a result, he would spend the majority of his final decade on lecture tours in the West and would found the Vedanta Society in New York City in 1894.

The Vedanta Society was envisioned as the Western branch of the Ramakrishna Mission, which was a monastic Hindu order. Vivekananda would serve as head of its first Western branch in New York until 1897, when his travels took him to England. He named Swami Abhedananda, also a disciple of Ramakrishna, to serve as its head from there. From there, the Vedanta Society established missions all over the United States, with its largest missions (besides New York) established in Southern California (with multiple centers from Santa Barbara to Hollywood) and Boston. Outside of the United States, there is a Vedanta Society in England, though the heart of the Ramakrishna Mission resides in Belur Math, Calcutta, India. Though there is also an International Vedanta Society, it is unaffiliated with the Ramakrishna Mission and its Vedanta centers, having been founded in 1989.

BELIEFS AND PRACTICES

Vedanta means, literally, "end or goal of the Vedas" referring to a category of philosophical and religious ideas that arose from the Upanishads, which are part of the Vedas. The Vedas contain most of the foundational ideas of Hinduism (the term Veda means "knowledge" in Sanskrit); they are also vast, meaning that various branches and interpretations emerge, privileging particular areas of Vedic sacred knowledge. Even those who fall under the umbrella of Vedanta are not uniform in belief. In adapting Hinduism to a Western audience, Vivekananda chose to build his version of Vedanta in a particularly syncretic mold: privileging those areas of the Upanishads that highlighted unity with other world religions and privileged the possibility of enlightenment to esoteric truths.

It is not surprising then—and given Vivekananda's message at the 1893 World's Parliament of Religion—that the Vedanta Society argues for the harmony of all religions. All religions are equally engaged in finding truth and a path toward the same God, even if that truth may take different doctrinal or ideological forms. Differences in religion are mainly the result of geographical, historical, and political forces, but are ultimately nonessential. Relatedly, and aligned with traditional Hindu belief, Vedantists believe in the unity of existence, meaning that everything in the world (including people) are manifestations of the divine oneness (or God, depending upon how one defines it). For human beings, our true self, or Atman, is inherently divine. Most people are unaware of their true nature due to "maya" or ignorance, thus the purpose of most Vedanta practice is to achieve awareness or enlightenment of this truth. This ignorance coupled with karma, which refers both to humans' actions and the result of their actions, ties us to and guarantees our reincarnation into subsequent lives until the results of our actions are nullified and we have realized the truth of reality.

Echoing traditional Hindu practices, Vedantists practice various forms of yoga (which means "path") to help them discover the reality of divine oneness. Vivekananda had emphasized raja-yoga, or the discipline of meditation, which emphasized individual practice, often at the hands of an instructor, or guru (similar to his own experience with Ramakrishna). However, Vedantists also practice jnana-yoga, or the path of knowledge, by reading or taking classes at various Vedanta centers; bhakti yoga, or the path of love, which usually involves the repetition of a mantra, often the name of God, or puja (worship) at a personal or communal altar; and karma-yoga, the path of work, which involves the performance of good works while simultaneously detaching oneself from their results. Vedantists emphasize the importance of ethical living and cultivating moral virtues, which include nonviolence, truthfulness, and cleanliness. These virtues are specifically targeted at those Vedantists living a monastic life, as did Swami Vivekananda (hence the precept of "chastity"). However, since many Vedantists choose not to live the life of the religious adept, the general emphasis is on self-control and living a life that diminishes one's ego.

INSTITUTIONS AND CULTURE

Today, the Vedanta Society operates much as it did when it was first founded by Swami Vivekananda. Each branch of the Vedanta Society is led by a swami, whose role it is to provide guidance to individual practitioners and the monastics who choose to live and operate in its various centers. However, much of the sustainability of the society comes through sustained interest in the writings of Swami Vivekananda, as a figure who sought to bring East and West together. With the advent of the internet (see the various websites for Vedanta centers, such as New York http://www.vedantany.org/ or Southern California, http://vedanta.org/), the spread of his message and the possibility of individual practice has meant that those without monastic aims can be a part of the Vedantist community.

See also: Hindu New Religious Movements; Occultism and Esotericism; Ramakrishna Mission; Theosophical Society, The; Theosophy; Vivekananda, Swami (1863–1902); Yoga.

Further Reading

Sharma, Jyotirmaya. 2012. *Cosmic Love and Human Apathy: Swami Vivekananda's Restatement of Religion.* New York: Harpercollins.

Vedanta Society. *Vedanta Magazine.* Available at: http://www.vedantauk.com/Magazine .aspx.

Vivekananda, Swami. 2004. *Practical Vedanta.* Belur Math, Howrah, Indian: Advaita Ashrama.

Violence and New Religious Movements

When the contemporary anticult movement began to take shape in the 1970s, one of its foundational ideas was that members of new or alternative religious groups were suffering harm by the very fact of their membership. Among the harmful behaviors attributed to "cults" by early anticult organizations like FREECOG, established to get adult children out of The Children of God, were the deprivation of liberty, sleep, and nutrition and exploitation of members in fundraising, proselytization, and sexual relationships, among other things. Efforts to associate new religions with violence, however, received an extraordinary boost when over nine hundred people died by murder and suicide at the Peoples Temple Agricultural Mission in Jonestown, Guyana, in November 1978.

Jonestown solidified a stereotype of dangerous cults in public opinion that has varied little since then, even as it has been applied to a diverse array of groups. A spate of events involving new religious movements in the 1990s appeared to confirm that stereotype. They included the deaths of more than eighty people at the Branch Davidians' Mount Carmel Center in 1993, the murders and suicides associated with The Order of the Solar Temple in 1994, the deadly release of sarin gas by members of Aum Shinrikyō in the Tokyo subway in 1995, and the suicides of members of Heaven's Gate in 1997. The actions of al-Qaeda terrorists in 2001 were also assimilated to the cult stereotype.

From that perspective, cult leaders are cynical manipulators who seek followers to exploit for monetary or sexual rewards. Cult members have somehow been bamboozled into membership, had their ability to reason clearly and exercise their free will compromised, and need to be rescued from the clutches of the cult before they come to even greater harm. Without a doubt, in the anticult view, cults do harm to their members and to society at large.

The homogenized image of dangerous cults, however, erases significant differences between groups and directs little attention to the specific contexts in which acts of violence have occurred. It also ignores overwhelming historical evidence that established religions throughout the world have also perpetrated and suffered from significant acts of violence. In fact, there is no inherent connection between new religions and violence, just as there is no inherent connection between more established religions and violence. Violence plays out in specific contexts in which multiple factors either contribute to or inhibit violent outcomes. It is essential, therefore, to consider any violent act in the context in which it occurred and to treat violent actions as the results of complex social processes that could potentially have turned out differently.

The beliefs and practices of a given group, its social context, whether it experiences significant opposition from cultural opponents, and many other factors come into play when assessing the potential for and analyzing the occurrence of violence. Acts of violence themselves can also be distinguished from each other. For example, violent acts within a group perpetrated by one member against another differ from collective actions of a group against outsiders, which in turn differ from violent actions of outsiders against a group or some of its members. The homogenizing effects of the anticult stereotype do not promote such

656   Violence and New Religious Movements

necessary distinctions and thus lead to skewed views of whatever violence does happen in connection with new religions.

INTRAGROUP VIOLENCE

To a substantial extent the violence that the early anticult movement attributed to new religions was in the eye of the beholder. Many of the early members of the Unification Church in the United States, for example, claimed to have willingly embraced the long, grueling hours of public proselytization for the sake of spreading Reverend Moon's (1920–2012) message. But there have been indisputable acts of violence committed within new religions. When the Children of God (later The Family International) were operating under the Law of Love instituted by their leader, David Berg (1919–1994), some members acted on Berg's understanding of children as sexual beings and engaged in abusive sexual relations with underage children. To its credit, The Family explicitly renounced all adult sexual contact with children in 1986, but that neither healed the wounds that had already occurred nor entirely salvaged the group's reputation.

The International Society for Krishna Consciousness had to face similar issues. In 1998, it published an exposé in its own *ISKCON Communications Journal* detailing years of physical, emotional, and sexual abuse in its boarding schools in India and the United States in the 1970s and 1980s. Like The Children of God, ISKCON attempted to put strong safeguards into place. In 1997, for example it established a Child Protection Office designed to help individual leaders of temples to identify, prevent, and report to legal authorities potential incidents of abuse.

Incidences of sexual abuse may expose the tensions between the roles of sexuality within the theology of a specific group and widely accepted social and legal norms. David Koresh (1959–1993) had multiple wives and engaged in sexual relations with underage girls. His actions were part of a complex theological scenario in which he, as the Lamb of God, was supposed to sire the twenty-four elders mentioned in the Book of Revelation as reigning in the Kingdom of God. Koresh was investigated by the Child Protective Services in Texas, but they could not substantiate allegations of child abuse, in part because those who accepted Koresh's New Light revelation helped to shield him. The near-total demise of the Branch Davidian community in 1993 cut off any opportunity for the kinds of reforms pursued by The Family and ISKCON.

Finally, in a few rare cases, new religions have actually ordered the murder of members or defecting members. In late 1988, for example, a member of Aum Shinrikyō died while undertaking extreme ascetic practices. In 1989, Shoko Asahara (1955–2018), Aum's leader, ordered the murder of a member who had participated in the cover-up of the death but who was threatening to leave and expose Aum. Similarly, Malcolm X (1925–1965), who had harshly criticized Elijah Muhammad's (1897–1975) moral failings, was assassinated by members of the Nation of Islam in 1965.

The 1978 deaths at Jonestown were a mix of suicides, where individuals ingested the poison willingly, and murder where it was forced upon them or their lives were ended by other means. The deaths of the Branch Davidians at the Mount Carmel Center included those who were killed as a direct result of Federal Bureau of Investigation actions, suicides, and murders at the hands of other members. The deaths of members of The Order of the Solar Temple were similarly mixed in their causes.

VIOLENCE AGAINST NEW RELIGIONS

New religions are incubators for innovative practices and ideas. Plural marriage among the early Mormons and the contemporary Fundamentalist Latter-day Saints and complex marriage in the Oneida community are among the many examples. Such practices can inflame opposition against a group because it departs from accepted norms. Generally, opposition remains ideological. The widely publicized stereotype of dangerous cults is a case in point. But opposition to new religions also frequently carries with it the plea for something to be done.

Agents of violence against new religions come from different quarters. It is beyond doubt that many early deprogrammings, for example, included forced kidnapping and other physical and emotional violence. Most attempts to enlist the government in the anticult movement have been focused on the courts, but in a few cases, such as the fifty-one-day siege at the Branch Davidians' Mount Carmel Center, law enforcement officials have taken violent actions that have resulted in deaths on both sides.

The series of raids in several countries against communal homes of The Family in the early 1990s, which put children into state custody separate from their parents, were certainly experienced as unnecessary state-sanctioned violence against members of new religions. The same holds for the 1984 raid by ninety state troopers that removed 112 children from the Twelve Tribes community in Island Pond, Vermont. A similar raid on the Texas Yearning for Zion ranch of the Fundamentalist Latter-day Saints led by Warren Jeffs took place in 2008; it eventually caused the removal of more than four hundred fifty children into the custody of the State of Texas. In both cases, the children were quickly returned.

Those examples show that the treatment of children and unconventional sexual practices, and especially their intersection, are particular flash points in the interactions of new religions with their social environments. While new religions may strive to maintain a low or moderate degree of tension with their social environments, various factors can prompt actions against new religions that take a violent turn. Whether such violence is justified remains a matter of contention that is usually adjudicated after the fact. But the perpetration of violence against new religions demonstrates again the descriptive and analytical bankruptcy of the stereotype of the dangerous cult.

NEW RELIGIONS' VIOLENCE AGAINST SOCIETY

In general, the fear that new religions will do violent harm to society far eclipses the number of cases in which something has actually happened. But such cases do

658　Violence and New Religious Movements

exist. Aum Shinrikyō is a prime example. As it became clearer that the group's hopes for a millennialist renovation of the world was unlikely to occur, external opposition grew, and internal defections threatened the integrity of the group, Asahara devised a plan that would simultaneously lash out at a society that had failed to embrace Aum and hasten the apocalyptic end of the world.

Many millennialist groups, like Aum, draw on the violent imagery of biblical books like Daniel and Revelation in which cosmic, natural, social, and religious catastrophes will herald the end of the current world and the dawn of a new one. But for most of them violence remains in the realm of rhetoric. Divine figures will be the ultimate perpetrators of the violence; faithful humans have only to wait and cultivate their personal piety so that they can be worthy of entering the new heaven and the new earth.

In a few cases, however, individuals have turned their millennialist rhetoric into action. Timothy McVeigh (1968–2001), for example, embraced the deeply racist and anti-semitic white supremacist millennialism of William Pierce's (1933–2002) novel, *The Turner Diaries* (1978). McVeigh saw himself as involved in an apocalyptic war for the soul of America and hoped that his 1995 bombing of the Alfred P. Murrah Federal Building in Oklahoma City, which took 168 lives, would ignite the Second American Revolution. A similar zeal for the total renovation of religious and political institutions, particularly the purification of the holy land of Saudi Arabia from the polluting presence of American troops and the restoration of the Islam practiced by the Prophet and his companions, has animated the terrorist activities of al-Qaeda. Both McVeigh and al-Qaeda saw themselves as the initiators of transformation, rather than patient bystanders.

See also: Al-Qaeda; Anticult Movement, The; Aum Shinrikyō; Brainwashing; Children of God/Family International, The; Church of Jesus Christ of Latter-day Saints, The; Cosmotheism; Courts and New Religious Movements; Cult; Deprogramming; FREECOG (Free the Children of God); Heaven's Gate; International Society for Krishna Consciousness (ISKCON); Jonestown; Koresh, David (1959–1993); Law Enforcement and New Religious Movements; Malcolm X (1925–1965); Moon, Rev. Sun Myung (1920–2012); Muhammad, Elijah (1897–1975); Oneida Community, The; Order of the Solar Temple, The; Twelve Tribes, The; Unification Church, The.

Further Reading

Bromley, David G., & J. Gordon Melton, eds. 2002. *Cults, Religion, and Violence*. Cambridge: Cambridge University Press.

Hall, John R, with Phillip D. Schuyler & Sylvaine Trinh. 2000. *Apocalypse Observed: Religious Movements, Social Order, and Violence in Europe, North America, and Japan*. New York: Routledge.

Juergensmeyer, Mark, Margo Kitts, & Michael Jerryson, eds. 2013. *The Oxford Handbook of Religion and Violence*. New York: Oxford University Press.

Lifton, Robert Jay. 1999. *Destroying the World to Save It: Aum Shinrikyo, Apocalyptic Violence, and Global Terrorism*. New York: Henry Holt.

Lincoln, Bruce. 2006. *Holy Terrors: Thinking about Religion after 9/11*, 2nd ed. Chicago: University of Chicago Press.

Wessinger, Catherine. 1999. *How the Millennium Comes Violently: From Jonestown to Heaven's Gate*. New York: Seven Bridges Press.

Wessinger, Catherine, ed. 2000. *Millennialism, Persecution, and Violence: Historical Cases*. Syracuse, NY: Syracuse University Press.

Vivekananda, Swami (1863–1902)

EARLY YEARS AND SPIRITUAL BEGINNINGS

Thirty years before becoming the undisputed star of the World's Parliament of Religion, Swami Vivekananda was born Narendranath Datta in Calcutta in 1863. His family's membership in an upper caste in Hindu society awarded him elite educational opportunities, which he used to pursue his early and burgeoning interest in religion and spirituality. He read voraciously and widely in Hindu scriptures, such as the Vedas, Bhagavad Gita, and the Upanishads, and in Western philosophy, science, and literature.

Gradually, his spiritual interests expanded as he began to participate in esoteric Hindu sects and freemasonry and he sought more immediate access to divine knowledge, through practice and not simply through reading. In 1881, he met Ramakrishna (1836–1886), known for his experience of mystical ecstasy and prophetic visions. In the company of his new guru Ramakrishna, Vivekananda shed the trappings of his previous, cushy life and eventually became a monk.

However, Vivekananda was not content to remain in a monastery and began traveling around India to spread the message of Ramakrishna (a function of the "Ramakrishna Mission") and later the West, a choice that would fundamentally alter the course of his life. Beginning his travels westward in 1893, he traveled to Japan, China, Canada, and the United States, adopting the name "Vivekananda" as he went, which means "bliss of discerning wisdom" in Sanskrit.

RELIGIOUS CELEBRITY AND THE WORLD'S PARLIAMENT OF RELIGION

The World's Parliament of Religion was the brainchild of Charles Bonney (1831–1903). In conjunction with the Chicago World's Fair, Bonney called the Parliament as a way of seeking unity among the many religious traditions of the world. Vivekananda wished to participate as a delegate of Hinduism, failing at first but eventually succeeding in procuring the necessary credentials as a "swami" among Hindu monastics.

Vivekananda took the Parliament by a storm, captivating people with his charisma, his gift for oratory, and his message of Hinduism's inherent inclusivity. He gave a number of speeches over the ensuing weeks of the Parliament, which highlighted the beliefs of Hinduism, while subtly critiquing the West's perception that its (Christian) institutions were superior. His speeches were published swiftly, becoming the resounding message of the Parliament and earning him instant celebrity status.

VEDANTA AND BEYOND

Following his success at the Parliament, Vivekananda undertook an extended lecture tour of the United States and United Kingdom. The lecture tour resulted in the founding of the Vedanta Society in New York in 1894, which, with outposts established after it, effectively became subsidiaries of the Ramakrishna Mission outside of India. Showing his adeptness at understanding the needs of his audience, Vivekananda molded Hindu doctrine to fit the needs of a Western audience, whose fascination with esoteric or occult knowledge was at a height. He emphasized the notion that the human soul had the potential to become divine and that all religious practice should be focused on channeling and harnessing that divinity through focused practice of the mind. He published extensively even as he traveled, gaining a wide audience, particularly in upper-class white society. His followers included actress Sarah Bernhardt (1844–1923), psychologist and scholar of religion William James (1842–1910), and inventor Nikola Tesla (1856–1943). He (among others) popularized the practice of yoga in his 1896 book, *Raja Yoga*, primarily its contemplative and meditative varieties.

Swami Vivekananda was a monk and disciple of Indian guru Ramakrishna. In the late nineteenth century, Vivekananda traveled west, ultimately making a splash at the World's Parliament of Religion in 1893. He founded the Vedanta Society in New York, bolstered by Western interest in the "esoteric" knowledge of Asian religious figures. (L. P. Mercer. *Review of the World's Religious Congresses*. Chicago: Rand McNally & Company, 1893)

Despite his popularity in the West, Vivekananda was a patriot at heart and sought, through his return there in 1897, to build India as a world power on its own and outside of British colonial rule. Though he would return to the United States in 1899, declining health ultimately prompted his return to Calcutta, where he resided at the monastery in Belur and continued to coordinate the work of the Ramakrishna mission. He died on July 4, 1902, reportedly from a stroke, while meditating and after a full day of teaching his disciples. Vivekananda's teachings continue to live on in his writings, which still enjoy circulation, and through the work of the Ramakrishna Mission in India and the Vedanta Society. As a result of his nationalistic views, his birthday, January 12, 1863, is celebrated as a national holiday in India.

See also: Charisma and Leadership in New Religious Movements; Hindu New Religious Movements; Occultism and Esotericism; Ramakrishna Mission; Vedanta Society, The; World's Parliament of Religion, The; Yoga.

Further Reading

Badrinath, Chaturvedi. 2006. *Swami Vivekananda, the Living Vedanta.* India: Penguin Books.

Sen, Amaya, & Narayani Gupta, eds. 2003. *Swami Vivekananda.* New Delhi: Oxford University Press.

Vivekananda, Swami. 2014. *The Complete Works of Swami Vivekananda.* 8 Volumes. Twelfth Edition. Belur Math, Howrah, Indian: Advaita Ashrama.

Vodou

Of the many new religions that emerged in the New World during and after the Atlantic slave trade, none is as notorious—and misunderstood—as Haitian Vodou. While popular culture retails images of voodoo dolls and tales of frightening

Vodou is a tradition that emerged in Haiti among enslaved Africans, particularly those of the Fon-Dahomey kingdom. Vodou involves the invocation of the lwa, intermediary deities or spirits, in order to create balance and harmony in a given community. Vodou rituals often incorporate elements of Catholicism and almost always involve music, drumming, and dancing as indicated by the depiction above of a Togolese Vodou (or Vodun) ceremony. (Siempreverde22/Dreamstime.com)

zombies hungry for human flesh, Vodou as it is actually practiced is a complex religious system that links human beings and the *lwa* (intermediary spirits) in a reciprocal relationship. Practitioners of Vodou serve the *lwa* through various rituals and the *lwa* in turn provide benefits to those with whom they interact. The term Vodou itself, meaning a set of deities, the service of those deities and spirits, and sacred energy, among other things, comes from the Fon-Dahomey African language and culture and came to Haiti with slaves who had been forcibly removed from their homelands.

ORIGINS

Although it is difficult to pinpoint a single origin, Vodou took shape during the late eighteenth century in the French colony of Saint-Domingue on the western third of the Caribbean island of Hispaniola, which is split between what is now Haiti and the Dominican Republic. The French imported enslaved Africans to work on their sugar plantations. With the aim of keeping their slaves docile, the colonial administrators intentionally broke up family and ethnic groups and imposed French Catholicism upon them. Consequently, when reports about "vaudoux" first surfaced, they revealed a blending of religious practices from Fon, Kongo, and other African groups. Vodou tradition holds that on August 14, 1791, a group of slaves met in northern Haiti to sacrifice a wild boar to the African deities and swore to overthrow the French. The developing Afro-Haitian religion thus served as a catalyst for the revolution that would produce Haitian independence, which was formally declared on January 1, 1804.

Independence meant the demise of the plantation system and the slavery that enabled it to flourish. Many newly freed slaves became subsistence farmers and settled in extended family compounds. Those rural compounds, called *lakous* in Haitian creole, became the incubators for the developing religion. Since the *lakous* were not linked into any overarching organization, Vodou, which most accurately refers to a cluster of related religious systems, took a variety of forms as different families focused on different spirits. As Vodou communities formed in urban areas, they were marked more by kinship established by initiation.

PRACTICES AND BELIEFS

Dancing, drumming, and other ritual actions are at the heart of Vodou practice. Ceremonies take place in an *ounfo* or sacred space, which is often a simple outdoor space with a roofed area for rituals. The focal point is a center post or *poto-mitan*, which links the sky, earth, and underworld. The roots of the *poto-mitan* reach all the way to Ginen or Africa, which connects the participants with their distant homelands.

An *oungan* (male) or *manbo* (female) presides over the *ounfo* and its rituals. The primary goal of ritual activity is to invite the *lwa* to visit the assembled community. Uninitiated persons may attend ceremonies, but those who have been initiated an *oungan* or *manbo*, the *ounsis*, claim a special, continuing relationship with the *lwa* and are described as their spouses. Different levels of spiritual insight or ritual knowledge (*konesans*) separate the uninitiated, the *ounsis* ("spouses" of the *lwa*) and the *oungan/manbo*.

Vodou cosmology recognizes a creator God, Bondye, but the deity is manifested in ritual through the various *lwa*. The *lwa* are divided into two major groups, *Rada* and *Petwo*, with the former being identified as "cool" and the latter as "hot" and "fiery." Among the prominent *lwa* are the female Ezili, many of whom have roots in Africa but some of whom have developed in Haiti. For example, Ezili Freda is a romantic *lwa* who loves fine clothing and focuses on attracting men. Ezili Danto is a creole *lwa* also associated with womanhood and eroticism. Both Ezili are associated with the Virgin Mary. Danbala, figured as a python, is believed to have created the world with Bondye; he is the source of energy and life force. Danbala is associated with Saint Patrick. All of the *lwa* have distinct personalities that are manifested when they possess their worshippers.

Reflecting the assimilation of some Catholic elements, ceremonies typically begin with Catholic prayers and invocations of the saints. Then a priest prepares the sacred space and the *oungan* or *manbo* draws the elaborate designs associated with each of the *lwa*, the *vévés*, on the ground. Drumming and singing continue and colorful flags adorned with sparkling sequins, each associated with one of the *lwa*, are waved to attract the spirits' attention. Animal sacrifices are placed on the *vévés* for the *lwa*.

The climax of the ritual is the appearance of the *lwa*. The *lwa* are said to mount humans as a rider mounts a horse and displace their normal consciousness. The *lwa* arrive to partake of the sacrificial sustenance that they need but they also infuse the gathering with their energy. They offer both admonishment and counsel to those who interact with them. Their presence benefits the community just as the community's attention to them sustains the *lwa*. Their interactions keep alive the memory of Africa and demonstrate the continuing power of Ginen in the present.

Vodou has traveled with the Haitian diaspora throughout the world.

In the United States, it has taken root in urban areas, such as New York and New Orleans, wherever there has been a concentration of Haitians. In the process, it has attracted adherents who have no direct connections either to Haiti or to Africa but who see Vodou as a religion open to all.

See also: Candomblé; Race and New Religious Movements; Santería.

Further Reading

Brown, Karen McCarthy. 2001. *Mama Lola: A Vodou Priestess in Brooklyn*. Updated edition. Berkeley: University of California Press.

Desmangles, Leslie G. 1992. *The Faces of the Gods: Vodou and Roman Catholicism in Haiti*. Chapel Hill: University of North Carolina Press.

Joseph, Celucien L., & Nixon S. Cleophat, eds. 2016. *Vodou in the Haitian Experience: A Black Atlantic Perspective*. Lanham, MD: Lexington Books.

Vorilhon, Claude (Raël) (1946–)

The call to prophesy generally comes unexpectedly. Individuals are wrenched out of their daily lives by contact with some sort of extraordinary power and given the task of speaking on its behalf. So it was in late 1973 with Claude Vorilhon, a French motor sports driver and journalist, poet, and singer-songwriter of modest accomplishments.

As he recounts his story, on December 13, 1973, he was walking near a dormant volcano overlooking Clermont-Ferrand in central southern France. He was stretching his legs during a break in a drive for pleasure and aimed to visit a crater named Puy-de-Lassolas, where he had been before for picnics with his family. That time, however, something unprecedented happened. Vorilhon saw a flashing red light through the fog and some sort of craft began to descend toward him. He quickly realized that it was a flying saucer and when it landed he met its inhabitant.

The alien, who stood around four feet tall, had long black hair, a black beard, and wore a green garment. He quickly engaged Vorhilon in conversation, affirming that he had come to earth this time specifically to converse with him. In a brief exchange Vorilhon learned that he had been chosen by the alien for "a very difficult mission" and that he should return the next day with a Bible and a means of taking notes.

The ensuing six-day conversation effectively transformed the relatively nondescript Frenchman into the prophet of a new religious movement. In his personal tutorial, the alien guided Vorhilon through a proper understanding of the Bible, or at least those parts that warrant careful reading. Vorilhon was taught that the true creators of life on earth were a race of advanced beings who live in other worlds. They are the Elohim (singular: Eloha) that the Bible mentions, but the true meaning of the term is "those who come from the sky." The Eloha informed Vorhilon that he had been chosen at a turning point in human history to bring their message to humanity. If humans were to accept that message and conform their lives to its requirements (including building an embassy to welcome the Elohim on their return), they, too, would be able to build a wonderful advanced civilization.

After that first encounter, which was memorialized in a book with the English title *The Book Which Tells the Truth* (1974), Vorilhon was well on the way to adopting the prophetic persona of Raël and becoming both the prophetic inspiration for and the organizational head of a new religion ultimately called the International Raëlian Movement. Raël's status and authority within the movement would continue to be reinforced, especially when he reported an even more extraordinary visit to the home planet of the Elohim in *Extraterrestrials Took Me to Their Planet* (1977).

Raël's message, founded on the charismatic authority bestowed on him through his encounters with the Elohim, has inspired tens of thousands of Raëlians to spread his message to the world, though precise numbers are difficult to determine. The Raëlian movement is organized hierarchically, with Raël at the top as the "Guide of Guides" and under him Bishop Guides, Priest Guides, Regional Guides, Assistant Priests, Organizers, and Assistant Organizers. The Raëlian ethic favors personal responsibility, respect for differences, the establishment of world peace, and the embrace of nonviolence. In accordance with their understanding of creation, Raëlians embrace science, including the production of genetically modified foods. But Raëlians reject the lynchpin of evolution, since it conflicts with their understanding of the work of the Elohim, which has lessened their credibility in scientific circles.

Like the founders of other new religions, Raël has been subject to criticism, including the charge that he plagiarized his writings from multiple sources. Raël's strong criticism of the Catholic Church has also earned him enmity. But the most controversial incident that the Raëlians have been involved in was the announcement in late 2002 by Clonaid, a spinoff from the Raëlian Movement, that a cloned baby girl, named Eve, had been born. The clamor for evidence did not produce anything persuasive, and the credibility of the Raëlian movement was again damaged.

See also: Raëlians, The; UFO Religions.

Further Reading

Palmer, Susan J. 2004. *Aliens Adored: Raël's UFO Religion.* New Brunswick, NJ: Rutgers University Press.

Partridge, Christopher, ed. 2003. *UFO Religions.* New York: Routledge.

Raël 2005. *Intelligent Design: Message from the Designers.* N.p.: Nova Distribution.

Tumminia, Diane G., ed. 2007. *Alien Worlds: Social and Religious Dimensions of Extraterrestrial Contact.* Syracuse, NY: Syracuse University Press.

Waite, Arthur Edward (1857–1942)

Many of the figures in England's occult revival in the late nineteenth and early twentieth centuries interacted with each other, moving from group to group in search of esoteric wisdom and practical rituals that would increase their spiritual mastery. The scholar and practitioner Arthur Edward Waite moved from Spiritualism to the Hermetic Order of the Golden Dawn, which he joined and left after six months in 1891 and then rejoined in 1896.

During his second period of membership in the Order, Waite achieved the second order of initiation in 1899. In the wake of the split within the group in the early 1900s, Waite assumed control over the London Isis-Urania Temple. He established the Independent and Rectified Rite, which steered the Order in the direction of the Christian mysticism that he preferred, as opposed to the ceremonial magic, which was the focus of Samuel Liddell Mathers (1854–1918).

When Waite's version of the Hermetic Order dissolved in 1914, he next established the Fellowship of the Rosy Cross, drawing on the Rosicrucian tradition. That new group jettisoned the focus on ancient Egyptian and other Pagan wisdom that had characterized the original Hermetic Order of the Golden Dawn. In an interpretive strategy similar to the Traditionalist and Perennialist philosophers, Waite instead sought the unified "Secret Tradition" that underlay all Western esoteric systems. He saw the Jewish Kabbalah as representative of that tradition and published several books on it.

Waite's quest for the mystical experience of union with the divine was complemented by his work as a scholar. His translations and original works covered a wide range of subjects. He translated two of the works of the French ceremonial magician Éliphas Lévi (né Alphonse Louis Constant, 1810–1875), *The Mysteries of Magic* (1891) and *Transcendental Magic* (1913). Waite found Lévi to be the most original and interesting interpreter of Western occult philosophy. Waite also wrote about the Kabbalah, Rosicrucianism, Freemasonry, alchemy, and a variety of topics in Christian mysticism. When he died, Waite had produced forty-six monographs; more than forty translated, edited, or introduced works; and scores of shorter pieces. He also devised some forty rituals for the groups that he led.

Today, Waite is most widely known for the Rider-Waite deck of tarot cards, illustrated by Pamela Coleman Smith (1878–1951), a member of the Hermetic Order of the Golden Dawn. In the short volume that he wrote to accompany the cards, Waite argued that the cards offered symbolic presentations of universal ideas.

See also: Crowley, Aleister (1875–1947); Hermetic Order of the Golden Dawn, The; Kabbalah; Lévi, Éliphas (1810–1875); Mathers, Samuel Liddell (1854–1918); Occultism and Esotericism; Rosicrucianism.

Further Reading

Butler, Alison. 2015. "Arthur Edward Waite." In Christopher Partridge, ed., *The Occult World*, pp. 283–287. New York: Routledge.

Gilbert, R. A. 1987. *A. E. Waite: Magician of Many Parts.* Wellingborough, Northamptonshire: Crucible.

Waite, Arthur Edward. 1887. *The Real History of the Rosicrucians.* Available at: https://www.sacred-texts.com/sro/rhr/index.htm.

Waite, Arthur Edward. 1911. *The Pictorial Key to the Tarot.* Available at: https://www.sacred-texts.com/tarot/pkt/index.htm.

Watch Tower Bible and Tract Society, The (Jehovah's Witnesses)

HISTORY

Known best for their persistent door-to-door campaigning, members of the Watch Tower Bible and Tract Society, better known as Jehovah's Witnesses, relish this reputation, if not the accompanying rudeness from those whose thresholds they darken. Yet, they expect such responses, given the nature of their message: that the end of the world is near. Those who do open their doors to Jehovah's Witnesses, however, learn that this apocalyptic message is grounded in a theology of hope.

The nineteenth-century United States was rife with (Christian) millennialism, particularly related to accurately predicting Christ's Second Coming ("Second Advent"). The most well-known instance of this type of date-setting was William Miller's (1782–1849) prediction that the Rapture would occur on October 22, 1844—a nonevent later known as "the Great Disappointment." While Miller's prediction failed, his millennialist beliefs, particularly as they related to a correct reading of the Bible, persisted and were reshaped into a number of different movements. The first, and arguably the most successful, was the Seventh-day Adventists, whose spiritual reinterpretation of Miller's failed prophecy skirted a possible religious crisis. Adventist preachers and writings were in high demand for those searching for a new set of biblical prophecies on which to latch. One such seeker was Charles Taze Russell (1852–1916).

After attending several meetings of Adventists hearing their sermons, in 1869, Russell was drawn to the teachings of Jonas Wendell (1815–1873). Besides taking his own stab at predicting Christ's return (1873), Wendell argued that the Bible did not support a view of eternal hell or of an immortal soul. Inspired by Wendell's interpretation of the Bible and his unorthodox conclusions, Russell founded his own Bible study group, later known as the "Bible student movement." Through his biblical studies, he distanced himself from Adventist teachings, specifically the belief that Christ would come to destroy the earth. Instead, he posited that Christ's death on the cross had atoned for all humanity's sin (thus making such total destruction unnecessary) and that when he did return, Christ would recreate Eden on earth. In fact, he argued that Christ's return would be invisible, since he would make himself known only during the final Battle of Armageddon. Based on calculations from the Bible, Russell argued that Christ had returned in 1874. Following these discoveries, Russell began publishing prolifically to spread his views on Christ's return, on the lack of eternal hell, and on the mortality of the soul.

Realizing that a formal institution was needed to spread his message, Russell and his fellow Bible students formed Zion's Watch Tower Tract Society in 1881; it was legally incorporated as the Watch Tower Bible and Tract Society in 1884. Though originally conceived as a business endeavor, not a formal religious society, as the movement grew, its need for a more formal religious structure evolved apace. Beyond the distribution of literature, Russell instituted a system of traveling preachers or "pilgrims."

Following his death in 1916, Russell was succeeded as president of the Society by Joseph Franklin Rutherford (1869–1942), who further consolidated the Society into a "theocratic structure" thought to mirror God's invisible governance on earth. Though his tenure as president was marked by controversy, it was Rutherford who would emphasize door-to-door preaching by the pilgrims and who would advocate for the name "Jehovah's Witnesses" based on a passage from Isaiah 43:10. Later presidents would continue to institute lasting changes in the church: the further expansion of missionary activity, creation of global branches of the Society, and an increased focus on moral code and proper living. Throughout all of this time, predictions of Christ's return would continue; as each date passed, another would rise to replace it.

BELIEFS AND PRACTICES

The Watch Tower Bible and Tract Society is a form of restorationist Christianity, modeling its beliefs on the apostolic church as revealed in the Bible. For them, the Bible is the final authority on everything. They believe it to be without error, though they are open to both literal and symbolic readings of the text. Jehovah's Witnesses also believe that God's meaning will be revealed gradually through progressive interpretations of the Bible. This evolution in knowledge accounts for the existence of earlier, less developed doctrines, such as the concept of eternal hell.

Accompanying Russell's belief that eternal hell was a fallacy was the idea of restitution. Once again distinct from Adventist beliefs, restitution rested on the idea that after a designated amount of time (originally thought to end in 1914, then adapted) all human beings since Adam would be given the chance to live eternal life on earth. Rutherford altered this doctrine slightly, noting that there were two classes of those given eternal life: the "anointed" and the "great multitude." The anointed were those Jehovah's Witnesses who joined the Society prior to 1935 (thought to correspond to the 144,000 who would survive Armageddon; see Rev. 14:1) and would be immediately resurrected to rule with Christ in God's Kingdom above earth. The great multitude, after a designated amount of time, would be resurrected to live in an earthly paradise.

670 Watch Tower Bible and Tract Society, The

Those of the great multitude enter a state of no-consciousness when they die. Since Witnesses do not believe in the immortal soul, there is no possibility of eternal torment once dead; either one ceases to exist or one is resurrected to live bodily and eternally on earth following the Battle of Armageddon. Satan—though his role is diminished given the lack of hell—has a role to play in the end. Jehovah's Witnesses believe that Satan (and his demonic followers) were cast down to earth from heaven in 1914, marking the beginning of the end of the world. Satan controls all human governments and his primary role is to mislead people and hinder the spread of biblical truth.

Less formal than traditional church services, Witnesses gather twice a week (occasionally more) in Kingdom Halls for "meetings," scheduled and run by church elders. The focus of these meetings is always textual in basis, involving readings from the Bible and the vast library of Watch Tower materials. Relatedly, the primary practice of the Jehovah's Witness is preaching: spreading the word about biblical prophecy by proselytizing in person and distributing the materials published by the Society.

Beyond their reputation as door-to-door evangelists, Jehovah's Witnesses are perhaps best known for what they do not do. Interpreting literally various passages from the Bible that prohibit the consumption of blood (e.g., Lev. 17:14 and Acts 15:28–29), Witnesses to do not accept blood transfusions. Though conflicts have arisen over this issue, this belief has also spurred medical innovations, such as the bloodless transplant. Additionally, Witnesses reject service in the military and patriotic gestures, in general, believing this constitutes idolatry (and allegiance to Satan over God); a similar logic is applied to their sparse liturgical calendar, which celebrates very few holidays (including birthdays).

CHURCH AND CULTURE

As originally intended under Russell, the congregations of the Watch Tower Bible and Tract Society are intended to be quite autonomous. While elements of this remain, such as the lack of formal creed, under Rutherford, the hierarchy became increasingly formalized. The "Governing Body," a group of anywhere between seven to eighteen members (always men), appoints all members of various society committees and oversees the governance of the entire institution and community, from the ninety worldwide branches to the local congregations. Since all Jehovah's Witnesses are tasked with preaching the message of the imminent end of the world, there is no formal clergy. There are those who hold various titles and administrative positions, such as elders who are tasked with presiding over local congregations. Though both men and women are expected to spread the word, most, if not all, official positions within the society are held by men.

According to their website, in 2017, the Watch Tower Bible and Tract Society counted 8.45 million "publishers," the term for anyone publicly baptized and formally converted to the faith, who have spent over two billion hours in the field. The term itself highlights the primary task of Jehovah's Witnesses, which is to aid in the publication and spread of their materials. The Society has published over

220 million copies of *The New World Translation of the Holy Scriptures*, its edition of the Bible, which has been translated into 160 languages. Their global success runs parallel to a history of persecution, particularly during the Holocaust, global legal struggles regarding the right to practice their beliefs, and failed predictions. Hardships aside, the Witnesses remain stalwart and prepared for the end, which they believe will come any day now.

See also: Healing, Health, and New Religious Movements; Millennialism; Miller, William (1782–1849); Millerites, The; Prophecy in New Religious Movements; Russell, Charles Taze (1852–1916); Seventh-day Adventism.

Further Reading

Holden, Andrew. 2002. *Jehovah's Witnesses: Portrait of a Contemporary Religious Movement.* New York: Routledge.

Jehovah's Witnesses. Available at: https://www.jw.org/en/.

Peters, Shawn Francis. 2000. *Judging Jehovah's Witnesses: Religious Persecution and the Dawn of the Rights Revolution.* Lawrence: University of Kansas Press.

Russell, Charles Taze. 1896–1904. *Studies in the Scripture.* Volumes I–VII. Available at: https://archive.org/details/StudiesInTheScripturesVolumes1-7.

White, Ellen G. (1827–1915)

BEGINNINGS AND GREAT DISAPPOINTMENTS

Defying nineteenth-century gender conventions, Ellen Gould White (née Harmon) was one of several women (see, e.g., Mary Baker Eddy (1821–1910)) who rose to religious leadership through alternative religious channels. White experienced a religious conversion in childhood, when, after being hit with a rock in her face, she began to turn her attention from the bodily and physical to the spiritual and heavenly. Plagued with bodily ailments and illness throughout her life, White's focus on the spirit over the material enabled her to have a sense of mastery and power often denied her and would come to characterize much of her religious thought.

In 1840, White and her family became affiliated with William Miller (1782–1849), a millenialist preacher who claimed he knew the precise date of the Rapture (the moment when all believing Christians would be lifted into Heaven; 1 Thess. 4:17). After the proposed date—October 22, 1844—passed (an event known as "The Great Disappointment"), the Millerites disbanded. However, the end of the Millerites marked the beginning of White's visions, which propelled her to religious leadership.

VISIONS AND A NEW CHURCH

In 1844, she experienced her first vision, wherein she ascended to heaven and foresaw Christ's imminent Second Coming ("Advent"). Most of White's visions and the many writings that followed were millennial in nature, focusing on preparing for the imminent end of days. This aligned her with a group of former Millerites, led by Hiram Edson (1806–1882) and her future husband, James White (1821–1881), who had reinterpreted the events of the Great Disappointment. Rather than physical

Rapture, what had occurred was a spiritual Rapture, which marked the end of the period of probation and the beginning of a period of judgment. Since God's judgment was now occurring, this preparation had to involve both spiritual and physical preparation. White's visions spoke to these needs.

Soon after her first visions, she married James White, who would become her greatest advocate and, at times, her publisher, with whom she would have four children. The Whites were among a loose association of people who became known as the Seventh-day Adventists—"Seventh Day" referring to their observing the Sabbath on Saturday and "Adventist" given their central focus on Christ's Return. The movement began to grow in the 1860s, made possible in great part by White's visions, prophecies, and publications.

White would also develop many of Seventh-day Adventism's most distinguishing features, in both theology and practice. Her most famous book, *The Great Controversy between God and Satan*, became a seminal text for the movement. In the book, she described past, present, and future as stages in a great battle between God and Satan, in which the former would ultimately rise victorious. However, it was her focus on temperance in food and drink and proper hygiene that drew the most attention. Since the body needed to be prepared for bodily resurrection at Christ's Second Advent, White proposed that a healthy, mostly vegetarian, diet was necessary. This led to the creation of Adventist sanitariums, which came to form the backbone of the Adventists' institutional structure. She published extensively on this subject as well, most notably her books *Christian Temperance and Biblical Hygiene* and *Healthful Living*.

DEFYING EXPECTATION

Though described as a powerful preacher, it was White's physical comportment when experiencing a vision that seemed to convince people of her authenticity. Witnesses described her as transitioning from a faint to feats of unimaginable strength, ceasing breathing altogether, and staring without blinking for hours. These acts defied the bounds of both her sex and her sickly constitution.

During her lifetime, she produced nearly fifty thousand pages of writing, including over forty books. Her magnum opus, *The Great Controversy*, underwent four editions and sold over half a million copies during her lifetime. White's abstemious lifestyle may have helped her live longer. Continuing to prophesy until the end, she died at home in 1915; her grave is now an Adventist Heritage site.

See also: Eddy, Mary Baker (1821–1910); Healing, Health, and New Religious Movements; Millennialism; Miller, William (1782–1849); Millerites, The; Prophecy and New Religious Movements; Seventh-day Adventism; Women in New Religious Movements.

Further Reading

Numbers, Ronald L. 2008. *Prophetess of Health: A Study of Ellen G. White*, 3rd ed. Grand Rapids, MI; Cambridge, U.K.: William B. Eerdmans Publishing Company.

White, Ellen G. 1858. *The Great Controversy between God and Satan*. Battle Creek, MI: James White.

White, Ellen G. 1890. *Christian Temperance and Bible Hygiene*. Battle Creek, MI: Good Health.

Wicca

Although it is sometimes used interchangeably with terms like Neopaganism or Contemporary Paganism, Wicca also has a more specific meaning. The formation of modern Wicca can be traced to the British colonial administrator, Gerald Gardner (1884–1964). Although Gardner claimed that an ancestor of his had been burned as a witch in 1640 in Scotland, most significant was his claim to have been initiated in 1939 into a surviving coven of the Old Religion of Wicca, which he originally spelled "Wica." Gardner identified his initiating high priestess as "Old Dorothy," (Dorothy Clutterbuck, 1880–1951), but her status as the person who initiated Gardner has been disputed.

Since the Witchcraft laws in England were not repealed until 1951, Gardner originally published a novel giving his account of ancient Wicca, *High Magic's Aid* (1949), under the pen name Scire. With all of his publications, Gardner did much to support what came to be known as the "myth of Wicca." With roots in Margaret Murray's *The Witch-Cult in Western Europe* (1921), the myth held that the pre-Christian religion of Europe had been a form of witchcraft (see www.geraldgardner.com). Despite efforts to stamp it out, it had survived centuries of Christian persecution. Now, it was being revived and its message spread throughout the world. Although the myth of contemporary Wicca being connected to the ancient past by an unbroken chain of transmission initially gained many adherents in contemporary Paganism, it was eventually decisively

Wicca is an eclectic form of contemporary Paganism. Practitioners may use tarot cards and the pentacle in their ritual practice. (Tarah Prout/Dreamstime.com)

disproved both by scholarly practitioners, such as Aidan A. Kelly (1940–), who founded his own Wiccan group, the New Reformed Orthodox Order of the Golden Dawn in 1967, and scholars outside of Paganism, such as Ronald Hutton (1953–).

Despite its uncertain mooring in an ancient past, Gardnerian Wicca attracted many adherents. As Gardner presented it, Wicca was an initiatory mystery religion, with three distinct degrees. Only those in the second or third degree could initiate another person into Wicca and only those in the third degree, High Priestess or Priest, could initiate someone into the third degree. Once initiated, members of a coven would be tutored in the secret knowledge of their group and warned against making it public. Gardner's books, for example, frequently mention that he was only disclosing information that had been permitted by his elders.

Although Gardner claimed that the Wicca he practiced had been handed down to him through an initiatory chain, his distinctive system was clearly influenced by various occult and esoteric currents. He spent some time, for example, with Aleister Crowley (1875–1947) who elevated Gardner to a high level within the Ordo Templi Orientis (OTO). After Crowley's death, Gardner considered himself for a while to be the leader of the OTO in Europe. When Gardner returned to England after his service in the East, he eventually settled in Highcliffe, Hampshire. There he encountered the Rosicrucian Order Crotona Fellowship. A subgroup of those Rosicrucians led him to his initiation by Old Dorothy. Gardner's form of Wicca thus bore traces of his long-standing fascinating with folklore, history, archaeology, occultism, and esotericism, including his belief in reincarnation.

Gardnerian Wicca focuses on a male God of the hunt and a female Goddess of fertility. Covens consist of twelve members, ideally six couples, under a single high priestess. Gardner himself initiated a series of high priestesses, with Doreen Valiente (1922–1999) being the most influential among them. Deriving in part from Gardner's earlier embrace of naturism, Gardnerian rituals were undertaken skyclad, or unclothed. Gardner recorded ritual instructions and other lore in a *Book of Shadows* (see https://www.sacred-texts.com /pag/gbos/index.htm) to which he frequently added. Each initiate was also encouraged to compose a personal Book of Shadows. Specific ritual occasions include the observation of the esbats and sabbats observed by other contemporary Pagans.

Particularly after the 1951 repeal of the British laws against Witchcraft, Gardner was very eager to publicize Wicca. He had moved to the Isle of Man in 1951 to become the "resident witch" at the newly established Folk-lore Center of Superstition and Witchcraft. After a dispute with the original owner, Gardner purchased the museum in 1954. Gardner continued to pursue publicity, even though some of it was negative, purportedly in an attempt to keep the "old religion" from extinction. Gardner's thirst for publicity eventually caused friction in his circle of Wiccans, and some of the dissidents following Valiente decided to separate from Gardner's group and form their own coven.

Gardner's influence can be seen in the many groups that can be traced back to him. Raymond Buckland (1934–2017), for example, claimed to introduce Gardnerian Wicca to the United States in 1964 after having been initiated by Gardnerian High Priestess Monique Wilson (1923–1982) the previous year. Buckland detailed his story in *Witchcraft from the Inside* (1971). He eventually started his own Wiccan tradition, Seax-Wica, which focused on Anglo-Saxon symbolism. Another influential figure in the Gardnerian tradition has been Alex Sanders (1926–1988). Although Sanders claimed to have been initiated into the craft by his grandmother early in his life, he was also initiated into Gardnerian Wicca by another High Priestess, Patricia Crowther (1927–). Like other initiates Sanders went on to found his own tradition, called Alexandrian Wicca. Sanders's wife Maxine later initiated Stewart Farrar (1916–2000). With his wife Janet (1950–), Farrar would establish his own coven and publish extensively.

See also: Crowley, Aleister (1875–1947); Gardner, Gerald (1884–1964); Gender and New Religious Movements; Neopaganism; Ordo Templi Orientis; Rosicrucianism.

Further Reading

Buckland, Raymond. 2001. *Witchcraft from the Inside: Origins of the Fast Growing Religious Movement in America*, 3rd ed. St. Paul, MN: Llewellyn Publishers.

Gardner, Gerald. 1959. *The Meaning of Witchcraft*. Thame, England: I-H-O Books, reprint.

Heselton, Philip. 2012. *Witchfather: A Life of Gerald Gardner*. 2 vols. Loughborough, UK: Thoth Publications.

Hutton, Ronald. 1999. *The Triumph of the Moon: A History of Modern Pagan Witchcraft*. New York: Oxford University Press.

Kelly, Aidan A. 1991. *Crafting the Art of Magic, Book I: A History of Modern Witchcraft, 1939–1964*. St. Paul, MN: Llewellyn Publishers.

Scire (Gerald Gardner). 1949 [1996]. *High Magic's Aid*. Hinton, WV: Godolphin House, reprint.

Women in New Religious Movements

From certain (often comparative) perspectives, the world of new religious movements has been particularly generative for women. Particularly in Abrahamic traditions, such as Christianity, the place of women has been treated with a certain ambivalence: women are touted as paragons of virtue and fortitude, while simultaneously being painted as weak and particularly susceptible to evil. Such interpretations have been historically reinforced in traditional religious institutions. Mounting feminist critiques in the nineteenth century bolstered by the advent of twentieth-century feminist theology has exposed entrenched patriarchy, leading some to seek change within existing institutions and others to seek alternatives. Many new religious movements that are not only populated but initiated by women have provided an alternative space of religious knowing and spiritual advancement outside of historically patriarchal institutions.

WOMEN POWERING NEW RELIGIOUS MOVEMENTS

Since more new religions dissolve than survive, it is particularly notable that several major new religions founded by women are among those considered the greatest success stories among scholars of new religions and practitioners alike.

Spurred by a variety of societal forces—global expansion, scientific innovation, social reform, political upheaval—beginning in the late eighteenth century and gathering steam in the nineteenth and twentieth centuries, women leaders of new religions abounded. As cultural landscapes shifted, so did the views of traditional gender roles, and women's opportunity for advancement and innovation increased exponentially. Ann Lee (1736–1784), better known as Mother Ann, led a small group of Christian sectarians known as the Shakers. Though she did not found the movement, her abilities in prophecy and preaching galvanized the group and sustained them through the transition from England to the United States. Ultimately, she would reveal herself to be the Second Coming of Christ in the flesh, thus initiating the millennium and necessitating the dissolution of traditional marital and sexual relationships (the remaining Shakers remain celibate to this day).

A little more than a half century later, Ellen Gould White (1827–1915) found herself in a similar prophetic and visionary role. White had been a member of the Millerites: a group of millennialist Christians who believed that Christ's Second Coming was imminent. After an event known as "The Great Disappointment," when the expected Rapture failed to occur, former Millerites grappled to understand what had occurred. White was among a small group who argued that a "spiritual Rapture" had occurred and that earth had now entered the period of judgment; this group would become the Seventh-day Adventists. White ascended to leadership status in the movement for her visions, which ultimately produced much of the theological and practical bases of the movement.

White was among a group of new religious leaders who made health and healing central to her religious message. The idea that sacred healing could occur in and through the female bodies, long sites of objectification and scrutiny, was appealing and revolutionary. Perhaps no leader was more engaged in the sacred work of wellness than Mary Baker Eddy (1821–1910) whose movement, Christian Science, grew from her discovery that God was Mind and that all material existence, including disease, was illusory. Like White, Eddy had been plagued by illness during her life and found no relief from modern medicine. After a crippling injury, Eddy consulted the Bible and discovered that the cure for her illness rested in her own mind and in the power of prayer. For women, whose bodies were so often circumscribed by society, the notion that they could have individual control of their bodies—and that their bodies were inherently divine—was a powerful thought. Also like White, Eddy composed her own sacred text in 1875, titled *Science and Health with Key to the Scriptures*, which still serves as the official pastor of all Christian Scientist congregations.

Sectarian Christian movements were not the only religions that grew from female innovation. In 1848, two sisters Kate (1837–1892) and Margaret (1833–1893) Fox experienced a series of unexplained phenomena in their home in Hydesville, New York. They soon discovered that these phenomena resulted from spirits attempting to communicate with the living. Both sisters discovered that they were mediums—those capable of communing with and even serving as conduits for spirits. Many mediums were women, since their perceived vulnerability to the supernatural made them likely sites of spiritual contact; the role awarded them with a degree of status and respect unavailable in many traditional religious systems at that time. The Fox sisters began holding séances to a growing clientele, spawning a religious movement—Spiritualism—which numbered in the millions at its height. Scholars have noted that many Spiritualists became women's rights activists, and vice versa, seeing the clear discrepancy between the equality and power women enjoyed in the movement and the inferior status they experienced outside.

Spiritualism spawned other religious movements, including Theosophy, arguably its most successful offshoot. Helena Petrovna Blavatsky (1831–1891) was a Russian immigrant who began holding séances after being initiating into Spiritualism. Soon, however, the discoveries made while channeling various spirits led her to create her own religion. Blavatsky claimed to be contacted by a group of divine beings, the Great Masters, who had been guiding human beings in their spiritual advancement for millennia. Though she would bear the title of cofounder of the Theosophical Society with Henry Steel Olcott (1832–1907), Blavatsky was the figurehead and spiritual center of the movement.

Both Theosophy and Christian Science would influence Elizabeth Clare Prophet (1939–2009) who, along with her husband Mark (1918–1973) founded the Church Universal and Triumphant. Mark and Elizabeth claimed to be visited by the "Ascended Masters"—the name for the supernatural beings whose initial contact with Guy (1878–1939) and Edna (1886–1971) Ballard spawned the I AM Activity, which was itself an offshoot of Theosophy. After Mark's death, Elizabeth took over as the undisputed leader of the Church, calling herself "Mother," a role she would ultimately divinize as the "Mother of the Flame" of the holy I AM.

NEW RELIGIONS THAT EMPOWER WOMEN

Female leaders of new religious movements presided over religions made up of men and women. However, there are also numerous new religions founded on notions of female empowerment or whose principles ensure that women play a central role in the movement from the hierarchy to the rank-and-file members. The new religious movement most synonymous with female empowerment is Neopaganism and its various offshoots. Neopagans are those who claim descent from or sympathy with ancient Pagan traditions, while also drawing inspiration from modern esoteric and magical traditions, New Age religions, and feminism. Though there are Neopagan traditions that celebrate maleness and male deities, very often the divine feminine and female deities are featured in ritual and belief. Wicca, perhaps the most well-known Neopagan sect, maintains worship of a goddess and a god and emphasizes that all creation, including human beings, bear both masculine and feminine traits. Goddess worship is a Neopagan movement that focuses specifically on the Goddess, both as a divine being and as an entity inherent in all women. Starhawk (1951–), a Dianic Wiccan, is often cited as the founder of the modern Goddess movement, whose book *The Spiral Dance* (1979) was hailed as a feminist religious text that critiqued the stultifying power of patriarchal religion (particularly Christianity) and emphasized the centrality of women to history and Pagan religious practice.

Following in the footsteps of nineteenth-century mediums and Spiritualists, twentieth-century "channels" claimed contact or visitation by supernatural entities or forces. Many of the earliest and most well-known channels were women, including JZ Knight (1946–) who channels Ramtha, an ancient spiritual being hailing from Atlantis. Though Channeling, as a tradition, is not populated exclusively by female channels nor is it traditionally touted as a feminist vehicle (as Spiritualism has been), women share an equal place with men as viable sites of spiritual contact.

It is not only women-driven religions that flip the script on patriarchy. Claude Vorilhon (1946–), better known as Raël, whose religion, Raëlism, maintains that human beings were created in a lab, not born through human reproduction, maintains that women are superior to men. When the Elohim return, women will serve as ambassadors between these divine beings and humanity. Similarly, though he was the exception, Bhagwan Shree Rajneesh (1931–1990) maintained that women are more spiritually advanced than men; men, in turn, were encouraged to develop feminine characteristics, which would make them stronger spiritual beings. Rajneesh populated the highest offices of his religious compound, Rajneeshpuram, with female officers and both men and women took on all roles in the community. Both Raëlism and the Rajneesh movement discouraged procreation so that both men and women could focus on spiritual advancement, thus releasing women from traditional roles of mother and homemaker.

THE SUBJUGATION OF WOMEN IN NEW RELIGIOUS MOVEMENTS

Notwithstanding these female messiahs and leaders and women-focused religions, new religious movements are not somehow free of patriarchy. The sexual and social exploitation of women is a common critique (one often yielded by anti-cult groups) of new religions, particularly when led by a charismatic male figure. David Koresh (1959–1993), leader of the Branch Davidians, after dissolving marital relationships, married numerous women among his followers, including some who were underage. Satchidananda (1914–2002), founder of Integral Yoga, was accused of sexual impropriety with numerous female converts, who claimed that he leveraged spiritual access for sex. Perhaps most egregious of all is NXIVM, whose founder Keith Raniere (1960–) was convicted of sex trafficking in 2019, a case built on the accusations of former recruits who alleged they had been forced into sexual slavery. Thus, women and women's bodies are still often sites of abuse and oppression in religious movements.

However, scholars have rejected typologies of new religious movements that characterize some as "neopatriarchal" and others as "feminist"; most new religions bear a mixture of both. Though Warren Jeffs (1955–) has become synonymous with sexual assault and child abuse, not all Fundamentalist Mormon sects operate in this way; some do not require polygamous marriages at all and many require consent by the woman before a marriage can occur. The "mainstream" Mormon Church practiced plural marriage from 1852–1890, but during that time women were granted the vote and many spoke out about the various ways that plural marriage empowered them by giving them a vital role in their community. The Nation of Islam, often critiqued for its protectionist attitude toward women, is fiercely defended by female members, who see the prescriptions for purity and domesticity as a means of reclaiming respect in a society that often denigrates black women. Though these women are required to wear the veil, they are also encouraged to pursue education and personal and professional advancement.

New religious movements have served as sites of both change and stasis for women over the last few centuries. Women found their voices through religious innovation or found patriarchal tropes reinforced in new forms. New religions often reflect the needs and culture around them and, thus, will continue to engage with questions of gender roles, feminism, and women's rights.

See also: Blavatsky, Helena Petrovna (1831–1891); Channeling; Church Universal and Triumphant, The; Eddy, Mary Baker (1821–1910); Fox, Kate (1837–1892), and Margaret (1833–1893); Fundamentalist Mormons; Gender and New Religious Movements; Goddess Worship; Healing, Health, and New Religious Movements; I AM Activity, The; Integral Yoga; Lee, (Mother) Ann (1736–1784); Mediums; Nation of Islam, The; Neopaganism; Prophet, Elizabeth Clare (1939–2009); Rajneesh, Shree Bhagwan/Osho (1931–1990); *Science and Health with Key to the Scriptures*; Seventh-day Adventism; Spiritualism; Starhawk (1951–); Theosophical Society, The; Theosophy; White, Ellen G. (1827–1915); Wicca.

Further Reading

Braude, Ann. 1989. *Radical Spirits: Spiritualism and Women's Rights in Nineteenth-Century America*. Bloomington: Indiana University Press.

Eller, Cynthia. 1995. *Living in the Lap of the Goddess: The Feminist Spirituality Movement in America*. Boston: Beacon Press.

Palmer, Susan J. 2004. "Women in New Religious Movements." In *The Oxford Handbook of New Religious Movements*. Volume I. New York: Oxford University Press.

Tøllefsen, Inga Bårdsen, & Christian Giudice. 2017. *Female Leaders in New Religious Movements (Palgrave Studies in New Religions and Alternative Spiritualities)*. Basingstoke, UK: Palgrave Macmillan.

Vance, Laura. 2015. *Women in New Religions*. New York: New York University.

World Church of the Creator, The

Creativity is a religious movement founded in 1973 by white supremacist Ben Klassen (1918–1993) as the Church of the Creator. Though he was born into a Mennonite family in Ukraine, Klassen gradually drifted away from Christianity. Eventually, he rejected Christian messages of love for enemies because he thought they contradicted the fundamental human imperative of survival. When he came

680   **World Church of the Creator, The**

to North America, Klassen moved into right-wing circles and became a member of the John Birch Society, but later left because he objected to the society's tolerance for Jews whom he saw as the enemies of the white race. Klassen eventually developed his own religious system based on his study of history and contemporary events.

Klassen saw himself as more a philosopher than an organizer of a movement for white supremacy. Creativity was loosely organized and it was on the verge of disintegration during the early 1990s before his death. Klassen had great difficulty in finding a suitable replacement, and his movement virtually receded back into the white supremacist corner of the cultic milieu. Only with the installment of Matthew Hale (1971–), who assumed formal leadership of the group in 1996 after Klassen's suicide in 1993, did the group reestablish a brief organizational unity. But when Hale was convicted in 2005 of soliciting a murder, the movement again devolved into fragments claiming to represent Creativity.

Klassen saw the white race as locked in a death struggle with its enemies, whom he identified as Jews, blacks, and assorted "mud peoples." Whites, he concluded, needed a religion that would support their necessary efforts to build "a whiter, brighter world." Rather than claiming divine inspiration, Klassen presented his conclusions in works, like *Nature's Eternal Religion* (1973) and *The White Man's Bible* (1981), as the result of a dispassionate examination of the facts of history and the contemporary world. He claimed to have discovered the destiny of his race set by the laws of nature. Creativity is a materialist rather than a supernatural religion that relies on Klassen's understanding of nature as having an end goal: the survival and flourishing of the white race.

Klassen had great ambitions for his works, identifying them as "sacred books." Hale also described them as the "church's bibles." Klassen summed up his teaching in a set of sixteen commandments, ironically modeled on the ten from the Hebrew Bible but having a very different substance. Klassen's commandments echo the sentiments in the "fourteen words" coined by a member of the white supremacist group The Order, David Lane (1938–2007), and widely recognized by white supremacists: "We must secure the existence of our people and a future for white children." The similarity shows how Creativity has been immersed in the overlapping subcultures of the radical right.

In Klassen's imagination, eventually, the membership of the Church of the Creator and the White Race would completely overlap. Creativity would become the religion of everyone on the planet once it had been purged of other, lesser, racial groups. The White Race itself constitutes the sacred for Klassen; it is the highest expression of Nature's plan, and since there is nothing that transcends Nature, it holds ultimate value and significance.

The vitriolic denigration of non-whites, the insistent oppositional exclusiveness of Klassen's ideology, and his advocacy for RaHoWa (Racial Holy War), despite Klassen's and Hale's frequent emphases that they only needed to change white people's minds, gave Creativity's rhetoric a violent edge. It is thus not surprising that members of the group in good standing and former members have been involved in multiple violent incidents. Although many plots to commit violence were foiled by law enforcement, on the July 4 weekend in 1999, Benjamin Smith

(1978–1999) conducted a series of shootings in Illinois and Indiana that eventually left two people dead and nine injured. Although Smith claimed that he had resigned from the Church of the Creator because he could not abide by its policy of peacefully attempting to change white people's minds, he was clearly influenced by the writings and statements of both Klassen and Hale.

See also: Christian Identity; Cosmotheism; Race and New Religious Movements.

Further Reading
Klassen, Ben. 1973. *Nature's Eternal Religion.* Milwaukee, WI: The Milwaukee Church of the Creator.

Klassen, Ben. 1981. *The White Man's Bible.* Milwaukee, WI: The Milwaukee Church of the Creator.

Klassen, Ben. 1991. *Against the Evil Tide: An Autobiography.* Otto, NC: The Church of the Creator.

Michael, George. 2009. *Theology of Hate: A History of the World Church of the Creator.* Gainseville: University Press of Florida.

World's Parliament of Religion, The

Physical remnants of the 1893 World's Fair and Columbian Exposition still adorn the landscape of Chicago, Illinois. Though less well known, the World's Parliament of Religion held in conjunction with the World's Fair has had equally long-lasting and, arguably, farther reaching effects than the Fair itself. Instead of an exhibition on the variety and innovation of the world's cultures, the World's Parliament brought together representatives of various world religions, such as Sikhism, Hinduism, Islam, Jainism, Buddhism, and homegrown new religions such as Spiritualism, and Christian Science, among others. These representatives gathered together from September 11 to 27, giving speeches along the way that combined their desire to educate, welcome, and, either explicitly or implicitly, proselytize to a rapt audience.

The World's Parliament was the brainchild of Charles Carroll Bonney (1831–1903) and represented a confluence of several global religious trends. First, it represented the burgeoning field of comparative religions. In both scholarly and liberal Christian circles, the project of comparative religions sought commonalities between religions, while simultaneously setting up Western religions as the most advanced and universal. Second, given the interest generated by Swami Vivekananda (1863–1902), a Hindu monk and breakout star of the Parliament, there was a clear pattern of Western fascination with the "occult" and "esoteric" traditions of the East. Third, the Parliament foretold the future impact of globalization: the common availability of innumerable religious ideas, texts, peoples, and movements.

The World's Parliament was deemed a resounding success and many of its stars remained in the United States, traveling the country on lecture circuits and even founding new religions along the way (such as the Vedanta Society). This moment of triumph for religions like Hinduism, Buddhism, Islam, in addition to their various sects and offshoots, was marred in the decades to come by anti-immigrant sentiment in the United States that produced prohibitive immigration laws, such as the Johnson-Reed Act (1924). These "old" religions were treated as "new" and "other" in the American context, even despite the ecumenism espoused by the World's Parliament of Religion.

However, following changes to immigration law in 1965 and an explosion of interest in world religions, the ethos of the World's Parliament experienced a renaissance. Beginning its centennial celebration in 1993, the World's Parliament was reborn, meeting more frequently (every four or five years) and in locations outside of the United States, such as Cape Town, South Africa and Toronto, Canada, while focusing on common themes of unity and universality in the face of divisive forces at work in the modern world.

See also: Globalization and New Religious Movements; Occultism and Esotericism; Vedanta Society, The; Vivekananda, Swami (1863–1902).

Further Reading

Barrows, John Henry. 1893. *The World's Parliament of Religion: An Illustrated and Popular Story of the World's First Parliament of Religions, held in Chicago in connection with the Columbian Exposition of 1893.* London: Review of Reviews Office.

Seager, Richard Hughes. 2009. *The World's Parliament of Religion: The East/West Encounter, Chicago, 1893.* Bloomington: Indiana University Press.

Vivekananda, Swami. 1893. "Sisters and Brothers of America." Available at: https://www.dnaindia.com/india/report-telling-the-world-about-hinduism-full-text-of-swami-vivekananda-s-historic-speech-in-1893-2164870.

Yoga

In the twenty-first century, yoga is everywhere. Synonymous with a more intentional, holistic, "Eastern" trend in modern fitness, yoga is practiced by millions of people who vary in their spiritual motives and degree of knowledge about the deeply religious origins of the practice. And the story of yoga's evolution from ancient Hindu discipline to global cultural phenomenon is definitively entwined with the creation and proliferation of various new religions.

EASTERN ORIGINS

Though the term "yoga" (translated as "to join or yoke") first appeared centuries before, yoga was popularized in India by the Yoga Sutras written by Hindu scholar Patanjali (whose dates of birth and death are disputed) around the turn of the Common Era. Yoga refers variously to a discipline, a school of philosophy, a particular religious tradition, bodily and mental techniques, or the goal of yoga itself (known as "raja" yoga); all relate, in some way, to the goal of release from the wheel of samskara or the endless cycle of birth, death, and reincarnation.

In Hinduism, most often yoga refers to a specific "path" or method of yoga, such as bhakti yoga (the path of worship), jnana-yoga (the path of knowledge), karma-yoga (the path of action), and hatha yoga (the path of force or physical technique). Each path can employ a variety of techniques to achieve the end of liberation, such as meditation, repetition of mantras, charitable work, physical discipline, and study of sacred Sanskritic texts. Depending upon the type of yoga, its methods may be practiced by monastic adepts alone (such as tantric yoga) and it is often transmitted on a one-to-one basis from guru to disciple. Both Buddhism and Jainism employ yoga in their religious practice as well.

COMING WEST

During the nineteenth and twentieth centuries, interest in the culture and religions of Asia was on the rise. Fueled by events such as the World's Parliament of Religion in 1893 and the lifting of restrictive immigration laws in 1965, yoga was brought to the West. Figures such as Swami Vivekananda (1863–1902) and Yogananda (1893–1952) introduced Hinduism to an audience clamoring for Asian religious ideas and techniques, so much so that Western branches of their brands of

Yoga is ubiquitous in contemporary society, though before it became synonymous with modern wellness, exercise classes (as depicted above), and a fascination with Asian religious life and culture, it was popularized as a Hindu practice of spiritual advancement. Practitioners of yoga choose from a variety of paths, some involving worship and others meditation or physical practice, but the aim is always release from the wheel of samskara, or the eternal cycle of birth, life, and death. (Hongqi Zhang /Dreamstime.com)

yoga soon arose: the Vedanta Society and the Self-Realization Fellowship, respectively. There were also those like Pierre Bernard (1875–1955), later "The Great Oom," who traveled to India and returned to the United States with religious knowledge that he transformed in the Tantrik Order.

The difference between those like Vivekananda and those like Bernard is clear: one is born a Hindu and hails from India, the other adopted a Hindu practice later in life. This can often lead to critiques regarding the authenticity of Hindu religious practices peddled by white Westerners. However, Vivekananda and Bernard are similar in the fact that they adapted yoga to fit their specifically Western audience. The Vedanta Society emphasized the importance of individual practice and spiritual catharsis, downplaying the more devotional and communal aspects of yogic practice. The Tantrik Order highlighted the sexual and esoteric aspects of tantric yoga, thereby appealing to those who wished for secret access to exotic practices. The modern varieties of yoga are numerous and arise from a variety of sources and interpretations, each of which claims to be a genuine manifestation of an ancient practice.

Interest only grew in the latter half of the twentieth century, culminating in the counterculture of the 1960s and 1970s when droves of "hippie" religious seekers turned to Eastern religion as an alternative to the Abrahamic religions of their context. Over time, general interest in yoga turned secular as many grew interested in the emotional and bodily benefits of yoga without pursuing it for religious ends. Yoga has also been subsumed into the general "Spiritual but not Religious" culture as one of many paths to spiritual enlightenment and truth. Today, a simple Google search will produce millions of hits for books, studios, ashrams, retreats, and fitness channels. For a term that was relatively unknown in the Western Hemisphere 150 years ago, its popularity and ubiquity is remarkable.

See also: Hindu New Religious Movements; International Society for Krishna Consciousness (ISKCON); Ramakrishna Mission; Self-Realization Fellowship (Yogananda); Spiritual but Not Religious; Tantrik Order, The; Vedanta Society, The; Vivekananda, Swami (1863–1902).

Further Reading

Jain, Andrea. 2015. *Selling Yoga: From Counterculture to Pop Culture*. Oxford; New York: Oxford University Press.

Miller, Barbara Stoler. 1995. *Yoga: Discipline of Freedom*. The Yoga Sutra *Attributed to Patanjali*. Berkeley: University of California Press.

Singleton, Mark, & Ellen Goldberg, ed. 2014. *Gurus of Modern Yoga*. Oxford; New York: Oxford University Press.

Yogi, Maharishi Mahesh (1918–2008)

Maharishi Mahesh Yogi was born Mahesh Prasad Varma in India. Like the lives of many Hindu ascetics, his early years are shrouded in mystery. However, the pivotal point in his life came in 1941 when he began serving as the secretary to Swami Brahmananda Saraswati (1868–1953), later called Guru Dev, a sannyasi, or one who had renounced professional life and material wealth. Even though he was a favorite pupil, Mahesh could not become his spiritual master's successor because he was not born in the Brahmin caste. Nonetheless, before he died, Guru Dev tasked Mahesh with spreading his message and teaching meditation throughout the world.

Throughout the 1950s and 1960s, beginning in India and then in Europe and the United States, Mahesh toured the world, spreading what would be called Transcendental Meditation (TM). Around this time, he assumed the name "Maharishi," which means "seer" and "Yogi," which means one who practices yoga. Called the Maharishi by his growing group of devotees, he came to fame when several famous individuals affiliated with the Maharishi, and publically practiced and proclaimed the gospel of TM. Most famous were the Beatles, for whom the Maharishi served as spiritual adviser. Soon thereafter, the Maharishi appeared on late night talk shows, the news, and magazine covers.

As his fame grew, so did the demand for TM and the diminutive Yogi himself. In response, the Maharishi published prolifically, including his own translation and commentary on the Bhagavad Gita. *Science of Being and Art of Living* was his best-selling book and is published in over a dozen languages. He also focused on educating future teachers of TM, holding courses in Europe and the United States. In 1972 he announced his plan to open thirty-six hundred centers for TM. He continued to tour, announcing the advance of the "Age of Enlightenment," a postmillennial period of peace and joy that would occur as more people came to the truth of TM. Eventually, he settled in the Netherlands, which would serve as the international headquarters of the TM movement and from where he broadcast his message until his death in 2008.

The Maharishi died weeks after his ninetieth birthday at his home in the Netherlands; both his funeral and burial were conducted in India. Dubbed the "Giggling Guru," he was remembered as a warm and welcoming person who lived the life of an ascetic without pretension or judgment. He or his likeness have featured in many pop cultural forms, including popular songs, films, and satires.

See also: Charisma and Leadership in New Religious Movements; Hindu New Religious Movements; Millennialism; New Age, The; Transcendental Meditation; Yoga.

Further Reading

Olson, Helena. 2001 [1967]. *Maharishi Mahesh Yogi: A Living Saint for the New Millennium: Stories of his First Visit to the U.S.A.* College Park, MD: Samhita Productions.

Yogi, Maharishi Mahesh. 1990 [1967]. *Maharishi Mahesh Yogi on the Bhagavad-Gita: A New Translation and Commentary, Chapters 1–6.* New York: Penguin Group.

Yogi, Maharishi Mahesh. 2001 [1963]. *Science of Being and Art of Living; Transcendental Meditation.* New York: Penguin Books.

Z

Zionist Churches (Africa)

Zion has long been a potent symbol in the Jewish and Christian traditions. Originally referring to a specific hill in the ancient city of Jerusalem (see 2 Sam. 5:7), by extension the term has been used to refer to the whole of Jerusalem, the land of Israel, the Jewish people (as in the phrase "daughters of Zion"), and also the world to come. Many religious movements have used the symbolism of Zion to depict ideal situations. The Church of Jesus Christ of Latter-day Saints, for example, has used "Zion" to refer to a place where the Saints are gathered, such as the Salt Lake Valley. The Rastafari contrasts Zion to Babylon and long to inhabit the utopia it describes.

The Zionist Churches that appeared in southern Africa in the latter stages of the nineteenth century also capitalized on that powerful symbolism. Zionism (distinct from the modern Jewish political movement) actually came to southern Africa from the United States. John Alexander Dowie (1847–1907), who was born in Scotland and later moved to Australia, came to the United States in 1893 for the Chicago World's Fair. Dowie had founded the International Divine Healing Association in 1887 and held healing meetings on the periphery of the Fair.

Dowie decided to stay in the Chicago area and at the end of 1899 established the intentional community of Zion City midway between Chicago and Milwaukee. Dowie welcomed people of all ethnicities, particularly the working-class and poor, to Zion City and promoted a sober lifestyle, including avoidance of drugs, alcohol, tobacco, gambling, pork, among other things. Dowie's acceptance of everyone and focus on healing attracted some six thousand residents by 1904. Dowie wrote about his work in the periodical *Leaves of Healing*, which gained an international readership.

The positive reception of *Leaves of Healing* in southern Africa led to the dispatching of missionaries from Dowie's Christian Catholic Apostolic Church to South Africa. There they worked with white South Africans to missionize the black population. The emphasis on healing and universalism proved equally attractive in South Africa, though eventually the white missionaries retreated from the scene and an array of Zionist churches under indigenous black leadership took shape, some of which had started before the arrival of the U.S. missionaries. For native Africans, Zion symbolized a refuge or shelter from life's harsh realities, including the racial oppression to which they were subjected, the possibility of a supportive utopian community directly in contact with God, and the revivification of the traditional homestead that sustained members of an extended family.

Zionist churches focus on this-worldly experiences of healing, blessing, and protection from evil. Doctrine is often not fully elaborated and varies from one church to another. African Zionist churches, like Dowie's Zion City, promote a conservative morality. Baptism of adults by threefold immersion in flowing water is an important ritual. It is common to see Zionists at rivers or by the sea, enacting ritual baptisms. Zionist services typically include singing hymns, prayer, preaching, and testimonies of healing. Prophets do the work of healing and pastoral care. One form of healing ritual involves members of the community laying hands on the petitioner, either by gently patting or jostling as a sign of support and (re)integration into the community.

Of the many Zionist churches, the Zion Christian Church is South Africa's largest, with some sixteen million members worldwide. It was formally founded in late 1924 or early 1925 by Engenas Barnabas Lekganyane (c. 1885–1948). In 1910, while he was training to become an Anglican missionary, Lekganyane had a dream in which he was instructed to found a new church that would heal and baptize. Lekganyane did not act immediately on his dream but soon sought healing from the Apostolic Faith Mission, which had been founded by a Boer South African and two of Dowie's missionaries who had also participated in the Azusa Street Pentecostal revival. He was then baptized and eventually joined a splinter group called the Zion Apostolic Church, later leaving that group to become part of the Zion Apostolic Faith Mission in 1920. Disagreements with church leadership finally led Lekganyane to establish the Zion Christian Church in 1924/1925.

Lekganyane's church does not use the white robes that so many Zionist groups wear. For ritual purposes, they adopt military attire and for everyday use they identify themselves with a silver star against a black cloth background pinned to their lapels. Rituals take place in the open air and the church has few dedicated buildings. The church has, following the example of Dowie, established its own Zion City in Moria, around fifty kilometers from Pietersburg in the Northern Transvaal. Members are expected to visit Moria at least once a year and more than a million do so, with Easter being a popular time.

Lekganyane died without naming a successor and his two surviving sons each ended up leading a faction of the church, with Edward (1928–1967) forming the larger group. Edward was more an administrator than a prophet and he helped spread the church throughout South Africa and build Moria into a true city. On his death he was succeeded by his son Barnabas (1954–) who continues to serve as bishop.

See also: African New Religious Movements; Church of Jesus Christ of Latter-day Saints, The; Church of the Lord (Aladura); Globalization and New Religious Movements; Healing, Health, and New Religious Movements; Kimbangu, Simon (1887–1951); Pentecostalism; Rastafari; Shembe, Isaiah (1865–1935).

Further Reading

Anderson, Allan H. 1999. "The Lekganyanes and Prophecy in the Zion Christian Church." *Journal of Religion in Africa* 29: 285–312.

Cabrita, Joel 2017. "Revisiting 'Translatability' and African Christianity: The Case of the Christian Catholic Apostolic Church in Zion." *Studies in Church History* 53: 448–475.

Zionist Churches (Africa)   689

Eyre, Ronald 1977. "The Long Search: African Religions; Zulu Zion." TV series. London: British Broadcasting System.

Sundkler, Bengt 1976. *Zulu Zion and Some Swazi Zionists*. New York: Oxford University Press.

Tishken, Joel, & Andreas Hauser 2015. "'Africa Always Brings Us Something New'; A Historiography of African Zionist and Pentecostal Christianities." *Religion* 45: 153–173.

Index

Note: Page numbers in **bold** indicate the location of main entries. Page numbers in *italics* indicate photos and illustrations.

Adi Da Samraj, **1–2**
  Adidam movement, 2, 93
  as the Bright (ultimate Divine Reality), 1–2
  early years, 1
  The Gnosticon, 2
  Hindu gurus and, 1–2
  identity formation and self-mythologizing of, 1
  influences on, 1
  transfer of charisma from prophet to book, 2, 93
Aetherius Society, the, **2–4**
  as audience cult, 4
  Cosmic Missions, 3
  history and founding, 2–3
  Jesus and, 3, 444, 625, 629
  King, George, and, xxxiii, xxxiv, 2–3, 444, 547, 624
  New Lord's Prayer, 3–4
  in Nigeria, 8
  teachings and practices, 2–4, 547
  The Twelve Blessings, xxxiv, 3, 444, 624–625
  as UFO religion, 624–625
African new religious movements, **4–8**
  Boko Haram, 6
  Candomblé, 8
  Chrislam, 6
  Christian movements, 7
  in Ghana, 8
  Islamic movements, 5–6
  Nazareth Baptist Church (South Africa), xxxii, 7, 577–578
  in Nigeria, 5–6, 8

  in South Africa, 7
  See also Candomblé; Zionist Churches (Africa)
Ahmadiyya movement, the, **8–11**
  Ahmad, Mirza Ghulam, and, 8–10, 384
  Ahmad, Mirza Masroor, and, 9
  beliefs and practices, 9–10
  caliphs, 9
  controversy and culture, 10
  conversion and, 8, 9, 129, 420
  death of Mirza Ghulam Ahmad, 9
  history and origins, 8–9
  messianism and, 8–9, 384
  millennialism and, 9
Alamo, Tony, **11–12**
  Alamo, Susan (Edith Opal Horn), and, 11
  beliefs and practices, 11–12
  choice of name, 11
  early years, 11
  Jesus and, 11
  police raid and sex trafficking conviction, 12, 351
  Tony Alamo Christian Ministries, 11
Ali, Noble Drew, **12–13**
  beliefs and teachings, 12–13, 218, 399–400
  death of, 13, 400–401
  early years, 12
  founding of Moorish Science Temple of America, xxxii, 12, 399
  Freemasonry and, 218
  The Holy Koran of the Moorish Science Temple of America (primary document), 401–404

692   Index

Ali, Noble Drew (*Continued*)
  See also Moorish Science Temple of
    America, the
Al-Qaeda, **13–15**
  affiliates, 14, 306
  beliefs and practices, 14
  bin Laden, Osama, and, 13–14
  history and origins, 13–14
  influence of Sayyid Qutb, 14
  ISIS and, xxxviii, 305–306, 307
  9/11 and, 14–15, 532, 655, 658
  Salafism and, 14, 531, 532
  al-Zawahiri, Ayman, and, 14
Amana Society, **15–16**
  beliefs and practices, 15–16
  German Pietism and, 15–16, 647
  history and founding, xxx, 15, 647
  marriage and, 16
  split into Amana Church Society and
    Amana Society, 16, 647
  utopianism and, 647
American Psychological Association,
  xxxvii, 25, 69, 130, 290, 579
Amish, the, **16–19**
  Amish farmer, *17*
  Amish Mennonites, 17
  Amman, Jakob, and, xxix, 17
  baptism, 18
  beliefs and practices, 16, 18
  Breaking Amish (television program), 19
  community unity, 18
  in contemporary culture, 18–19
  history and origins, xxix, 17
  internet technology and, 440
  Old Order Amish, 17
  Pennsylvania Dutch language, 18
  sects and communities, 17–18
  self-sufficiency and isolation, 18
  Witness (film), 18–19
Anamadim, **19–20**
  Ana's Creed, 20
  eating disorders and, 19–20
  history and origins, 19
  Pro-Ana websites, 19–20
  Project Shapeshift and, 19
  Thin Commandments, 20
Anthroposophy, **20–22**
  Anthroposophical Society, xxxii, 22
  beliefs and practices, 21, 464
  criticism and controversy, 21–22
  history and origins, xxxii, 21, 591

Kandinsky, Wassily, and, 34
modern environmental movement and,
  22, 185–186, 207
Nazism and, 21–22
Steiner, Rudolf, and, xxxii, 21–22, 185,
  464, 591
Theosophy and, 20–21, 185, 464, 591
Anticult movement, the, **22–25,** *148,*
  149–150
  Aum Shinrikyō and, 41
  Brahma Kumaris and, 66
  brainwashing and, 68–69, 130–131
  CESNUR and, 85
  charisma and, 93
  children and, 98, 99
  Christianity and, 149
  Church of Jesus Christ of Latter-day
    Saints and, 23
  Citizens Engaged in Reuniting Families
    and, 23
  conspiracy theories and, 127–128
  contemporary anticult movement, 24–25
  conversion and, 131
  countercult movements, 23–24
  The Cult Project and, 282
  deprogramming and, 24–25, 142, 150,
    160–161
  exit counseling and, 190
  gender and, 66
  Hassan, Steven, and, 253
  history of, 22–23
  I Am Activity and, 280
  Info-Cult/Info-Secte and, 282, 283
  INFORM and, 285–286, 287
  insider/outsider problem and, 289, 290
  International Society for Krishna
    Consciousness and, 23, 24, 299,
    301–302
  Judaism and, 23–24
  Landmark Forum and, 346
  Love Israel Family and, 358
  propositions of, 24–25
  Satanic Panic and, 128
  Shakers and, 22–23
  Unification Church and, 23, 24, 98,
    130–131, 340
  See also Cult Awareness Network;
    FREECOG (Free the Children of
    God); International Cultic Studies
    Association, the (the American
    Family Foundation)

Index

Anti-semitism
Christian Identity and, 109, 110, 508, 620
Farrakhan, Louis, and, 198
National Youth Alliance and, 133
Odinism and, 466, 467
Paganism and, 429
The Protocols of the Elders of Zion, 109
Silver Legion of America and, 55
The Turner Diaries and, 658
white supremacy and, 508
World Church of the Creator and, 508
Apostates, **25–27**
of Church of Jesus Christ of Latter-day Saints, 26
of Church of Satan, 26
of Church of Scientology, 26
definition of, 25
ISIS and, 25–26, 305, 306
of new religious movements, 26, 165–166
reasons for apostasy, 26
of Theosophy, 26
See also Disaffiliation and ex-membership in new religious movements
Applewhite, Marshall, and Bonnie Lu Nettles, **27–32**
beliefs and teachings, 27–29, 259–260
Christian Arts Center, 27, 28, 258
death of Bonnie Lu Nettles, xxxvi, 29, 260
death of Marshall Applewhite, 29–30, 95, 261
as "Do" and "Ti," 28–29
early years and backgrounds, 27, 258
'88 Update (pamphlet by Applewhite), 30, 260
identification with "two witnesses," 27–28, 29, 258, 260
Know Place (retreat center), 27, 28, 258
"Last Chance to Evacuate Earth before It's Recycled" (edited videotape transcript by Applewhite) (primary document), 30–32
millennialism and, 28
mysticism and, 417
See also Heaven's Gate
Aquino, Michael, xxxvi, 121–122, 538, 601–602
Art and new religious movements, **32–35**

abstract and modern art, 32, 34
art as spiritual practice, 32–33
art historians and critics, 33
Bosch, Hieronymus, 32
Catholicism, 32
Chagall, Marc, 32
Christian Science, 34–35
En Joong, Kim, 32
Federation of Damanhur (Italy), 33
Houghton, Georgiana, 34
Judaism, 32
Kandinsky, Wassily, 34
Klint, Hilma, 34
Malevich, Kazimir, 33
Mathieu, Georges, 32
Michelangelo, 32
new religious movements' influence on artists, 33–35
Theosophy, 33–34
Asahara, Shoko, **35–36**
Agonshū member, 35, 312
beliefs and prophecies, 35–36, 39–40
charisma and, 92
conspiracy theories and, 127
early years, 35
founding of Aum Shinrikyō, xxxvii, 35–36, 38–39
messianism and, 386
millennialism and, 35–36, 312, 658
Tokyo subway sarin attack (1995), xxxvii, 36, 38, 40–41, 127, 142, 312, 386, 472, 655
trial and execution of, 36, 40, 142
violence and, 656, 658
See also Aum Shinrikyō
Ásatrú, **36–38**
Ásatrú Alliance, 38
Ásatrú Free Assembly (later Ásatrú Folk Assembly), 37–38, 467
beliefs and practices, 36
ethnicity and, 36–37
groups and organizations, 37–38
history of, 36
Icelandic Ásatrú Fellowship, 38
Odinism and, 466, 467
Odinist Fellowship, 37, 38
Paganism and Neopaganism, 36–38, 429
white supremacy and, 508
Wolfling Kindred (group), 38
Yggdrasil (tree of life), 36, *37*

694 Index

Asian Exclusion Act, repeal of, 1, 148
Association for Research and
 Enlightenment (ARE), xxxiii, 84. *See
 also* Cayce, Edgar
Asuza Street Revival, xxxi, 7, 484–485,
 569
Aum Shinrikyō, **38–41**
 history and founding, xxxvii
 millennialism and, 35–36, 38–39, 41, 92,
  312, 389, 658
 Tokyo subway sarin attack (1995),
  xxxvii, 36, 38, 40–41, 127, 142, 312,
  386, 472, 655
Aurobindo, Sri, **41–43**
 beliefs and teachings, 42–43
 collective meditation at Auroville
  ashram, *42*
 death of, 43, 267
 early years, 41–42
 founding of first ashram in India, xxxii
 Integral Yoga and, 291–292
 The Life Divine, 42
 Richard, Mira, and, 42–43, 267, 291
 Sri Auroville Ashram, xxxv, 43
 The Synthesis of Yoga, 42
Ayahuasca, **43–45**
 Harner, Michael J., and, 575
 Irineu, Mestre (Raimundo Irineu Serra),
  and, 44–45
 Santo Daime and, 44, *44*
 uses and forms, 43

Baba, Meher, **47–49**, *48*
 "Baba O'Riley" (The Who), 48
 beliefs and teachings, 47–48
 on drug use, 48
 early years, 47
 first visit to United States, xxxiii
 on Real Control, 48
 on Real Existence, 47, 48
 on Real Knowledge, 48
 on Real Love, 47
 on Real Renunciation, 47–48
 on Real Sacrifice, 47–48
 on Real Surrender, 48
 vow of silence, xxxii, 47
Babism, **49–51**
 beliefs and practices, 49–50
 execution of the Báb, xxx
 messianism and, 49–50

millennialism and, 49–50
origins and history, 49
Shia Islam and, 49, 50
Siyyid 'Alí Muhammad announces
 himself as Báb, xxx
Bahá'í, **51–54**
 Babism and, 49, 50
 beliefs and practices, 51–53
 dual branches of, 53
 institutions and culture, 53
 mission of Bahá'u'lláh begins, xxx
 origins and background, xxx, 51
 in popular culture, 53
Bainbridge, William Sims, 150, 151, 551
Ballard, Edna, 55, 124, 213, 279, 280, 677
Ballard, Guy W., **54–58**
 beliefs and teachings, 54–55, 279–280
 Church Universal and Triumphant and,
  124, 125
 controversy and prosecution, 213–214,
  280, 497
 death of, 55
 early years and influences, 54
 founding of I Am Activity, xxxiii,
  54–55, 124, 237, 279, 497, 677
 "Guy Ballard's Initial Encounter with
  Saint Germain" (primary document),
  55–58
 Saint Germain and, xxxii, 54–57, 124,
  237, 279, 280, 497
 See also I AM Activity, the
Beats, 1, 241
Berg, David Brandt, 100–103, 152, 159,
 214–215, 447, 656. *See also* Children of
 God (the Family International)
Berg, Philip, xxxiv, 325, 416
Bernard, Pierre, xxxi, 464, 565–566,
 599–600, 684
Bey, Hakim, **58–59**
 beliefs and teachings, 58
 criticism and controversy, 58
 early years and travels, 58
 on pederasty, 58
 Sufism and, 58, 595
 on temporary autonomous zones (TAZ),
  58
Bin Laden, Osama, 13–14, 306
Black Judaism, **59–61**
 Beth B'Nai Abraham (New York City),
  xxxii, 60

Crowdy, William Saunders, and, 59–60
Ford, Arnold Josiah, and, 60
Matthew, Wentworth Arthur, and, 60
Blavatsky, Helena Petrovna, **61–63**, *62*
Anthroposophy and, 21–22
beliefs and teachings, 61–63, 608–610
Cayce, Edgar, and, 84
death of, 63, 321, 608
early life, 61
founding of Theosophical Society, xxx,
61–62, 209, 227, 237, 239–240,
606–607
fraud and deception, 213
Isis Unveiled, 62–63
Judge, William Quan, and, 320–321
later years and legacy, 62–63
Lévi, Éliphas, and, 356
Mathers, Samuel Liddell, and, 371
as medium, 374, 464, 608
Olcott, Henry Steel, and, 468, 469
Ouspensky, P. D., and, 477
The Secret Doctrine, 63
Spiritualism and, 61–62, 587–588, 677
Steiner, Rudolf, and, 592
Boko Haram, 6
Book of Mormon, The, **63–66**
content and reception, 65–66
revelation and translation, 63–65
Brahma Kumaris, **66–67**
beliefs and practices, 66
Brahma Kumaris World Spiritual
University, 67
Dada Lekhraj and, xxxiii, 66
environmentalism and, 67
Hinduism and, 66, 266
history and founding, xxxiii, 66
known as "Daughters" of Brahma, 66
millennialism and, 66
Brainwashing, **67–70**
American Psychological Association on,
xxxvii, 25, 69, 130, 290, 579
as explanation for conversion, 68–69
Kent, Steven, and, 69
military and intelligence services, 67
rise and fall of theories of, 69
scholarly and popular examinations of,
68
Zablocki, Benjamin, and, 69
See also Singer, Margaret Thaler
Branch Davidians, **70–74**

children and, 99
conversion and, 129
Davidian Seventh-day Adventists and,
xxxiv, 71–72, 150, 350, 563
history and founding, xxxiv, 71–72
McVeigh, Timothy, and, 133
music and, 414
Roden, Ben and Lois, and, xxxiv
Ross, Rick Alan, and, 527
scriptures and, 446
as sect, 150
sex and, 566–567
siege of Mount Carmel Center, xxxvii,
70, *70,* 73, 95, 110, 128, 140, 340, 342,
350, 352, 370, 384–385, 389, 414, 444,
472, 527, 655, 657
trial of, 140–141
violence and, 656, 657
women and, 678
See also Koresh, David
Breatharianism, **74–75**
beliefs and practices, 74, 207
criticism and controversy, 74, 257
groups and leaders, 74

Caddy, Eileen, **77–78**
beliefs and teachings, 77–78
early years, 77
Findhorn Foundation and, 77–78,
201–202, 434, 526
God Spoke to Me (primary document),
202–205
Opening Doors Within, 77–78
Caddy, Peter, 77, 78, 201–202, 434, 526
Campbell, Colin, 155–156, 556
Candomblé, **78–81**
in Africa, 8
beliefs and practices, 80–81
in Brazil, 8, 79–80
globalization and, 241
healing, 80–81
history and origins, xxix, 78–80
orixás, 80
outside Brazil, 8, 80
symbolism, *79*
Cao Dai, **81–83**
beliefs and practices, 81–82
denomination, 82–83
history and founding, 81
temples, 82, *82*

696 Index

Cayce, Edgar, **83–85**
  beliefs and teachings, 83–84
  channeling and, 86
  criticism and controversy, 84
  crystals and, 145
  early years, 83–84
  founding of Association for Research
    and Enlightenment, xxxiii, 84
  known as "Sleeping Prophet," 83, 434
  mediums and, 374
CESNUR (the Center for the Study of
  New Religions), **85–86**
  history and founding, xxxvii, 85
  Introvigne, Massimo, and, 85
Channeling, **86–90**
  Butts, Robert, and, 87
  Church of Jesus Christ of Latter-day
    Saints and, 86
  definition of, 86
  history of, 86–88
  Kimbangu, Simon, and, 86
  Knight, JZ, and, 87–88, 89
  Lazaris and, 88
  reception and controversies, 89
  Roberts, Jane, and, 86–87
  Schucman, Helen, and, 88
  significant figures, 86–88
Chaos Magick, **90–91**
  beliefs and practices, 90–91
  Carroll, Peter J., and, 90–91
  debate and controversy, 91
  history and founding, 90, 360–361
  Illuminates of Thenateros and, 91
  as results-based magic, 90
  Sherwin, Ray, and, 90–91
Charisma and leadership in new religious
  movements, **91–95**
  Adi Da Samraj and, 2, 93
  ancient texts and, 492
  anticult movement and, 93
  Asahara, Shoko, and, 30, 92
  Blavatsky, Helena Petrovna, and, 63
  claiming charisma, 92–93
  Eddy, Mary Baker, and, 93
  Farrakhan, Louis, and, 422
  Father Divine and, 198
  fraud and, 213, 214
  Hinkins, John-Roger, and, 406
  Hubbard, L. Ron, and, 94, 275
  Japanese new religious movements and,
    309, 312

Koresh, David, and, 93–94, 678
LaVey, Anton Szandor, and, 348
maintaining charisma, 93–94
Malcolm X and, 507
millennialism and, 388–389
Moon, Rev. Sun Myung, and, 92, 240,
  398
Pentecostalism and, 484
Peoples Temple and, 491
prophecy and, 493–494
Rajneesh, Shree Bhagwan, and, 266
Rastafari and, 520
routinizing charisma, 94–95
Seymour, William J., and, 484
Smith, Joseph, and, 92, 94–95, 581
Spiritualism and, 587
theories and categories, 91–92
Vivekananda, Swami, and, 587, 659
Vorilhon, Claude (Raël), and, 664
Weber, Max, on, 91–92, 94
White, Ellen G., and, 92–93
Wovoka and, 385
Chen Tao, **95–97**
  Chen, Hon Ming, and, xxxviii, 95–96
  *God's Descending on Clouds (Flying
    Saucers) to Save People,* xxxviii, 96
  history and origins, 95–96
  move to United States, 107
  prophecy of Christ's return, xxxviii, 96,
    496
  as UFO religion, 106, 625
Children and new religious movements,
  97–100
  Branch Davidians and, 99
  childbearing and childrearing, 97–98
  Church of Jesus Christ of Latter-day
    Saints and, 97–98
  concern for minors, rumors and
    realities, 98–99
  Oneida Community and, 98
  Peoples Temple and, 98–99
  Satanic Panic and, 99
  Shakers and, 98
  See also Children of God (the Family
    International); Indigo Children
Children of God (the Family
  International), **100–103**
  Berg, David Brandt, and, 100–103, 152,
    159, 214–215, 447, 656
  criticism and controversies, 102
  death of David Berg, 102–103

Index **697**

history and founding, xxxiv, 100–101
Law of Love, 102
MO Letters, 101, 102
See also FREECOG (Free the Children of God)
Chinese new religious movements, **103–108**
Buddhism and, 104, 106
Chen Tao, 106, 107
Christianity and, 104, 105, 106
Confucianism and, 104
Daoism and, 104, 106
Falun Gong, 106
Islam and, 104, 105
movements outside of China, 107
new (new) religions, 105–106
new (old) religions, 104–105
Qigong, 107
Taiping movement, 105–106
Christadelphians, **108–109**
beliefs and practices, 108
millennialism and, 108
Christian Identity, **109–111**
beliefs and practices, 109–110
Branch Davidians, 110
British Israelism and, 109, 110
Ford, Henry, and, 109
history and origins, 109–110
millennialism and, 110
The Order or Silent Brotherhood, 110
Posse Comitatus, 110
Smith, Gerald L. K., and, 109–110
Tree of Life synagogue shooting and, 110
Weaver, Randy, and, 110
Christian Science, **111–114**
beliefs and practices, 112–113
church and culture, 113–114
First Church of Christ, Scientist (Boston), *112*
healing and, 111–114, 255
history and origins, xxxi, 111–112
See also Eddy, Mary Baker
Church of All Worlds, the, **114–115**
Green Egg, 115
history and founding, xxxv, 114–115
Paganism and, 114–115
Zell, Tim, and, 114–115
Church of Jesus Christ of Latter-day Saints, the, **115–119**
beliefs and practices, 117–118

The Book of Mormon (film), 119
The Book of Mormon (text), 23, 63–66, 86, 92, 116, 187, 239, 444, 447, 459–460, 580, 642
Doctrine and Covenants, 65, 117
ends practice of plural marriage, xxxi
"The First Vision," xxix, 92, 116, 117, 119, 580
history and founding, xxix, 115–117
institution and culture, 118–119
Word of Wisdom, 118, 205–206, 256–257
See also Fundamentalist Mormons; Smith, Joseph
Church of Satan, the, **120–122**
Aquino, Michael, and, xxxvi, 121–122, 538, 601–602
doctrines and practices, 120
history and founding, xxxiv, 120–122
LaVey, Anton Szandor, and, xxxiv, xxxv, 120–122, 129, 151, 242, 347–349, 373, 414, 537, 538, 556, 601
organization, 121
The Satanic Bible, xxxv, 120, 122, 242, 347, 361, 538
schisms and further developments, 121–122
See also Temple of Set, the
Church of the Lord (Aladura), **123–124**
beliefs and practices, 123–124
history and founding, xxxii, 123
Ositelu, Josiah Olunowo, and, 123–124
Church Universal and Triumphant, the, **124–126**
beliefs and practices, 125
challenges, 126
Gnosticism and, 243
history and founding, 124–125
prophecy and, 495–496
Prophet, Elizabeth Clare, and, 124–126, 497–498, 677
Prophet, Mark L., and, 124, 677
Theosophy and, 464
See also Prophet, Elizabeth Clare
Climate change
Eco-Paganism and, 177
environmentalism and, 186
The Farm and, 197
food and, 207
religious denial of, 545

698 Index

Conspiracy theories, **126–128**
  about new religions, 127–128
  in new religions, 127
Conversion, **128–132**
  brainwashing and, 130–131
  definition of, 128–129
  history and concept of, 128–130
  models and, 131–132
Cosmotheism, **132–133**
  McVeigh, Timothy, and, 132–133
  The Turner Diaries (Pierce) and, 133
Course in Miracles, A, **134–139**
  beliefs and practices, 134–135
  history and publication, xxxvi, 134
  Preface (primary document), 136–139
  reception and controversies, 135–136
  Schucman, Helen, and, xxxvi, 88, 134,
    135–136, 435
Courts and new religious movements,
  139–143
  Aum Shinrikyō and, 142
  Branch Davidians and, 140–141
  Christian Science and, 141
  Church of Babalu and, 140
  Church of Jesus Christ of Latter-day
    Saints and, 139–140
  Church of Scientology and, 141
  Church of the Flying Spaghetti Monster
    (Pastafarianism) and, 141
  *Church of the Lukumi Babalu Aye v.
    Hialeah,* 140
  Employment Division v. Smith, 140
  FREECOG and, 142
  Fundamentalist Latter-day Saints and,
    141–142
  legal issues and criminal proceedings,
    141–142
  Native American Church and, 140
  NXIVM and, 142
  religious liberty, 139–141
Crowley, Aleister, **143–144**
  Argenteum Astrum and, 90
  The Book of Law, xxxi, 144, 474
  early years, 143
  Grant, Kenneth, and, 247–248
  Hermetic Order of the Golden Dawn
    and, 143, 262, 263, 371
  legacy of, 144
  occultism and, 143–144, 208, 225, 356,
    360, 465
  Ordo Templi Orientis and, 144, 218,
    225, 248, 265, 474–475, 603, 674

  Paganism and, 427
  in popular culture, 144
  sex magick and, 360, 361
  See also Thelema
Crystals, **145–147**
  Alper, Frank, and, 145
  Atlantis and, 145
  Cayce, Edgar, and, 145
  history of, 145
  New Age and, 146–147
  Reiki and, 146
  uses of, 145
  Vogel, Marcel, and, 145–146
Cult, **147–151**
  anticult movement, 149–150
  audience cults, 151
  Christian polemicists on, 149
  client cults, 151, 551, 557
  cult movements, 151
  definition of, 147
  derogatory use of the term, 149
  historical developments, 148–149
  Niebuhr, H. Richard, on, 147–148
  scholarly understandings, 147–148
  sects and, 150–151
  Stark, Rodney, and William Sims
    Bainbridge on, 150, 151, 551
  as useful scholarly concept, 150–151
  Weber, Max, on, 147
  Wilson, Bryan, and, 148
  Yinger, J. Milton, on, 148
  See also Anticult movement, the
Cult Awareness Network, **152–155**
  bankruptcy declared by, xxxvii, 154
  decline and demise of, 153–154
  history and founding, xxxv, 152
  Jason Scott case, 153–154
  Kisser, Cynthia, and, 153, 154, 555
  new CAN, 154
  Ross, Rick, and, 153–154, 527–528
  services, 152–153
Cultic milieu, **155–156**
  Campbell, Colin, on, 155–156
  definition of, 155
  Partridge, Christopher, on occulture,
    155–156

Damanhur, **157–159**
  Airaudi, Oberto (Falco Tarassaco), and,
    33, 157
  beliefs and practices, 157–158
  environmentalism and, 158

history of, 157
Temples of Humankind, xxxvii, 33, 157, 158, *158*
Deprogramming, **159–161**
exit counseling and, 160–161
history and origins, 159
rationale, 159–160
See also Exit counseling; Patrick, Ted
Diagnostic and Statistical Manual of Mental Disorders, 20
Diamond Mountain Center, **161–162**
history and founding, 161
McNally, Christie, and, 161–162
Roach, Michael, and, 161–162
Diamond Way, the, **162–163**
criticism and controversy, 163
history of, 162–163
Karma Kagyu lineage of, 162–163
Nydahl, Ole, and, 162–163
sixteenth Karmapa (Ranjung Rigpe Dorje), 162, 163
teachings of, 162–163
Dianetics, **164–165**
concepts of, 164
history and publication, xxxiii, 164
reception and challenges, 164
See also Hubbard, L. Ron
Disaffiliation and ex-membership in new religious movements, **165–168**
apostasy and atrocity tales, 165–166
Children of God and, 167
Church of Scientology and, 165, 166
"cult" and, 167
Fundamentalist Latter-day Saints (FLDS) and, 166, 167
new religions and, 167
NXIVM and, 167
Shakers and, 165–166
varieties of disaffiliation, 166–167
Divine Principle, **168–169**
authority of, 444–445
Completed Testament Age canon and, 168, 397–398, 445, 632
contents and concepts, 168–169, 339–340, 385, 444–445, 565, 631
history and publication, xxxiv, 168, 339, 631
messianism and, 385
sexuality and, 565
Druidry, **169–171**
Bonewits, Isaac, and, 170
Eco-Paganism and, 176

Gardner, Gerald, and, 225
groves (local groups), 170
history and origins, 169–170
Neopaganism and, 169, 186
Reformed Druids of North America (RDNA), 170
Zell, Tim, and, 170
Dudeism, **171–172**
attitude and ritual, 171–172
The Big Lebowski (film) and, 171
as open source religion, 171
origins of, 171

Eating disorders, 19–20
Eckankar, **173–175**
Eck (symbol), *173*
history and founding, xxxiv, 173–174
Klemp, Harold, and, 174–175
membership and teachers, 175
Movement of Spiritual Inner Awareness and, 407
Twitchell, Paul, and, 173–175
Eco-Paganism, **175–177**
climate change and, 177, 186
ecological practices and ideology, 176–177
food and, 207
Goddess movement and, 246
healing and, 176–177
history and origins, 175–176
Eddy, Mary Baker, 34–35, **177–183**, *178*
beliefs and teachings, 112–113, 178–179
criticism and controversies, 179–180
death of, 112, 180
Divine Science discovered by, xxx
early life, 177–178
fall and near-death experience, xxx, 111, 178, 255
founding of Church of Christ, Scientist (Christian Science), xxxi, 111–112, 178–179, 255
later life and legacy, 179–180
publication of *Science and Health with Key to the Scriptures,* xxxi
Quimby, Phineas, and, xxx, 111, 178, 255, 501–502
Retrospection and Introspection (primary document), 180–181
Science and Health with Key to the Scriptures (primary document), 181–183
See also Christian Science

700 Index

Elan Vital (Divine Light Mission), **183–184**
beliefs and practices, 183–184
history and founding, 183–184
Maharaj, Shri Hans Ji, and, 183, 184
Prem Rawat Foundation, 183, 184
primary aim of, 184
Rawat, Prem, and, 183–184
Words of Peace Global, 183, 184
Emerson, Ralph Waldo, 416, 448, 453, 556, 597, 611, 618, 619
Environmentalism and new religious movements, **185–187**
Anthroposophy and, 22, 185–186, 207
climate change, 186
Druidry and, 186
forms of, 185–186
Ghost Dance movement, 185
history and origins, 184–186
Neopaganism and, 186
New Age religions and, 186
Silent Spring (Carson) and, 185–186
See also Eco-Paganism
Essene groups, **187–188**
Dead Sea Scrolls and, 187–188
diversity of, 188
Essene Church, 188
Vero Essene Yahad, 188
Evans, Warren Felt, 449, 502, 572–574
Exclusive (Plymouth) Brethren, **188–190**
Darby, John Nelson, and, 188–189
history and founding, 188–189
humanitarian services, 189–190
worship ("meetings"), 189
Exit counseling, **190–191**
anticult movement and, 190
history of, 190–191
Patrick, Ted, and, 190
rejection of brainwashing hypothesis and, 191

Falun Gong, **193–195**
beliefs and practices, 194–195
coordinated movement, body postures, and meditation, *194*
Dharma Wheel, 194–195
history and founding, xxxvii, 193–194
Li, Hongzhi, and, xxxvii, 193–195
scientific nature of, 195
silent protest of, xxxviii

Farm, The, **195–197**
beliefs and aims, 195–196
book publishing company, 197
Gaskin, Stephen, and Ina May, and, xxxv, 195–197
history and founding, xxxv, 195–196
nonprofit organizations, 197
present day, 197
Farrakhan, Louis, **197–198**
early years, 197
Malcolm X and, 197, 198
Muhammad, Elijah, and, 197–198, 411
Nation of Islam and, 197–198, 411
split from Wallace Dean Muhammad, xxxvi, 198
Father Divine, **198–200**
charisma and, 198
early life and influences, 198–199
legacy of, 199–200
New York and International Peace Mission Movement, 199–200
Fillmore, Charles, xxxi, 199, 207, 450
Talks on Truth (primary document), 452–454
See also Unity School of Christianity
Fillmore, Myrtle, xxxi, 450, 546, 638–639.
See also Unity School of Christianity
Findhorn Foundation, the, **200–205**
Caddy, Eileen and Peter, and, 201–202
God Spoke to Me (primary document), 202–205
history and founding, xxxiv, xxxv, 200–201
Maclean, Dorothy, and, 77, 201–202, 434
Spangler, David, and, 78, 201–202, 434, 557
See also Caddy, Eileen; Caddy, Peter
Food and new religious movements, **205–208**
Church of Jesus Christ of Latter-day Saints and, 205–206
climate change and, 207
environmentalism and, 207
fasting, 207
Heaven's Gate and, 207
International Peace Mission Movement and, 206
preparing holy vessels, 205–206
Rastafarianism and, 206

Index

Seventh-day Adventists and, 206
spiritualizing food, 207
Unity School of Christianity and, 207
Fortune, Dion, **208–209**
early years, 208
founding of Society of the Inner Light, 208
published works, 209
Fourth Way, the, **209–211**
beliefs and methods, 210
Gurdjieff, G. I., and, 209–210, 250–251
history and founding, 209–210, 250–251
Fox, Kate, and Margaret, **211–212**
death of, 212
history of Spiritualism and, 587, 589
Kardecism (Spiritism) and, 326
mass séances, 211
mediums and, 374, 375, 676–677
"rappings" and, xxx, 211, 212, 236–237, 676–677
as Spiritualist celebrities, 211–212
Spiritualist movement founded by, xxx, 211–212, 374, 587, 676–677
Fraud and deception in new religions, **212–214**
challenges of proof of, 212–213, 214
"dangerous cults" stereotype and, 213
history of, 212
I AM Activity prosecutions, 213–214
Peoples Temple and, 213
Theosophical Society and, 213
FREECOG (Free the Children of God), **214–215**
history and founding, xxxv, 214–215
organization of, 214
Patrick, Ted, and, xxxv, 102, 142, 215, 482
Freemasonry, **215–219**
beliefs and practices, 217–218
history and origins, 215–217
lodges, 217
National Treasure (film) and, 215, 218
Prince Hall Freemasonry, 217–218
religious legacy and cultural influence, 218–219
Washington, George, and, *216*
Freezone Scientology, **219–221**
beliefs and practices, 219–221
history and origins, 219–220

Hubbard, L. Ron, and, 219–220, 221
Miscavige, David, and, 219–220, 552
Rathbun, Mark "Marty," and, 220–221, 552
Fundamentalist Mormons, **221–224**
controversy and culture, 223–224
Edmunds-Tucker Act and, 223
Fundamentalist Church of Latter-day Saints, xxxviii, xxxix
history of, 221–222
Jeffs, Warren, and, xxxviii, xxxix
statutory rape and child abuse charges, xxxviii, xxxix
varieties of belief and practice, 222–223
Yearning for Zion (YFZ) Ranch raid, xxxviii, 142, 223–224, 351, 657

Gardner, Gerald, **225–226**
Book of Shadows, 225, 428, 429, 674
criticisms and controversies, 225
early years, 225
Gardnerian Wicca, 144, 225, 360, 526, 673–675
Goddess Worship and, 225
High Magic's Aid, 673
magic and, 360
Neopaganism and, 225, 360, 427–428
occultism and, 208, 225, 465
Rosicrucian Order, Crotona Fellowship (ROCF) and, 526
See also Urantia Book, The
Gender and new religious movements, **226–230**
Church of Jesus Christ of Latter-day Saints and, 228–229
definitions, 226
Dianic Wiccans and, 229
dissolving gender binaries, 226–228
gender divisions, 229
Heaven's Gate and, 227–228
Islamic new religious movements and, 229
Millennialist Christians and, 227
Neopaganism and, 228, 229
Postmillennialist movements and, 227
Rastafarianism and, 229
reinforcing gender norms, 228–229
Satanism and, 229
Scientology and, 229

Ghost Dance Movement (Wovoka),
230–236, 237
American Indian Movement (AIM) and,
233
Arapaho Indians participating in "round
dance," *231*
beliefs and practices, 232–233
Black Elk Speaks (Neihardt) and, 233
Bureau of Indian Affairs (BIA) and,
231–232
"cult" and, 233
cultural legacy, 233
end of, xxxi
ghost shirts, 232
history and origins, xxxi, 230–231
messianism and, 385
millennialism and, 185, 230, 389, 425,
494
Native American Church and, 425
Parker, Mrs. Z. A., description of a
Lakota Ghost Dance (primary
document), 235–236
prophecy and, 494
Wilson, Jack (Wovoka), and, xxxi, 230,
232–233, 234
Wounded Knee incident (1973) and,
233
Wounded Knee massacre (1890), xxxi,
231, 233
Wovoka's Messiah Letter (primary
document), 234
Ghosts, the paranormal, and new religious
movements, **236–238**
children and, 237–238
dealing with the deceased, 236–238
Kardecism and Spiritism, 237
mythical creatures and, 238
Raëlism, 238
Spiritualism, 236–237
Theosophy, 237
vampirism and, 238
Globalization and new religious
movements, **238–242**
Church of Jesus Christ of Latter-day
Saints and, 239
Church of Satan and, 242
Church of Scientology and, 242
definition of globalization, 238–239
immigration and, 240, 241
Immigration and Nationality Act of
1965 and, 240

International Society for Krishna
Consciousness (ISKCON) and, 240,
241
Neopaganism and, 242
Shakers and, 239
Soka Gakkai and, 240
Theosophical Society and, 239–240
Unification Church and, 240–241
Gnostic groups, **243–244**
Church of Scientology, 243
definitions, 243
Elan Vital, 244
Heaven's Gate, 243–244
history of, 243
Revolution of Consciousness, 243
Goddess Worship, **244–247**
beliefs and varieties, 245–246
contemporary culture and, 246
criticism and controversy, 247
Eco-Paganism and, 246–247
history and origins, 244–245
Neopaganism and, 244–247
Wicca and, 245–246
Grant, Kenneth, **247–249**
beliefs and teachings, 248–249
Crowley, Aleister, and, 247–248
early years, 248
founding of Isis Lodge, 248
Ordo Templi Orientis (OTO) and,
248
Typhonian Order and, 248–249
Guénon, René, **249–250**
beliefs and teachings, 249–250
early years, 249
Gnostic Church of France and, 249
*Introduction to the Study of the Hindu
Doctrines,* 249
legacy of, 250
*Theosophy: History of a Pseudo
Religion,* 250
Gurdjieff, G. I., **250–251**
beliefs and teachings, 250–251
early years, 250
founding of the Fourth Way, xxxii,
209–210, 251, 413, 464, 477–478,
593
occultism and, 250
Ouspensky, P. D., and, xxxii, 209–210,
250–251, 464, 477–478
"self-remembering," 478
"The Work," 251

Index

703

Hale-Bopp Comet, xxxviii, 29, 260–261, 389, 441, 548

Hare Krishna movement. *See* International Society for Krishna Consciousness (ISKCON)

Hassan, Steven, **253–254**
anticult movement and, 253–254
early years, 253
founding of Freedom of Mind Resource Center, 253

Healing, health, and new religious movements, **254–258**
asceticism, 254–255
Christian Science, 255–256
Church of Jesus Christ of Latter-day Saints, 256–257
mental health, 257
Mesmerism, 255
modern medicine and, 255–257
New Thought, 255
Pentecostalism, 256
Quimby, Phineas, and, 255
Scientology, 257
Seventh-day Adventists, 257
syncretic religious systems, 256

Heaven's Gate, **258–261**
beliefs and practices, 27–29, 30–32
death of Bonnie Lu Nettles, xxxvi, 29, 260
death of Marshall Applewhite, 29–30, 95, 261
'88 Update (pamphlet), 30, 260
The Evolutionary Level Above Human, 28, 29, 31, 44, 207, 228, 259, 369, 377, 389, 417, 496, 548, 565
food and, 207
founders, 27–32, 258–259
gender and, 227–228
Gnosticism and, 243–244
Hale-Bopp Comet and, xxxviii, 29, 260–261, 389, 441, 548
history and origins, 27–29, 258–260
Human Individual Metamorphosis, xxxvi, 29, 259
"Last Chance to Evacuate Earth before It's Recycled" (edited videotape transcript by Applewhite) (primary document), 30–32
millennialism and, 28, 207, 389, 441, 545, 565

ritual suicide event, xxxviii, 29–30, 228, 260–261, 377, 389, 441, 496, 544, 548
See also Applewhite, Marshall, and Bonnie Lu Nettles

Hermetic Order of the Golden Dawn, the, **261–262**
beliefs and practices, 261–262
Freemasonry and, 261
history and founding, xxxi, 261

Hermeticism, **262–264**
Crowley, Aleister, and, 263
history and origins, 262–263
Neopaganism and, 263
Rosicrucianism and, 263

Hindu new religious movements, **264–267**
ashram of Maharishi Mahesh Yogi, *264*
counterculture and, 265–266
Elan Vital, 267
Hindu-born and Hindu-inspired, 266–267
history of, 264–265
International Society for Krishna Consciousness (ISKCON), 265
Maharishi Mahesh Yogi and, 266
Movement for Spiritual Inner Awareness, 266
Osho Movement, 266
Self-Realization Fellowship, 266–267
Transcendental Meditation, 266
Vedanta Society, 265

Holy Order of MANS, the, **267–268**
beliefs and practices, 268
Blighton, Earl Wilbur, and, 268
history and founding, 267–268

Holy Piby, The, **269–272**
"The Call of a Prophet," 270
"Ethiopia Anointed," 271
excerpts (primary document), 270–272
"The Heavens Open," 270
history and publication, xxxii, 269
"The Mighty Angel," 272
"Rejoicing in Heaven," 271
Rogers, Robert Athyli, and, 269
"Shepherd Anointed," 271–272

Hoodoo, **272–273**
beliefs and practices, 272–273
definitions, 272
history of, 272
legacy of, 273
magic and, 360

704 Index

Hubbard, L. Ron, **273–277**, *274*
  Battlefield Earth, 543
  Dianetics, xxxiii, 164, 219, 257, *274,*
    276, 543, 548, 550
  Dianetics (system), 164, 219, 257, 275,
    479–480, 548, 550, 552
  "Dianetics: The Evolution of a Science"
    (*Astounding Science Fiction* article),
    164, 219, 276
  founding of Church of Scientology,
    xxxiii, 275–276
  Kingslayer, 543
  life story, 273–275
  organization and succession, 276–277
  See also Scientology

I AM Activity, the, **279–281**
  beliefs and practices, 279–280
  criticism and controversy, 280
  history and founding, xxxiii, 54–55,
    124, 237, 279, 497, 677
  influence of, 280–281
  See also Ballard, Guy W.
Indigo Children, **281–282**
  background and context, 281
  commercialism and, 282
  criticism and controversy, 282
  texts and proponents, 281
Info-Cult/Info-Secte, **282–284**
  beliefs and goals, 282–283
  The Cult Project, 282–283
  history and origins, 282
  Kropveld, Mike, and, 282–283
INFORM (the Information Network on
  Religious Movements), **284–288**
  Barker, Eileen, and, 284–285
  Barker, Eileen, interview with (primary
    document), 286–288
  history and founding, 284–285
  mission and goals, 284–286
Insider/outsider problem, the, **288–290**
  definition of, 288–289
  history of, 288–289
  scholarship on, 290
  stereotypes of "cults" and, 290
Integral Yoga, **291–292**
  Aurobindo, Sri, and, 291–292
  history and origins, 291
  Integral Yoga Institute, 291
  Satchidananda Ashram (Yogaville), 292,
    292

International Cultic Studies Association,
  the (the American Family Foundation),
  293–296
  beliefs and practices, 293–294
  history and founding, xxxviii, 293–294
  Langone, Michael, interview with
    (primary document), 294–296
  publishing program, 293–294
International Peace Mission Movement,
  296–298
  Baker, George, and, 296–297
  beliefs and practices, 297–298
  cultural legacy, 298
  history and founding, 296–297
International Society for Krishna
  Consciousness (ISKCON), **299–305**
  anticult movement and, 23, 24
  beliefs and practices, 300–301
  Bhagavad-gītā As It Is, preface
    (primary document), 302–305
  bhakti yoga and, 300–301
  children and, 99
  culture and controversy, 301–302
  globalization and, 240, 241
  Hindu new religious movements and,
    265
  history and founding, xxxiv, 240,
    299–300, 492
  intragroup violence and, 656
  marriage and, 368
  Prabhupada, A. C. Bhaktivedanta
    Swami (Abhay Charan De), and, 240,
    299–301
  science and, 546–547
ISIS, **305–307**
  al-Qaeda and, xxxviii, 305–306, 307
  future of, 306–307
  ideology and aims, 306
  impact of, 307
  millennialism and, 306
  origins and background, 305–306
  al-Zarqaw, Abu Musab, and, 305–306

Japanese new religious movements,
  309–313
  Agonshū, 311–312
  Aum Shinrikyō, 312
  Soka Gakkai, 310–311
  Tenrikyō, 310
Jediism, **313–314**
  beliefs and practices, 313–314

Index   **705**

census statistics, xxxviii, 313
internet technology and, 441–442
online resources, 314
Star Wars (film) and, 313, 314
Temple of the Jedi Order, 313–314
Jehovah's Witnesses. *See* Watch Tower
Bible and Tract Society, the
Jesus Movement, 11, 620
Jews for Jesus, **314–317**
beliefs and practices, 315–316
controversy and culture, 316
history and origins, 315
millennialism and, 315–316
Rosen, Martin "Moishe," and, 315, 316
Jones, Rev. Jim, **317–320**
in California, xxxiii, 318–319
early life, 317
founding of Community Unity, xxxiii,
318
in Indiana, 317–318
in Jonestown, 319–320
"revolutionary suicide," 98–99, 320,
389, 491, 647
See also Peoples Temple
Judge, William Quan, **320–321**
beliefs and teachings, 320–321
early years, 320
founding of *The Path,* 320
founding of Theosophical Society, xxx,
320, 606, 607

Kabbalah, **323–326**
beliefs and practices, 324–325
Berg, Philip, and, xxxiv, 325, 416
Brandwein, Yehuda Tzvi, and, xxxiv,
325
founding of Kabbalah Centre (New
York), xxxiv, 325–326
history and origins, 323–324
tree of life, *324*
Kardecism (Spiritism), **326–328**
beliefs and practices, 327–328
history and origins, 326–327
legacy of, 328
Rivail, Hippolyte Léon Denizard, and,
326–327
Spiritualism as distinct from, 326
Kimbangu, Simon, **328–334**
beliefs and teachings, 329–330
Church of Jesus Christ on Earth and,
213, 241, 329–330

early years, 328
"The Kimbanguist Catechism" (primary
document), 330–332
"Psalms of Kimbangu" (primary
document), 332–334
public ministry of, xxxii, 329
King, George
founding of Aetherius Society, xxxiii,
2–3, 444, 547, 624
The Twelve Blessings and, xxxiv, 3, 444,
624–625
See also Aetherius Society, the
Knight, JZ (Ramtha), **334–335**
beliefs and teachings, 334–335
criticism and controversy, 335
early years, 334
first encounter with Ramtha, xxxvi,
334
Ramtha's School of Enlightenment, 335
Kopimism, **335–337**
beliefs and practices, 336
criticism and controversy, 336
formal recognition of in Sweden, xxxix,
336
Gerson, Isak, and, 335–336
history and founding, 335–336
internet technology and, 335
membership, 336–337
Nipe, Gustave, and, 335–336
Korean new religious movements,
337–340
Chŭngsan religions, 338–339
Daesun Jinri-hoe, 339
Jeung San Do, 338–339
Taejonggyo, 338
Tonghak and Ch'ondogyo, 337–338
Unification Church, 339–340
Won Buddhism, 339
Koresh, David, **340–343**
Bible studies and, 341
charisma and, 93
early years, 340–341
last letter to his attorney (primary
document), 342–343
new light of, 341–342
See also Branch Davidians

Landmark Forum, the (est), **345–347**
beliefs and practices, 345–346
Erhard, Werner, and, 345–346
history and founding, 345

706   Index

LaVey, Anton Szandor, 129, 151, **347–349,**
   373, 414, 537, 556, 601
   as the "Black Pope," 347–348
   founding of the Church of Satan, xxxiv,
      120–122
   influence of, 349
   influences on, 347
   personality of, 348
   The Satanic Bible, xxxv, 120, 122, 242,
      347, 361, 538
Law enforcement and new religious
   movements, **349–353**
   Alamo Christian Ministries and, 351
   arrests, raids, and standoffs, 350–351
   Branch Davidians and, 350
   children and, 351
   Children of God and, 351
   Christian Patriot Movement and,
      350–351
   Church of Jesus Christ of Latter-day
      Saints and, 350
   future and reform, 352
   Moorish Science Temple of America
      and, 351–352
   Nation of Islam and, 352
   Osho Movement and, 351
   policing new (black) religions,
      351–352
Lee, (Mother) Ann, **353–356**
   early years, 353
   journey to New World, xxix, 354
   legacy of, 355–356
   messianism and, 354–355
   millennialism and, 355
   as prophet, 353–354
   Shakers and, 353–356
Lévi, Éliphas, **356–357**
   criticism and controversy, 357
   early years, 356
   legacy of, 356–357
   occultism and, 356
   pentagrams and, 356
   published works, 356
Lourdes apparitions, xxx, 364–365. *See
   also* Marian apparitions
Love Israel Family, the, **357–358**
   anticult movement and, 358
   beliefs and practices, 357–358
   Erdman, Paul, and, 357–358
   history and founding, xxxv, 357–358

Maclean, Dorothy, 77, 201–202, 434
Magic and new religious movements,
   359–362
   black magic, 361
   Chaos Magick, 90, 360–361
   Christian Science and, 361
   Church of Satan and, 361
   Evans-Pritchard, E. E., on, 359
   Hoodoo and, 360
   magic as religion, 359–361
   Neopaganism and, 360
   Pentecostals and, 361
   white magic, 361
Malcolm X, **362–364,** *363*
   assassination of, xxxiv, 364
   conversion of, xxxiii, 362
   criticism and controversy within Nation
      of Islam, 363
   hajj of, 363–364
   Muhammad, Elijah, and, 362–363
Marian apparitions, **364–366**
   Chapel of the Apparitions (Fatima), *364*
   at Fatima, 365–366
   at Lourdes, xxx, 364–365
   Marian devotional culture, 365–366
   in modern age, 366
   to Soubirous, Bernadette (St.
      Bernadette), xxx, 364–365
Marriage and relationships in new
   religious movements, **366–370**
   Branch Davidians, 370
   breaking marital bonds, 368–369
   Children of God, 369
   Church of Jesus Christ of Latter-day
      Saints and, 367
   concerns over regulating relationships,
      369–370
   holy matrimony, 366–368
   International Society for Krishna
      Consciousness (ISKCON) and, 368
   Neopaganism and, 368–369
   Oneida Community, 367
   Osho Movement, 369
   plural marriage, 367
   Raëlians, 369
   Shakers and, 368
   Wicca and, 368–369
Mathers, Samuel Liddell, **370–371**
   criticism and controversy, 371
   early years, 371

founding of Hermetic Order of the Golden Dawn, 371

Media and new religious movements, **372–374**
Church of Jesus Christ of Latter-day Saints and, 373
Church of Scientology and, 373
cult stereotypes and, 372–373
memoirs, 372
"noisy apostates" and, 372

Mediums, **374–375**
fraud and, 375
gender and, 374–375
history of, 374
varied experiences of, 374

Membership and new religious movements, **375–377**
initiation and, 376–377
process of membership, 375–376
total commitment requirement and, 377
varieties of membership, 376–377

Mesmerism, **377–380**
Eddy, Mary Baker, and, 380
history and origins, 378–379
hypnotism and, 379
Mesmer, Franz Anton, and, xxix, 378–379
offshoots and cultural significance, 380
theory and practice, *378,* 378–380

Messianic Judaism, **380–383**
beliefs and practices, 382
critique and contemporary culture, 382–383
history and origins, 380–381
millennialism and, 381, 383

Messianism and new religious movements, **383–386**
Haile Selassie I of Ethiopia and, 385–386
history of messianism, 383–384
Koresh, David, and, 384–385
Lee, Mother Ann, and, 384
messiahs in new religions, 384–386
millennialism and, 384, 385, 386
Moon, Rev. Sun Myung, and, 385
Wovoka and, 385

Millennialism, **386–390**
Ahmadiyya movement and, 8, 9–10
Asahara, Shoko, and, 35–36, 312, 386, 658

Aum Shinrikyō and, 35–36, 38–39, 41, 92, 312, 389, 658
Babism and, 49–50
Book of Revelation and, 28
Brahma Kumaris and, 66
Branch Davidians and, 73, 389
Cao Dai and, 82
Chen Tao and, 95, 106
Children of God and, 149, 369, 648
Christadelphians and, 108
Christian Identity and, 110, 388
Chŭngsan religions and, 339
Church of Jesus Christ of Latter-day Saints and, 390
concept and origins, 387
coronation of Haile Selassie I and, 414
Cosmotheism and, 133
Exclusive (Plymouth) Brethren and, 413
food and, 205, 207
gender norms and, 227
general patterns of belief, 387–389
Ghost Dance Movement (Wovoka) and, 185, 230, 389, 425, 494
Heaven's Gate and, 28, 207, 389, 441, 545, 565
historical and modern varieties, 389–390
I AM Activity and, 279
ISIS and, 306, 388, 390, 531
Jews for Jesus and, 315–316
Lee, (Mother) Ann, and, 355
Malcolm X and, 363
marriage and, 366
membership requirements and, 377
Messianic Judaism and, 381, 383
messianism and, 384, 385, 386
Millerites and, 388, 392, *393,* 394, 561
Moorish Science Temple and, 400
Movement for the Restoration of the Ten Commandments of God and, 404–405
Nation of Islam and, 363
New Age and, 433
Oneida Community and, 388, 454
Order of the Solar Temple and, 473
Pentecostalism and, 483, 486
Peoples Temple and, 389
postmillennialism, 387–388
premillennialism, 387
Prophet, Elizabeth Clare, and, 498

708 Index

Millennialism (*Continued*)
  Raëlians and, 511
  Rosicrucianism and, 524
  Russell, Charles Taze, and, 528, 529
  Seventh-day Adventists and, 71, 388,
    562, 671, 676
  Shakers and, 389, 570, 571
  3HO and, 614
  Transcendental Meditation and, 616
  Twelve Tribes and, 620, 621
  UFO religions and, 625
  Unification Church and, 631
  utopianism and, 645
  Watch Tower Bible and Tract Society
    and, 388, 394, 668
  white supremacy and, 388, 508, 658
Miller, William, **390–392**
  early history, 390–392
  *Evidence from Scripture and History of
    the Second Coming of Christ*
    (primary document), 394–397
  "The Great Disappointment," xxx,
    391–392
  published works, 391
Millerites, the, **392–397**
  beliefs and practices, 392–393
  *Evidence from Scripture and History of
    the Second Coming of Christ*
    (primary document), 394–397
  history of, 390–393
  Miller, William, and, 392–393
  millennialism and, 388, 392, *393,* 394,
    561
Mind Cure theory and movement, xxx,
  380, 448, 451, 501–502
Miscavige, David, 219–220, 552
Moon, Hak Ja Han, 169, 213, 340, 368,
  385, 397, 398, 417, 565, 631, 632, 633
Moon, Heung Jin, 398, 633
Moon, Hyo Jin, 398, 633
Moon, Hyun Jin, 398, 633
Moon, In Jin, 633
Moon, Kook Jin, 633
Moon, Rev. Sun Myung, **397–399**
  beliefs and teachings, 168–169
  charisma and, 92, 240, 398
  first "Blessing" (mass marriage)
    ceremony, xxxiv
  founding of Holy Spirit Association for
    the Unification of World Christianity
    (the Unification Church), xxxiii

  leadership of, 398
  prophetic persona, 397–398
  True Parents of humankind (with Hak
    Ja Han Moon), 169, 213, 340, 385,
    397, 398, 417, 565, 631, 632, 633
  See also Divine Principle; Unification
    Church, the
Mooney, James, 234–236
Moorish Science Temple of America, the,
  399–404
  beliefs and practices, 399–400
  death of Drew Ali and aftermath, 13,
    400–401
  as ethnic religion, 507
  formal incorporation of, xxxii
  Freemasonry and, 526
  history and origins, xxxii, 399
  Moorish Manufacturing Corporation
    and, 547
  Newark location, 420
  Rosicrucianism and, 526
  science and, 547
  See also Ali, Noble Drew
Mount Carmel Center, siege of, xxxvii, 70,
  70, 73, 95, 110, 128, 140, 340, 342, 350,
  352, 370, 384–385, 389, 414, 444, 472,
  527, 655, 657
Movement for the Restoration of the Ten
  Commandments of God, the, **404–406**
  beliefs and practices, 405
  history and founding, 404–405
  mass murder, xxxviii, 404, 406
  millennialism and, 404–405
  prophecy and, xxxviii, 405–406
Movement of Spiritual Inner Awareness,
  406–408
  beliefs, practices, and organization,
    407–408
  Hinkins, John-Roger, and, xxxv, 406
  history and founding, xxxv, 406–407
  membership, 408
Muhammad, Elijah, **408–411**, *409*
  beliefs and teachings, 410–411
  conversion of, xxxiii, 409–410
  death of, xxxvi, 411
  Fard, W. D., and, xxxiii, 408–410
  Farrakhan, Louis, and, 197–198, 411
  Malcolm X and, 362–363
  Nation of Islam and, 197–198, 408–411
Muhammad, Wallace (Warith) Dean,
  xxxvi, 198, 411, 422

Index

Mungiki, **411–412**
  beliefs and practices, 411–412
  history and origins, 411
Murray, John, 634
Murray, Margaret, 428, 673
Murray, Valgard, 38
Music and new religious movements, **412–415**
  Candomblé and, 413
  Darby, John Nelson, and, 413–414
  Gurdjieff, G. I., and, 413
  hip-hop, 415
  Koresh, David, and, 414
  Mesmer, Franz Anton, and, 413
  music as a tool, 414–415
  music as sacred practice, 412–414
  Neopaganism and, 414
  Rastafari and, 414
  Yogananda, Paramahansa, and, 412–413
Mysticism, **415–417**
  contemporary mystical movements, 416–417
  definition of, 415
  Emerson, Ralph Waldo, on, 416–417
  history of, 415–416
  Kabbalah, 416–417
  Neo-Sufi movements, 416
  New Age Gnostic movements, 417

Nation of Gods and Earths, the (the Five Percent Nation), **419–420**
  history and origins, 419
  influence of, 419–420
  Smith, Clarence 13X, and, 419, 507
Nation of Islam, the, **420–423**
  beliefs and practices, xxxiii, 421–422
  death of Elijah Muhammad, xxxvi, 411, 422
  Farrakhan, Louis, and, 422
  history and origins, 420–422
  Malcolm X and, xxxiii, 421–422
  Muhammad, Elijah, and, 197–198, 408–411, 420–422
  Muhammad, Wallace (Warith) Dean, and, xxxvi, 198, 411, 422
Nation of Yahweh, the, **423–424**
  criticism and controversy, 424
  history and founding, 423
  prophecy and, 423
  RICO convictions, 424
  teachings and practices, 423

Native American Church, the, **424–426**
  beliefs and practices, 425
  in contemporary society, 426
  Employment Division v. Smith, 426
  history and origins, 424–425
Nazareth Baptist Church, xxxii, 7, 577–578
Neopaganism, **426–432**
  Ásatrú and, 38
  beliefs and practices, 429–431
  conversion and, 132
  Crowley, Aleister, and, 427
  Druidry and, 169
  Eco-Paganism and, 175–177
  environmentalism and, 186
  Gardner, Gerald, and, 225, 360, 427–428
  gender and, 228, 229
  globalization and, 242
  Goddess movement and, 244–247
  history and origins, 426–429
  internet communication and, 242
  magic and, 360
  marriage and sexuality, 368, *427,* 430
  music and, 414
  occultism and, 144, 263
  Wicca and, 229, 360, 428, 430
  Wiccan Rede and, 246, 430
Nettles, Bonnie Lu. *See* Applewhite, Marshall, and Bonnie Lu Nettles
New Age, the, **432–436**
  controversy, 436
  diffusion of, 435–436
  emergence of, 434–435
  history of, 433
  See also Caddy, Eileen; Cayce, Edgar; *Course in Miracles, A;* Findhorn Foundation, the; Knight, JZ (Ramtha)
New Cathar Church, the, **436–438**
  beliefs and practices, 436–437
  Bereslavskii, Veniamin Iakovlevich, and, 437–438
  history of, 436–437
  legacy of, 437
New Church, the, **438–439**
  beliefs and practices, 438–439
  history and founding, xxix, 438
  membership, 439
  Swedenborg, Emanuel, and, 438–439

710 Index

New religions on/and the internet,
439–443
conversion and recruitment, 440–441
Heaven's Gate, 441
"I'm a Mormon" campaign, 440
Jediism, 441–442
Kopimism, 442
Otherkin and Vampirism, 442
religious controversies of the digital
frontier, 442–443
religious innovation and the internet,
440–441
virtual religions, 441–442
New scriptures and new religious
movements, **443–447**
Bhagavad-Gītā As It Is, 445
Children of God and, 447
Church of Scientology and, 447
claiming authority, 444–445
Divine Principle, 444–445
The Holy Piby, 446
Intelligent Design, 445–446
Koresh, David, and, 444, 446
making interpretations, 445–446
making scriptures, 446
opposition to new scriptures,
446–447
Raëlian movement and, 446
New Thought, **447–454**
beliefs, practices, and varieties,
449–450
history of, 448–449
modern iterations and cultural legacy,
450–451
Talks on Truth (primary document),
452–454
9/11 attacks
al-Qaeda and, xxxviii, 14–15, 532, 655,
658
Salafism and, 532–533
Norman, Ernest, xxxiv, 547, 629, 630
Norman, Ruth, xxxiv, xxxv, 547,
629–630
Noyes, John Humphrey, **454–456,** *455*
early years, 454
Oneida Community founded by, xxx,
455–456, 469–472
revelation of, 454–455
NXIVM, **456–457**
beliefs and practices, 456
criticism and controversy, 456–457

history and founding, 456
Raniere, Keith, and, xxxix, 456–457

Oahspe, **459–463**
Chapter 1 (primary document), 460–463
contents and teachings, 460
history and publication, xxxi, 459
length and organization, 459–460
Newbrough, John Ballou, and, 459
Occultism and esotericism, **463–466**
Anthroposophy, 464
Church Universal and Triumphant,
464–465
The Fourth Way, 464
Hermetic Order of the Golden Dawn,
465
I AM Activity, 464–465
Neopaganism, 465
occult in England, 465–466
Satanism, 465
Thelema, 465
Theosophy, 464
Western esotericism in Asia, 463–465
Occulture, 155–156, 556, 557
Odinism, **466–468**
Christensen, Else, and, 467
history and origins, 466–467
McNallen, Stephen, and, 467
Odinist Fellowship, 467
Wotansfolk, 467
Olcott, Henry Steel, **468–469**
early years, 468
founding of Theosophical Society, xxx,
468–469, 606, 607
legacy of, 469
Oneida Community, the, **469–472**
beliefs and practices, 471
dissolution of, xxxi
history and founding, xxx, 469–471
legacy of, 472
Mansion House, *470*
Noyes, John Humphrey, and, xxx,
455–456, 469–472
Order of the Solar Temple, the, **472–474**
beliefs and practices, 473
Di Mambro, Joseph, and, 472–474
history and origins, 473
ritual murder-suicide, xxvii, 472–473,
474
Ordo Templi Orientis, **474–475**
beliefs and practices, 474–475

Index 711

history and origins, 474
Osho Movement, the. *See* Rajneesh/Osho
Movement, the
Ositelu, Josiah Olunowo, 123–124
Otherkin, **475–477**
beliefs and practices, 475–476
criticism and controversy, 476
history and origins, 475
Ouspensky, P. D., **477–478**
Blavatsky, Helena Petrovna, and,
477
*The Fourth Way: A Record of Talks and
Answers Based on the Teachings of
G. I. Gurdjieff,* 477–478
Gurdjieff, G. I., and, xxxii, 209–210,
250–251, 464, 477–478
Tertium Organum, 477

Parham, Charles Fox, 483–484, 568–569
Parsons, John Whiteside, **479–480**
"Babalon Working," 479
Crowley, Aleister, and, 479
Hubbard, L. Ron, and, 479–480
Thelema and, 479
Partridge, Christopher, 155–156, 556
Pastafarianism (Church of the Flying
Spaghetti Monster), **480–481**
beliefs and practices, 480
controversy, 480–481
depicting the deity, *481*
history of, xxxviii, 480
Patrick, Ted, **482**
career of, 482
contemporary anticult movement and,
24
conviction of, xxxvi, 142, 160, 190,
482
deprogramming and, 68, 102, 130, 159,
160, 190, 482
founding of FREECOG, xxxv, 102, 142,
215, 482
Love Israel Family and, 358
Pentecostalism, **483–487**
Asuza Street Revival and, xxxi, 7,
484–485, 569
beliefs and practices, 485–486
global denominations, 486–487
history and origins, 483–485
McPherson, Aimee Semple, and, *484,*
485, 487
Seymour, William, and, 484, 506

Peoples Temple, **487–492**
in Guyana, 490–491
history and founding, xxxiii, 487–489
Jonestown, 319–320
life for members, 489–490
move to Guyana from California,
xxxiii
"revolutionary suicide," 98–99, 320,
389, 491, 647
revolutionary suicide of, xxxvi, 320
See also Jones, Rev. Jim
Pierre, Bernard, xxxi. *See also* Tantrik
Order, the
Poole, Elijah. *See* Muhammad, Elijah
Prabhupada, A. C. Bhaktivedanta,
492–493
Bhagavad-Gītā As It Is, 302–305, 445,
492
early years, xxxiv, 492
founding of International Society for
Krishna Consciousness, xxxiv,
299–300, 492
See also International Society for
Krishna Consciousness (ISKCON)
Prophecy in new religious movements,
493–497
Abrahamic religions and, 493
Church of Jesus Christ of Latter-day
Saints and, 494
Church Universal and Triumphant and,
495–496
claiming prophethood, 493–495
failed prophecies and their
consequences, 495–496
Ghost Dance movement and, 494
Heaven's Gate and, 496
Millerites and, 495
Nation of Islam and, 494
Pentecostalism and, 495
Prophet, Elizabeth Clare, **497–499**
assumes leadership of Summit
Lighthouse, xxxv, 497
early years, 497
end-times prediction of, xxxvii, 498
founding of Church Universal and
Triumphant, xxxv, 497–498
millennialism and, 498
Pursel, Jach (Lazaris), **499–500**
beliefs and teachings, 499–500
as channel, xxxv, 435, 499–500
criticism and controversy, 500

Quimby, Phineas, **501–503,** *502*
  early years, 501
  Eddy, Mary Baker, and, xxx, 111, 178,
    255, 380, 448–449, 501–502, 546
  Evans, Warren Felt, and, 449
  healing and, 255
  legacy of, 502
  mesmerism and, 380, 448, 501–502, 546
  Mind Cure theory and movement, xxx,
    380, 448, 501–502
  New Thought and, 448–449, 450, 501,
    502, 546
  published works, 449, 502

Race and new religious movements,
    505–509
  black ethnic religions, 506–508
  Christian Identity, 508
  colonialism, 505, 508
  Commandment Keepers, 507
  Curse of Ham, 505, 507
  International Peace Mission Movement,
    506
  interracial utopias, 506
  Moorish Science Temple, 507
  Nation of Islam, 507
  Pentecostalism, 506
  Rastafarianism, 508
  religions of white supremacy, 508
  slavery, 505–506, 507
Raëlians, the, **509–513**
  beliefs, practices, and organizations,
    511–512
  The Book Which Tells the Truth, 509,
    664
  controversies, 512
  history and origins, 509–511
  human cloning and, xxxviii, 369, 511
  *Intelligent Design: Message from the
    Designers,* 445, 446, 625
  marriage and, 369
  science and, 511
  symbol of, *510*
  as UFO religion, *510*
  Vorilhon, Claude, and, 369, 445,
    509–510, 512, 544, 547, 644–645
Rajneesh, Shree Bhagwan/Osho, **513–514**
  beliefs and teachings, 513–514
  early years, 514–515
  first ashram in India, xxxv
  followers of, 513

Rajneesh/Osho Movement, the, **514–516**
  beliefs and practices, 514–515
  city of Rajneeshpuram (Oregon), xxxvi,
    515–516
  history and origins, 514–515
Ramakrishna Mission, **516–519**
  beliefs and practices, 517–518
  history and origins, 517
  organization and later history, 518–519
Rastafari, **519–524**
  beliefs and practices, 521–522
  coronation of emperor Haile Selassie I
    of Ethiopia, xxxiii, 520–522
  history and origins, 520–521
  impact of, 522
  The Promised Key (primary document),
    523–524
Rathbun, Mark "Marty," 220–221, 552
Rathbun, Valentine, 22–23, 165–166
Restorationist Christianity, 108, 669
Richard, Mira, 42–43, 267, 291. *See also*
  Aurobindo, Sri
Rosicrucianism, **524–527**
  beliefs and practices, 525
  first published texts, xxix
  founding of Rosicrucian Fellowship,
    xxxii
  history and origins, 524–525
  orders and societies, 525–527
  Rosicrucian Order, Crotona Fellowship
    (ROCF), 525–526
Ross, Rick Alan, **527–528**
  Cult Awareness Network (CAN) and,
    153–154, 527–528
  as deprogrammer, 153–154, 527–528
  early career, 527
Russell, Charles Taze, **528–530**
  early years, 528
  founding of Watch Tower Bible and
    Tract Society, xxxi, 528–529,
    668–669
  life and legacy, 529
  published works, 529

Salafism, **531–533**
  branches of, 532
  early history, 532
  evolution and beliefs, 531–532
  9/11 and, 532–533
Santería, **533–535**
  beliefs and practices, 534–535

dancing, *533*
history and origins, 533–534
second diaspora, 535
Satanic Panic, **536**
McMartin Preschool case and trial,
xxxvi, 536
publication of *Michelle Remembers,*
xxxvi, 536, 567
Satanism, **537–539**
esoteric Satanism, 538
history and origins, 537–538
rationalist Satanism, 538
types of, 538
See also Church of Satan, the
Sathya Sai Baba Movement, the, **539–541**
beliefs and practices, 540
declares himself reincarnation of Sai
Baba of Shirdi, xxxiii, 539
early life, 539–540
institution and legacy, 541
miraculous feats, xxxiii, 539–540
Sathya Sai International Organization
(SSIO), 540–541
Schucman, Helen, xxxvi, 88, 134, 135–
136, 435
*Science and Health with Key to the
Scriptures,* **541–543**
content and features, 542–543
sales, 542
writing and publication of, 542
Science fiction and new religious
movements, **543–545**
Church of Scientology, 543
Church of the Flying Spaghetti Monster,
544
from fiction to religion, 543–544
Star Wars (film), 544
stranger than fiction, 544–545
UFO religions, 544
Science, technology, and new religious
movements, **545–549**
Church of Scientology, 548
Galileo Galilei, 545
Heaven's Gate, 548
International Society for Krishna
Consciousness (ISKCON), 546–547
Kopimism, 548
Moorish Science Temple, 547
New Thought, 546
religions of the future, 548–549
technology and mythology, 546–548

UFO religions, 547
Unarius Academy of Science, xxxiv,
547, 628–630
Scientology, **549–553**
as client cult, 551
criticism and controversies, 550,
552–553
history and origins, xxxiii, 549–550
Miscavige, David, and, 94, 128,
219–220, 277, 552
practices and beliefs, 551–552
Ron's Orgs, xxxvi, 220
See also Dianetics; Freezone
Scientology; Hubbard, L. Ron
Sect, **553–555**
dangerous sectes, 555
definition and connotations, 553
religious sects, 553–555
Seekers, **555–557**
conversion and, 557
cults and, 557
Emerson, Ralph Waldo, and, 556
occulture and, 556–557
rejection of external authorities by,
556
Self-Realization Fellowship (Yogananda),
558–561
beliefs and practices, 559–560
culture and controversy, 560
Kriya yoga, 559
origins and founding, 558–559
Seventh-day Adventism, **561–564**
beliefs and practices, 562–563
culture and controversy, 563
early history and origins, 561–562
millennialism and, 71, 388, 562, 671,
676
White, Ellen G., and, xxx, 495, 562,
563, 671–672
Sex, sexuality, and new religious
movements, **564–568**
Children of God and, 566
Church of Jesus Christ of Latter-day
Saints and, 566–567
Oneida Community and, 565
Osho Movement and, 566
sexual experimentation, 564–566
sexual exploitation, 566–567
sexual orientation, 567
Shakers and, 564–565
Unification Church and, 565

714   Index

Seymour, William, **568–570**
  Asuza Street Revival and, 569
  early years and religious beginnings,
    568–569
  later years and legacy, 569
  Parham, Charles Fox, and, 484
  Pentecostalism and, 484, 506,
    568–569
Shakers, the, **570–574**
  anticult movement and, 22–23
  beliefs and practices, 571–572
  children and, 98
  Compendium of the Origin, History,
    Principles, Rules and Regulations,
    Government, and Doctrines . . .
    (primary document), 572–574
  disaffiliation and ex-membership,
    165–166
  globalization and, 239
  history and origins, 570–571
  legacy and future, 572
  marriage and, 368
  Rathbun, Valentine, and, 22–23,
    165–166
  sexuality and, 564–565
  two remaining modern-day members,
    xxxix, 572
  See also Lee, (Mother) Ann
Shamanism, **575–577**
  Andrews, Lynn V., on, 576
  Castenada, Carlos, on, 575
  definition of, 575
  Eliade, Mircea, on, 575
  Harner, Michael J., on, 575–576
  neo-shamanism, 576
Shembe, Isaiah, **577–578**
  beliefs and teachings, 577–578
  early years, 577
  Nazareth Baptist Church and, xxxii, 7,
    577–578
Singer, Margaret Thaler, **578–580**
  anti-secte movement influenced by, 555
  APA Task Force on Deceptive and
    Indirect Methods of Persuasion and
    Control, 25, 69, 579
  on brainwashing and coercive
    persuasion, 25, 68–69, 527, 579
  Cults in Our Midst, 579
  early career, 578–579
  lawsuits brought against APA by, 579
Smith, Clarence 13X, 419, 507, 637

Smith, Joseph, **580–582**
  beliefs and teachings, 580–582
  death and legacy, 582
  early life, 580
  "The First Vision," xxix, 92, 116, 117,
    119, 580
  founding of Church of Jesus Christ of
    Latter-day Saints, 580–582
  murder of Hyrum and Joseph Smith Jr.,
    xxx, 582
  visitation of angel Moroni, 580
  See also Book of Mormon, The; Church
    of Jesus Christ of Latter-day Saints,
    the
Soka Gakkai, **582–584**
  controversies, 584
  globalization and, 240
  history and founding, xxxii, 310,
    582–583
  music and, 413
  practices, 311, 583–584
Spiritual but not Religious, **584–587**
  beliefs and varieties, 585–586
  history of, 585
  meaning of, 584–585
  modern spirituality and, 586
Spiritualism, **587–590**
  alternative healing and, 589
  beliefs and practices, 588–589
  cultural legacy, 589
  Fox, Kate, and Margaret, xxx, 211–212,
    374, 587, 676–677
  history and background, 587–588
  Swedenborg, Emanuel, and, 588,
    596–598
  Theosophy and, 587–589
  See also Mediums
Starhawk, **590–591**
  beliefs and teachings, 590
  early years, 590
  Goddess movement and, 245, 590, 678
  Neopaganism and, 176
  Reclaiming tradition and, 428, 430, 590
  "Religion from Nature, Not
    Archaeology" (primary document),
    431–432
  The Spiral Dance, 428–429, 590, 678
Stark, Rodney, 115–116, 119, 131, 150, 151,
  551, 554–555, 557
Steiner, Rudolf, **591–592**
  Anthroposophical Society and, xxxii

Anthroposophy and, xxxii, 21–22, 185, 464, 591
Blavatsky, Helena Petrovna, and, 592
early years, 591
environmentalism and, 185
racial theories, 21–22, 592
Theosophical Society and, xxxii, 21–22
Theosophy and, 21
Subud, **592–594**
beliefs and practices, 593
history and origins, 592–593
World Subud Association, 593
Sufi new religious movements, **594–596**
Hazrat Inayat Khan and, xxxii, 595
modern Sufism, 595
Subud, 595
Sufi belief and practice, 594–595
syncretic Sufi traditions, 595
Universal Sufism, 595
Swedenborg, Emanuel, **596–598**
early years, 596
New Church and, 438–439
published works, 596–597
Spiritualism and, 588, 596–598
visions of, xxix, 596, *597*

Tantrik Order, the, **599–601**
beliefs and practices, 600
Bernard, Pierre, and, xxxi, 599–600
culture and controversies, 600–601
history and founding, xxxi, 599–600
Tarot cards, 356, 435, 667, *673*
Temple of Set, the, **601–602**
Aquino, Michael, and, xxxvi, 121–122, 538, 601–602
Barrett, Ronald Keith, and, 602
beliefs and practices, 601–602
history and founding, xxxvi, 601
Thelema, **602–606**
beliefs and practices, 602–603
The Book of Law, xxxi, 144, 474
The Book of Law (primary document), 603–606
Crowley, Aleister, and, xxxi
history and origins, 602
occultism and esotericism, 465
Parsons, John Whiteside, and, 479
Theosophical Society, the, **606–607**
Anthroposophy and, 21–22

Blavatsky, Helena Petrovna, and, xxx, 61–62, 209, 227, 237, 239–240, 606–607
fraud and, 213
globalization and, 239–240
history and origins, xxx, 606
judge, William Quan, and, xxx, 320, 606, 607
Olcott, Henry Steel, and, xxx, 468–469, 606, 607
organization and institution, 607
Steiner, Rudolf, and, xxxii, 21–22
Theosophy, **608–610**
apostates and, 26
art and, 33–34
beliefs and practices, 609–610
Church Universal and Triumphant and, 464
ghosts and, 237
history and background, 608
occultism and esotericism, 464
Spiritualism and, 587–589
Steiner, Rudolf, and, 21
Theosophy: History of a Pseudo Religion, 250
Thoreau, Henry David, **610–612**
Asian influence, 1, 611–612
criticism and controversy, 611, 612
death of, 612
early life and Transcendentalism, 610–611
The Maine Woods, 611
as surveyor, 611–612
Walden, 611
A Week on the Concord and Merrimack Rivers, 611
Wild Fruits, 612
3HO, **612–615**
beliefs and practices, 613–614
history and founding, xxxv, 612–613
modern day, 614–615
Yogi Bhajan and, xxxv, 612–614
Tokyo subway sarin attack (1995), xxxvii, 36, 38, 40–41, 127, 142, 312, 386, 472, 655
Transcendental Meditation, **615–617**
beliefs and practices, 616
history and origins, 615–616
institution and cultural legacy, 617
Yogi, Maharishi Mahesh, and, xxxiv, 615, 685

716 Index

Transcendentalism, **617–620**
  Asian influence, 1
  beliefs and practices, 618–619
  culture and legacy, 619
  "Hedge's Club," xxix, 618
  history and origins, 617–618
  See also Thoreau, Henry David
Turner Diaries, The (Pierce), 133, 388, 658
Twelve Tribes, the, **620–621**
  beliefs and practices, 620–621
  history of, 620
  ritual life, 621
  Vine Church and, 620

UFO religions, **623–626**
  Aetherius Society, 624–625
  Chen Tao, 95–96, 106
  Chen Tao and, 106, 625
  flying saucers and, 544, 623, 625
  Gnosticism and, 243–244
  history of, 623–625
  Ministry of Universal Wisdom, 624
  Nation of Islam, 625
  New Age and, 433
  Raëlians, 238, 369, *510,* 547, 567, 624,
    625
  science and, 547
  science fiction and, 544
  stories of sightings and contacts,
    623–624
  The Urantia Book and, 625
  See also Heaven's Gate
Umbanda, **626–628**
  history and origins, 626–627
  practices and beliefs, 627–628
Unarius Academy of Science, the,
  628–630
  beliefs and practices, 629–630
  history and founding, xxxiv, 547, 629
  Norman, Ernest and Ruth, and, xxxiv,
    547, 629, 630
Unification Church, the, **630–633**
  anticult movement and, 150
  Completed Testament Age canon, 168,
    445, 632
  conversion and, 368
  "cults" and, 630–631, 632
  death of Rev. Moon, 632–633
  globalization and, 240–241
  history and founding, xxxiii, 631–632
  intragroup violence and, 656

  in Japan, 240, 340
  in Korea, 339–340
  marriage and mass weddings, xxxiv, 98,
    368, 565, 632
  memoirs, 372, 398
  messianism and, 385
  Moon's prophetic persona, 397–398
  as New Age Gnostic movement, 417
  successors to Rev. Moon, 398, 633
  in United States, 340, 632
  See also Divine Principle; Moon, Rev.
    Sun Myung
Unitarian Universalism, **634–636**
  beliefs, 635
  history of, 634–635
  institution and culture, 635
United Nuwaubian Nation of Moors, the,
  636–638
  beliefs and practices, 636–637
  conflicts, 637
  history and origins, 636
  York, Dwight D. "Malachi," and,
    636–637
Unity School of Christianity, **638–640**
  beliefs and practices, 639–640
  Fillmore, Charles and Myrtle, and, xxxi,
    450, 546, 638–639
  origins and founding, 638–639
  unity in contemporary society, 640
Urantia Book, The, **640–645**
  challenges, 642–643
  contents, 641–642
  history and publication, xxxiv, 640–641
  "The Meaning of Jesus" (primary
    document), 643–645
Utopianism in new religious movements,
  645–648
  general characteristics, 646
  historical examples, 646–647
  modern utopian movements, 647–648

Valley of the Dawn, the, **649–650**
  healing and, 650
  history and origins, 649
  rituals and ritual spaces, 649–650
Vampirism, **650–652**
  beliefs and practices, 651–652
  community and culture, 652
  history and origins, 650–651
  membership and, 376
  Otherkin and, 476

Temple of the Vampire (TOV), xxxvii, 238, 544, 651–652
Vedanta Society, the, **652–654**
  beliefs and practices, 653–654
  history and founding, xxxi, 265, 652–653
  institutions and culture, 654
  Ramakrishna Mission and, 517, 518–519
  Vivekananda, Swami, and, xxxi, 265, 517, 653–654, 659–660
Violence and new religious movements, **655–659**
  intragroup violence, 656–657
  violence against new religions, 657
  violence against society, 657–658
Vivekananda, Swami, **659–661**
  early years and spiritual beginnings, 659
  as religious celebrity, 659
  Vedanta Society and, xxxi, 265, 517, 653–654, 659–660
  World's Parliament of Religion and, xxxi, 265, 659, 681
  See also Vedanta Society, the
Vodou, **661–663**
  Haitian Revolution and, xxix
  history and origins, 661–662
  Petro ritual, xxix
  practices and beliefs, 662–663
Vorilhon, Claude (Raël), **664–665**
  The Book Which Tells the Truth, 509, 664
  criticism and controversy, 665
  Intelligent Design: Message from the Designers, 445, 446, 625
  science and, 547
  science fiction and, 544
  visits from Elohim, xxxv, 228, 664, 665
  See also Raëlians, the

Waite, Arthur Edward, **667–668**
  Hermetic Order of the Golden Dawn and, 667
  occultism and, 465, 667
  Rider-Waite deck of tarot cards, 667
  Spiritualism and, 667
Watch Tower Bible and Tract Society, the (Jehovah's Witnesses), **668–671**
  beliefs and practices, 669–670
  church and culture, 670–671
  healing and, 255–256

history and founding, xxxi, 528–529, 668–669
  meetings, 670
  millennialism and, 388, 394, 668
  Millerites and, 392, 394, 668
  The New World Translation of the Holy Scriptures, 670
  restorationist Christianity and, 669
  Russell, Charles Taze, and, xxxi, 528–529, 668–669
  The Watch Tower (tract), 529
Weber, Max, 91–92, 94, 147, 493, 553–554
White, Ellen G., **671–672**
  charismatic authority and, 92–93
  early years, 671
  founding of Seventh-day Adventists and, xxx, 495, 561, 562, 563, 671–672, 676
  The Great Controversy, 562, 672
  Great Disappointment, 671–672, 676
  Millerites and, 71, 495, 676
  prophecy and, 495, 562, 563, 672
White supremacy
  Ásatrú and, 37, 508
  Ballard, Edna, and, 55
  Christian Identity and, 110, 127, 351, 388, 508
  conspiracy theories and, 127
  millennialism and, 388, 508, 658
  Odinism and, 466, 467
  The Order and, 37, 133
  religions of, 508
  The Turner Diaries and, 658
  World Church of the Creator and, 508, 679–680
Wicca, **673–675**
  Buckland, Raymond, and, 428, 675
  Crowther, Patricia, and, 428, 675
  Gardner, Gerald, and, 144, 225, 360, 526, 673–675
  gender and, 229
  Goddess Worship and, 245–246
  history of, 673–674
  marriage and, 368–369
  Neopaganism and, 229, 246, 360, 428, 430
  New Reformed Orthodox Order of the Golden Dawn, 674
Wilson, Jack. *See* Ghost Dance Movement (Wovoka)

718 Index

Women in new religious movements,
675–679
Blavatsky, Helena Petrovna, 677
Eddy, Mary Baker, 676
Fox, Kate, and Margaret, 676–677
Lee, (Mother) Ann, 676
new religions that empower women,
677–678
Prophet, Elizabeth Clare, 677
subjugation of women, 678–679
White, Ellen Gould, 676
World Church of the Creator, the, **679–681**
beliefs and practices, 680–681
history and origins, 679–680
Klassen, Ben, and, 679–681
white supremacy and, 508
World's Parliament of Religion, the, **681–682**
Bonney, Charles Carroll, and, 659, 681
history of, 681
immigration and, 681–682
introduction of yoga to the West and,
683
reception and success of, 681–682
Vivekananda, Swami, and, xxxi, 265,
681
Wounded Knee massacre, xxxi. *See also*
Ghost Dance Movement (Wovoka)
Wovoka. *See* Ghost Dance Movement
(Wovoka)

Yearning for Zion (YFZ) Ranch, xxxviii,
142, 223–224, 351, 657
Yoga, **683–685**
Bernard, Pierre, and, 684
Eastern history and origins of, 683
Self-Realization Fellowship
(Yogananda) and, 683–684

Spiritual but not Religious culture and,
684
Tantrik Order and, 684
Vedanta Society and, 684
Vivekananda, Swami, and, 683
Western history of, 683–684
World's Parliament of Religion and,
683
See also Integral Yoga
Yogi, Maharishi Mahesh, **685–686**
beliefs and teachings, 615, 685
celebrity acolytes of, 266, 685
death and legacy, 686
early years, 685
global tour of, xxxiv
published works, 685
Rishikesh ashram of, *264*
Transcendental Meditation and, 266,
615, 685

Zell, Tim, 114–115, 170, 429
Zen Buddhism
Beats and, 1, 241
Erhard Seminars Training (est) and,
345, 346
Rajneesh/Osho and, 514
Zionist Churches (Africa), **687–689**
beliefs and practices, 7, 688
Dowie, John Alexander, and, 687–688
history and origins, xxxii, 687
Lekganyane, Engenas Barnabas, and,
688
symbol of Zion, 687
Zion Christian Church (South Africa),
xxxii, 688
Zion City (Dowie), 687, 688
Zion City (Lekganyane), 688

About the Authors

Eugene V. Gallagher is Rosemary Park Professor of Religious Studies Emeritus at Connecticut College. He has taught a wide range of courses, and his previous books include *The Religious Studies Skills Book*, *Reading and Writing Scripture in New Religious Movements*, and *The New Religious Movements Experience in America.* His work has been published in such journals as *History of Religions* and *Nova Religio.*

Lydia Willsky-Ciollo is associate professor of religious studies at Fairfield University. She is an American religious historian who specializes in nineteenth-century religious thought, culture, and innovation. She is the author of *American Unitarianism and the Protestant Dilemma* and has published articles in *Nova Religio*, the *New England Quarterly*, *Journal of Religious History,* and other journals.